Renaissance Thought and Its Sources

Paul Oskar Kristeller, a preeminent intellectual historian of the Renaissance, is Frederick J. E. Woodbridge Professor Emeritus of Philosophy at Columbia University. **Michael Mooney,** his former student, is Associate Provost at Columbia University.

RENAISSANCE THOUGHT AND ITS SOURCES

Paul Oskar Kristeller

EDITED BY

MICHAEL MOONEY

New York   Columbia University Press   1979

Library of Congress Cataloging in Publication Data

Kristeller, Paul Oskar, 1905–
   Renaissance thought and its sources.

   Includes bibliographical references and index.
   1. Philosophy, Renaissance.   2. Humanism—History.
3. Science, Renaissance.   4. Art, Renaissance.
5. Literature, Medieval—History and criticism.
6. Renaissance—Sources.   I. Mooney, Michael.
II. Title.
B775.K73   190′.9′024   79–15521
ISBN 0–231–04512–3

Columbia University Press
New York   Guildford, Surrey

To the Memory of
Ernest Abrahamson

Contents

Editor's Preface

The origin of *Renaissance Thought and Its Sources* is simple and clearly remembered. Shortly after Paul Oskar Kristeller, in 1976, completed the final lectures of "Philosophical Literature of the Renaissance," the popular graduate course he gave at Columbia University nearly every other year since 1939, I put to him the obvious question: Would he now, in the relative leisure of his retirement, prepare the definitive study of Renaissance philosophy? His reaction was immediate and somewhat surprised: Absolutely not, he replied. We—meaning the company of scholars—are not yet in a position to do that. My generation might be, he added a bit playfully, but surely not his, and in any event, everything he might say on the subject had already been published. That was a pity, I thought, since the essays to which he referred were scattered, some even out of print, and no single work offered the comprehensive view of Renaissance thought and its sources that his graduate course had achieved.

Two events in 1977, nearly simultaneous, gave new life to my hope for a general text. A casual mention of the idea to John D. Moore, editor-in-chief of Columbia University Press, led to a round of discussions and an eventual proposal, while a letter to Professor Kristeller from a British publisher inquired whether he would be interested in its reissuing some titles now out of print. Out of these events came the concept of the volume and the plan for publication.

Although we at first considered a much larger book, the collection we settled on was one nearly given us ready-made. Over the course of the last twenty-five years, Professor Kristeller has been called upon to deliver several series of sponsored lectures, and more by coincidence than design the order of these assignments has formed a systematic presentation of the sources of Renaissance thought and a survey of some of its central themes: the Martin Classical Lectures that he gave in 1954 treated "The Classics and Renaissance Thought"; the Wimmer Lecture of 1961 concerned "Renaissance Philosophy and the Medieval Tradition"; two lectures given in 1963 at the Cini Foundation in Venice addressed the relationship between Renaissance thought and Byzantium; the Arensberg Lectures of 1965 explored "Renaissance Concepts of Man"; and three faculty seminars held in 1975 at the University of Colorado at Boulder examined "Philosophy and Rhetoric from Antiquity to the Renaissance." With the addition of an article on "Humanism and Scholasticism," a justly celebrated paper of 1944, we had the structure of the survey we had intended and the comprehensive presentation we had sought.

Were it not for their separate origins, the essays of the book might even be called organic. Part One shows the classical sources of Renaissance thought and gives its essential physiognomy, indicating the humanist, Aristotelian, and Platonist traditions to which the other essays in the volume continually refer. Part Two and Part Three present Renaissance thought in its immediate context—the Middle Ages, both Greek and Latin—and show the continuity and distinctiveness of its representative strains within the movements of this age. Against this background, Part Four offers a thematic study of Renaissance thought, examining three elements of a subject for which Renaissance thinkers are often credited with particular originality: the conception of man, his dignity, his destiny, and his grasp of truth. Part Five forms a summary of the whole from the perspective of a theme that is at the heart of Renaissance intellectual life, if not of the Western tradition at large: the relation of language to thought, words to ideas, prudence to science, and rhetoric to philosophy. Within these rubrics, the ancient and seemingly insoluble contest between our literary and philosophical traditions—a *paragone*, in fact, that marks much of contemporary Renaissance scholarship—is explored, and in the closing pages thoughts are offered on the shape and outcome of that conflict in our own times.

Since the essays were written in various contexts and at various times, there is some repetition in the handling of themes, but this seemed to us on the whole more instructive than annoying and thus we did not attempt to remove all instances of it. The text, however, has been thoroughly reviewed and occasional changes made, and the notes, which contain a large amount of related literature and serve to document points that the text can merely summarize, have been revised and brought up to date. The book is introduced by an essay in which Professor Kristeller reviews the half century of his scholarly life, telling of changes he finds in the field of Renaissance scholarship and in his own perceptions, and identifying the challenges he sees facing the field at this juncture.

What the author writes there of himself and his field will serve to give point to what I take to be the life of the book as a whole. Throughout a long and distinguished career, Professor Kristeller has earned, and cherished, a reputation as a careful, meticulous historian of ideas, a *Geisteswissenschaftler* in the best German tradition, well-grounded in philosophy, philology, and history, and the master of the classical and several modern languages. Among colleagues he is known as a scholar's scholar, one who does not shy from the task of preparing, as he had these last twenty years, a multi-volume "Finding List of Uncatalogued or Incompletely Catalogued Humanistic Manuscripts of the Renaissance in Italian and Other Libraries" (*Iter Italicum,* 2 volumes to date [London: The Warburg Institute, and Leiden: E. J. Brill, 1963–67] and 4 volumes to follow). This love for the texts and his intimate acquaintance with them explains, of course, why he is so tolerant in his approach to Renaissance thought, why he cannot, for example, accept the notion of Renaissance humanism as a single philosophy; it is simply too large a reality, has too many representatives and too many interests to be defined by a set of common philosophical ideas.

Yet, without sacrificing a whit of this scholarly caution, he is not without his preferences and is not incapable of applying to Renaissance thinkers as to those of every other age the criteria by which he himself would judge what is truthful and of enduring value. From his doctoral work on Plotinus, to his post-graduate study of Ficino, to his lifelong reading of Kant, he has made no secret of his sympathy with those ideas that we know as the "Platonic" tradition: the belief that reality is always more than what it appears to be; that we can with effort and persistence come to know it and know it truly; that there are ideals of duty and propriety that regulate our actions and we should seek to know and follow them; that there is a final unity in the universe such that nothing, however insignificant in appearance, is ultimately lost. His commitment to Plato and Plato's followers wafts gently through the pages of this volume, never obscuring or prejudicing the historical account, but always there, hovering, until it is permitted, in a rendering of modernity and its tendencies in the closing pages, full expression. Such a graceful blending of severe historical scholarship and a sturdy commitment to a set of values is nearly a lost art in our times, and it is refreshing to find it so successfully carried out here.

With the exception of the introductory essay, prepared especially for this volume, all essays in the book were first given as lectures, some repeated on a number of occasions, and all undergoing a rather continual refinement leading to the form in which they are found here. Those appearing here as essays 12, 13, and 14 have not until now been published. The rest have been published previously, some in several languages.

Presented originally as the Charles Beebe Martin Classical Lectures at Oberlin College, February 22–26, 1954, the essays forming Part One, Renaissance Thought and Classical Antiquity, were first published as *The Classics and Renaissance Thought* (Cambridge, Mass.: Harvard University Press, 1955), and were reprinted with other papers in *Renaissance Thought: The Classic, Scholastic, and Humanist Strains* (New York: Harper Torchbooks, 1961), pp. 3–91. They have also appeared in an Italian version by Fabrizio Onofri in *La tradizione classica nel pensiero del Rinascimento* (Florence: La Nuova Italia, 1965); in a German version by Renate Schweyen-Ott in *Humanismus und Renaissance, I: Die antiken und mittelalterlichen Quellen,* ed. Eckhardt Kessler (Munich: Wilhelm Fink, 1974), pp. 11–86; and in a Japanese version by Morimichi Watanabe in *Runessansu no shisō* (Tokyo: University of Tokyo Press, 1977). A Hungarian edition is now in preparation.

Part Two, Renaissance Thought and the Middle Ages, brings together two papers of similar compass but separate provenance. "Humanism and Scholasticism in the Italian Renaissance" (essay 5) was given originally as a lecture at Connecticut College on March 9, 1944, and again at Brown University on December 14, 1944. It was first published in *Byzantion* 17 (1944–45): 346–74, from which it was later reprinted in the Bobbs-Merrill Reprint Series in European History. It also appeared in *Studies in Renaissance Thought and Letters* (Rome: Edizioni di Storia e Letteratura, 1956), pp. 553–83, and in *Renaissance Thought: The Classic, Scholastic, and Humanist Strains* (New York: Harper Torchbooks, 1961), pp. 92–119. Italian, German, and Japanese versions appear in the same collections, indicated above, in which the chapters of Part One are contained. The Italian version also appeared earlier in *Humanitas* 5 (1950): 988–1015. A Hebrew version is now in preparation.

"Renaissance Philosophy and the Medieval Tradition" (essay 6) was originally given as the 15th Wimmer Lecture at St. Vincent's College, Latrobe, Pa., on October 25, 1961, and was published under the same title by The Archabbey Press, Latrobe, Pa., in 1966. It has also appeared in *Renaissance Concepts of Man and Other Essays* (New York: Harper Torchbooks, 1972), pp. 110–55. A German version appears in the same collection in which the chapters of Part One are contained, and an Italian version by Simonetta Salvestroni is included in the recent volume, *Concetti rinas-*

cimentali dell'uomo e altri saggi (Florence: La Nuova Italia, 1978), pp. 81–133.

Essays 7 and 8, presented here as Part Three, Renaissance Thought and Byzantine Learning, were originally delivered in Italian at the Fondazione Giorgio Cini in Venice on September 13 and 14, 1963. The first (essay 7) was published in Italian in *Lettere Italiane* 16 (1964): 1–14, and was reprinted, without notes, in *Venezia e l'Oriente fra Tardo Medioevo e Rinascimento,* ed. Agostino Pertusi (Florence: Sansoni, 1966), pp. 19–33, in which volume (pp. 103–16) the second paper (essay 8) was also published, it too without notes. They appeared for the first time in English, and with notes, in *Renaissance Concepts of Man and Other Essays* (New York: Harper Torchbooks, 1972), pp. 64–85 and 86–109, and have also appeared in a German version by Renate Schweyen-Ott in *Humanismus und Renaissance, I: Die antiken und mittelalterlichen Quellen,* ed. Eckhardt Kessler (Munich: Wilhelm Fink, 1974), pp. 145–76.

The essays forming Part Four, Renaissance Concepts of Man, were originally delivered as the Arensberg Lectures under the auspices of the Francis Bacon Foundation at the Claremont Graduate School and University Center on May 17, 19, and 21, 1965. They were first published in the volume *Renaissance Concepts of Man and Other Essays* (New York: Harper Torchbooks, 1972), pp. 1–63. An Italian version by Simonetta Salvestroni is now available in *Concetti rinascimentali dell'uomo e altri saggi* (Florence: La Nuova Italia, 1978), pp. 3–78.

The three essays of Part Five, Philosophy and Rhetoric from Antiquity to the Renaissance, were originally delivered at a Faculty Colloquium at the University of Colorado at Boulder on November 27–29, 1975, and are published here for the first time.

In preparing the volume we have incurred a number of debts that we are pleased to acknowledge, and in the first instance to the several institutions and publishing houses that permitted us to reprint material for which they hold copyrights: Oberlin College of Oberlin, Ohio; the Harvard University Press, Cambridge, Massachusetts; the international review *Byzantion* in Brussels; St. Vincent's College, Latrobe, Pennsylvania, and its Archabbey Press; the Francis Bacon Foundation of Claremont, California; and Harper & Row Publishers of New York. In preparing the lectures on "Philosophy and Rhetoric from Antiquity to the Renaissance" and in revising them for publication here, Professor Kristeller received much helpful information from Professors James Hutton, Stephan Kuttner, and Emil Polak, as well as from colleagues at the University of Colorado at Boulder, where he first gave the series, and at the Folger Shakespeare Library in Washington, at Dumbarton Oaks, the University of Delaware, the University of Virginia, Georgia State University, and at the thirteenth conference on medieval studies at Western Michigan University, where he repeated the last paper. Hugh Van Dusen of Harper & Row and John D. Moore of Columbia University Press gave us their friendly support when we were planning the volume, and Dalli C. Bacon retyped the notes when that became necessary. Debra Ann Bolka had a large hand in preparing the index.

The volume is dedicated to the memory of Ernest Abrahamson, close friend and fellow student of Professor Kristeller at Heidelberg, who like him was able to leave Germany for Italy and to emigrate from there to this country, where until his untimely death in 1956 he taught at Howard University, St. John's College, and Washington University in St. Louis.

M. M.

New York
March 1979

Renaissance Thought and Its Sources

Introduction

The essays brought together in this book were all originally composed as lectures, and this accounts for their broad and comprehensive topics. The general statements presented in the course of each lecture cannot be fully documented, and are at best approximations that require many nuances and qualifications in view of the rich and diverse source material that no scholar can hope to master or present. These statements are not intended as self-contained, abstract propositions that may be taken out of context and argued about without reference to the concrete historical facts and sources which they attempt to describe.

Since each essay is a unit in itself, they sometimes overlap, and there are a few more or less extensive repetitions which the reader, I hope, will overlook or forgive. Moreover, since the essays were written at different times and with a different focus, there may be some apparent inconsistencies or contradictions. As a matter of fact, I have sometimes been criticized for being inconsistent when I said or wrote different things at different times, and also for being too consistent when I have failed to change or correct my views over the years. I like to think that I have maintained my basic views over this long time, but have perhaps changed my emphasis here and there, under the impact of newly studied sources and problems, and in response, more often negative than positive, to changing fashions.

The essays were written between 1944 and 1975, while the research on which they draw goes back at least to 1931 when I first entered the field of Renaissance studies, whereas some of their premises may even go back to my earlier work as a student of philosophy and the classics in the 1920s. Since I am thus presenting here the partial results of nearly fifty years of work, it may be in order to indicate briefly how I arrived at my views and how I came to develop them.

I was educated in a *Humanistisches Gymnasium* in Berlin in which I learned a great deal of Greek, Latin, French, and German literature as well as history and mathematics. I read extensively for myself, and acquired an interest in classical music and art history that I have sustained throughout my life. By the time I graduated, I had read Plato in school and Kant at home. At the university, I studied ancient philosophy under Ernst Hoffmann, Kant under Rickert, Hegel under Kroner, existentialism under Jaspers and Heidegger, classical literature under Jaeger and Norden, and medieval history under Hampe and Baethgen. My dissertation dealt with Plotinus and was published in 1929.

I entered the field of Renaissance studies in 1931 when I decided to study Marsilio Ficino as a representative of Renaissance Platonism, after having studied Plato and Plotinus whom he had both translated and interpreted. At that time, the old works of Burckhardt and Voigt were still considered fundamental, and detailed research on Italian humanism was being continued by Bertalot and others. On the other hand, Dilthey's studies and his method of *Geistesgeschichte* exerted a wide influence on scholars in several fields, and Hans Baron was publishing his first contributions to Florentine humanism. Ernst Cassirer, who had given much attention to neglected Renaissance thinkers in his early history of epistemology, published in 1927 a major contribution to Renaissance philosophy in a series of the *Bibliothek Warburg* which included other important studies on the art and thought of the Renaissance by Panofsky, Saxl, and others. I also had to cope with Italian scholarship on Ficino and his time which included the older work by Della Torre and the more recent studies by Saitta and others.

When I was in Italy from 1934 to 1939, I became familiar with the scholarly work of Gentile and Mercati, of Novati, Sabbadini, and many others, and with the first writings of Garin. While I finished writing my book on the philosophy of Ficino and edited his unpublished writings, my interests expanded from Ficino to his associates and contemporaries, to his sources and influence, and I read many scholastic and humanist texts. I learned to appreciate the contributions of local history and of eighteenth-century erudition that are so indispensable for Italian scholarship. I also became aware of the wealth of unpublished and untapped manuscript material preserved but almost hidden in Italian and other libraries. Thus the ground was laid for bringing out a series of unpublished humanistic texts (which is still continuing) and for preparing an extensive list of uncatalogued manuscripts (of which two volumes have appeared so far).

When I came to the United States in 1939, I had just found the evidence that Ficino and Florentine Platonism, in addition to its known dependence on ancient and medieval Platonism and on early Renaissance humanism, also had direct links with Aristotelian scholasticism, and this was the subject of the first lecture I gave and published in this country at the invitation of Roland Bainton.

After I came to Columbia University in the fall of 1939, I was encouraged to expand my interest from Ficino and Florentine Platonism to the much broader area of Renaissance philosophy and Renaissance intellectual history. I had to give a lecture course on the entire subject, to supervise dissertations, to read articles and review books for several periodicals, and to participate in various bibliographical enterprises. I was drawn into the activities of the *Journal of the History of Ideas*, founded by Arthur Lovejoy and inspired by his work, and into several enterprises that tended to organize and develop Renaissance studies on an interdepartmental basis: the New England Renaissance Conference and the Renaissance Committee of the American Council of Learned Societies, both initiated and guided by Leicester Bradner; the Columbia University Seminar on the Renaissance, founded by John Randall, Marjorie Nicolson, and others; and later the Renaissance Society of America, organized by Josephine Bennett and others. I also became familiar with the work of Dean P. Lockwood, B. L. Ullman, Ernest K. Wilkins, and other American scholars who had worked on Renaissance humanism.

I was impressed with the work of Haskins and Thorndike and with the activities of the Mediaeval Academy of America, and the "revolt of the medievalists" against the cult and very concept of the Renaissance prompted me to attempt an interpretation of the Renaissance that would take into account the legitimate objections of the medievalists. The extensive list of Medieval and Renaissance Latin Translations and Commentaries, a large international project which I helped to organize with James Hutton, Martin McGuire, Mario Cosenza, and others, is intended to document the tradition of all ancient authors in the West and to establish on a factual basis the share that each century had in this tradition. Through my close connection with John Randall and Ernest Moody, I came to appreciate the importance of Renaissance Aristotelianism, and of the scholarly traditions that go back to Renan and Duhem. I became interested in Pomponazzi and in the tradition to which he belonged. This led me to investigate the history of the Italian universities, and especially their curriculum, and the developments and interrelations of the various academic and scholarly disciplines as reflected in this curriculum, in the learned professions, and in the classifications of the arts and sciences. These studies were never concluded in a book, but they were the basis for many of my lectures and articles.

I thus reached the conclusion, first summarized in what is essay 5 in this volume, that in Renaissance Italy, humanism and Aristotelian scholasticism were not so much two ideologically opposed currents, let alone the representatives of a new and old philosophy, but two coexisting areas of interest. Humanism was based on the *studia humanitatis* (i.e., grammar, rhetoric, poetry, history, and moral philosophy), and Aristotelian scholasticism on the philosophical disciplines (i.e., logic, natural philosophy, metaphysics, and again moral philosophy). A study of the literary production as well as of the teaching activities associated with the humanists and with the scholastics showed that they developed, at least in part, from two branches of learning that had flourished in medieval Italy: humanism was linked with the medieval rhetoric of the *ars dictandi* and *ars arengandi,* and scholastic philosophy with the secular Aristotelianism of the medical schools of Salerno, Bologna, Padua, and other centers.

Further research on specific manuscripts and texts that I was able to pursue on my visits to many European libraries helped me to fill in many details and to add a few qualifications, but in spite of many objections, I have not been driven to change my basic views. This may be due to my stubborn character or narrow perspectives, but also to my conviction (which may be just another aspect of the same thing) that such matters do not, or should not, depend on opinions or preferences, but on the testimony of the texts and documents. History, and especially the history of thought and philosophy, has its own "scientific method." A historical interpretation derives its validity, not from the authority of the scholars who endorse it, or from its agreement with conventional views (which may be wrong) or with current fashions (which constantly change), but from its agreement with the primary sources, that is, with the original texts and documents of the past. I tried to formulate my views on the basis of such primary sources, and I am ready to change them (or to see them changed by others) when they are confronted with primary sources that contradict them.

Apart from the course of my own work, often diverted but also stimulated by teaching, lectures, congresses, and correspondence, I have no doubt been affected and influenced more than I know by the work of other scholars, old and young, and by the steady change and progress in the state of scholarship. After the time when I first began to work on Renaissance subjects, and even after I first formulated my general interpretations, a large number of new books and articles appeared which I had to study and examine critically, some of them challenging, and others very instructive. Perhaps even more important than the comprehensive studies on the thought of the Renaissance are the new monographs, text editions, and bibliographies that have appeared over the last few decades. Scholarly periodicals, many of them new, have become so numerous and diversified that it is now almost impossible to keep up with them in a satisfactory way. I have tried my best to learn from the new studies as far as I have come across them, and to take them into account when restating my general views on the respective subject. But the pressure to read new secondary studies makes it increasingly difficult to keep reading the primary sources, many of which are available only in rare old editions or even in manuscripts.

Yet when I compare the state of scholarship at the present time with that of fifty years ago, the difference consists not merely in the number of books and articles that have been added to the body of available material, or in the changes in interpretations and opinions or in the emphasis placed on certain problems or areas of investigation. As it seems to me, several more fundamental changes have occurred, not only in the content and method of scholarship, but also in its style and external organization. These developments are by no means peculiar to the study of Renaissance thought, or even to Renaissance studies in general, but characterize the world of scholarship at large and merely affect our field as a part of that broader world. These changes have by now become so pervasive that younger scholars take them for granted, but I may be permitted to point out that a number of the facts of life of present scholarship, good and bad, did not exist, at least not to the same extent, when I began my scholarly career, and that I have seen them develop and am hence aware of their comparative novelty.

When I began my work in Germany and Italy, scholarship in any one field, whether philosophy or history, classical or Romance philology, was very much a matter of a few individuals working in small circles, each of them based in a single university or institute and critical of all others, if indeed they paid any attention to the others at all. There were few visiting lecturers and relatively few congresses, and for a scholar to meet another scholar, a formal introduction or a chance occasion was required.

Scholarly life in America was always more informal and also more gregarious. The large number of widely scattered colleges, universities, and other institutions favored the practice of guest lectures and the organization of professional societies in the various major fields that held annual conventions and thus encouraged personal contacts and a wide exchange of information and ideas. When these national meetings became too large, and hence impersonal and colorless, smaller conventions and conferences began to be held in increasing number, some of them nationwide but limited to more specific subjects, others regional or local. More recently, small conferences on very specialized topics have become fashionable, and often their proceedings are published. International congresses, not unknown in the past, have become increasingly frequent since World War II when it seemed necessary to reestablish contacts and cooperation between scholars of different countries. To organize and attend scholarly congresses has become a major occupation, and many people are convinced that the discussion of problems at congresses of any size or composition will instruct and enlighten the participants in a way they could not hope for when engaged in lonely reading, thinking, or writing at their desk or in the library. Some people even seem to think that scholarly conventions, like the church synods and councils of old, will settle debates and controversies and sanction conclusions that are the result of previous work and may serve in turn as the starting point for later investigations.

Other developments in recent decades have also tended to favor research on all levels, and Renaissance studies have had their appropriate share in them. Specialized research institutes and postdoctoral fellowships have multiplied over the years, giving to young and also to older scholars the opportunity to do concentrated work on their own chosen projects for a year or two.

No less important is the progress made in recent decades as far as library facilities and the bibliographical control of the pertinent literature are concerned. The Union List of Serials and more recently the National Union Catalogue make it easy to locate and to borrow any volume available in the United States, whereas the printed catalogues of the British Library, the Bibliothèque Nationale, and the bibliographical centers in Rome, Madrid, and East Berlin help to locate rare books and obtain microfilms of them. Also the cataloguing of manuscripts has made great progress during the last fifty years, although there are still major gaps that can be filled only by traveling or by circular letters. American scholars also have access to many university and other research libraries that have been built up with foresight and generosity over many decades to a size and quality that may stand comparison with the best European libraries, except for manuscripts and rare books, and that surpass them in the quality of their catalogues and reference services, and in the easier access to their stacks. In many areas, current bibliographies and other reference works, including national bibliographies, make it easy to find many, if not all, books and articles needed for the study of a given subject, and even greater claims are made for the printouts of computerized catalogues and bibliographies.

But the changes in scholarship over this last half century go beyond its mere organization; there has also occurred a gradual but profound change in the content of recent scholarship, and in the problems to which it addresses itself. I should like to single out two approaches that are not entirely unrelated to each other and that are both very important for the study of Renaissance thought: the history of ideas, and the trend towards interdepartmental studies.

The program of *Geistesgeschichte,* inspired by the work of Dilthey, received a powerful impulse in Germany in the 1920s. With somewhat different overtones, it was taken up in this country by Arthur Lovejoy and embodied in his work and in the *Journal of the History of Ideas* that was founded by him and still continues along the lines defined by him and his closest associates. The history of ideas, even more than *Geistesgeschichte,* tries to coordinate the work done in different fields, such as the history of philosophy and the sciences, of religion and the arts. It deals not only with the thought of professional philosophers, but also of scientists and theologians, economists and political theorists, poets and artists. It stretches from antiquity to the present century, and although its center of attention is the Western world, forays into Oriental and primitive thought are not excluded. It makes the assumption that problems, concepts, and terms, though subject to constant change and development, represent a world of living discourse that is for us both understandable and significant and helps us to interpret the past and also to formulate our own thought which lives in continuity with it.

Whereas the older scholarly tradition in the history of thought had concentrated on the systems of major individual thinkers, the history of ideas has focused on the way specific problems and concepts have been treated by a variety of thinkers, great and small, professional or popular. This approach has suggested entirely new lines of research, and even of bibliographical investigations. It has made many lesser or marginal thinkers more important because of the treatment they gave to a certain problem or concept, whereas this same problem may have occupied only a minor place in the systems of the leading thinkers who have traditionally dominated the study of the history of metaphysics, cosmology, epistemology, or logic.

The history of ideas also makes it easier to view the history of philosophy proper within the context and against the background of a more broadly conceived intellectual history, since it is a fact that professional philosophers received many of their concepts and ideas from the civilization surrounding them, just as their original ideas tended in turn to influence and to transform that civilization. The history of ideas is thus a welcome supplement to the history of philosophy, but it is not a substitute for it. Philosophy, just as the sciences or the arts, has its own specific tradition, and there are essential points in the thought of each modern philosopher that are more adequately understood in relation to his predecessors in antiquity or in later times than to the vague ideas of his own non-philosophical contemporaries. There are, as it were, two dimensions to the understanding of a philosopher, an artist, or a scientist, and it should be possible to combine both of them, or to pursue one of them without denying the other.

The other recent development to which we have alluded and which affects the study of the Renaissance is the rise of interdepartmental studies. It began perhaps with *Altertumswissenschaft* and the program of the *Bibliothek Warburg* in the 1920s, and was taken up in the work of the Mediaeval Academy and of the Renaissance Society and of their regional and local counterparts in this country. Just as a complete understanding of Greek and Roman antiquity needs the study of history and archaeology, and of other special disciplines, and not only the conventional classical scholarship limited to ancient literature alone, so the study of the Middle Ages and of the Renaissance calls for a comprehensive synthesis of the knowledge provided for the respective period by such different academic disciplines as political, economic, and institutional history, English, Germanic, and Romance literature, church history and theology, the history of art and music, philosophy, and the sciences.

A mere juxtaposition of these findings is easy but meaningless. More important and more difficult is a synthesis and comprehensive interpretation of the results attained in the different disciplines, and this is, at least at the beginning, a program and an ideal rather than an accomplished fact. Nevertheless, the movement towards interdepartmental studies and programs has been beneficial for Renaissance studies in a variety of ways. It has facilitated an exchange of information and methods between the various disciplines. It has encouraged the students of English literature, who in this country represent a populous guild, to turn from the overcrowded areas of their specific field to some less cultivated subjects and problems in neighboring fields. It has prompted the students of Italian literature to pay greater attention to some neglected areas of their very large field because these areas acquire greater interest as sources or counterparts of important developments outside of Italy. Moreover, the modern system of academic disciplines and departments and their teaching programs are far from complete or adequate. They omit many areas of medieval and Renaissance civilization, or fail to discover them because they lack the names of their modern counterparts. On the other hand, an interdepartmental program can accommodate such necessary subjects as palaeography or Neolatin literature that no department would readily emphasize, or the history of rhetoric or grammar that have barely been made relevant by calling them literary criticism and linguistics.

Finally, Renaissance philosophy is studied by few philosophers and taught in few departments of philosophy, but it has a firm place in any program of Renaissance studies where the students of the arts and of literature want to learn something about the philosophy of their period, and the teachers of literature and history, art history and musicology will continue to study the philosophical sources of their period, whether or not their philosophical colleagues care to give them any help or guidance. I may say from my own experience that I have encountered a greater interest in Renaissance philosophy among students of history, literature, art, and music, than among professional philosophers, and I am afraid my work must show the effects of the circumstance that I have had to address my courses and my lectures more often to students and colleagues in neighboring disciplines than to professional philosophers.

Having spoken of the changes that have occurred in Renaissance scholarship during the last fifty years or so, I should like to add a few remarks about its future tasks and prospects as far as they may be envisaged from our present perspective. For a study of the intellectual history of the Renaissance, a good deal has been accomplished in the recent past, but much more remains to be done, partly along the same lines of investigation that have been followed until now. In order to have a firm basis for a study of the sources, the bibliographical task of listing the pertinent manuscripts and early printed editions should be continued and completed, as far as possible. The manuscripts and editions should not only be enumerated, but they should be cross-indexed by authors and by topics to facilitate a further study of individual thinkers and problems. Such indices will also disclose the relative popularity of a given author or problem in their own time, something that does not always coincide with the importance attached to them, rightly or wrongly, by modern historians.

Whereas all texts, in manuscripts or editions, must be listed, not all of them deserve close study, and even fewer of them justify the considerable effort of a new critical edition. However, the critical editing of the more important thinkers, and of the more significant or influential works by lesser thinkers, remains a major desideratum of scholarship. The editions that have been started for Petrarch, Bruni, Valla, Manetti, Cusanus, Landino, Ficino, Pico, Pomponazzi, and others should be completed, and a number of other more or less important philosophers and humanists should be made available in good editions. It is true that any old edition or manuscript may now be read in microfilm, but it is also true that no single manuscript offers an accurate text, whereas the critical edition will give not only a correct text, but also provide the necessary annotation for variants and sources.

A great many Renaissance thinkers, some of them important, require new monographs based on a direct and complete knowledge of their writings. Old studies are often unreliable, and it has been shown in more than one instance that a direct reading of an author's works will quickly dispose of certain conventional labels and judgments that have been repeated for centuries. School labels such as Platonism, Averroism, or nominalism should be used with the greatest care or even avoided to make room for a detailed and accurate description of an author's real opinions as expressed in his writings.

Apart from monographs on individual thinkers, the history of many concepts and problems needs further elucidation, as does the history of certain schools and currents that were recognized as such by their members and contemporaries, and not merely by later historians. The impact of individual ancient and medieval thinkers on the Renaissance requires further careful study, and attention should be given to the copies and editions of their writings, to their translations, commentaries, and summaries produced during the Renaissance, as well as to their quotations in the works of Renaissance thinkers. We need in turn further studies on the influence exercised by Renaissance thinkers on subsequent centuries, on the Enlightenment, on Romanticism, and on modern and contemporary thought. We need more work on the history of the various philosophical disciplines and of their cross connections with other branches of learning, the sciences and the arts. A further study of the place philosophy occupied at the universities will go a long way to bridge the gap between intellectual and institutional or social history. A synthesis of our scholarly findings, in the form of an encyclopaedia or of a detailed handbook, should be one of our goals and will have to be attempted sooner or later, although the present state of our knowledge does not give much hope for a quick or lasting success, especially when the attempt is made by an individual scholar or even by a small group of scholars.

Yet in all these efforts toward a study of Renaissance philosophy, our orientation should be guided by a concern for the central problems and traditions that go back to Greek philosophy and to which Renaissance philosophy, placed between medieval and modern philosophy, attempted to make its own distinctive contribution. In this way, the charge of a merely antiquarian concern for old-fashioned ideas will be refuted, apart from the fact that any old-fashioned idea, if it had any merit at all, may become fashionable again at any time.

The progress made in Renaissance scholarship in recent years, and the talent and competence of several generations of scholars younger than I, should give us great hope for the further development of our field of study. On the other hand, several factors of a more general nature represent a serious threat to scholarship in general, and thus also to Renaissance scholarship. The steady decline of our educational system makes it increasingly difficult for future scholars to acquire the linguistic and other skills essential for the serious pursuit of historical studies, and the exclusive emphasis on the contemporary world which has reached the proportions of a "cultural revolution" undermines any interest the lay public may have in the past. The scholar is under constant pressure, not to attain new knowledge through fresh research, but to communicate to the general public all that is known, as he should, and to communicate it in a diluted and sometimes distorted fashion, as he should not. Thus he may be led, as a result of popular pressure and weak training, to cultivate a kind of fake scholarship instead of the real thing, relying on translations rather than on the original texts, on secondary rather than on primary sources, on vague clichés instead of precise concepts, on abstract formulas instead of concrete nuances, and concerning himself with fashionable theories and ideologies rather than with the historical facts and documents, and with artificial problems that are in vogue but unrelated to the historical events and hence uncapable of any satisfactory solution.

Within the academic world, historical, literary, and philosophical scholarship, now usually labeled as the humanities, has to compete with the professional disciplines of law and medicine, with the practical training programs for engineers, businessmen, journalists, and social workers, and more directly with the natural and social sciences. Even within the humanities, the intellectual historian has to defend himself against the claims, often excessive and intolerant, of the social historian, the literary critic, and the analytical philosopher. There is a widespread quest for broad syntheses and a contempt for details and nuances, while specialization is constantly deplored but practised, as it has been ever since the twelfth century at least.

We must still hope that these threats to the future of our work will not prevail, but will be overcome, at least to some extent. We hope for a better education, both of our general population and our future scholars, for a better public understanding of what we are trying to do, and for greater tolerance within the academic community that will preserve or restore to our subject the place which it needs for its existence and further development. Finally, there should be no restriction of scholarly investigations on political or ideological grounds. The scholar just as the scientist has the right and duty to follow his natural curiosity rather than to satisfy a popular interest or to favor a specific political cause. He must be free to investigate his problems and to advance knowledge as best he can. If this knowledge is thought to have undesirable political or social consequences, it is the responsibility of the statesman and the citizen (and also of the scholar *qua* citizen) to prevent these consequences, but not to stop the pursuit and acquisition of knowledge as such.

Natural curiosity, changing perspectives, and the new combination of various elements of our old knowledge will continue to open up the way for new subjects and problems, methods and interpretations, will draw attention to new sources hitherto neglected, and will help to correct older theories that are no longer tenable. We should not replace "traditional scholarship" by new methods and theories, as some people claim, but rather use both old and new methods for the greatest possible expansion of our knowledge. The younger generations of competent students and scholars must be able and willing to learn from their teachers what there is to be learned before they can proceed to make their own new contributions, just as we old scholars who were once young did in our time. The validity of all scholarly contributions will not be decided by the preconceptions of academic cliques or claques, or by the shifting bias of intellectual fashion designers and opinion makers, but by the uncorrupted judgment of future scholars willing and able to reexamine the evidence. I hope there will be such scholars, and I for one am willing to face their judgment and to have my errors corrected by them.

For the future health of our profession, we also need reflection on the methods of historical scholarship and its place within the broader system of our culture and experience. A beginning was made by the philosophers of history from Vico to Hegel, and by the methodologists of history from Droysen to Marrou and from Dilthey and Rickert to Cassirer. In this country and in recent decades, there has been a strange lack of concern for these problems. As a result, the various scholarly disciplines have remained unaware of their own method, i.e., both of the methodological features common to all of the fields, and of those peculiar to some or only one of them. The competing claims of facts and interpretation, of evidence and theory have not been clarified. On the other hand, recent philosophers, whether concerned with logic or with the philosophy of science, have tended to neglect or misunderstand the methods of the historical investigation and the nature of the evidence on which its claim to validity as a branch of knowledge is based. We need an epistemology of historical scholarship that will unite the different disciplines into a common enterprise and assign to it its appropriate place in a comprehensive theory and philosophy of culture.

The world of scholarship, once called the republic of letters, is or should be autonomous. It has its own domain and tradition, its recruits and loyalties, its enemies and traitors. If it yields to political or social pressures, it does so at its own risk, and must consider the price it pays and whether that price is worth paying. For it is our task as scholars to preserve and to keep alive what is valuable in our cultural tradition. Our civilization, and especially its external aspects, such as monuments, libraries, and institutions, have always been, and will continue to be, exposed to destruction and continuing transformation. The changes are brought about by new ideas, but also by the sheer succession of different human generations. It is the task of philosophers and historians to continue the discussion of old and new problems within the framework of our past. This work depends on the transmission of knowledge and the preservation of books.

We have the right and duty to communicate our findings and to express our views as best we can. We should not advertise them beyond their merit, or bully our critics, but patiently await the verdict of our successors. We have no power over the future. Our hopes may be deluded, and the fruits of our labor rejected or forgotten. We should like to believe that the past and present will always contribute to the future and be encompassed in it, and also that what is past has a life in itself and a potential future. This is a faith which we cannot prove, though it may sustain us. We can only know and do what is given to us, and we must leave the outcome to the natural and human forces that govern the world and that we hope may be guided in the end by a higher law and providence.

ONE

RENAISSANCE THOUGHT AND CLASSICAL ANTIQUITY

Introduction

Ever since I received training in classical philology and wrote my doctoral dissertation on a Greek philosopher, I have retained, in the face of the changing winds of fashionable opinion, a firm belief in the continuing value of classical studies and of a classical education. Thus I have never failed, in my efforts to understand certain philosophical writers of the Renaissance period, to pay due attention to the influences exercised upon them by classical antiquity, and I should like in these essays to present in a more comprehensive manner my views on this important subject, as fully as the available space and the state of my information will permit.

Since philosophical and historical no less than political discussions are apt to sink into confusion through the use of vague and ill-defined notions, and since I feel unable to discuss my subject without using some of the general terms traditionally applied to it, I should like to explain first how I plan to use some of these terms.

The meaning of the term "Renaissance" has been the subject of an unending controversy among recent historians, who have been debating about the value, the distinctive characteristics, the time limits, and the very existence of that historical period.[1] I shall not repeat or refute any of the arguments proposed by others, but merely state that by "the Renaissance" I understand that period of Western European history which extends approximately from 1300 to 1600, without any preconception as to the characteristics or merits of that period, or of those periods preceding and following it. I do not pretend to assert that there was a sharp break at the beginning or end of "the Renaissance," or to deny that there was a good deal of continuity. I should even admit that in some respects the changes which occurred in the twelfth and thirteenth or in the seventeenth and eighteenth centuries were more profound than the changes of the fourteenth and fifteenth. I merely maintain that the so-called Renaissance period has a distinctive physiognomy of its own, and that the inability of historians to find a simple and satisfactory definition for it does not entitle us to doubt its existence; otherwise, by the same token, we should have to question the existence of the Middle Ages, or of the eighteenth century.

The Renaissance is a very complex period and it encompassed, just as do the Middle Ages or any other period, a good many chronological, regional, and social differences. Not being able to do equal justice to all aspects of the Renaissance, I shall focus our attention, though not exclusively, upon Italy in the fifteenth and early sixteenth centuries. Whereas the cultural differences between Italy and Northern Europe were no less marked during the high Middle Ages than during the Renaissance, in the fifteenth century Italy, along with the Low Countries, attained a position of intellectual leadership in Western Europe which she had not possessed in the preceding age. If Europe during the Middle Ages had one or several renaissances, as some scholars believe, Italy's share in these earlier "renaissances" was rather limited. On the other hand, if the Renaissance of the fifteenth century, seen against the background of the French Middle Ages, does not appear to some historians like a rebirth of Europe, it certainly appeared to its contemporaries, against the background of the Italian Middle Ages, like a rebirth of Italy.

Moreover, I shall not discuss the Renaissance in terms of a few outstanding and well-known thinkers and writers alone, but I shall rather try to draw a cultural map of the period, taking into account the vast amount of information hidden away in the bibliographies of early editions, in the collections and catalogues of manuscript books, and in the records of schools, universities, and other learned institutions. This approach will enable us also to view the great writers of the period in a better perspective, and to judge in each case whether we are dealing with the representative expression of a broad trend of thinking or with the isolated and original contribution of an individual mind.

If we try to understand the thought and philosophy of the Renaissance, or of any other period, we are of course confronted with a variety of currents and of individual writers, which defies any attempt at a general description. The task becomes even more complex if we extend our view beyond the area of "philosophy" in the narrow and technical sense, characterized by professional traditions and the discipline of method, into the vast field of general thought embodied in the writings of poets and prose authors, of scholars, scientists, and theologians. To some extent the historian of philosophy is driven to follow this course, since the very meaning of philosophy, the emphasis it puts on certain problems, its relations to other fields of intellectual endeavor, the place it occupies in the system of culture, are apt to undergo a continuous change. On the other hand, our task is simplified in so far as we are not considering Renaissance thought in its originality or in its entire content but merely in its relation to classical antiquity.

This relation in turn calls for one further preliminary remark. To be sure, the world of classical antiquity, and especially its literature and philosophy, seems to possess a solid reality which, like a high mountain range, has remained above the horizon for many centuries. Yet on closer inspection, it becomes apparent that the use made of this heritage by later generations has been subject to many changes. Each period has offered a different selection and interpretation of ancient literature, and individual Greek and Latin authors as well as their individual writings have seen more or less deep ebbs and tides of popularity at different times. Hence we shall not be surprised to learn that the Renaissance attitude towards classical antiquity differed in many ways from that of medieval or modern times. Modern classicism, which originated in the eighteenth century and continues to influence our approach to the classics, though it has been modified since then by various currents of historical, archaeological, and anthropological scholarship, has tended to focus our attention upon the literature and thought of the early and classical Greek period down to the fourth century B.C., and to a lesser degree upon Roman literature to the first century A.D.; whereas the later phases of Greek and Latin literature, and especially of its doctrinal and scientific literature, have been comparatively neglected.

Medieval Europe, on the other hand, lived for many centuries in the direct tradition of Roman antiquity, used the Latin language as a medium for its learning and much of its literature and business, and knew some though not all of the ancient Roman poets and prose authors quite thoroughly, yet was with a few exceptions unfamiliar with the Greek language and with its classical literature. Moreover, the early Middle Ages, from the time of the Latin Church Fathers, were concerned with the problem of reconciling the study of the pagan classics with the teachings and commands of Christianity, a problem which received added urgency from the fact that the learning of the period was almost entirely in the possession of the Catholic clergy. During the later Middle Ages, and more specifically between the middle of the eleventh and the end of the thirteenth centuries, profound changes occurred in the intellectual culture of Western Europe. A growing professional interest developed in philosophy and in the sciences, which was kindled by Arabic influences and nourished by a flood of Latin translations, from the Arabic and from the Greek, through which many writings of Aristotle and of a few other Greek philosophers, of Euclid and Ptolemy, Galen and Hippocrates became for the first time available to Western students. This later medieval interest in the works of certain Greek philosophers and scientists must be clearly distinguished from the earlier medieval study of the classical Latin poets and prose writers. Actually, there was a conflict between the representatives of the *artes*, that is, of the liberal arts and the scientific and philosophical disciplines, and the followers of the *authores*, that is, of the great books, and by the thirteenth century the latter tendency had suffered a decisive, though perhaps temporary, defeat.[2]

The Renaissance attitude towards the classics inherited some features from the Middle Ages, but was different from the earlier and later medieval approach, as well as from that of modern classicism. Renaissance scholars continued or resumed the study of the Latin authors that had been cultivated by the medieval grammarians, but greatly expanded and improved it, and also pursued it for its own sake. They were not anti-Christian, but as laymen they did not subordinate the development of secular learning to its amalgamation with religious or theological doctrine. Moreover, they added the study of the Greek language and of its entire literature, going far beyond the limits of science and of Aristotelian philosophy. Finally, guided by their enthusiasm for everything ancient, and by the conscious program of imitating and reviving ancient learning and literature, Renaissance scholars had a much more comprehensive interest in ancient literature than either medieval or modern students. They did not despise late or minor authors, in spite of a widespread preference for Cicero or Vergil, and even accepted many apocryphal works as authentic. As a result of this broad interest, classical studies occupied in the Renaissance a more central place in the civilization of the period, and were more intimately linked with its other intellectual tendencies and achievements, than at any earlier or later time in the history of Western Europe.

1.

The
Humanist
Movement

If we are to understand the role of classical studies in the Renaissance, we must begin with the humanist movement. The term "humanism" has been associated with the Renaissance and its classical studies for more than a hundred years, but in recent times it has become the source of much philosophical and historical confusion. In present discourse almost any kind of concern with human values is called "humanistic," and consequently a great variety of thinkers, religious or antireligious, scientific or antiscientific, lay claim to what has become a rather elusive label of praise.

We might ignore this twentieth-century confusion, but for the direct impact it has had upon historical studies. For many historians, knowing that the term "humanism" has been traditionally associated with the Renaissance, and seeing that some features of the modern notion of "humanism" seem to have their counterparts in the thought of that period, have cheerfully applied the term "humanism" in its vague modern meaning to the Renaissance and to other periods of the past, speaking of Renaissance humanism, medieval humanism, or Christian humanism, in a fashion which defies any definition and seems to have little or nothing left of the basic classicist meaning of Renaissance humanism.[1] This seems to me a bad example of that widespread tendency among historians to impose the terms and labels of our modern time upon the thought of the past. If we want to understand the philosophy of the Renaissance or of any other period, we must try not only to separate the interpretation of the authentic thought of the period from the evaluation and critique of its merits, but also to recapture the original meaning in which that period employed certain categories and classifications which either have become unfamiliar to us or have acquired different connotations.

In the case of the term "humanism," its historical ancestry has become pretty clear as a result of recent studies. The term *Humanismus* was coined

in 1808 by the German educator, F. J. Niethammer, to express the emphasis
on the Greek and Latin classics in secondary education as against the rising
demands for a more practical and more scientific training.[2] In this sense, the
word was applied by many historians of the nineteenth century to the
scholars of the Renaissance, who had also advocated and established the
central role of the classics in the curriculum, and who in some German cities
had founded in the sixteenth century the same schools which were still carrying on that tradition in the nineteenth. The term *Humanismus,* in the specific sense of a program and ideal of classical education, cannot be dismissed because of its comparatively recent origin. For it is derived from
another, similar word, "humanist," whose origin can be traced back to the
Renaissance itself. *Humanista* in Latin, and its vernacular equivalents in
Italian, French, English, and other languages, were terms commonly used in
the sixteenth century for the professor or teacher or student of the humanities, and this usage remained alive and was well-understood until the eighteenth century.[3] The word, to judge from its earliest appearance known so
far, seems to have originated in the student slang of the Italian universities,
where the professor of the humanities came to be called *umanista,* after the
analogy of his colleagues in the older disciplines, to whom the terms *legista,*
jurista, canonista, and *artista* had been applied for several centuries.

The term *humanista,* coined at the height of the Renaissance period, was
in turn derived from an older term, that is, from the "humanities" or *studia
humanitatis.* This term was apparently used in the general sense of a liberal
or literary education by such ancient Roman authors as Cicero and Gellius,
and this use was resumed by the Italian scholars of the late fourteenth century.[4] By the first half of the fifteenth century, the *studia humanitatis* came
to stand for a clearly defined cycle of scholarly disciplines, namely grammar, rhetoric, history, poetry, and moral philosophy,[5] and the study of each
of these subjects was understood to include the reading and interpretation of
its standard ancient writers in Latin and, to a lesser extent, in Greek. This
meaning of the *studia humanitatis* remained in general use through the sixteenth century and later, and we may still find an echo of it in our use of the
term "humanities."

Thus Renaissance humanism was not as such a philosophical tendency or
system, but rather a cultural and educational program which emphasized and
developed an important but limited area of studies. This area had for its
center a group of subjects that was concerned essentially neither with the
classics nor with philosophy, but might be roughly described as literature. It

was to this peculiar literary preoccupation that the very intensive and extensive study which the humanists devoted to the Greek and especially to the
Latin classics owed its peculiar character, which differentiates it from that of
modern classical scholars since the second half of the eighteenth century.
Moreover, the *studia humanitatis* includes one philosophical discipline, that
is, morals, but it excludes by definition such fields as logic, natural philosophy, and metaphysics, as well as mathematics and astronomy, medicine,
law, and theology, to mention only such fields as had a firmly established
place in the university curriculum and in the classification schemes of the
period. This stubborn fact seems to me to provide irrefutable evidence
against the repeated attempts to identify Renaissance humanism with the
philosophy, the science, or the learning of the period as a whole.[6]

On the other hand, if we want to apply the Renaissance term "humanist"
to the medieval period, which did not use it, we may choose to call "humanists" certain Carolingian scholars such as Alcuin or Lupus of Ferrières,
or certain twelfth-century authors such as John of Salisbury or the grammarians of Orléans and Chartres, because of the affinity of their learned interests with those of the Italian humanists of the Renaissance. But if we call
St. Thomas Aquinas a "humanist" because of his indebtedness to the Greek
philosopher Aristotle, we might as well apply the same label to all other
Aristotelian philosophers of the later Middle Ages, and also to all medieval
mathematicians, astronomers, medical authors, or jurists, due to their
dependence upon such ancient authorities as Euclid, Ptolemy, Galen, or the
Corpus Juris; and thus we shall have deprived ourselves of a very helpful
distinction indeed. Hence I should like to ask you to keep the Renaissance
meaning of "humanities" and "humanist" well in mind whenever I use the
term "humanism" in these essays, and to forget our modern uses of the
word as completely as you can.

The central importance of literary preoccupations in Renaissance humanism might be illustrated by the professional status of the humanists, most of
whom were active either as teachers of the humanities in secondary schools
or universities, or as secretaries to princes or cities, and by the bulk of their
extant writings, which consists of orations, letters, poems, and historical
works and which is in part still unpublished or even unsifted. It cannot be
our task in this work to give an account of the professional activities of the
humanists or of their contributions to Neolatin literature and to the various
vernacular literatures. I merely want to point out that Renaissance humanism
must be understood as a characteristic phase in what may be called the rhe-

torical tradition in Western culture. This tradition is as old as the Greek Sophists, and it is very much alive in our own day, although the word "rhetoric" has become distasteful to many people. For the studies of speech and composition, of English and creative writing, of advertisement and business correspondence are nothing but modern varieties of the age-old rhetorical enterprise that tries to teach oral and written expression by means of rules and models. Since the rhetorician offers to speak and to write about everything, and the philosopher tries to think about everything, they have always been rivals in their claim to provide a universal training of the mind. This rivalry appeared in Plato's polemic against the Sophists; it continued throughout the later centuries of Greek antiquity in the competing schools of the philosophers and of the rhetoricians;[7] it was largely forgotten among the Romans and their successors in the early Middle Ages, for the simple reason that they had a strong rhetorical, but no philosophical, tradition; it reappeared in various ways in the high Middle Ages with the rise of philosophical studies,[8] and again in the Renaissance when humanistic learning began to compete with the scholastic tradition of Aristotelian philosophy. The relation between the two traditions has been complicated by the fact that the rhetoricians ever since Isocrates have been concerned with morals and have liked to call themselves philosophers, whereas the philosophers ever since Aristotle have tended to offer their own version of rhetoric as a part of philosophy.

The historical significance of rhetoric cannot be fully understood unless we take into consideration not only the rhetorical theories of philosophers such as Aristotle and his scholastic successors, or of rhetoricians who tried to combine rhetoric and philosophy such as Cicero, but also the rhetoric of the rhetoricians, that is, of the authors professionally concerned with the practice of speaking and writing. In medieval Italy, this profession was strongly represented from the late eleventh century on by the so-called *dictatores* who taught and practiced, on the basis of textbooks and models, the eminently practical art of composing documents, letters, and public speeches.[9] It has become clear as a result of recent investigation that the humanists of the Renaissance were the professional successors of the medieval Italian *dictatores,* and inherited from them the various patterns of epistolography and public oratory, all more or less determined by the customs and practical needs of later medieval society. Yet the medieval *dictatores* were no classical scholars and used no classical models for their compositions. It was the novel contribution of the humanists to add the firm belief that in order to write and to speak well it was necessary to study and to imitate the ancients. Thus we can understand why classical studies in the Renaissance were rarely, if ever, separated from the literary and practical aim of the rhetorician to write and to speak well. This practical and professional connection provided a strong incentive towards classical studies and helped to supply for them the necessary manpower for their proper development. I cannot help feeling that the achievements of a given nation or period in particular branches of culture depend not only on individual talents but also on the available professional channels and tasks into which these talents can be drawn and for which they are trained. This is a subject to which cultural and social historians apparently have not yet paid sufficient attention.

If we try to survey the contributions of the Renaissance humanists to classical scholarship, it will be helpful to distinguish between the Latin and the Greek fields. In the field of Latin studies, there was a much closer connection with the rhetorical and practical interests just mentioned, and also with the scholarly traditions of the Middle Ages, although we should keep in mind that these traditions had been less cultivated in Italy, the cradle of Renaissance humanism, than in the Northern countries, and had suffered a decline even in France during the period immediately preceding the Renaissance.

Most attention has been paid to the humanist discoveries of classical Latin authors unknown or neglected during the Middle Ages. The merit of these discoveries has been unduly disparaged with the remark that the manuscripts found by the humanists were written during the Middle Ages, and that the respective authors were consequently not unknown or in need of discovery. If an ancient Latin text survived only in one or two Carolingian manuscripts, and if there are but scanty traces of its having been read during the subsequent centuries, the fact that such a text was found by a humanist and made generally available through numerous copies does constitute a discovery. On the other hand, the fact that some classical Latin authors such as Vergil or Ovid or Seneca or Boethius were widely known throughout the Middle Ages does not refute the equally obvious fact that some other authors such as Lucretius or Tacitus or Manilius were discovered by the humanists. It would be wrong to maintain that classical Latin literature as a whole was neglected during the Middle Ages, or to deny that a certain nucleus of it was commonly studied. It would be equally wrong to deny that as a result of the humanist discoveries the available patrimony of Latin literature was extended almost to its present limits, and that the writings added to the medieval nucleus included, besides less important texts, also some that have been important and influential. Moreover, the case of such a central author as Cicero shows that the dividing line between the medieval nucleus and the humanist discoveries may separate the individual works of the same writer. For whereas some of his works, such as the *De inventione* and the *De officiis,* were commonly used during the Middle Ages, his *Brutus,* his letters and many of his orations were rediscovered by the humanists.

Less sensational but perhaps more effective was the tremendous activity of the humanists as copyists, and later as editors, of the Latin classics. The wide diffusion and popularity of the Latin classics in the sixteenth century and afterwards would not have been possible without the printing press. In the fourteenth and fifteenth centuries, the introduction of paper as a cheaper writing material and the organization of a regular trade in manuscript books had a similar effect, and the enormous number of manuscript copies of the Latin classics from these centuries has escaped general attention because they have been rarely used by modern editors because of their late origin. Along with the copying and editing of the Latin authors, the humanists developed the techniques of textual and historical criticism, studied Latin orthography, grammar, and rhetoric, ancient history and mythology, as well as archaeology, epigraphy, and antiquarian subjects.

Finally, the humanists produced a vast body of commentaries on the various Latin authors, which are the direct result of their teaching activity and in which they incorporated their philological and historical knowledge as well as their critical judgment. This body of literature is undoubtedly related to the commentaries on Latin authors written by medieval grammarians, but the extent of this connection remains to be investigated, and there is reason to believe that the humanist commentaries became gradually more critical and more scholarly in the course of the Renaissance period.[10]

The humanist study of Greek was much less affected by the tradition of rhetorical practice or by Western medieval precedents. Greek books and Greek instruction were rare exceptions during the Middle Ages;[11] consequently, the work of the humanists appears much more novel when attention is focused on the Greek rather than on the Latin classics. On the other hand, the study of the Greek classics had flourished more or less continually during the medieval centuries in the Byzantine East, and Renaissance humanists in their Greek studies were clearly influenced by scholarly contacts with their Byzantine colleagues. The extent of this influence, not only on the acquisition of particular knowledge but also on the approach and attitude of

Western scholars towards Greek literature, cannot yet be estimated.[12] As is well-known, the humanists introduced Greek into the curriculum of all universities and of the better secondary schools of Western Europe, and they also imported from the Byzantine and later Turkish East, through purchase and through less honorable means, a large number of manuscripts containing almost the entire body of extant Greek literature, which was thus deposited in Western libraries and diffused through handwritten copies and printed editions.

But since the knowledge of Greek was comparatively rare even during the Renaissance, whereas Latin remained the common vehicle of learning and instruction, the general diffusion of Greek literature depended no less on Latin translations than on editions of the original Greek texts. Thus it was an important, though not yet sufficiently appreciated, achievement of the Renaissance scholars that they gradually translated into Latin almost the entire body of Greek literature then known, and introduced it into the mainstream of Western thought. Whereas comparatively few writings had been translated from Greek into Latin in ancient times, during the later Middle Ages a large body of such translations was made which covered mainly writings on mathematics, astronomy, and medicine, besides the philosophical works of Aristotle. The Renaissance humanists supplied many new versions of the same works which had been translated before, and the relative merits of these competing medieval and humanist translations have been debated with some passion, but not yet sufficiently investigated.[13] More obvious are the merits of the humanists in those numerous cases where they translated works of Greek antiquity for the first time. The catalogue of these translations cannot yet be given in the present state of our knowledge, but it appears certain that the body of newly translated material includes practically all of Greek poetry, historiography, and oratory, much of Greek patristic theology and of non-Aristotelian philosophy, and even some additional writings on the sciences of mathematics and medicine. The authors all or most of whose writings thus became known to Western readers include Homer and Sophocles; Herodotus and Thucydides; Xenophon, Isocrates, Demosthenes, Plutarch, and Lucian; Epicurus, Sextus, and Plotinus, to mention only a few writers of obvious merit or influence. Again, the dividing line between works translated in the Middle Ages and first translated during the Renaissance often separates the individual writings of the same author, as is the case with Plato, Hippocrates, Galen, and Ptolemy, with many Aristotelian commentators and patristic theologians, and even with Aristotle. Thus it will be apparent that both in the Latin and in the Greek fields, the Middle Ages possessed a significant selection of classical sources, but that Renaissance humanism extended its knowledge almost to the entire range of its extant remains, that is to the point where modern scholarship has made its further discoveries from palimpsests and papyri.

When we try to assess the contributions of the humanists to the philosophical thought of the Renaissance, we must mention in passing the attempts at a reform of logic, due to Valla, Agricola, Ramus, and Nizolius, which were in part guided by rhetorical considerations, but represent an episode of great historical significance. Yet the most extensive and direct expression of the thought of the humanists proper must be sought in a body of their writings that we have not yet mentioned, namely their treatises and dialogues, many of which deal, as might be expected, with moral questions, including educational, political, and religious problems.[14]

Most of these treatises, whether their authors are Petrarch or Salutati, Bruni or Valla, Poggio or Filelfo, Francesco Barbaro or Leone Battista Alberti, are the works of consummate writers and scholars, but must appear somewhat amateurish to a reader acquainted with the works of the greater Greek, scholastic, or modern philosophers. They often seem to lack not only originality, but also coherence, method, and substance, and if we try to sum up their arguments and conclusions, leaving aside citations, examples, and commonplaces, literary ornaments, and digressions, we are frequently left with nearly empty hands. Thus I have not been convinced by the attempts to interpret these humanistic treatises as contributions to speculative thought or to find in humanist philology the seeds of Vico's philosophy of language, although the eighteenth-century philosopher certainly inherited his erudition and his interest in history and literature from the humanists. Nevertheless the humanist treatises are important in many ways and deserve a more thorough study than they have received. They please through the elegance and clarity of their style and their vivid personal and historical flavor as well as through their well-selected and mellowed classical wisdom. They also air or express interesting opinions on matters that occupied the heart and thought of the authors and their contemporaries. They derive added importance from the fact that some of the genuine and more concrete problems of moral philosophy were apparently neglected by the professional philosophers of the time, and thus the humanists prepared the ground for a more systematic treatment of the same problems by later philosophers. This seems to be the function of poets, writers, and amateur thinkers at any time when the professional philosophers are absorbed in technicalities and refuse to discuss certain basic problems.

If we remember the range and extent of humanist scholarship and literature, we shall not be surprised to learn that Isocrates, Plutarch, and Lucian were among their favorite authors, but that the ancient writer who earned their highest admiration was Cicero. Renaissance humanism was an age of Ciceronianism in which the study and imitation of Cicero was a widespread concern, although the exaggeration of this tendency also found its critics. Cicero's influence in the Renaissance has been the subject of more than one study,[15] and we can merely try to state in a few words some of the main features of this influence. Above all, Cicero's rhetorical works provided the theory, and his orations, letters, and dialogues the concrete models for the main branches of prose literature, whereas the structure of his well-cadenced sentences was imitated in all kinds of literary compositions. Through his philosophical writings, he served as a source of information for several schools of Greek philosophy and also as a model of that eclectic type of thinking which was prepared to take its crumbs of knowledge wherever it could find them, and which also characterizes many of the humanist treatises. Finally, the synthesis of philosophy and rhetoric in his work provided the humanists with a favorite ideal, namely, the combination of eloquence and wisdom, an ideal which pervades so much of Renaissance literature. It is true that many of the minor humanists were quite satisfied with eloquence alone, or convinced that enough wisdom would come along with it without further effort; whereas many others took shallow commonplaces for wisdom. Yet we should also remember that many of the greater humanists such as Petrarch and Salutati, Valla and Bruni, Alberti and Pontano, Erasmus, More, and Montaigne were able to add genuine wisdom to their eloquence.

After the middle of the fifteenth century, the influence of humanistic learning spread outside the limits of the *studia humanitatis* into all areas of Renaissance culture, including philosophy and the various sciences. This was due not only to the fashionable prestige of the humanities, but also to the fact that practically every scholar received a humanistic training in secondary school before he acquired professional training in any of the other disciplines at the university. On the other hand, some of the humanists also began to realize that a thorough study of philosophy should be added to the *studia humanitatis*.[16] Consequently, we find a number of important thinkers in the fifteenth century, such as Cusanus, Ficino, and Pico, and many more in the sixteenth, who combined a more or less thoroughgoing humanist

background with solid philosophical achievements which were derived from
different origins.[17] I believe that the discussion of Renaissance humanism in
its original meaning has been confused by the attempts to claim these philosophers as an integral part of it, and thus to identify humanism with all or
most of Renaissance philosophy. On the other hand, these thinkers should
be taken into account if we wish to understand the indirect influence of
humanism on Renaissance thought, an influence which in many ways was
even more important than its direct contribution.

The pervasive influence of humanism on all aspects of Renaissance culture and especially on its philosophical thought is a vast subject of which we
can mention only a few major points. Some influential aspects of Renaissance humanism are characteristic of the age and not necessarily due to classical influences. There is the emphasis on man, on his dignity and privileged
place in the universe, which was forcefully expressed by Petrarch, Manetti,
and other humanists, and later elaborated or criticized by many philosophers.[18] This idea was undoubtedly implied in, and connected with, the concept and program of the *studia humanitatis,* and it has provided the opening
entry for many modern interpretations of humanism, whenever the specific
content of the humanities was left out of account.

Another characteristic feature is the tendency to express, and to consider
worth expressing, the concrete uniqueness of one's feelings, opinions, experiences, and surroundings, a tendency which appears in the biographical and
descriptive literature of the time as well as in its portrait painting, which is
present in all the writings of the humanists, and which finds its fullest philosophical expression in Montaigne, who claims that his own self is the main
subject matter of his philosophy.[19] This tendency has been adequately described by Burckhardt, who called it "individualism," and those who have
debated the individualism of the Renaissance have missed this point entirely
when they understand by individualism merely the existence of great individuals, or the nominalist emphasis on the reality of particular things as
against universals.

Yet more relevant to our purpose are those aspects of humanist influence
which are directly connected with its fundamental classicism. I am inclined
to find its traces in the taste for elegance, neatness, and clarity of style and
literary form which distinguishes the writings of many, if not all, Renaissance scientists and philosophers, and which is not always or entirely a mere
external feature. More obvious is the ubiquity of classical sources, quotations, and ideas in Renaissance thought that were either introduced or popu-

larized by the work of the humanists. Without impairing the originality of achievement, this classical element appears in one way or another in all areas, in the visual arts as in the various sciences. Although nearly nothing was known about ancient music, ancient musical theories were used to justify certain innovations of the time, and the humanist reform of handwriting from which our Roman characters are derived was based on the Carolingian minuscule which they mistakenly thought to be the script of the ancient Romans. Livy and Polybius affected the political thought of Machiavelli, Plato that of Thomas More, and Tacitus the theorists of the later sixteenth century. There was no thinker in the sixteenth century who did not use, besides the traditional texts of Aristotle, Cicero, and Boethius, the newly acquired writings of Plato and the Neoplatonists, of Plutarch and Lucian, of Diogenes Laertius, of Sextus and Epictetus, or the aprocryphal works attributed to the Pythagoreans, Orpheus, Zoroaster, and Hermes Trismegistus.

One more effect of humanism upon Renaissance thought consisted of the repeated attempts to revive or restate the philosophical doctrines of particular ancient thinkers or schools, which in a sense represent the application to philosophy of the revival or renaissance of ancient learning which was one of the favorite slogans of the humanists, and from which the much-debated modern name of the period derives its origin. Whereas the tendency of most humanists was rather eclectic, some of them, and also certain other philosophers with a humanist background, preferred a restatement of some particular ancient doctrine. Thus we find a kind of Christianized Epicureanism in Valla; whereas the natural philosophy of Epicurus found an advocate, after the end of the Renaissance proper, in Gassendi, and even influenced some aspects of Galileo's physics. Stoic philosophy had a wide influence on the moral thought of the Renaissance, until it found a systematic and learned interpreter towards the very end of the period in Justus Lipsius, whose writings exercised a strong influence on the moralists of the subsequent centuries. Various brands of ancient skepticism were adopted, with some modifications, by Montaigne, Sanchez, and others before they came to influence early modern thought down to Bayle and Hume. This tendency also supplies the broader context for at least some aspects of Renaissance Platonism, Aristotelianism, and Christianity.

Thus I should like to understand Renaissance humanism, at least in its origin and in its typical representatives, as a broad cultural and literary movement, which in its substance was not philosophical but had important philosophical implications and consequences. I have been unable to discover in

the humanist literature any common philosophical doctrine, except a belief
in the value of man and the humanities and in the revival of ancient learning. Any particular statement gleaned from the work of a humanist may be
countered by contrary assertions in the writings of contemporary authors or
even of the same author. On the other hand, the common cultural orientation
and background might be combined in the case of each author with any set
of philosophical or scientific or theological opinions or cognitions, and actually came to cut across all national, religious, philosophical, and even professional divisions of the period. Since the entire range of Greek philosophical and scientific literature was made more completely available to the
West than it had been in the Middle Ages or in Roman antiquity, there was a
large store of new ideas and notions that had to be tried out and appropriated
until its lesson was finally exhausted, and it is this process of intellectual fermentation which characterizes the period and which accounts at least in part
for the difference between Thomas Aquinas and Descartes. For only after
this process had been completed, did seventeenth-century philosophy make
its new beginning on the basis of early physical science, whereas the heritage of the Renaissance continued to feed many secondary currents of
thought down to the nineteenth century.

2.

The Aristotelian Tradition

Among the many philosophers of classical antiquity, two thinkers have
exercised a wider and deeper influence upon posterity than any others, Plato
and Aristotle. The controversy and interplay between Platonism and Aristotelianism has occupied a central place in many periods of Western
thought, and even the modern student who receives but an elementary introduction to Greek philosophy will inevitably get acquainted with the
thought, and with some of the writings, of Plato and Aristotle. This over-
whelming importance of Plato and Aristotle is due to two factors which are
in a sense related to each other: the intrinsic greatness of their thought and

the preservation of their writings. Aside from such authors as Sextus Empiricus, Epictetus, Alexander of Aphrodisias, and the Neoplatonists, who represent the latest phases of ancient thought, Plato and Aristotle are the only important Greek philosophers whose writings have been extant, either completely or to a considerable extent. Neither their predecessors such as Heraclitus, Parmenides, or Democritus, nor their successors such as Chrysippus, Panaetius, or Posidonius have been so fortunate, and others such as Theophrastus and Epicurus have fared but slightly better.

Historians of Western thought have often expressed the view that the Renaissance was basically an age of Plato, whereas the Middle Ages had been an age of Aristotle. This view can no longer be maintained without considerable qualifications. In spite of a widespread revolt against the authority of Aristotle, the tradition of Aristotelianism continued to be very strong throughout the Renaissance period, and in some ways it even increased. On the other hand, Platonism had its own medieval roots and precedents, and even during the Renaissance its precise place and the extent of its influence are somewhat elusive and difficult to define, in spite of its undoubted depth and vigor. Nevertheless, Aristotle's influence in the Renaissance was clearly linked with a tradition that originated in the later Middle Ages, and Platonism was understood by its representatives and their contemporaries as a revival. These circumstances may explain why I am going to discuss Aristotle's influence before that of Plato, although Aristotle was Plato's pupil and presupposed the philosophy of his teacher in many ways.

If we want to understand the impact of Aristotle upon later thought, we must remember some curious facts connected with the transmission of his writings.[1] When Aristotle died in 322 B.C., he left a very extensive body of writings which consisted of two completely different kinds. On the one hand, there was a large group of dialogues and other popular treatises which had been published during his lifetime and which continued to be widely read through many centuries until they were finally lost towards the end of antiquity. These popular writings of Aristotle were praised for their literary elegance, and apparently the most famous among them were composed in Aristotle's earlier years and were comparatively close to Plato in their philosophical opinions. The second group of Aristotle's writings, which is the one that has come down to us, represents a collection of the lecture courses he delivered in his school in Athens. These courses served no literary purpose, but in turn they are highly technical in character, very detailed in their reasoning and in the information supplied, and fairly systematic in their over-all arrangement, forming a vast encyclopaedia of philosophical and scientific knowledge. The systematic writings of Aristotle were not published in his lifetime, and were for several centuries available only in the library of his school where they were studied by his pupils and successors, and in a few large research libraries such as Alexandria where they were accessible to other advanced students of philosophy.

The Aristotelian corpus as we know it was finally published during the first century B.C., and even some time after that date it does not seem to have been widely read or studied. Until the second century A.D., outside the circle of scholars trained in the Aristotelian school, the systematic writings of Aristotle exercised little influence upon the development of ancient thought, and it would be anachronistic to assume such an influence as a major factor in the Platonic Academy, in Stoicism, Epicureanism, or Skepticism, in Philo or in the early Christian thinkers. At the same time, the works and thoughts of Aristotle were transmitted, studied, interpreted, and supplemented by a long series of Aristotelian philosophers in his school, among whom the earliest, Theophrastus, and the last, Alexander of Aphrodisias, are best known to us. Alexander, who lived around 200 A.D., was one of the most authoritative commentators of Aristotle; it was he who modified the Aristotelian doctrine in a more naturalistic and anti-Platonic direction, denying, for example, the immortality of the soul, a point on which Aristotle had been somewhat ambiguous.

The rise of the Neoplatonic school, which was founded in the third century A.D. and dominated Greek thought down to the end of antiquity in the sixth century, also marks an important phase in the history of Aristotelianism. During that period, Aristotelianism disappeared as a separate school tradition, yet the Neoplatonists themselves were committed to a synthesis of Plato and Aristotle. Consequently, the systematic writings of Aristotle were no less thoroughly studied than the dialogues of Plato; Aristotelian doctrine, especially in logic and natural philosophy, was extensively appropriated, and some of the best and most voluminous commentaries on Aristotle, such as those of Simplicius, are due to members of this school. One Neoplatonic treatise, Porphyry's introduction to the *Categories*, became almost an integral part of the Aristotelian corpus.

The fact that Aristotle was appropriated and in a sense preserved by the Neoplatonists left profound traces in the later history of Aristotelianism. In trying to follow this history through the Middle Ages, we must distinguish, as for all philosophical and scientific writings of Greek antiquity, three main traditions: the Byzantine, the Arabic, and the Latin.[2] The place of Aristotle in the Byzantine tradition has not yet been, to my knowledge, sufficiently investigated.[3] Yet it is apparent that the writings of the Aristotelian corpus were preserved and transmitted in their original Greek text by Byzantine scholars and copyists, and a number of extant Byzantine commentaries on Aristotle show that the study of his works and thought was by no means neglected. As far as I can determine, the study of Aristotle among the Byzantines was not separated from, or opposed to, the study of Plato and of the ancient Greek poets, nor was it especially connected with theology, except in some very late authors who had been subjected to Western, Latin influences. If I am not mistaken, it was this Byzantine Aristotle, allied with Neoplatonism and literature as an integral part of the classical heritage, whom some of the Greek scholars of the fifteenth century carried with them into their Italian exile and who exercised some influence upon the Aristotelian studies of the later Renaissance.

Very different, and for its impact upon the Western Middle Ages, more important, was the history of Aristotle among the Arabs.[4] When the Arabs began to translate the works of Greek literature that interested them, they largely omitted the Greek poets, orators, and historians, and centered their efforts on the most authoritative writers in such fields as mathematics and astronomy, medicine, astrology and alchemy, and philosophy. The translated Greek works provided the nucleus of subject matter in these disciplines, to which the Arabs subsequently added their own contributions. As far as philosophy is concerned, the Arabs acquired an almost complete corpus of Aristotle's systematic writings, along with some Neoplatonic and other commentaries on them, and a certain number of Neoplatonic treatises. Thus the Arabs inherited Aristotle from the Neoplatonic tradition of late antiquity, and consequently their understanding of Aristotle was affected by Neoplatonic interpretations and accretions which they were never able to eliminate completely.

On the other hand, Aristotle attained among the Arabs an authority and doctrinal preponderance that he had never possessed in Greek antiquity to the very end. Apparently the Arabs did not acquire the complete writings of Plato and the major Neoplatonists, and thus the sheer bulk of Aristotle's writings, along with their commentaries and the apocrypha, outweighed all other Greek philosophical literature available to them. Moreover, these writings imposed themselves by the solidity of their content and by the systematic and encyclopaedic character of the corpus, which lent itself to painstaking study and which comprised, besides such disciplines as logic, rhetoric, poetics, ethics, and metaphysics, also a number of others which have since been detached from philosophy as separate sciences, such as economics and psychology, physics and natural history. The Aristotelian corpus, supplemented by medicine and mathematics, seemed to represent a complete encyclopaedia of learning whose various writings coincided with the branches of knowledge as such. The authority of Aristotle was probably further enhanced by that of Galen, who was strongly influenced by Aristotelian philosophy and exercised a similar influence upon Arabic medicine, especially since some of the most important Arabic thinkers combined philosophy and medicine in their work. Thus the major Arabic philosophers, such as Avicenna and Averroes, were commentators and followers of Aristotle, and Averroes even tended to reduce the Neoplatonic additions and to attain a purer understanding of Aristotle. As is well known, the Aristotelianism of the Arabs, and especially that of Averroes, exercised a powerful influence upon Jewish thought of the later Middle Ages, where Maimonides was the leading representative of Aristotelianism, and strongly affected the philosophy of the Christian West even after its tradition had come to a sudden end in the Islamic world itself as a result of new religious and political developments.

If we want to understand the history of thought and learning in the Western Latin Middle Ages, we must first of all realize that it had its foundation in Roman, not Greek antiquity. The Romans produced, under the impact of Greek models, a distinguished literature in poetry and in prose; they appropriated the grammatical and rhetorical learning of the Greeks; and they made a lasting original contribution in the field of jurisprudence; but they did not develop a significant philosophical tradition. Rome and the other Western centers had flourishing schools of rhetoric, but no schools of philosophy comparable to those of Athens and Alexandria. The efforts to develop a technical vocabulary for philosophical discourse in the Latin language remained in the beginning stages until the end of antiquity.

Few outstanding works of Greek philosophers were translated into Latin, and the philosophical literature produced by the Romans was mostly of a popularizing nature. Among the Greek sources of this literature Aristotle occupies a very minor place, compared with the Platonists, Stoics, Skeptics, or Epicureans. He appears to be unknown to, or to have no importance for, Lucretius, Seneca, or St. Augustine; and even Cicero is chiefly acquainted with the published works of Aristotle that are now lost and barely mentions the systematic writings which dominated the later tradition. The one significant exception is represented by one of the latest writers of Roman antiquity, Boethius, who translated at least two of Aristotle's logical works, the *Categories* and the treatise *On Interpretation*, along with Porphyry's introduction.

During the early Middle Ages, the Latin West was largely cut off from the richer Greek tradition and restricted to the indigenous resources of Roman literature, which, as we have noted, was weak in philosophy. The body of secular learning provided in the monastic and cathedral schools of the period was limited to the elementary encyclopaedia of the seven liberal arts, that is, grammar, rhetoric, dialectic, arithmetic, geometry, astronomy, and music. In this scheme, which prevailed to the eleventh century, grammar was the leading subject, which included at times the study of the Latin poets. Philosophy was represented only by dialectic, that is, elementary logic, and this subject was largely based on the Aristotelian treatises translated by Boethius. Philosophy in the broad sense of the word as known to the ancient Greeks was almost forgotten, and the only author who made a genuine contribution to philosophical thought in that period, Scotus Eriugena, was an isolated figure distinguished for his acquaintance with Greek Neoplatonism.

This situation was completely changed through the remarkable rise of philosophical, theological, and scientific studies that began during the second half of the eleventh century and culminated in the thirteenth. During that period, the body of learning expanded steadily until it surpassed the traditional limits of the seven arts. A large number of writings on philosophy, on the sciences and the pseudo sciences were translated from Arabic and from Greek, which introduced precious material previously unavailable in Latin and tended to stimulate and transform Western thought.[5] Among the philosophical authors thus translated, Proclus and other Neoplatonic authors were well represented, but the most extensive and most important body of literature consisted of the nearly complete corpus of Aristotle, accompanied by a few Greek commentaries, and by a much larger body of Arabic commentaries, especially those of Avicenna and Averroes. The writings of Aristotle and his Greek commentators as well as of Proclus were in part translated from the original text, to be sure, but the selection of subjects and authors clearly reflects the Arabic rather than the ancient Greek tradition of philosophy.

At the same time, new institutions of higher learning developed, the universities, which differed considerably from the earlier schools in their curriculum, textbooks, and methods of instruction.[6] The instruction centered around the *lectura,* the continuous reading and exposition of a standard text, and the *disputatio,* the public discussion of a proposed thesis with the help of formalized arguments. These forms of instruction produced the two main types of medieval scholarly literature, the commentary and the question. The subject matter of university instruction was fixed during the thirteenth century at Paris and the other Northern universities in the system of four faculties: theology, law, medicine, and arts or philosophy. Whereas the teaching of theology was based on the Bible and on Peter Lombard's *Sentences,* and that of law on the *Corpus Juris* of Justinian and on Gratian's *Decretum,* the instruction in medicine and in philosophy came to be based on some of the new translations from the Greek and Arabic. The philosophical disciplines thus became for the first time in the Latin world subjects of separate instruction, and the texts adopted for this instruction, after some resistance, were the writings of Aristotle along with those of Averroes and other commentators. The chief subjects were logic and natural philosophy, whereas ethics and metaphysics attained the status of elective courses only. Thus the writings of Aristotle had become by the middle of the thirteenth century the basis of philosophical instruction at the universities. They owed this position not merely to Arabic precedent, but also to the solidity of their content and to their systematic and encyclopaedic character. Aristotle was not studied as a "great book," but as a textbook that was the starting point for commentaries and questions and supplied a frame of reference for all trained philosophical thinkers even when they ventured to reinterpret him, or to depart from his doctrine, according to their own opinions.

The Aristotelianism of the later Middle Ages was characterized not so much by a common system of ideas as by a common source material, a common terminology, a common set of definitions and problems, and a common method of discussing these problems. There was offered a variety of interpretations for many passages in Aristotle, and a variety of solutions for the most debated problems, some of which grew out of medieval philosophical preoccupations rather than from Aristotle's own writings. The understanding of this vast and complex philosophical literature has made much progress in recent years, yet it is still hampered by the failure to distinguish clearly between philosophy and theology, which were separate disciplines, by an excessive faith in such general labels as Thomism, Scotism, Ockhamism, and Averroism, and by a tendency to focus attention too exclusively on St. Thomas Aquinas and his school.

The Aristotelian philosophers of the thirteenth and fourteenth centuries were engaged in the discussion of numerous detailed problems, especially in logic and physics, and offered a great variety of solutions for each of them. Whereas it might be possible to group them roughly according to the stand taken on a particular issue, they may show a very different alignment with reference to some other issue.[7] Thomas Aquinas went farthest among his contemporaries in his attempt to reconcile Aristotelian philosophy and Christian theology, and his writings are distinguished by their clarity and coherence. Yet in his own time, he enjoyed no monopoly of authority or of orthodoxy; his teachings were in competition with many others, and sometimes even condemned, and much of his work belongs, by medieval standards, to theology rather than to philosophy. His authority was soon established within his own Dominican order, but outside that order, the doctrines of Duns Scotus and of William of Ockham were much more influential, and the important developments in logic and physics which took place during the fourteenth century at Oxford and Paris were largely due to the Ockhamist school.

Most ambiguous and controversial of all is the term Averroism which has been applied by historians to one particular trend of medieval Aristotelianism.[8] If we understand by Averroism the use of Averroes' commentary on Aristotle, every medieval Aristotelian including Aquinas was an Averroist. If we limit the term to all those thinkers who made a neat distinction between reason and faith, Aristotelian philosophy and Christian theology, practically all teachers of philosophy, as distinct from the theologians, took that position, from the later thirteenth century through the fourteenth and later. Finally, if we mean by Averroism the adherence to one distinctive doctrine of Averroes, namely the unity of the intellect in all men, we are singling out a much smaller group of thinkers who still differ among each other on the numerous other questions which occupied and divided the Aristotelian philosophers of the period. Hence it will be best to use these labels with great caution, and to emphasize the fact that the Aristotelian tradition of the later Middle Ages comprised a great variety of thinkers and of ideas held together by a common reference to the corpus of Aristotle's writings, which constituted the basic material of reading and discussion in the philosophical disciplines.

I seem to have given an undue share of space to a discussion of medieval rather than Renaissance developments. Yet it has been my intention to show how Aristotle had become by the early fourteenth century "the master of those who know," in order to emphasize the additional fact, which is less widely known, that this Aristotelian tradition, though exposed to attacks and subject to transformations, continued strongly and vigorously to the end of the sixteenth century and even later. The failure to appreciate this fact is due to various reasons. Historians, like journalists, are apt to concentrate on news and to forget that there is a complex and broad situation which remained unaffected by the events of the moment. They also have for some time been more interested in the origins than in the continuations of intellectual and other developments. More specifically, many historians of thought have been sympathetic to the opponents of Aristotelianism in the Renaissance, whereas most of the defenders of medieval philosophy have limited their efforts to its earlier phases before the end of the thirteenth century, and have sacrificed the late scholastics to the critique of their contemporary and modern adversaries.

Yet we have learned through recent studies that the chief progress made during the later fourteenth century in the fields of logic and natural philosophy was due to the Aristotelian, and more specifically, to the Ockhamist school at Paris and Oxford. During the fifteenth and sixteenth centuries, university instruction in the philosophical disciplines continued everywhere to be based on the works of Aristotle; consequently, most professional teachers of philosophy followed the Aristotelian tradition, used its terminology and method, discussed its problems, and composed commentaries and questions on Aristotle. Only a few individual thinkers and schools have been studied so far, and the large extent of this tradition, and of its proportional share in the philosophical literature of the Renaissance period, is not generally realized. This Aristotelian orientation of the university philosophers can be traced at Paris,[9] Louvain, and other centers far into the sixteenth century, although it has not been studied very much. It disappears from sight at Oxford and Cambridge after the end of the fourteenth century, but there is reason to believe that this is due to lack of scholarly attention rather than lack of facts or source materials.[10] It flourished, in close alliance with Catholic theology, well into the seventeenth century at Salamanca, Alcalà, and Coimbra, and the influence of this Spanish neoscholasticism extended, through its most famous representative, Franciscus Suarez, well beyond the borders of the

Iberian peninsula or of Catholicism.[11] Also at the German universities, Aristotelianism was strong and productive through the fifteenth century, and continued to flourish long after the Protestant Reformation, for in spite of Luther's dislike for scholasticism, and thanks to the influence of Melanchthon, Aristotle remained the chief source of academic instruction in the philosophical disciplines.[12] Thus it is not surprising if even later philosophers who turned far away from scholasticism, such as Bacon, Descartes, Spinoza, or Leibniz, still show in their terminology, in their arguments, and in some of their doctrines the traces of that tradition which was still alive in the schools and universities of their time, although we should realize that these thinkers absorbed at the same time also different influences which we might roughly describe as humanistic, Platonist, Stoic, or Skeptical.[13]

We have not yet spoken about the place of Aristotelianism in Italy, a country which differed from the rest of Europe in many respects even during the Middle Ages and which occupied such an important position during the Renaissance period. The customary views on the Italian Renaissance might easily lead us to believe that Aristotelian scholasticism flourished in medieval Italy as in the North, but was abandoned in Italy sooner than elsewhere under the impact of Renaissance humanism. The actual facts suggest almost exactly the opposite. Up to the last decades of the thirteenth century, instruction at the Italian universities was almost entirely limited to formal rhetoric, law, and medicine. Scholastic theology was largely confined to the schools of the mendicant orders; and those famous scholastic theologians and philosophers who happened to be Italian, such as Lanfranc, Anselm, Peter Lombard, St. Bonaventura, and St. Thomas Aquinas, did most of their studying and teaching at Paris and other Northern centers. After some earlier appearance at Salerno and Naples, Aristotelian philosophy became for the first time firmly established at Bologna and other Italian universities towards the very end of the thirteenth century,[14] that is, at the same time that the first signs of a study of the Latin classics began to announce the coming rise of Italian humanism. Simultaneously with humanism, Italian Aristotelianism developed steadily through the fourteenth century under the influence of Paris and Oxford, became more independent and more productive through the fifteenth century,[15] and attained its greatest development during the sixteenth and early seventeenth centuries, in such comparatively well-known thinkers as Pomponazzi, Zabarella, and Cremonini. In other words, as far as Italy is concerned, Aristotelian scholasticism, just like classical humanism, is fundamentally a phenomenon of the Renaissance period whose ultimate roots can be traced in a continuous development to the very latest phase of the Middle Ages.

The greatest difference between this Italian Aristotelianism and its Northern counterpart, aside from the times of their respective rise and decline, is related to the organization of the universities and their faculties or schools. In Paris and the other Northern centers, philosophy was taught in the faculty of arts, which also included what was left of the seven liberal arts, and which served as preparation for the three higher faculties of law, medicine, and theology, especially for the latter. At Bologna and the other Italian centers, there were only two faculties, that of law and that of the arts. There never was a separate faculty of theology. Within the faculty of arts, medicine was the most important subject of instruction, logic and natural philosophy were considered as preparatory for medicine and occupied the second place, whereas grammar, rhetoric, and moral philosophy, mathematics and astronomy, theology and metaphysics came last. As in the North, logic and natural philosophy were considered the most important philosophical disciplines and taught on the basis of Aristotle and his commentators, but this instruction was and always remained linked with medicine and unrelated to theology.

Under the misleading name of "Paduan Averroism," some phases of this Italian Aristotelianism have been studied during the last hundred years or so, but much of the literature produced by it remains unpublished or unread. It consists in commentaries and questions on the works of Aristotle, and in independent treatises on related problems. The labels used for it such as Thomism, Scotism and Ockhamism, Averroism and Alexandrism are, as usual, inadequate. Their work consists, like that of their Northern predecessors and contemporaries, in a detailed discussion of many minute questions where each particular issue was likely to produce a variety of solutions and a different alignment of individual thinkers. Again they agree in their method and terminology, and in their constant reference to Aristotle and his commentators, but there are few philosophical doctrines common to all of them. The separation between philosophy and theology, reason or Aristotle and faith or religious authority, was consistently maintained, without leading to a direct conflict or opposition. Besides rational argument, sense perception or experience was emphasized as the major or only source of natural knowledge, and this might justify us in speaking of a kind of empiricism. In the sixteenth century, Averroes' doctrine of the unity of the intellect for all men continued to be discussed, although it was accepted only by some of the Aristotelian philosophers. At the same time, the related problem of immortality became the center of discussion through a famous and controversial treatise of Pomponazzi, who rejected the unity of the intellect but maintained that the immortality of the soul cannot be demonstrated on rational or Aristotelian principles. Later Aristotelians such as Zabarella participated in the discussion on the nature of the cognitive method, and formulated the doctrine that natural knowledge proceeds through analysis from the observed phenomena to their inferred causes, and returns through synthesis from the latter to the former, a doctrine that was at least partly rooted in the Aristotelian tradition and influenced in turn so anti-Aristotelian a scientist as Galileo.[16]

Among the Aristotelian philosophers of the Italian Renaissance, the strongest influences were apparently those of Ockhamism and of the so-called Averroism, which were gradually modified by various contemporary developments. At the same time, Thomism and Scotism continued to flourish among the theologians. Scotism seems to have been the more active and more widely diffused current, but the Italian Renaissance produced such authoritative Thomists as Caietanus, and the Dominican teaching affected many other theologians, and also such non-Thomist philosophers as Ficino and Pomponazzi. If we add to this the authority attached to Thomas by the Jesuits and by the Council of Trent, and the increasing use of his *Summa,* instead of Peter Lombard's *Sentences,* as a textbook of theology, we may very well say that the sixteenth century marks a notable advance over the thirteenth and fourteenth centuries in the relative role and importance of Thomism, and a conspicuous step towards that adoption of Thomism as the official philosophy of the Catholic Church which was finally codified in 1879.[17]

After this all-too-brief discussion of Renaissance Aristotelianism in its close relations to the later Middle Ages, I should like to mention those changes and modifications which it underwent under the impact of the new attitudes of the period, and especially of classical humanism. The keynote of this change was sounded by Petrarch when he suggested that Aristotle was better than his translators and commentators, and the general tendency was to take Aristotle out of his isolation as a textbook authority into the company of the other ancient philosophers and writers.[18]

Western scholars learned from their Byzantine teachers to study the works of Aristotle in the Greek original. Humanist professors began to lecture on

Aristotle as one of the classical Greek authors, and Aristotelian philosophers who had enjoyed a humanist education were led to refer to the original text of their chief authority. Although practically the whole corpus of Aristotle's works had been translated into Latin during the later Middle Ages, the Renaissance humanists used their increased knowledge of the Greek language and literature to supply new Latin versions of Aristotle which competed with their medieval predecessors and gradually penetrated into the university curriculum. The merits of these humanist translations in relation to the medieval ones have been debated ever since their own time, and obviously vary according to the abilities of the individual translators. They show a better knowledge of syntax, idioms, and textual variants, and also a greater freedom in word order, style, and terminology. The changes in terminology were a serious matter in an author who served as a standard text in philosophy, and the net result was to present an Aristotle who was different from that of the medieval tradition.

Moreover, there were a few additions made to the Aristotelian corpus, and some of the writings previously available acquired a novel importance or a novel place in the system of learning. The *Eudemian Ethics* was translated for the first time, and so were the *Mechanics* and some other writings of the early Aristotelian school. The *Theology* of Aristotle, an apocryphal work of Arabic origin and Neoplatonic tendency, was used to emphasize the agreement between Plato and Aristotle, and the fragments of Aristotle's lost early writings were collected for the same purpose.[19] The humanists who considered moral philosophy as a part of their domain and often held the chair of ethics continued to use the *Nicomachean Ethics* and *Politics* as their main texts, and thus were led to give to Aristotle's doctrine an important share in their eclectic views on moral, educational, and political questions.

Aristotle's *Rhetoric,* which in the Middle Ages had been neglected by the professional rhetoricians and treated by the scholastic philosophers as an appendix to the *Ethics* and *Politics,* became during the sixteenth century an important text for the humanist rhetoricians.[20] The *Poetics,* not completely unknown to the Latin Middle Ages,[21] as scholars had long believed, but still comparatively neglected, attained through the humanists a wide circulation and became in the sixteenth century the standard text which gave rise to a large body of critical discussion and literature;[22] and it is curious to note that the authority of Aristotle's *Poetics* attained its climax in the same seventeenth century which witnessed the overthrow of his *Physics.* Finally, if we pass from the humanist scholars to the professional philosophers and scientists, it appears that the most advanced work of Aristotle's logic, the *Posterior Analytics,* received greater attention in the sixteenth century than before, and that at the same time an increased study of Aristotle's biological writings accompanied the contemporary progress in botany, zoology, and natural history.[23]

With reference to those works of Aristotle which were and remained the center of instruction in logic and natural philosophy, the most important changes derived from the fact that the works of the ancient Greek commentators became completely available in Latin between the late fifteenth and the end of the sixteenth centuries and were more and more used to balance the interpretations of the medieval Arabic and Latin commentators. The Middle Ages had known their works only in a very limited selection or through quotations in Averroes. Ermolao Barbaro's complete translation of Themistius and Girolamo Donato's version of Alexander's *De anima* were among the most important ones in a long line of others. When modern historians speak of Alexandrism as a current within Renaissance Aristotelianism that was opposed to Averroism, they are justified in part by the fact that the Greek commentators, that is, Alexander and also Themistius, Simplicius, and many others, were increasingly drawn upon for the exposition of Aristotle. In a more particular sense, Alexander's specific notion that the human soul was mortal received more attention from the Aristotelian philosophers. Thus the change and increase in Aristotelian source material led in many instances to a doctrinal change in the interpretation of the philosopher or in the philosophical position defended in the name of reason, nature, and Aristotle, and these doctrinal changes were further enhanced under the impact of both classical and contemporary ideas of different, non-Aristotelian origin. Thus Pomponazzi, who is rightly considered an outstanding representative of the Aristotelian school, emphasizes such non-Aristotelian doctrines as the central position of man in the universe and the importance of the practical rather than the speculative intellect for human happiness, which are both of humanistic origin; defends the Stoic doctrine of fate against Alexander of Aphrodisias; and follows Plato and the Stoics in stressing that moral virtue is its own reward, vice its own greatest punishment.[24] Such amalgamations of diverse doctrines are bound to occur in any genuine philosophical tradition dedicated to the pursuit of truth rather than of orthodoxy, and they become harmful only when they are used to distort the historical facts or to bolster the dogmatic claims of a particular tradition.

The gradual nature of the change which affected Renaissance Aristotelianism and which I have been trying to describe is apparent when we compare the works of two outstanding Aristotelian philosophers of the early and of the late sixteenth century. Jacopo Zabarella, who represents the later phase, had acquired a full command of the Greek Aristotle and of his ancient commentators, and thus he has been praised by modern scholars not only as a good philosopher but also as one of the best and most lucid Aristotelian commentators of all ages. Pietro Pomponazzi, who died in 1525, knew no Greek and was still deeply imbued with the traditions of medieval Aristotelianism, but he eagerly seized upon the new source material made available by his humanist contemporaries and derived from Alexander the idea that the immortality of the human soul could not be demonstrated on rational or Aristotelian principles. Thus the classical scholarship of the humanists, applied to Aristotle and to his Greek commentators, had an indirect but powerful effect upon the continuing tradition of philosophical Aristotelianism through the sixteenth century and afterwards.

Our picture of the Renaissance attitude towards Aristotle would be incomplete if we failed to discuss the strong currents of anti-Aristotelianism which have been often exaggerated or misunderstood but which do occupy an important place in Renaissance thought. The rebellion against the authority of Aristotle or at least against his medieval interpreters is indeed a recurrent feature in the writings of many Renaissance thinkers from Petrarch to Bruno and Galileo. When we examine this polemic in each case for its reasons, content, and results, instead of taking its charges and claims at their face value, we are led to the conclusion that the anti-Aristotelianism of the Renaissance laid the ground for certain later developments, to be sure, but that it was in its own time neither unified nor effective. When we listen to Petrarch's attacks against Aristotle and his medieval followers, we are apt to forget that the Aristotelianism which he attacked had been established at the universities for hardly a hundred years, and in Italy even more recently. Thus a younger generation tends to believe that it is overthrowing a tradition of many centuries when in fact this tradition had been barely established by its fathers or grandfathers.

The humanist attacks against scholasticism from which Aristotle himself was often exempted are known from several documents of the fifteenth century, from Leonardo Bruni to Ermolao Barbaro.[25] This polemic turned out to be ineffective inasmuch as the humanists criticized the bad style of their opponents, their ignorance of classical sources, and their preoccupation with supposedly unimportant questions, but failed to make positive contributions to the philosophical and scientific disciplines with which the scholastics were concerned. If we keep in mind the cultural and professional divisions of the period, and the flourishing state of Aristotelian philosophy in Renaissance Italy, we are inclined to view this polemic in its proper perspective, that is, as an understandable expression of departmental rivalry and as a phase in the everlasting battle of the arts of which many other examples may be cited from ancient, medieval, or modern times.[26] Only in some instances did Renaissance humanists succeed in attacking their scholastic opponents on their own ground. There was a persistent tendency which began with Valla and culminated in Ramus and Nizolius to reform Aristotelian logic with the help of rhetoric, and during the latter part of the sixteenth century as well as much of the seventeenth, Ramism was a serious rival of Aristotelian logic in the schools of Germany, Great Britain, and America.[27] On the other hand, the Spanish humanist Vives in his *De tradendis disciplinis* made the ambitious attempt to substitute a classical and humanist encyclopaedia of learning for the medieval one and exercised a deep and wide influence on Western education.

Renaissance Platonism, which many historians have been inclined to oppose to medieval Aristotelianism, was not as persistently anti-Aristotelian as we might expect. Its most influential representatives were either impressed by the Neoplatonic synthesis of Plato and Aristotle, or even directly affected by medieval Aristotelianism. Thus Marsilio Ficino would follow both Plato and Aristotle, though according the higher place to Plato, a view which is reflected in Raphael's School of Athens, and Pico della Mirandola expressly defended the medieval Aristotelians against the humanist attacks of Ermolao Barbaro.[28]

It was only during the sixteenth century that Aristotelianism began to be attacked in its central territory, that is, in natural philosophy. A series of brilliant thinkers, not unaffected by Aristotelianism or other traditions, but original in their basic intention, people like Paracelsus, Telesio, Patrizi, Bruno, and others, began to propose rival systems of cosmology and of natural philosophy which made an impression upon their contemporaries and have been of lasting interest to historians of Renaissance thought.[29] They failed to overthrow the Aristotelian tradition in natural philosophy, not because they were persecuted, or because their opponents preferred vested interests and habits of thought to the truth, but because their impressive doctrines were not based on a firm and acceptable method. Aristotelian natural philosophy, rich in subject matter and solid in concepts, could not possibly

be displaced from the university curriculum as long as there was no comparable body of teachable doctrine that could take its place. This was not
supplied by the humanists, the Platonists, or the natural philosophers of the
later Renaissance, who could dent but not break the Aristotelian tradition.
The decisive attack upon the natural philosophy of the Aristotelians came
from Galileo and the other physicists of the seventeenth century.

This momentous event in the history of modern thought has often been
represented rather crudely as a victory of "Science" and the "Scientific
Method" over superstition or a mistaken tradition. There is no such thing as
Science or the Scientific Method, but there is a complex body of various
sciences and other forms of knowledge whose unity remains an ideal program, and there are various methods of attaining valid knowledge and of
judging its validity. In the period preceding Galileo with which we are concerned, the various sciences differed in their traditions and mutual relations.
Mathematics and astronomy were largely separate from philosophy and the
Aristotelian tradition, and made notable advances during the sixteenth century without affecting that tradition in a serious way.[30] Medicine was another science distinct from philosophy, but more closely linked to it since
medicine and philosophy were considered as parts of the same study and career, and since such medical authorities as Galen and Avicenna were Aristotelians. Nevertheless, notable progress was made in such medical disciplines as anatomy and surgery, that were based on observation and
comparatively removed from the philosophical and medical theories of the
time.

On the other hand, natural philosophy as then understood and taught from
the works of Aristotle, comprised such sciences as physics and biology.
Even the development of these two sciences took a different course with reference to Aristotelianism. In biology, great progress was made during the
sixteenth century and even afterwards within the framework of the Aristotelian tradition. In physics, on the other hand, the very conception of Aristotelian physics had to be overthrown in order to make room for modern
physics. The Aristotelian physics of the later Middle Ages and of the Renaissance was not as wrong or absurd as older scholars had assumed, nor
was Galileo as unaffected by it as he himself or some of his modern admirers believed.[31] Yet for the Aristotelians, physics was a matter of qualities, not of quantities, and its objects on earth were essentially different from
the stars in heaven. Consequently, Aristotelian physics was closely linked

with formal logic, but separated from mathematics and even to some extent from astronomy.

Galileo, the professional mathematician and astronomer who claimed to be a natural philosopher, postulated a new physics based on experiments and calculations, a physics of quantities that had for its foundation not formal logic, but mathematics, and that was to be closely related to astronomy.[32] Once this new physics had been firmly established in its methods and had begun to yield more and more specific results, it was bound to undermine the prestige of traditional Aristotelian physics and eventually to drive it from its place in the curriculum. This happened during the seventeenth and early eighteenth centuries, and it could not possibly have happened in the sixteenth. Our impatient enthusiasm for the achievements of a later period should not prompt us to read them back into an earlier epoch or to blame the latter for not having anticipated them. To be sure, individual thinkers are always capable of startling insights, but a large group of people is likely to change its modes of thought rather slowly unless it is suddenly shaken by fashion, by violent experiences, or by political compulsion.

Thus we may conclude that the authority of Aristotle was challenged during the Renaissance in different ways and for different reasons, but that it remained quite strong, especially in the field of natural philosophy. This was due not so much to professional inertia as to the wealth and solidity of subject matter contained in the Aristotelian writings, to which its critics for some time could not oppose anything comparable. The concepts and methods that were bound to overthrow Aristotelian physics were just being discussed and prepared during the sixteenth century, but did not bear visible and lasting fruits before the seventeenth. The anti-Aristotelian revolution which marks the beginning of the modern period in the physical sciences and in philosophy had some of its roots and forerunners in the Renaissance period, but did not actually occur until later. The Renaissance is still in many respects an Aristotelian age which in part continued the trends of medieval Aristotelianism and in part gave it a new direction under the influence of classical humanism and other different ideas.

3.

Renaissance
Platonism

Plato's influence on Western thought has been so broad and profound, and in spite of occasional voices of dissent, so continuous, thàt a great contemporary thinker has been able to state that the history of Western philosophy may be characterized as a series of footnotes to Plato.[1] Yet if we examine the actual ideas of those thinkers who have professed their indebtedness to the Athenian philosopher or who have been called Platonists by themselves or by others, we do not only find, as might be expected, a series of different interpretations and reinterpretations of Plato's teachings and writings; we are also confronted with the puzzling fact that different Platonists have selected, emphasized, and developed different doctrines or passages from Plato's works. Hardly a single notion which we associate with Plato has been held by all Platonists, neither the transcendent existence of universal forms nor the direct knowledge of these intelligible entities, neither spiritual love nor the immortality of the soul, let alone his outline of the perfect state. Thus it is possible for two thinkers who have been conventionally and perhaps legitimately classified as Platonists to have very different philosophies, or even to have not a single specific doctrine in common. The term Platonism does not lend itself very well as a middle term to the arithmetic or syllogistics of sources and influences, unless the specific texts and notions involved in each case are spelled out in all their detail.

Moreover, ever since classical antiquity, Platonist philosophers have tried not so much to repeat or restate Plato's doctrines in their original form as to combine them with notions of diverse origin, and these accretions, like the tributaries of a broadening river, became integral parts of the continuing tradition. They are as necessary for a proper understanding of the history of Platonism as they might be misleading if used uncritically for an interpretation of Plato himself. It is only during the last 150 years or so that modern scholarship has attempted to cleanse the genuine thought of Plato from the mire of the Platonic tradition. This effort has yielded in part very solid results, yet today we are beginning to feel that there has been a tendency to exaggerate the differences between Plato and later Platonism, and to over-look certain genuine features in Plato's thought that may be alien to modern science and philosophy but served as a starting point for his earlier interpre-ters.[2] Thus an archaeologist who tries to remove the crust of later centuries from a Greek statue must be careful not to damage its incomparably subtle surface.

This complex and even elusive nature of the Platonic tradition is partly due to the character of Plato's thought and writings. Among all major Greek philosophers until Plotinus, Plato had the unique fortune of having his works, as far as we can tell, completely preserved. These works are literary compositions written and published in different periods of a long and event-ful life. They are in the form of dialogues which sometimes end without ap-parent conclusion and in which different views are proposed and discussed by different persons. Since Plato rarely speaks in his own name, it seems difficult to identify his own definite opinions, or to separate them from those of Socrates, Parmenides, and his other characters. Moreover, some of the most coherent passages are presented in the ambiguous form of myths, sim-iles, or digressions. Finally, the different dialogues, though not completely unrelated in their subject matter, fail to suggest any order or connection that might lead to a philosophical system. Modern scholarship has tried to over-come these difficulties through the historical method, to establish a chrono-logical sequence for the authentic dialogues, and to supplement their content with the statements of Aristotle and others about Plato's oral teaching. This historical approach was foreign to the Platonist scholars of classical antiq-uity. They merely collected all works attributed to Plato in a single edition, thus giving them the appearance of a systematic order which to us seems ar-tificial. In this manner, a number of apocryphal pieces found their way into the Platonic corpus and continued to influence the subsequent tradition, al-though the authenticity of certain Platonic works was already questioned in antiquity.

Plato's influence upon later Greek thought was dependent not only on his dialogues which were generally available to the reading public, but also on the school which he founded and which continued as an institution for many centuries until 529 A.D. Since Plato left no systematic writings to his school, and since even his oral teaching was apparently not of a dogmatic character, the philosophical tradition in his Academy was subject to much greater changes and fluctuations than in the other philosophical schools of antiquity.

Plato's immediate successors in the Academy modified his doctrine as we
know it hardly less than did another pupil, Aristotle,[3] and during the third
century B.C. the Academy turned towards a more or less radical skepticism
to which it clung for more than two hundred years. In the meantime, Plato's
dialogues were read and admired outside his school and strongly affected the
thought of such Stoic philosophers as Panaetius and Posidonius.

Around the beginning of our era, a popular and somewhat eclectic kind of
Platonism that borrowed various elements from Aristotle and especially from
Stoicism had replaced Skepticism in the Athenian Academy, had established
a kind of school in Alexandria and perhaps in other centers, and had begun
to pervade the thought of a widening circle of philosophical and popular
writers.[4] This movement, which is now commonly called Middle Platonism,
made at least one important contribution to the history of Platonism, for it
formulated the doctrine, ever since attributed to Plato but hardly found in his
dialogues, that the transcendent ideas or intelligible forms are concepts of a
divine intelligence. Middle Platonism had many elements in common with
the Neopythagoreanism which flourished during the first centuries of our era
and forged many Platonizing works under the name of Pythagoras and his
early pupils, and with the Hermetics, a circle of pagan theologians who
flourished in Alexandria and composed a corpus of writings that were attributed to the Egyptian divinity Hermes Trismegistus.[5] When Philo the
Jew, and after him the Alexandrian Church Fathers Clement and Origen,
made the first attempts to combine the teachings of Biblical religion with
Greek philosophy, it was the Platonism popular at their time which supplied
the most numerous and most important doctrinal elements. Thus the ground
was well prepared both among pagans and Christians when philosophical
Platonism was revived during the third century A.D. in Alexandria by Am-
monius Saccas and by his great pupil, Plotinus.

This school, which called itself Platonic and which modern historians
have named Neoplatonic to emphasize its differences from Plato, chose
Plato's dialogues for its chief philosophical authority, but tried to fit Plato's
scattered doctrines into a coherent system and to incorporate in it other ideas
derived from the Stoics and especially from Aristotle. As a comprehensive
synthesis of Greek thought, Neoplatonism thus dominated the latest phase of
ancient philosophy and bequeathed its heritage to subsequent ages. Beneath
the surface of the common school tradition, there are many significant differences of doctrine that have not yet been fully explored. To the genuine elements derived from Plato, Plotinus added a more explicit emphasis on a hi-

erarchical universe that descends through several levels from the transcendent God or One to the corporeal world, and on an inner, spiritual experience that enables the self to reascend through the intelligible world to that supreme One; whereas the physical world is conceived, probably under the influence of Posidonius, as a web of hidden affinities originating in a world soul and other cosmic souls. In Proclus, one of the last heads of the Athenian school, Neoplatonism attains its most systematic and even schematic perfection. In his *Elements of Theology* and *Platonic Theology* all things and their mutual relations are neatly defined and deduced in their proper place and order; and the concepts of Aristotle's logic and metaphysics, divested of their specific and concrete reference, are used as elements of a highly abstract and comprehensive ontology.[6] As a commentator, Proclus applied this neat and scholastic system to some of Plato's dialogues, just as other members of the school applied it to Aristotle. And as the leading philosophy of the period, Neoplatonism supplied practically all later Greek Church Fathers and theologians with their philosophical terms and concepts, most of all that obscure father of most Christian mysticism who hides under the name of Dionysius the Areopagite, and whose writings owed a tremendous authority to the name of their supposed author, a direct disciple of St. Paul the Apostle.

The Platonic tradition during the Middle Ages, which has been the subject of much recent study, followed again three different lines of development.[7] In the Byzantine East, the original works of Plato and of the Neoplatonists were always available, and the study of Plato was surely often combined with that of the ancient Greek poets and of Aristotle.[8] The prevalence of Plato over Aristotle within a synthesis of both was justified by Neoplatonic precedent, and the tendency to harmonize Plato rather than Aristotle with Christian theology was amply sanctioned by the Greek patristic authors. In the eleventh century, Michael Psellos revived the interest in Platonic philosophy and set an influential precedent by combining with it the *Chaldaic Oracles,* attributed to Zoroaster, and the *Corpus Hermeticum.* In the fourteenth and fifteenth centuries, Gemistus Pletho attempted another revival of Plato's philosophy based on Proclus and Psellos. He even aimed at a philosophical reform of the falling Greek Empire and gave, after the model of Proclus, an allegorical explanation of the Greek divinities, which exposed him to the charge that he wanted to restore ancient paganism.[9] Certainly he was convinced that Plato and his ancient followers were the representatives of a very old pagan theology which has for its witnesses the writings attributed to

Hermes Trismegistus and Zoroaster, Orpheus and Pythagoras, and which parallels both in age and content the revelation of the Hebrew and Christian Scriptures. Through his teaching and writing, through his pupils, and through the violent reaction of his theological and Aristotelian opponents, Pletho did a good deal to awaken Platonic scholarship and philosophy in the Byzantine Empire during its last decades; and thanks to Pletho's stay in Italy and to the activities of his pupil, Cardinal Bessarion, and of other Greek scholars devoted or opposed to him, this development had important repercussions in the West until and beyond the end of the fifteenth century.[10]

Among the Arabs, Plato's position was inferior to that of Aristotle and consequently less important than in antiquity or in the Byzantine Middle Ages.[11] Whereas the corpus of Aristotle was almost completely translated into Arabic, only a few works of Plato, such as the *Republic*, the *Laws*, and the *Timaeus*, were made available, supplemented by a number of other Platonist writings. On the other hand, the Arabs derived many Platonist conceptions from the Aristotelian commentators, and they possessed at least two Aristotelian apocrypha, the *Liber de causis* and the *Theologia Aristotelis*, whose doctrinal content was based entirely on Proclus and Plotinus. Arabic philosophers such as Alfarabi wrote a paraphrase of Plato's *Laws*, and even the faithful Aristotelian commentator, Averroes, composed a paraphrase of Plato's *Republic*. Under the influence of the Arabic tradition, medieval Jewish thought included a strong Neoplatonic current. Avicebron (ibn Gabirol), whose *Fountain of Life* exercised a strong influence in its Latin version, also belongs to this tradition, and the peculiar form of medieval Jewish mysticism known as the Cabala contains several ideas derived from Neoplatonic and other late ancient philosophies.[12] Moreover, among both the Arabs and their Jewish disciples, the occult sciences of astrology, alchemy, and magic were cultivated in close connection with the genuine philosophical and scientific disciplines. These pseudo sciences also derived their traditions from the later phases of Greek antiquity, and they were or became associated with Platonist and Hermetic philosophy, with which they actually shared such notions as the world soul and the belief in the numerous hidden powers or specific affinities and antipathies of all things natural.

Roman antiquity, though poor in specific philosophical achievements, as we have seen, gave a larger share to the Platonic tradition than it did to Aristotle. Cicero, who had been a student at the Athenian Academy, reflected in his philosophical writings not only the Skepticism which had dominated that school for several centuries, but also the first phases of that eclectic or

Middle Platonism which was just beginning to replace it. Further Middle Platonic ideas appear in Apuleius, occasionally in Seneca, and in Calcidius' commentary on the *Timaeus;* whereas Neoplatonism was the basis for the writings of Macrobius, and for Boethius' influential *Consolation of Philosophy.* Of Plato's own works, Latin readers possessed only the partial versions of the *Timaeus* due to Cicero and Calcidius; the version of Plotinus attributed to Victorinus was probably not extensive, and certainly did not survive very long. The most important representative of Platonism in ancient Latin literature was St. Augustine, who acknowledged his debt to Plato and Plotinus more frankly than most of his modern theological admirers.[13] Typical Platonist doctrines, such as the eternal presence of the universal forms in the mind of God, the immediate comprehension of these ideas by human reason, and the incorporeal nature and the immortality of the human soul, are persistently asserted in his earlier philosophical as well as in his later theological writings, and they do not become less Platonist because they are combined with different Biblical or specifically Augustinian conceptions or because Augustine rejected other Platonic or Neoplatonic doctrines that seemed incompatible with the Christian dogma. Augustine's repeated assertion that Platonism is closer to Christian doctrine than any other pagan philosophy went a long way to justify later attempts to combine or reconcile them with each other.

During the early Middle Ages, when philosophical studies were not much cultivated in Western Europe, the most important text translated from the Greek was the corpus of writings attributed to Dionysius the Areopagite, who was also identified with the patron saint of St. Denis near Paris.[14] And the only author who had philosophical significance, Johannes Scotus Eriugena, was strongly imbued with Neoplatonic conceptions which were accessible to him in their original Greek sources. When philosophical studies began to flourish with the rise of scholasticism after the middle of the eleventh century, Augustinianism, which comprised many Platonist elements, became the prevailing current. This was quite natural, since the writings of Augustine represented the most solid body of philosophical and theological ideas then available in Latin. It was supplemented by Boethius' *Consolation,* by his logical works and his translations from Aristotle and Porphyry, and by Calcidius' partial translation and commentary of Plato's *Timaeus.* There was thus a body of source material available for philosophical study before the new translations from the Arabic and Greek were added, and this material was for the most part Platonist in character and in-

cluded at least one work of Plato, the *Timaeus*. Hence it is significant that in
one of the most important centers of early scholasticism, at the cathedral
school of Chartres, the *Timaeus* was apparently used as a textbook in natural
philosophy, as a number of glosses and commentaries coming from that
school would seem to indicate.[15] And a strange and long neglected Platonist
work, the so-called *Altividius,* seems to have been composed during the
same century.[16]

When the new translations brought about a vast increase in philosophical
and scientific literature, Aristotle and his commentators gradually gained the
upper hand, as we have seen, and hence during the thirteenth century Aristotelianism became the prevailing current of Western thought. Yet at the
same time, Platonism also profited from the new translating activity. The
versions from the Greek included two dialogues of Plato, the *Phaedo* and
the *Meno,* the work of Nemesius of Emesa, and a number of treatises by
Proclus, such as the *Elements of Theology* and the commentary on the *Parmenides,* which contains part of Plato's own text.[17] On the other hand, we
find among the versions from the Arabic not only the Aristotelian commentators who contained much Neoplatonic material, but also the *Liber de
Causis,* Avicebron's *Fons vitae,* and a vast amount of astrological and
alchemical literature that transmitted, or pretended to transmit, many notions
of Platonist or Hermetic origin. Hence we are not surprised to find Augustinian or Neoplatonic notions even in the thought of many Aristotelian philosophers of the thirteenth and early fourteenth centuries. On the other hand,
the Augustinian tradition persisted as a secondary current during that period,
and the speculative mysticism of Master Eckhart and his school drew much
of its inspiration from the Areopagite, Proclus, and other Neoplatonic
sources.

During the Renaissance, these medieval currents continued in many quar-
ters. German speculative mysticism was succeeded in the Low Countries by
the more practical *Devotio Moderna* which exercised a wide influence in
Northern Europe.[18] The Augustinian trend in theology and metaphysics
went on without interruption; the increasing religious literature for laymen
contained strong Augustinian elements, and even some of the Platonizing
works written in Chartres during the twelfth century still found attentive
readers. Yet although several elements of medieval Platonism survived during the Renaissance, it would be wrong to overlook the novel or different
aspects of Renaissance Platonism. They were partly due to the impact of
Byzantine thought and learning, for the Eastern scholars who came to Italy

for a temporary or permanent residence after the middle of the fourteenth century familiarized their Western pupils with Plato's writings and teachings, and with the controversy on the merits of Plato and Aristotle. While Chrysoloras was staying in Italy, he suggested the first Latin translation of Plato's *Republic*. Pletho's visit in Florence in 1438 left a deep impression, and the debate on Plato and Aristotle was continued in Italy by his pupils and opponents and by their Western followers. The most important document of the controversy is Bessarion's defense of Plato which drew on Western sources and which exercised some influence until the sixteenth century.[19] Other documents related to this debate have but recently attracted attention, or are still in need of further exploration.

Even more important was the impulse given by the Italian humanists of the period. Petrarch was not well acquainted with Plato's works or philosophy, but he was the first Western scholar who owned a Greek manuscript of Plato sent to him by a Byzantine colleague,[20] and in his attack on the authority of Aristotle among the philosophers of his time, he used at least Plato's name. This program was then carried out by his humanist successors. They studied Plato in the Greek original, and many of the dialogues were for the first time translated into Latin during the first half of the fifteenth century, including such works as the *Republic*, the *Laws*, the *Gorgias* and part of the *Phaedrus*. Some of these translations, like those of Leonardo Bruni, attained great popularity.[21] Other Platonist authors of antiquity were also made available in new Latin versions, and in the eclectic thought of the literary humanists Plato and his ancient followers occupied their appropriate place. Finally, at a time when a revival of everything ancient was the order of the day, and when restatements of many ancient philosophies were being attempted as a philosophical sequel to classical humanism, a revival of Platonism in one form or another was bound to occur.

However, Renaissance Platonism, in spite of its close links with classical humanism, cannot be understood as a mere part or offshoot of the humanistic movement. It possesses independent significance as a philosophical, not merely as a scholarly or literary, movement; it is connected both with the Augustinian and Aristotelian traditions of medieval philosophy; and thanks to the work of three major thinkers of the late fifteenth century, it became a major factor in the intellectual history of the sixteenth, and even afterwards.

The earliest and greatest of the three, Nicolaus Cusanus, was indebted to German and Dutch mysticism as well as to Italian humanism.[22] In his philosophical thought, which has many original features, notions derived from

Plato, Proclus, and the Areopagite play a major part. He interprets the ideas in the divine mind as a single archetype which expresses itself in each particular thing in a different way, and he stresses the certainty and exemplary status of pure mathematical knowledge, to mention only a few facets of his complex thought that show his link with the Platonic tradition.

The most central and most influential representative of Renaissance Platonism is Marsilio Ficino, in whom the medieval philosophical and religious heritage and the teachings of Greek Platonism are brought together in a novel synthesis.[23] As a translator, he gave to the West the first complete version of Plato and of Plotinus in Latin, adding several other Neoplatonic writings; and in adopting Pletho's conception of a pagan theological tradition before Plato, he translated also the works attributed to Pythagoras and Hermes Trismegistus that were bound to share the popularity and influence of Renaissance Platonism. In his *Platonic Theology* he gave to his contemporaries an authoritative summary of Platonist philosophy, in which the immortality of the soul is emphasized, reasserting to some extent the Thomist position against the Averroists. His Platonic Academy with its courses and discussions provided for some decades an institutional center whose influence was spread all over Europe through his letters and other writings. Assigning to the human soul the central place in the hierarchy of the universe, he gave a metaphysical expression to a notion dear to his humanist predecessors; whereas his doctrine of spiritual love in Plato's sense, for which he coined the term Platonic love, became one of the most popular concepts of later Renaissance literature. His emphasis on the inner ascent of the soul towards God through contemplation links him with the mystics, whereas his doctrine of the unity of the world brought about by the soul influenced the natural philosophers of the sixteenth century.

Closely associated with the Florentine Academy, but in many ways different from Ficino, was his younger contemporary, Giovanni Pico della Mirandola.[24] In his thought, which did not reach full maturity, the attempt was made to achieve a synthesis between Platonism and Aristotelianism. His curiosity encompassed also Arabic and Hebrew language and thought, and as the first Western scholar who became acquainted with the Jewish Cabala, he made the influential attempt to reconcile the Cabala with Christian theology and to associate it with the Platonist tradition. His *Oration* on the dignity of man became the most famous expression of that humanist credo to which he gave a novel philosophical interpretation in terms of man's freedom to choose his own destiny.[25]

The place of Platonism in sixteenth-century thought is rather complex and difficult to describe.[26] Unlike humanism or Aristotelianism, it was not identified with the teaching traditions in the literary or philosophical disciplines, and its institutional connections were slender and somewhat uncertain. Some of Plato's dialogues were among the standard prose texts that were read in all courses in Greek at the universities and secondary schools of the period, and this accounted for a wide diffusion of his philosophical ideas. In the academies—a new type of institution, half learned society and half literary club, which flourished especially in Italy throughout the century and afterwards—lectures and courses on the so-called philosophy of love, often based on Platonizing poems and always influenced by Plato's *Symposium* and its commentators, were a common feature, especially in Florence, where the memory of Ficino's Academy was never forgotten. Yet Francesco Patrizi's attempts to introduce courses on Platonic philosophy at the universities of Ferrara and Rome were of short duration, and a similar course given for several decades at Pisa was entrusted to scholars who taught Aristotle at the same time and thus were led to compare and to combine Plato with Aristotle rather than to give him an undivided allegiance.

Nevertheless it would be a mistake to underestimate the importance of sixteenth-century Platonism, or to overlook its almost ubiquitous presence, often combined with humanism or Aristotelianism or other trends or ideas, but always recognizable in its own distinctive physiognomy. In the course of the century, the works of Plato and of the ancient Platonists, and the connected writings attributed to Orpheus and Zoroaster, to Hermes and the Pythagoreans, were all printed and reprinted in the Greek original and in Latin translations, and likewise the writings of the Renaissance Platonists such as Cusanus, Ficino, and Pico were widely read and diffused, and some of this material even found its way into the vernacular languages, especially French and Italian. By that time, this body of literature supplied scholars and readers with the largest and most substantial alternative for, or supplement to, the works of Aristotle and his commentators. No wonder that its impact was felt in many fields and areas of thought and learning, although it would be difficult, if not impossible, to bring these various facets of Platonism under one common denominator or to establish very precise relationships among them.

Among the philosophers we find some who would try to combine Plato and Aristotle, like Francesco Verino, Jacopo Mazzoni, and the Frenchman Jacobus Carpentarius, best known for his sinister role during the Massacre of St. Bartholomew. Others professed their undivided allegiance to Plato, like Francesco da Diacceto, Ficino's successor in Florence, the Spaniard Sebastian Fox Morcillo, and the greatest of all, Francesco Patrizi. Yet the influence of Plato and Platonism extended far beyond the circle of those who wanted to be known as followers of that tradition. The natural philosophers of the time who are best known for their original speculations, like Paracelsus, Telesio, or Bruno, were strongly indebted to the Platonic tradition. Telesio, who distinguishes between two souls, is a thorough empiricist when dealing with the lower soul, to which he assigns our ordinary functions and activities, but follows the Platonists in his treatment of the higher, immortal soul. Bruno is a Platonist not only in his *Heroic Enthusiasts,* where he develops a theory of love derived from the *Symposium* and its interpreters, but also in his metaphysics, where he borrows his concept of the world soul from Plotinus and follows Cusanus on other important points.[27] The broad stream of astrological and alchemical literature, which continued and even increased during the sixteenth century, also presupposes such notions as a world soul or the inner powers and affinities of things celestial, elementary, and composite, notions that go back to Arabic sources that were still widely used in these circles, but which derived new impetus and dignity from the Greek and modern Platonist writers and from the Hermetic works associated with them.

On the other hand, we note that certain Aristotelian philosophers like Nifo, who wanted to defend the immortality of the soul, made use of the arguments given in Plato's *Phaedo* or in Ficino's *Platonic Theology,* and that even the more "naturalistic" among the Renaissance Aristotelians, like Pomponazzi or Cremonini, were willing to accept certain specific Platonist doctrines. For the humanists unfriendly to the Aristotelian tradition, Plato and his school always held much attraction. John Colet was much impressed by the Areopagite, and we now have direct evidence that he was in touch with Marsilio Ficino.[28] Sir Thomas More translated the life and a few letters of Pico into English, and his noted *Utopia,* however original in its content, could hardly have been conceived without the reading of Plato's *Republic.*[29] Erasmus, in the *Enchiridion* and the later part of the *Praise of Folly,* endorsed a somewhat diluted form of Platonism when he opposed the higher folly of the inner spiritual life to the lower folly of ordinary existence, and Peter Ramus used at least the name of Plato in his bold attempt to replace the traditional Aristotelian logic of the schools. In France, scholars like Lefèvre d'Etaples, Charles de Bouelles, Symphorien Champier, and others received many of their ideas from Cusanus and Ficino,[30] Pico apparently affected Zwingli,[31] and his Christian cabalism was adopted by Reuchlin and by many other Platonizing theologians.[32] A few scholars have even discovered Platonist elements in the theology of Calvin.[33] Theologians like Ambrosius Flandinus, who opposed both Pomponazzi and Luther, composed commentaries on Plato, or like Aegidius of Viterbo, general of the Augustinian Hermits, wrote a commentary on the *Sentences* "ad mentem Platonis."[34] When the Lateran Council of 1513 condemned Averroes' unity of the intellect and promulgated the immortality of the soul as an official dogma of the Church, we are inclined to see in this event an effect of Renaissance Platonism upon Catholic theology, especially since the Platonist Aegidius of Viterbo endorsed and perhaps inspired the decision, whereas the leading Thomist, Caietanus, opposed it,[35] since he departed on this issue, as on some others, from the position of Aquinas, and held with Pomponazzi that the immortality of the soul could not be demonstrated.

Aside from the professional theologians, religious writers and poets like Marguerite of Navarre, the poets of the Lyon circle and Joachim Du Bellay were impressed by the Platonist appeal to contemplation and inner experience.[36] Ficino's notion of Platonic love, that is, of the spiritual love for another human being that is but a disguised love of the soul for God, and some of his other concepts, found favor with such contemporary poets as Lorenzo de' Medici and Girolamo Benivieni, and this Platonizing poetry had among its successors in the sixteenth century Michelangelo and Spenser, besides many minor Italian, French, and English authors in whom the Platonist element is not always easy to distinguish from the common pattern of "Petrarchism."[37] It is not correct to say, as do some scholars, that Dante, Guido Cavalcanti, or Petrarch were poets of Platonic love, but they were thus interpreted by Ficino, Landino, and others, and thus it was possible for their imitators in the sixteenth century to merge their style and imagery with those of the genuine Platonist tradition.

Ficino's doctrine of Platonic love was repeated and developed not only in many sonnets and other poems of the sixteenth century, but also in a large body of prose literature which grew up around the literary academies and became fashionable with the reading public: the *trattati d'amore*.[38] These dialogues or treatises discuss in different forms the nature and beneficial effects of spiritual love in the Platonist manner, and also a variety of related Platonist doctrines like the immortality of the soul or the existence and knowledge of the pure Ideas. Among the numerous authors who contributed to this

literature and who tended to popularize but also to dilute the teachings of
Platonism, we find, besides many now forgotten, such influential writers as
Bembo and Castiglione, for whom Platonist philosophy was but a passing
fancy, and also a poet like Tasso, whose philosophical prose writings have
not yet been sufficiently studied, and such serious philosophers as Francesco
da Diacceto, Leone Ebreo, and Francesco Patrizi. Giordano Bruno's *Eroici
Furori* also belongs in this tradition. Finally Plato's doctrine of divine
madness as expressed in the *Ion* and *Phaedrus* appealed to many poets and
literary critics who would either add this Platonic doctrine to an otherwise
Aristotelian system of poetics, or use it as the cornerstone of an anti-Aristotelian theory, as was done by Patrizi.[39]

In the theory of painting and of the other visual arts, which was not yet
combined with poetics in a single system of aesthetics, as happened in the
eighteenth century,[40] the analogy between the conceptions of the artist and
the ideas of the divine creator which appears in Cicero, Seneca, Plotinus,
and other Middle and Neoplatonic authors was adopted by Duerer and by
many later critics.[41] Moreover, the expression of philosophical ideas of Platonist origin has been discussed and partly established in the iconography of
the works of such masters as Botticelli, Raphael, and Michelangelo.[42] If we
pass from the visual arts to the theory of music, which in the sixteenth century constituted a separate branch of literature unrelated to poetics or the
theory of painting, we notice again that Plato is praised and cited by Franchino Gafurio, by Vincenzo Galilei, the father of the great scientist, and by
other musical theorists of the time.[43] The extent of this "musical Platonism" has not been investigated, and its precise links with the philosophical tradition remain to be defined. Yet it is worth noting that Ficino
was an enthusiastic amateur in music and wrote several shorter treatises on
musical theory. It is conceivable and even probable that the passages on
musical proportions in Plato's *Timaeus,* together with Ficino's extensive
commentary on them, made a strong impression on those professional musi-
cians who had a literary education and were familiar with the fame and authority of Plato and his school.

Of even greater interest is the impact of Renaissance Platonism upon the
sciences, a subject that has been much debated by recent historians. Again,
a distinction must be made between the different sciences, which then as
now differed so much in method, subject matter, sources, and traditions.
Obviously, the history of technology and engineering would show no traces
of Platonist, or for that matter of Aristotelian, influence.[44] In natural history

also, where the Aristotelian tradition prevailed, Platonism hardly made itself felt. Yet in medicine, astrological and alchemical theories exercised a good deal of influence during that time, and the medical writings of Ficino, which embodied some of his philosophical and astrological views, were widely read, especially in Germany. Yet the main impact of Platonism, as might be expected, was felt in the mathematical sciences, which had been most cultivated and respected by Plato and his followers.[45] Mathematicians who were concerned with the theoretical and philosophical status of their science, and philosophers who wanted to emphasize the certainty and importance of methematical knowledge, would be inclined to recur either to the number symbolism of the Pythagoreans that had been associated with Platonism since late antiquity, or to the belief in the nonempirical a priori validity and certainty of mathematical concepts and propositions that goes back to Plato himself and that had been reemphasized by some, though not by all, representatives of the Platonic tradition. This belief was shared but not emphasized by Plotinus or Ficino, who were more concerned with other features of the Platonic tradition, but it was strongly expressed and applied by Cusanus.

In the sixteenth century when the doctrines of Plato and Aristotle were compared with each other, the superiority of quantitative over qualitative knowledge was considered one of the characteristic points of the Platonic position, and against this background it is quite significant that the Platonist Patrizi emphasized the theoretical priority and superiority of mathematics over physics.[46] This position had great potentialities at a time when mathematics was rapidly progressing and when the question arose whether the qualitative physics of the Aristotelian tradition should be replaced by a quantitative physics based on mathematics and in a way reducible to it. Hence there is no wonder that some of the founders of modern physical science should have been attracted by at least this feature of Platonism.

In the case of Kepler, no doubt seems possible that his cosmology is rooted in Renaissance Platonism, from which he borrowed not only his mathematical conception of the universe but also his notion of cosmic harmony and, at least in his earlier period, his belief in number symbolism and astrology. To understand the validity of Kepler's laws of planetary motion, the modern student of astronomy does not need to be concerned with his Platonist cosmology. Yet the historian of science will do well to recognize that the positive scientific discoveries of the past were never unrelated to the theoretical and philosophical assumptions of the investigating scientist, whether they were true or false from our point of view, whether consciously expressed or tacitly accepted by him. Even if we want to say that Kepler discovered his laws in spite of, and not on account of, his Platonist cosmology, as historians we cannot be concerned only with those parts of his work and thought that have been accepted as true by later scientists, but we must also understand his errors as well, as an integral part of his scientific and philosophical thought. Otherwise, the history of science becomes nothing but a catalogue of disconnected facts or a modern version of hagiography.

Whereas Kepler's link with the Platonic tradition has been generally admitted, though frequently regretted, the question of Galileo's Platonism has been a more controversial matter.[47] It has been pointed out that, because of his known dislike for the Aristotelian tradition, he tended to attribute to Aristotle views which he opposed and which are not always consistent with each other or with the text of Aristotle. It also must be admitted that he borrowed much more from that tradition than one might expect, including such important notions as the distinction between analysis and synthesis in the method of scientific knowledge. His atomism and his distinction between primary and secondary qualities is ultimately derived from Democritus, and his conviction that mathematical relations can be exactly reproduced by material conditions is radically opposed to Plato. On the other hand, his claims for the absolute certainty of mathematical knowledge are truly Platonic, and his demand that nature should be understood in quantitative, mathematical terms is no less in line with the Platonist position of his time because he rejects the Pythagorean number symbolism often associated with it. Finally, in the famous passage where he also refers to Plato's theory of reminiscence, he states not merely that first principles are evident without demonstration, as any Aristotelian would have granted, but that they are spontaneously known and produced by the human mind, which is specifically Platonic.[48] The fact that there are Aristotelian, Democritean, and novel elements in Galileo's thought does not disprove that Platonic notions are also present in it, and as long as we are inclined to attribute any significance to these latter notions, we are entitled to assign to Galileo a place in the history of Platonism.

With the beginning of a new period of philosophical and scientific thought in the seventeenth century, the Platonic tradition ceases to dominate the development as a separate movement, but continues to influence a number of secondary currents and the thought of many leading thinkers. In the case of Descartes, his indebtedness to scholastic terminology and arguments is now generally admitted, but it has also been shown, though this is less widely known, that he borrowed important elements in ethics from the Stoics, and in epistemology and metaphysics from Platonism.[49] Spinoza's thought contains many Platonist elements, and his notion of the intellectual love of God has been connected with the love speculation of the Renaissance and especially with Leone Ebreo. It is even easier to point out the Platonizing elements in Malebranche, Leibniz, Kant, and Goethe. Even England, where the prevailing philosophical and scientific tradition seems to be represented by Bacon, Locke, and Hume, by Boyle and Newton, produced in the seventeenth century a group of interesting thinkers, the so-called Cambridge Platonists, who professed their allegiance to Platonism and actually constitute the most important phase of professed Platonism after the Florentine Academy.[50] Thus it is not surprising to find strong Platonizing tendencies in the late Berkeley, in Shaftesbury, and in Coleridge, authors who in turn exercised a rather wide influence.

Thus I hope that it has become apparent that Renaissance Platonism, in spite of its complex and somewhat elusive nature, was an important phenomenon both for its own period and for the subsequent centuries down to 1800. We must resign ourselves to the fact that in most cases the Platonist elements of thought are combined with doctrines of a different origin and character, and that even the professed Platonists did not express the thought of Plato in its purity, as modern scholars understand it, but combined it with more or less similar notions that had accrued to it in late antiquity, the Middle Ages, or more recent times. Yet if we understand Platonism with these qualifications and in a broad and flexible sense, it was a powerful intellectual force throughout the centuries, and we shall understand its nature best if we realize that until the rise of modern Plato scholarship, Plato appealed to his readers not only through the content of his inimitable dialogues, but also through the diverse and often complicated ideas which his commentators and followers down to the sixteenth and seventeenth centuries had associated with him.

4.

Paganism
and
Christianity

You might easily raise the question whether the problem I propose to discuss in this chapter is relevant to the general topic of these essays, and there is no doubt that I feel quite unequipped to deal with it appropriately. Yet although philosophical thought has its own distinctive core which ought to be always considered in its own terms, its history in a broader sense can rarely be understood without taking into account the religious as well as the scientific and literary currents of a particular age. In the period we have been discussing in these essays, religious events such as the Protestant and Catholic Reformations were of such momentous importance, and their significance in relation to the Renaissance has been the subject of so much debate, that even a short and superficial account of Renaissance thought would be incomplete without some consideration of the Reformation. Some scholars have seemingly avoided this problem by treating the Reformation as a new epoch, different from, and in a sense opposed to, the Renaissance. We prefer to consider the Reformation as an important development within the broader historical period which extended at least to the end of the sixteenth century, and which we continue to call, with certain qualifications, the Renaissance.

Obviously, it cannot be our task to describe the original contributions made by the reformers to religious thought, let alone the changes in ecclesiastic institutions brought about by their initiative, or the political and social factors which accounted for their popularity and success. In accordance with our general topic, we shall merely try to understand in which ways, positive or negative, the classicism of the Renaissance exercised an influence upon the religious thought of the period, and especially upon the Reformation.

Many historians of the last century tended to associate the Italian Renaissance and Italian humanism with some kind of irreligion and to interpret the

Protestant and Catholic Reformations as expressions of a religious revival which challenged and finally defeated the un-Christian culture of the preceding period.[1] The moral ideas and literary allegories in the writings of the humanists were taken to be expressions, real or potential, overt or concealed, of a new paganism incompatible with Christianity. The neat separation between reason and faith advocated by the Aristotelian philosophers was considered as a hypocritical device to cover up a secret atheism, whereas the emphasis on a natural religion common to all men, found in the work of the Platonists and Stoics, was characterized as pantheism.[2] This picture of the supposed paganism of the Renaissance which was drawn by historians with much horror or enthusiasm, depending on the strength of their religious or irreligious convictions, can partly be dismissed as the result of later legends and preconceptions. In part, it may be traced to charges made against the humanists and philosophers by hostile or narrow-minded contemporaries, which should not be accepted at their face value.[3]

Most recent historians have taken quite a different view of the matter.[4] There was, to be sure, a good deal of talk about the pagan gods and heroes in the literature of the Renaissance, and it was justified by the familiar device of allegory and strengthened by the belief in astrology, but there were few, if any, thinkers who seriously thought of reviving ancient pagan cults. The word pantheism had not yet been invented,[5] and although the word atheism was generously used in polemics during the later sixteenth century,[6] there were probably few real atheists and barely a few pantheists during the Renaissance. The best or worst we may say is that there were some thinkers who might be considered, or actually were considered, as forerunners of eighteenth-century free thought. There was then, of course, as there was before and afterwards, a certain amount of religious indifference and of merely nominal adherence to the doctrines of the Church. There were many cases of conduct in private and public life that were not in accordance with the moral commands of Christianity, and there were plenty of abuses in ecclesiastic practice itself, but I am not inclined to consider this as distinctive of the Renaissance period.

The real core of the tradition concerning Renaissance paganism is something quite different: it is the steady and irresistible growth of nonreligious intellectual interests which were not so much opposed to the content of religious doctrine as competing with it for individual and public attention. This was nothing fundamentally new, but rather a matter of degree and of emphasis. The Middle Ages was certainly a religious epoch, but it would be wrong to assume that men's entire attention was occupied by religious, let alone by theological, preoccupations. Medieval architects built castles and palaces, not only cathedrals and monasteries. Even when the clerics held the monopoly of learning, they cultivated grammar and the other liberal arts besides theology, and during the High Middle Ages, when specialization began to arise, nonreligious literature also expanded. The thirteenth century produced not Thomas Aquinas alone, as some people seem to believe, or other scholastic theologians, but also a vast literature on Roman law, medicine, Aristotelian logic and physics, mathematics and astronomy, letter-writing and rhetoric, and even on classical Latin poetry, not to mention the chronicles and histories, the lyric and epic poetry in Latin and in the vernacular languages. This development made further progress during the Renaissance period, as a glance at the inventory of a manuscript collection or at a bibliography of printed books will easily reveal, and it continued unchecked during and after the Reformation, whatever the theologians of that time or later times may have felt about it. If an age where the nonreligious concerns that had been growing for centuries attained a kind of equilibrium with religious and theological thought, or even began to surpass it in vitality and appeal, must be called pagan, the Renaissance was pagan, at least in certain places and phases. Yet since the religious convictions of Christianity were either retained or transformed, but never really challenged, it seems more appropriate to call the Renaissance a fundamentally Christian age.

To prove this point, it would be pertinent in the first place to state that the medieval traditions of religious thought and literature continued without interruption until and after the Reformation, and that Italy was no exception to this rule. The study of theology and canon law, and the literary production resulting from it, tended to increase rather than to decline, a fact that is often overlooked because historians of these subjects have paid less attention to that period than to the earlier ones, except for the material directly connected with the Reformation controversies. German mysticism was succeeded during the very period with which we are concerned by the more practical and less speculative *Devotio Moderna* in the Low Countries, a movement that produced such an important document as the *Imitation of Christ,* contributed to a reform of secondary education all over Northern Europe, and had a formative influence on such thinkers as Cusanus and Erasmus.[7] Effective preachers made a deep impression on the learned and unlearned alike all over fifteenth-century Italy, and sometimes led to revivalist movements and political repercussions, of which Savonarola is the most

famous but by no means an isolated instance.[8] In
rest of Europe, the religious guilds directed the activ
ercised a tremendous influence upon the visual arts, ї
Partly in connection with these guilds, an extensive rel.
popular character was circulated, which was composed ї
by laymen, but always addressed to the latter and usually
languages. These facts, along with the persistence of church
tutions, and worship, would go a long way to prove the religio   ₋pa-
tions of the Renaissance period.

Yet we are not so much concerned with the undoubted survival of medieval Christianity in the Renaissance as with the changes and transformations
which affected religious thought during that period. As a distinguished historian has put it,[10] Christianity is not only medieval, but also ancient and
modern, and thus it was possible for Christian thought during the Renaissance to cease being medieval in many respects, and yet to remain Christian.
This novelty is apparent in the new doctrines and institutions created by the
Protestant and Catholic Reformations, a topic on which I shall not attempt to
elaborate. I shall merely show that the humanist movement, as we have tried
to describe it in our first chapter, had its share in bringing about those
changes in religious thought.

The view that the humanist movement was essentially pagan or anti-
Christian cannot be sustained. It was successfully refuted by the humanists
themselves when they defended their work and program against the charges
of unfriendly theologians of their own time. The opposite view, which has
had influential defenders in recent years, namely that Renaissance humanism
was in its origin a religious movement,[11] or even a religious reaction against
certain antireligious tendencies in the Middle Ages,[12] seems to me equally
wrong or exaggerated. I am convinced that humanism was in its core neither
religious nor antireligious, but a literary and scholarly orientation that could
be and, in many cases, was pursued without any explicit discourse on religious topics by individuals who otherwise might be fervent or nominal
members of one of the Christian churches. On the other hand, there were
many scholars and thinkers with a humanist training who had a genuine concern for religious and theological problems, and it is my contention that the
way they brought their humanist training to bear upon the source material
and subject matter of Christian theology was one of the factors responsible
for the changes which Christianity underwent during that period.[13] The most
important elements in the humanist approach to religion and theology were

...ck upon the scholastic method and the emphasis upon the return to ... classics, which in this case meant the Christian classics, that is, the Bible and the Church Fathers.

In order to understand the significance of these attitudes, we must once more go back to antiquity and the Middle Ages. Christianity originated in a Jewish Palestine which had become politically a part of the Roman Empire and culturally a part of the Hellenistic world. At the time when the new religion began to spread through the Mediterranean area, its sacred writings which were to form the canon of the New Testament were composed in Greek, that is, in a language which showed the marks of a long literary and philosophical tradition, and in part by authors such as Paul, Luke, and John, who had enjoyed a literary and perhaps a philosophical education. In the following centuries, the early Apologists, the Greek Fathers, and the great Councils were engaged in the task of defining and developing Christian doctrine and of making it acceptable to the entire Greek-speaking world. Thus the reading and study of the Greek poets and prose writers was finally approved, with some reservations, whereas the teachings of the Greek philosophical schools were subjected to careful examination, and everything that seemed incompatible with Christian doctrine was rejected, but whatever appeared compatible was used to bolster and to supplement Christian theology. After the precedent of Philo the Jew, Clement of Alexandria and the other Greek Fathers went a long way in adding Greek philosophical methods and notions, especially Stoic and Platonist, to the doctrinal, historical, and institutional teachings contained in the Bible, and in creating out of these diverse elements a novel and coherent Christian view of God, the universe, and man.

At the same time, a similar synthesis of ancient and Christian elements was achieved by the Latin Fathers of the Western Church. Writers like Arnobius, Cyprian, Lactantius, and Ambrose embody in their writings the best grammatical and rhetorical training, based on the Roman poets and orators, that was available in their time. Jerome added to his consummate Latin literary education that Greek and Hebrew scholarship which enabled him to translate the entire Bible from the original languages into Latin. Augustine, the most important and complex of them all, was not only an excellent and cultured rhetorician according to the standards of his time, but also made use of the allegorical method to justify the study of the ancient Roman poets and prose writers.[14] Furthermore, Augustine was a learned and productive philosophical and theological thinker, who left to posterity a substantial body of writings in which traditional religious doctrine was enriched with more elaborate theological ideas like the City of God, original sin, and predestination, and also with philosophical conceptions of Greek and especially Neoplatonic origin, like the eternal forms in the divine mind, the incorporeality and immortality of the soul, conceptions which appear more prominently in his earlier, philosophical writings, but which he did not completely abandon even in his later years when he was engaged in Church administration and in theological controversies with the heretics of his time.

Thus Christianity, during the first six centuries of its existence, which still belong to the period of classical antiquity, absorbed a large amount of Greek philosophical ideas and of Greek and Latin literary traditions, so that some historians have been able to speak, with a certain amount of justification, of the humanism of the Church Fathers. In recent years, it has become customary among theologians and historians to ignore or to minimize the indebtedness of Philo, Augustine, and the other early Christian writers to Greek philosophy.[15] I must leave it to the judgment of present-day theologians and their followers whether they are really serving their cause by trying to eliminate from Christian theology all notions originally derived from Greek philosophy. Certainly those historians who follow a similar tendency and deny the significance of Greek philosophy for early Christian thought can be corrected through an objective study of the sources.

During the early Middle Ages, the Latin West had very limited philosophical and scientific interests, as we have seen, but it continued as best it could the grammatical and theological studies sanctioned by Augustine and the other Latin Fathers; and a number of Spanish, Irish, Anglo-Saxon and Carolingian scholars achieved distinction in this way. In the history of theology, a marked change from the pattern of the patristic period occurred with the rise of scholasticism after the eleventh century.[16] What was involved was not merely the influx of additional philosophical sources and ideas, both Platonist and Aristotelian, of which we have spoken in the preceding essays. Much more important was the novel tendency to transform the subject matter of Christian theology into a topically arranged and logically coherent system. There was no precedent for this either in the Bible or in Latin patristic literature, although certain Greek writers like Origen and John of Damascus had paved the way. The desire for a topical arrangement found its expression in the collections of sentences and church canons which culminated in the twelfth century in the *Libri Sententiarum* of Peter Lombard and the *Decretum* of Gratian which for many centuries were to serve as the standard textbooks of theology and of canon law. At the same time, the rising interest in Aristotelian logic led to the endeavor, first cultivated in the schools of Bec, Laon, and Paris, to apply the newly refined methods of dialectical argument to the subject matter of theology, which thus became by the standards of the time a real science. It is this method of Anselm, Abelard, and Peter Lombard which dominates the theological tradition of the high and later Middle Ages, including Bonaventura, Aquinas, Duns Scotus, and Ockham, not the older method of Peter Damiani or St. Bernard, who tried in vain to stem the rising tide of scholasticism and whose influence was hence confined to the more popular and practical, less scientific areas of later religious literature.

If we remember these facts concerning the history of theology in the West, we can understand what it meant for a Renaissance humanist with religious convictions to attack scholastic theology and to advocate a return to the biblical and patristic sources of Christianity. It meant that these sources, which after all were themselves the product of antiquity, were considered as the Christian classics which shared the prestige and authority of classical antiquity and to which the same methods of historical and philological scholarship could be applied.[17] Thus Petrarch shuns the medieval theologians except St. Bernard and a few other prescholastic writers and quotes only early Christian writers in his religious and theological remarks.[18] Valla laments the harmful influence of logic and philosophy upon theology and advocates an alliance between faith and eloquence. Erasmus repeatedly attacks the scholastic theologians and emphasizes that the early Christian writers were grammarians but no dialecticians. In his rejection of scholastic theology and his emphasis on the authority of Scripture and the Fathers, even Luther no less than John Colet is in agreement with the humanists, whereas the attempt to combine the study of theology with an elegant Latin style and a thorough knowledge of the Greek and Latin classics characterizes not only many Italian humanists and Erasmus, but also Melanchthon, Calvin,[19] Hooker, and the early Jesuits.

If we try to assess the positive contributions of humanist scholarship to Renaissance theology, we must emphasize above all their achievements in what we might call sacred philology.[20] Valla led the way with his notes on the New Testament, in which he criticized several passages of Jerome's Vulgate on the basis of the Greek text. He was followed by Manetti, who made a new translation of the New Testament from Greek into Latin and of the Psalms from Hebrew into Latin, a work which has not yet been sufficiently studied.[21] Erasmus' edition of the Greek New Testament is well-known. It is this humanist tradition of biblical philology which provides the background and method for Luther's German version of the entire Bible from the Hebrew and Greek, as well as for the official revision of the Vulgate accomplished by Catholic scholars during the second half of the sixteenth century,[22] and for the official English version completed under King James I. The theological exegesis of the Bible and of its various parts had always been an important branch of Christian literature ever since patristic times. It was temporarily overshadowed, though by no means eliminated, by the predominance of Peter Lombard's *Sentences* in the theological curriculum of the later Middle Ages, but it derived new force in the sixteenth century from the emphasis of Protestant theology upon the original source of Christian doctrine. To what extent the exegesis of that period was affected by the new methods and standards of humanist philology seems to be a question which has not yet been sufficiently investigated.[23]

An even wider field was offered to humanist scholarship by the large body of Greek Christian literature of the patristic and Byzantine period. Some of this material had been translated into Latin towards the end of antiquity and again during the twelfth century. Yet it is an established fact not sufficiently known or appreciated that a large proportion of Greek patristic literature was for the first time translated into Latin by the humanists and humanistically trained theologians of the fifteenth and sixteenth centuries.[24] This applies to many important writings of Eusebius, Basil, and John Chrysostom, of Gregory of Nazianzus and Gregory of Nyssa, not to mention many later or lesser authors, or the writings which had been known before and were now reissued in presumably better Latin versions.

Early in the fifteenth century, Leonardo Bruni translated Basil's letter which defended the reading of the pagan poets on the part of Christian students, and this welcome support of the humanist program by a distinguished Church author attained a very wide circulation and was even used in the classroom outside of Italy.[25] About the same time, Ambrogio Traversari, a monk with a classical training, dedicated a considerable amount of his energy to the translating of Greek Christian writers, thus setting an example to many later scholars, clerics, and laymen alike. These Latin versions attained great popularity as the numerous manuscript copies and printed editions may prove. They were often followed by vernacular translations and, in the sixteenth century, by editions of the original Greek texts. Thus we must conclude that the Renaissance possessed a much better and more complete knowledge of Greek Christian literature and theology than the preceding age, and it is an interesting question, which to my knowledge has not yet been explored, whether or to what extent the newly diffused ideas of these Greek authors exercised an influence on the theological discussions and controversies of the Reformation period.

Whereas a considerable proportion of Greek Christian literature was thus made available to the West through the labors of the humanists, the writings of the Latin Church Fathers had been continuously known through the Middle Ages and never ceased to exercise a strong influence on all theologians and other writers. Yet in this area also humanist scholarship brought about significant changes. The humanists were fully aware of the fact that authors like Ambrose and Lactantius, and especially Jerome and Augustine, belong to the good period of ancient Latin literature, and hence must be considered "Christian classics." Consequently, some of their works were included in the curriculum of the humanistic school, as in that of Guarino,[26] and regularly listed as recommended readings by humanist educators like Bruni, Valla, Erasmus, and Vives. Thus the Latin Fathers were read in the humanistic period no less than before, but they were grouped with the classical Latin writers rather than with the medieval theologians, and this fact could not fail to bring about a change in the way in which they were read and understood.

Moreover, the new philological methods of editing and commenting which the humanists had developed in their studies of the ancient authors were also applied to the Latin Church Fathers. We know in the case of Augustine that many manuscript copies and printed editions of the fifteenth century were due to the efforts of humanist scholars, and that Vives composed a philological commentary on the *City of God,* with which he was said in true humanist fashion to have restored St. Augustine to his ancient integrity. The application of humanist scholarship to Latin patristic literature culminated in the work of Erasmus, who prepared for a number of the most important writers critical editions of their collected works. His example was followed by Protestant and Catholic scholars alike, and later in the sixteenth century the pope appointed a special committee of scholars for the purpose of publishing the writings of the Fathers in new critical editions.[27]

Another field in which humanist scholarship was applied to the problems which concerned the churches and theologians was the study of ecclesiastic history. The critical methods developed by the humanists for the writing of ancient and medieval history on the basis of authentic contemporary documents and evidence were first applied to church history by Valla in his famous attack on the Donation of Constantine. In the sixteenth century, the Magdeburg Centuriatores used this method to rewrite the whole history of the church from the Protestant point of view, and later in the century Cardinal Baronius and his assistants undertook the same task for the Catholic side.[28]

The humanist interest in early Christian literature was not limited to philological and historical preoccupations, but also had its doctrinal consequences in philosophy and theology. Just as the philological study of the pagan philosophers led the way towards a revival of Platonism and of other ancient philosophies, and more specifically to a new kind of Aristotelianism, so the humanistic study of the Bible and of the Church Fathers led to new interpretations of early Christian thought that are characteristic of the Renaissance and Reformation period. Thus the attempt to interpret the Epistles of Paul without the context and superstructure of scholastic theology was made by scholars like Ficino, Colet, and Erasmus before it had such powerful and decisive results in the work of Luther.[29] Even more significant and more widespread was the influence exercised during the Renaissance by St. Augustine, and hence I should like to discuss, as briefly as possible, some aspects of Renaissance Augustinianism.[30]

The terms "Augustinianism" or "the Augustinian tradition" cover almost as many different meanings as the term "Platonism," since a thinker may be called an Augustinian for many reasons. The cause of this ambiguity is the same as in the case of Plato: the great variety and complexity of Augustine's work. Before he had become a bishop and a dogmatic theologian, Augustine had been a rhetorician, a philosopher, and a heretic who underwent a conversion, and all these elements and experiences left their traces in his writings. Augustine is a preacher, a moral teacher, and a political thinker, an expositor of the Bible, an autobiographer, a skeptic and Neoplatonic philosopher, a rhetorically trained writer who finds a justification for the study of the pagan poets, a systematic theologian who continues the work of the Greek Fathers, and a vigorous opponent of heresies who formulated or sharpened the doctrines of original sin, grace, and predestination. All these elements were potential sources of inspiration for later readers of Augustine's works.

During the early Middle Ages, Augustine's influence was chiefly felt in the fields of theology proper, education, and political thought. During the rise of scholasticism in the eleventh and twelfth centuries, Augustine's works supplied the chief philosophical and theological inspiration, and most of the early scholastics have been rightly called Augustinians. During the thirteenth and fourteenth centuries when Aristotle became predominant among the philosophers and theologians, Augustinianism survived as an important secondary current, and even the Aristotelians preserved many traces of Augustinian influence. At the same time, the theology of the mystics, and the broad stream of popular religious literature remained unaffected by Aristotle and faithful to the spirit of Augustine.

The influence of Augustine during the Renaissance period followed in part the same lines taken during the preceding centuries. The Augustinian current in scholastic philosophy and theology can be traced through the fifteenth century and afterwards, and the popular religious literature affected by his ideas increased in volume during the same period. Among the leaders of the *Devotio Moderna* in the Low Countries, Augustine was, after the Bible, the leading authority, as he also had been with St. Bernard and the German mystics.

Yet besides these traditional lines of Augustinian influence, whose importance should not be underestimated, we also note certain attitudes towards Augustine that seem to be of a different type. For Petrarch, who ignores and dislikes scholastic theology but always emphasizes his religious convictions, Augustine was a favorite author who exercised a decisive influence upon his spiritual development. Aside from numerous citations, two instances deserve special mention. When Petrarch composed his most personal work, the *Secretum,* he gave it the form of a dialogue between Augustine and the author, and it is Augustine who takes the part of the spiritual guide who resolves the doubts and questions of the poet. In the famous letter describing his climbing of Mont Ventoux, Petrarch tells us that he took Augustine's *Confessions* out of his pocket, opened them at random, and found a passage which appropriately expressed his own feelings: "Men go to admire the heights of the mountains, the great floods of the sea, the shores of the ocean, and the orbits of the stars, and neglect themselves." Thus it was the Augustine of the *Confessions,* the man who eloquently expresses his feelings and experiences, not the dogmatic theologian, who impressed Petrarch and other later humanists and helped them to reconcile their religious convictions with their literary tastes and personal opinions. Only Erasmus, who had done so much for the text of Augustine, was unsympathetic to his theology and to his interpretation of the Bible, preferring that of St. Jerome, and significantly enough was taken to task for it by Catholics and Protestants alike.

Another strand of Augustinian influence in the Renaissance may be found among the Platonists of the period. Augustine's witness in favor of Plato and the Platonists, already utilized by Petrarch against the authority of Aristotle, was eagerly cited by all philosophers sympathetic to Platonism from Bessarion to Patrizi. At least some of these Platonists also derived important philosophical ideas from the writings of Augustine. Thus Cusanus, who was in many ways affected by the thought of Augustine, took from one of his letters the term "learned ignorance," which he used to describe the characteristic method of his speculation. Ficino not only states that his allegiance to the Platonic school was partly determined by the authority of Augustine, but also derived from a direct reading of Augustine's works some very essential elements of his philosophy, as a more detailed analysis of his works would easily show. To mention only one example, when Ficino in the preface to his main philosophical work announces his intention of interpreting Plato's philosophy primarily in terms of the soul and of God, he is clearly following the lead of St. Augustine. Yet it is again characteristic that Ficino seems to know Augustine mainly from such well-known works as the *Confessions,* the *City of God,* and the *De Trinitate,* and from those early philosophical and Platonist writings that have been minimized by the theological admirers of the great Church Father, whereas he apparently showed less interest in Augustine's later theological writings.

Very different but no less powerful was the influence which Augustine exercised upon the theological writers, both Protestant and Catholic, of the sixteenth and seventeenth centuries. It was the theology of the later writings of Augustine, with their emphasis on predestination, sin, and grace, which was taken up by Luther and Calvin and their successors, whereas the theologians of the Catholic Reformation, and later the Jansenists and Oratorians, derived very different theological ideas from the interpretation of Augustine's thought. It is true that these theological developments were far removed from the interests and ideas of Renaissance humanism, but it seems reasonable to remember that the authority granted to Augustine, to the other patristic writers, and to Scripture itself has something to do with the humanist emphasis on ancient sources and with their contempt for the medieval tradition of scholastic theology.

I think we are now at last prepared to offer a meaningful interpretation of the term "Christian humanism" that is so often applied to the Renaissance or to earlier periods.[31] Confining the term humanism, according to the Renaissance meaning of the words humanist and humanities, to the rhetorical, classical, and moral concerns of the Renaissance humanists, regardless of the particular philosophical or theological opinions held by individual humanists, and of the theological, philosophical, scientific, or juristic training which individual scholars may have combined with their humanist education, we might choose to call Christian humanists all those scholars who accepted the teachings of Christianity and were members of one of the churches, without necessarily discussing religious or theological topics in their literary or scholarly writings. By this standard, practically all Renaissance humanists, before and after the Reformation, were Christian humanists, since the alleged cases of openly pagan or atheistic convictions are rare and dubious. But it is probably preferable to use the term Christian humanism in a more specific sense, and to limit it to those scholars with a humanist classical and rhetorical training who explicitly discussed religious or theological problems in all or some of their writings. In this sense, neither Aquinas nor Luther were Christian humanists, for the simple reason that they were theologians, but not humanists as that term was then understood, although Luther presupposes certain scholarly achievements of humanism. On the other hand, we must list among the Christian humanists not only Erasmus, Vives, Budé, More, and Hooker, but also Calvin, the elegant Latin writer and commentator of Seneca; Melanchthon, the defender of rhetoric against philosophy, who had more influence on many aspects of Lutheran Germany than Luther himself and who was responsible for the humanistic tradition of the German Protestant schools down to the nineteenth century; and finally the Jesuit fathers, many of whom were excellent classical scholars and Latin writers, and who owed part of their success to the good instruction offered in their schools and colleges in the then fashionable humanistic disciplines.

The tradition of humanist learning by no means came to an end with the Protestant or Catholic Reformations, as might appear if we look only for the headlines of the historical development. It survived as vigorously as did the tradition of Aristotelian scholasticism, cutting across all religious and national divisions, flourishing at Leyden and Oxford no less than at Padua and Salamanca, and exercising as formative an influence upon the minds of the philosophers and scientists trained in the schools and universities of the seventeenth and eighteenth centuries.

We have at last reached the end of our long and rapid journey, and it is time for me to sum up my impressions and recollections. We might state briefly that the period which we call the Renaissance attained a much more accurate and more complete acquaintance with ancient Latin and especially Greek literature than had been possible in the preceding age. We have tried to show with a few examples taken from the history of philosophy and theology that this acquaintance was not merely a matter of study and of imitation, but that the ideas embodied in ancient literature served as a ferment and inspiration for the original thought of the period, and account at least in part for the intellectual changes which occurred more slowly in the fifteenth and more rapidly in the sixteenth centuries. These examples could easily be multiplied from the history of philosophy as well as from all other areas of intellectual and cultural history.

With the seventeenth century, there begins a new period in the history of Western science and philosophy, and the traditions of the Renaissance begin to recede into the background. Beginning about the middle of the sixteenth century, scholars started to be more conscious of their originality, and to notice the progresses made by their own time in comparison with classical antiquity.[32] The invention of printing and the discovery of America were now emphasized to illustrate this progress, and during the seventeenth century, the famous battle of the ancients and moderns led to a clearer distinction between the sciences, in which modern times had by now surpassed the achievements of the ancients, and the arts, in which the ancients could never be surpassed though perhaps equaled. Consequently, when a new wave of classicism arose during the eighteenth century, it was limited to literature and poetry, to the visual arts, and to political thought, but omitted the natural sciences in which the ancients could no longer be considered as masters.

We are now living in a time in which this wave of eighteenth-century classicism has nearly spent its force. Classical scholarship has become a highly specialized tool in the hands of a few brave experts who have greatly expanded the knowledge of their predecessors, at least in certain areas of their discipline, but who have seemed to lose, through no fault of their own, more and more ground with the nonspecialists and with the people at large. Those who are not trained classical philologists now have reason to envy any medieval century for at least its Latin learning, and there are many professional educators and many important sectors of public opinion that seem to be completely unaware of the existence, let alone the importance, of humanistic scholarship. The situation is such that many responsible scholars are rightly worried. Yet I am inclined to hope and to expect that the interest in the classics and in historical learning will be continued and even revived, for I am firmly convinced of their intrinsic merit and believe that it cannot fail to impose itself again, although perhaps in a form different from the one to which we are accustomed, and more in accordance with the needs and interests of our time and society. Thus the study of the history of civilization and the reading of the classical authors in translations perform a useful service in college education. The wheel of fashion which in modern times seems to have replaced the wheel of fortune that appears so frequently in the art and literature of the Middle Ages and of the Renaissance, is likely to bring back at some time that taste for clarity, simplicity, and conciseness in literature and in thought that has always found its nourishment in the works of antiquity.

The natural desire to overcome the limits of our parochial outlook in time as well as in place may stimulate the interest in the classics; for they have not only a direct appeal for our own time, but also hold many clues for the understanding of medieval and early modern thought, which contains in turn the direct roots of our own contemporary world. It is true that each generation has its own message, and each individual may make his own original contribution. The effect of the classics upon Renaissance thought and literature may show us that it is possible to learn from the past and to be original at the same time. Originality is greatly to be admired, but it is a gift of nature or providence; it cannot be taught, and I doubt that it is harmed by knowledge or increased by ignorance.

I do not wish to give the impression that I want to elevate the ideal of scholarship at the expense of other more fundamental and more comprehensive ideals, or that I ignore the limitations of historical learning. We all are, or want to be, not merely scholars, but citizens, persons who work, persons who think, if not philosophers, and human beings. Historical knowledge, as Jacob Burckhardt said, does not make us shrewder for the next time, but wiser forever.[33] It gives us perspective, but it does not give us answers or solutions to the moral, social, or intellectual problems which we face. No amount of information will relieve us of the choices in judgment and in action which we are compelled to make every day. There are unique feelings and experiences in every person's external and spiritual life that have never, or rarely and imperfectly, been expressed by the thinkers and writers of the past. The world of Western civilization, wide and rich in comparison with our present time and society which is but a part of it, is itself small and limited when compared with the entire history of mankind, with the existence of animals, of plants, and of silent nature on our planet, or with the huge, if not infinite, extent in space and time of our visible universe. Exclusive concern for historical scholarship may isolate us from all those persons who for geographical, social, or educational reasons cannot participate in it and who as human beings yet demand our sympathetic understanding.

Finally, the record of the past in which all battles are decided and many pains forgotten, whereas the most distinguished characters, actions, and works stand out more clearly and in a more final form than they did in their own time, may lull us into a false security and indolence in view of the pains we have to suffer, the decisions we have to make, the actions and works we have to accomplish, without yet knowing the outcome, or the value they may have if and when they appear in turn as a settled and hardened past to a future observer. All these objections and doubts are true, and should be always remembered. Nevertheless, I hope you will accept with patience this plea for classical scholarship and historical knowledge, since it comes from a person who is not a member of the guild of philologists or historians, and allow me to conclude with a word of Erasmus which he gave as a reply to those theologians who criticized his ideal of scholarship, and which we might easily adapt to our somewhat different situation: "Prayer, to be sure, is the stronger weapon (in our fight against vice) . . . yet knowledge is no less necessary."[34]

TWO

RENAISSANCE THOUGHT AND THE MIDDLE AGES

5.

Humanism and Scholasticism in the Italian Renaissance

Ever since 1860, when Jacob Burckhardt first published his famous book on the civilization of the Renaissance in Italy,[1] there has been a controversy among historians as to the meaning and significance of the Italian Renaissance.[2] Almost every scholar who has taken part in the discussion felt it was his duty to advance a new and different theory. This variety of views was partly due to the emphasis given by individual scholars to different historical personalities or currents or to different aspects and developments of the Italian Renaissance. Yet the chief cause of the entire Renaissance controversy, at least in its more recent phases, has been the considerable progress made during the last few decades in the field of medieval studies. The Middle Ages are no longer considered as a period of darkness, and consequently many scholars do not see the need for such new light and revival as the very name of the Renaissance would seem to suggest. Thus certain medievalists have questioned the very existence of the Renaissance and would like to banish the term entirely from the vocabulary of historians.

In the face of this powerful attack, Renaissance scholars have assumed a new line of defense. They have shown that the notion embodied in the term "Renaissance" was not an invention of enthusiastic historians of the last century, but was commonly expressed in the literature of the period of the Renaissance itself. The humanists themselves speak continually of the revival or rebirth of the arts and of learning that was accomplished in their own time after a long period of decay.[3] It may be objected that occasional claims of an intellectual revival are also found in medieval literature.[4] Yet the fact remains that during the Renaissance scholars and writers talked of such a revival and rebirth more persistently than at any other period of European history. Even if we were convinced that it was an empty claim and that the humanists did not bring about a real Renaissance, we would still be forced to admit that the illusion itself was characteristic of that period and that the term Renaissance thus had at least a subjective meaning.

Without questioning the validity of this argument, I think that there are also some more objective reasons for defending the existence and the importance of the Renaissance. The concept of style as it has been so successfully applied by historians of art[5] might be more widely applied in other fields of intellectual history and might thus enable us to recognize the significant changes brought about by the Renaissance, without obliging us to despise the Middle Ages or to minimize the debt of the Renaissance to the medieval tradition.

Moreover, I should like to reexamine the relation between the Middle Ages and the Renaissance in the light of the following consideration. Scholars have become so accustomed to stress the universalism of the medieval church and of medieval culture and also to consider the Italian Renaissance as a European phenomenon that they are apt to forget that profound regional differences existed even during the Middle Ages. The center of medieval civilization was undoubtedly France, and all other countries of Western Europe followed the leadership of that country, from Carolingian times down to the beginning of the fourteenth century.[6] Italy certainly was no exception to that rule; but whereas the other countries, especially England, Germany, and the Low Countries, took an active part in the major cultural pursuits of the period and followed the same general development, Italy occupied a somewhat peculiar position.[7] Prior to the thirteenth century, her active participation in many important aspects of medieval culture lagged far behind that of the other countries. This may be observed in architecture and music, in the religious drama as well as in Latin and vernacular poetry in general,[8] in scholastic philosophy and theology,[9] and even, contrary to common opinion, in classical studies.

On the other hand, Italy had a narrow but persistent tradition of her own which went back to ancient Roman times and which found its expression in certain branches of the arts and of poetry, in lay education and in legal customs, and in the study of grammar and of rhetoric.[10] Italy was more directly and more continually exposed to Byzantine influences than any other Western European country. Finally, after the eleventh century, Italy developed a new life of her own which found expression in her trade and economy, in the political institutions of her cities, in the study of civil and canon law and of medicine, and in the techniques of letter-writing and of secular eloquence.[11] Influences from France became more powerful only with the thirteenth century, when their traces appeared in architecture and music, in Latin and vernacular poetry, in philosophy and theology, and in the field of classical studies.[12] Many typical products of the Italian Renaissance may thus be understood as a result of belated medieval influences received from France, but grafted upon, and assimilated by, a more narrow, but stubborn and different native tradition. This may be said of Dante's *Divine Comedy,* of the religious drama which flourished in fifteenth century Florence, and of the chivalric poetry of Ariosto and of Tasso.

A similar development may be noticed in the history of learning. The Italian Renaissance thus should be viewed not only in its contrast with the French Middle Ages, but also in its relation to the Italian Middle Ages. The rich civilization of Renaissance Italy did not spring directly from the equally rich civilization of medieval France, but from the much more modest traditions of medieval Italy. It is only about the beginning of the fourteenth century that Italy witnessed a tremendous increase in all her cultural activities, and this enabled her, for a certain period, to wrest from France her cultural leadership in Western Europe. Consequently, there can be no doubt that there was an Italian Renaissance, that is, a cultural Renaissance of Italy, not so much in contrast with the Middle Ages in general or with the French Middle Ages, but very definitely in contrast with the Italian Middle Ages. It appears from a letter of Boccaccio that this general development was well-understood by some Italians of that period,[13] and we should keep this development constantly in mind if we want to understand the history of learning during the Italian Renaissance.

The most characteristic and most pervasive aspect of the Italian Renaissance in the field of learning is the humanist movement. I need hardly say that the term "humanism," when applied to the Italian Renaissance, does not imply all the vague and confused notions that are now commonly associated with it. Only a few traces of these may be found in the Renaissance. By humanism we mean merely the general tendency of the age to attach the greatest importance to classical studies, and to consider classical antiquity as the common standard and model by which to guide all cultural activities. It will be our task to understand the meaning and origin of this humanist movement which is commonly associated with the name of Petrarch.

Among modern historians we encounter mainly two interpretations of Italian humanism. The first interpretation considers the humanist movement merely as the rise of classical scholarship accomplished during the period of the Renaissance. This view which has been held by most historians of classical scholarship is not very popular at present. The revival of classical studies certainly does not impress an age such as ours which has practically abandoned classical education, and it is easy to praise the classical learning of the Middle Ages in a time which, except for a tiny number of specialists, knows much less of classical antiquity than did the Middle Ages. Moreover, in a period such as the present, which has much less regard for learning than for practical achievements and for "creative" writing and "original" thinking, a mere change of orientation, or even an increase of knowledge, in the field of learning does not seem to possess any historical significance. However, the situation in the Renaissance was quite different, and the increase in, and emphasis on, classical learning had a tremendous importance.

There are indeed several historical facts which support the interpretation of the humanist movement as a rise in classical scholarship. The humanists were classical scholars and contributed to the rise of classical studies.[14] In the field of Latin studies, they rediscovered a number of important texts that had been hardly read during the Middle Ages.[15] Also in the case of Latin authors commonly known during the Middle Ages, the humanists made them better known, through their numerous manuscript copies [16] and printed editions, through their grammatical and antiquarian studies, through their commentaries, and through the development and application of philological and historical criticism.

Even more striking was the impulse given by the humanists to the study of Greek. In spite of the political, commercial, and ecclesiastic relations with the Byzantine Empire, during the Middle Ages the number of persons in Western Europe who knew the Greek language was comparatively small, and practically none of them was interested in, or familiar with, Greek classical literature. There was almost no teaching of Greek in Western schools and universities, and almost no Greek manuscripts in Western libraries.[17] In the twelfth and thirteenth centuries, a great number of Greek texts were translated into Latin, either directly or through intermediary Arabic translations, but this activity was almost entirely confined to the fields of mathematics, astronomy, astrology, medicine, and Aristotelian philosophy.[18]

During the Renaissance, this situation rapidly changed. The study of Greek classical literature which had been cultivated in the Byzantine Empire throughout the later Middle Ages, after the middle of the fourteenth century began to spread in the West, both through Byzantine scholars who went to Western Europe for a temporary or permanent stay, and through Italian scholars who went to Constantinople in quest of Greek classical learning.[19] As a result, Greek language and literature acquired a recognized place in the curriculum of Western schools and universities, a place which they did not lose until the present century. A large number of Greek manuscripts was brought from the East to Western libraries, and these manuscripts have formed the basis of most of our editions of the Greek classics. At a later stage, the humanists published printed editions of Greek authors, wrote commentaries on them, and extended their antiquarian and grammatical studies as well as their methods of philological and historical criticism to Greek literature.

No less important, although now less appreciated, were the numerous Latin translations from the Greek due to the humanists of the Renaissance. Almost the whole of Greek poetry, oratory, historiography, theology, and non-Aristotelian philosophy was thus translated for the first time, whereas the medieval translations of Aristotle and of Greek scientific writers were replaced by new humanist translations. These Latin translations of the Renaissance were the basis for most of the vernacular translations of the Greek classics, and they were much more widely read than were the original Greek texts. For in spite of its remarkable increase, the study of Greek even in the Renaissance never attained the same general importance as did the study of Latin which was rooted in the medieval tradition of the West. Nevertheless, it remains a remarkable fact that the study of the Greek classics was taken over by the humanists of Western Europe at the very time when it was affected in the East by the decline and fall of the Byzantine Empire.

If we care to remember these impressive facts, we certainly cannot deny that the Italian humanists were the ancestors of modern philologists and historians. Even a historian of science can afford to despise them only if he chooses to remember that science is the subject of his study, but to forget that the method he is applying to this subject is that of history.

However, the activity of the Italian humanists was not limited to classical scholarship, and hence the theory which interprets the humanist movement merely as a rise in classical scholarship is not altogether satisfactory. This theory fails to explain the ideal of eloquence persistently set forth in the writings of the humanists, and it fails to account for the enormous literature of treatises, of letters, of speeches, and of poems produced by the humanists.[20] These writings are far more numerous than the contributions of the humanists to classical scholarship, and they cannot be explained as a necessary consequence of their classical studies. A modern classical scholar is not supposed to write a Latin poem in praise of his city, to welcome a distinguished foreign visitor with a Latin speech, or to write a political manifesto for his government. This aspect of the activity of the humanists is often dismissed with a slighting remark about their vanity or their fancy for speech-making. I do not deny that they were vain and loved to make speeches, but I am inclined to offer a different explanation for this side of their activity. The humanists were not classical scholars who for personal reasons had a craving for eloquence, but, vice versa, they were professional rhetoricians, heirs and successors of the medieval rhetoricians,[21] who developed the belief, then new and modern, that the best way to achieve eloquence was to imitate classical models, and who thus were driven to study the classics and to found classical philology. Their rhetorical ideals and achievements may not correspond to our taste, but they were the starting point and moving force of their activity, and their classical learning was incidental to it.

The other current interpretation of Italian humanism, which is prevalent among historians of philosophy and also accepted by many other scholars, is more ambitious, but in my opinion less sound. This interpretation considers humanism as the new philosophy of the Renaissance, which arose in opposition to scholasticism, the old philosophy of the Middle Ages.[22]

Of course, there is the well-known fact that several famous humanists, such as Petrarch, Valla, Erasmus, and Vives, were violent critics of medieval learning and tended to replace it by classical learning. Moreover, the humanists certainly had ideals of learning, education, and life that differed from medieval modes of thinking. They wrote treatises on moral, educational, political, and religious questions which in tone and content differ from the average medieval treatises on similar subjects.

Yet this interpretation of humanism as a new philosophy fails to account for a number of obvious facts. On one hand, we notice a stubborn survival of scholastic philosophy throughout the Italian Renaissance, an inconvenient fact that is usually explained by the intellectual inertia of the respective philosophers whom almost nobody has read for centuries and whose number, problems and literary production are entirely unknown to most historians. On the other, most of the works of the humanists have nothing to do with philosophy even in the vaguest possible sense of the term. Even their treatises on philosophical subjects, if we care to read them, appear in most cases rather superficial and inconclusive if compared with the works of ancient or medieval philosophers, a fact that may be indifferent to a general historian, but which cannot be overlooked by a historian of philosophy.

I think there has been a tendency, in the light of later developments, and under the influence of a modern aversion to scholasticism, to exaggerate the opposition of the humanists to scholasticism, and to assign to them an importance in the history of scientific and philosophical thought which they neither could nor did attain. The reaction against this tendency has been inevitable, but it has been equally wrong. Those scholars who read the treatises of the humanists and noticed their comparative emptiness of scientific and philosophical thought came to the conclusion that the humanists were bad scientists and philosophers who did not live up to their own claims or to those of their modern advocates. I should like to suggest that the Italian humanists on the whole were neither good nor bad philosophers, but no philosophers at all.[23]

The humanist movement did not originate in the field of philosophical or scientific studies, but it arose in that of grammatical and rhetorical studies.[24] The humanists continued the medieval tradition in these fields, as represented, for example, by the *ars dictaminis* and the *ars arengandi,* but they gave it a new direction toward classical standards and classical studies, possibly under the impact of influences received from France after the middle of the thirteenth century. This new development of the field was followed by an enormous growth, both in quantity and in quality, of its teaching and literary production. As a result of this growth, the claims of the humanists for their field of study also increased considerably. They claimed, and temporarily attained, a decided predominance of their field in elementary and secondary education, and a much larger share for it in professional and university education. This development in the field of grammatical and rhetorical studies finally affected the other branches of learning, but it did not displace them. After the middle of the fifteenth century, we find an increasing number of professional jurists, physicians, mathematicians, philosophers, and theologians who cultivated humanist studies along with their own particular fields of study. Consequently, a humanist influence began to appear in all these other sciences. It appears in the studied elegance of literary expression, in the increasing use made of classical source materials, in the greater knowledge of history and of critical methods, and also sometimes in an emphasis on new problems. This influence of humanism on the other sciences certainly was important, but it did not affect the content or substance of the medieval traditions in those sciences. For the humanists, being amateurs in those other fields, had nothing to offer that could replace their traditional content and subject matter.

The humanist criticism of medieval science is often sweeping, but it does not touch its specific problems and subject matter. Their main charges are against the bad Latin style of the medieval authors, against their ignorance of ancient history and literature, and against their concern for supposedly useless questions. On the other hand, even those professional scientists who were most profoundly influenced by humanism did not sacrifice the medieval tradition of their field. It is highly significant that Pico, a representative of humanist philosophy, and Alciato, a representative of humanist jurisprudence, found it necessary to defend their medieval predecessors against the criticism of humanist rhetoricians.[25]

Yet if the humanists were amateurs in jurisprudence, theology, medicine, and also in philosophy, they were themselves professionals in a number of other fields. Their domains were the fields of grammar, rhetoric, poetry, history, and the study of the Greek and Latin authors. They also expanded into the field of moral philosophy, and they made some attempts to invade the field of logic, which were chiefly attempts to reduce logic to rhetoric.[26]

Yet they did not make any direct contributions to the other branches of philosophy or of science. Moreover, much of the humanist polemic against medieval science was not even intended as a criticism of the contents or methods of that science, but merely represents a phase in the ''battle of the arts,'' that is, a noisy advertisement for the field of learning advocated by the humanists, in order to neutralize and to overcome the claims of other, rivaling sciences.[27] Hence I am inclined to consider the humanists not as philosophers with a curious lack of philosophical ideas and a curious fancy for eloquence and for classical studies, but rather as professional rhetoricians with a new, classicist idea of culture, who tried to assert the importance of their field of learning and to impose their standards upon the other fields of learning and of science, including philosophy.

Let us try to illustrate this outline with a few more specific facts. When we inquire of the humanists, it is often asserted that they were free-lance writers who came to form an entirely new class in Renaissance society.[28] This statement is valid, although with some qualification, for a very small number of outstanding humanists like Petrarch, Boccaccio, and Erasmus. However, these are exceptions, and the vast majority of humanists exercised either of two professions, and sometimes both of them. They were either secretaries of princes or cities, or they were teachers of grammar and rhetoric at universities or secondary schools.[29] The opinion so often repeated by historians that the humanist movement originated outside the schools and universities is a myth which cannot be supported by factual evidence. Moreover, as chancellors and as teachers, the humanists, far from representing a new class, were the professional heirs and successors of the medieval rhetoricians, the so-called *dictatores,* who also made their career exactly in these same two professions. The humanist Coluccio Salutati occupied exactly the same place in the society and culture of his time as did the *dictator* Petrus de Vineis one hundred and fifty years before.[30] Nevertheless there was a significant difference between them. The style of writing used by Salutati is quite different from that of Petrus de Vineis or of Rolandinus Passagerii. Moreover, the study and imitation of the classics which was of little or no importance to the medieval *dictatores* has become the major concern for Salutati. Finally, whereas the medieval *dictatores* attained considerable importance in politics and in administration, the humanists, through their classical learning, acquired for their class a much greater cultural and social prestige. Thus the humanists did not invent a new field of learning or a new professional activity, but they introduced a new, classicist style into the traditions of medieval Italian rhetoric. To blame them for not having invented rhetorical studies would be like blaming Giotto for not having been the inventor of painting.

The same result is confirmed by an examination of the literary production of the humanists if we try to trace the medieval antecedents of the types of literature cultivated by the humanists.[31] If we leave aside the editions and translations of the humanists, their classical interests are chiefly represented by their numerous commentaries on ancient authors and by a number of antiquarian and miscellaneous treatises. Theoretical works on grammar and rhetoric, mostly composed for the school, are quite frequent, and even more numerous is the literature of humanist historiography. Dialogues and treatises on questions of moral philosophy, education, politics, and religion have attracted most of the attention of modern historians, but represent a comparatively small proportion of humanist literature. By far the largest part of that literature, although relatively neglected and partly unpublished, consists of the poems, the speeches, and the letters of the humanists.

If we look for the medieval antecedents of these various types of humanist literature, we are led back in many cases to the Italian grammarians and rhetoricians of the later Middle Ages. This is most obvious for the theoretical treatises on grammar and rhetoric.[32] Less generally recognized, but almost equally obvious is the link between humanist epistolography and medieval *ars dictaminis*. The style of writing is different, to be sure, and the medieval term *dictamen* was no longer used during the Renaissance, yet the literary and political function of the letter was basically the same, and the ability to write a correct and elegant Latin letter was still a major aim of school instruction in the Renaissance as it had been in the Middle Ages.[33]

The same link between humanists and medieval Italian rhetoricians which we notice in the field of epistolography may be found also in the field of oratory. Most historians of rhetoric give the impression that medieval rhetoric was exclusively concerned with letter-writing and preaching, represented by the *ars dictaminis* and the somewhat younger *ars praedicandi,* and that there was no secular eloquence in the Middle Ages.[34] On the other hand, most historians of Renaissance humanism believe that the large output of humanist oratory, although of a somewhat dubious value, was an innovation of the Renaissance due to the effort of the humanists to revive ancient oratory and also to their vain fancy for speech-making.[35] Only in recent years have a few scholars begun to realize that there was a considerable amount of secular eloquence in the Middle Ages, especially in Italy.[36] I do not hesitate to conclude that the eloquence of the humanists was the continuation of the medieval *ars arengandi* just as their epistolography continued the tradition of the *ars dictaminis*. It is true, in taking up a type of literary production developed by their medieval predecessors, the humanists modified its style according to their own taste and classicist standards. Yet the practice of speech-making was no invention of the humanists, of course, since it is hardly absent from any human society, and since in medieval Italy it can be traced back at least to the eleventh century.[37]

Even the theory of secular speech, represented by rules and instructions as well as by model speeches, appears in Italy at least as early as the thirteenth century. Indeed practically all types of humanist oratory have their antecedents in this medieval literature: wedding and funeral speeches, academic speeches, political speeches by officials or ambassadors, decorative speeches on solemn occasions, and finally judicial speeches.[38] Some of these types, to be sure, had their classical models, but others, for example, academic speeches delivered at the beginning of the year or of a particular course or upon conferring or receiving a degree, had no classical antecedents whatsoever, and all these types of oratory were rooted in very specific customs and institutions of medieval Italy. The humanists invented hardly any of these types of speech, but merely applied their standards of style and elegance to a previously existing form of literary expression and thus satisfied a demand, both practical and artistic, of the society of their time. Modern scholars are apt to speak contemptuously of this humanist oratory, denouncing its empty rhetoric and its lack of "deep thoughts." Yet the humanists merely intended to speak well, according to their taste and to the occasion, and it still remains to be seen whether they were less successful in that respect than their medieval precedessors or their modern successors. Being pieces of "empty rhetoric," their speeches provide us with an amazing amount of information about the personal and intellectual life of their time.

In their historiography, the humanists succeeded the medieval chroniclers, yet they differ from them both in their merits and in their deficiencies.[39] Humanist historiography is characterized by the rhetorical concern for elegant Latin and by the application of philological criticism to the source materials of history. In both respects, they are the predecessors of modern historians.[40] To combine the requirements of a good style and those of careful research was as rare and difficult then as it is at present. However, the link between history and rhetoric that seems to be so typical of the Renaissance was apparently a medieval heritage. Not only was the teaching of history in the medieval schools subordinate to that of grammar and rhetoric, but we also find quite a few medieval historiographers and chronists who were professional grammarians and rhetoricians.[41] Even the Renaissance custom of princes and cities appointing official historiographers to write their history seems to have had a few antecedents in medieval Italy.[42]

Most of the philosophical treatises and dialogues of the humanists are really nothing but moral tracts, and many of them deal with subject matters also treated in the moralistic literature of the Middle Ages. There are, to be sure, significant differences in style, treatment, sources, and solutions. However, the common features of the topics and literary patterns should not be overlooked either. A thorough comparative study of medieval and Renaissance moral treatises has not yet been made so far as I am aware, but in a few specific cases the connection has been pointed out.[43] Again it should be added that the very link between rhetoric and moral philosophy which became so apparent in the Renaissance had its antecedents in the Middle Ages. Medieval rhetoric, no less than ancient rhetoric, was continually quoting and inculcating moral sentences that interested the authors and their readers for their content as well as for their form. Moreover, there are at least a few cases in which medieval rhetoricians wrote treatises on topics of moral philosophy, or argued about the same moral questions that were to exercise the minds and pens of their successors, the Renaissance humanists.[44]

Less definite is the link between humanists and medieval Italian rhetoricians in the field of Latin poetry. On the basis of available evidence, it would seem that in the Italian schools up to the thirteenth century verse-making was less cultivated than in France. Throughout the earlier Middle Ages, historical and panegyric epics as well as verse epitaphs were composed abundantly in Italy, yet prior to the thirteenth century her share in rhythmical and didactic poetry seems to have been rather modest.[45] It is only after the middle of the thirteenth century that we notice a marked increase in the production of Latin poetry in Italy, and the appearance of the teaching of poetry in the schools and universities. This development coincides with the earliest traces of Italian humanism, and it is tempting to ascribe it to French influences.[46]

The same may be said with more confidence of the literature of commentaries on the Latin classics, which are the direct result of school teaching. It is often asserted that Italy throughout the Middle Ages was closer to the classical tradition than any other European country. Yet if we try to trace the type of the humanist commentary back into the Middle Ages, we find hardly any commentary on a Latin poet or prose writer composed in Italy prior to the second half of the thirteenth century, whereas we find many such commentaries, from the ninth century on, written in France and the other Western countries that followed the French development.[47] Only after 1300, that is, after the earliest phase of humanism, did Italy produce an increasing number of such commentaries. Also, there is very little evidence of antiquarian studies in Italy prior to the latter part of the thirteenth century.[48]

Whereas we have abundant information about the reading of the Latin poets and prose writers in the medieval schools of France and other Western countries, and whereas such centers as Chartres and Orléans in the twelfth and early thirteenth centuries owed much of their fame to the study of the Latin classics,[49] the sources for Italy are silent during the same period and begin to speak only after the middle of the thirteenth century.[50] It was only after the beginning of the fourteenth century that the teaching of poetry and the classical authors became firmly established in the Italian schools and universities, to continue without interruption throughout the Renaissance.[51] Italian libraries, with the one exception of Monte Cassino, were not so well furnished with Latin classical poets as were some French and German libraries, and it has been noticed that the humanists of the fifteenth century made most of their manuscript discoveries not in Italy but in other countries. The conclusion seems inevitable that the study of classical Latin authors was comparatively neglected in Italy during the earlier Middle Ages and was introduced from France after the middle of the thirteenth century.[52] The Italian humanists thus took up the work of their medieval French predecessors just about the time when classical studies began to decline in France, and whereas the classical scholarship of the earliest humanists in its range and method was still close to the medieval tradition, that of the later Renaissance developed far beyond anything attained during the Middle Ages. Consequently, if we consider the entire literary production of the Italian humanists we are led to the conclusion that the humanist movement seems to have originated from a fusion between the novel interest in classical studies imported from France toward the end of the thirteenth century and the much earlier traditions of medieval Italian rhetoric.

We have seen that the humanists did not live outside the schools and universities, but were closely connected with them. The chairs commonly held by the humanists were those of grammar and rhetoric,[53] that is, the same that had been occupied by their medieval predecessors, the *dictatores*. Thus it is in the history of the universities and schools and of their chairs that the connection of the humanists with medieval rhetoric becomes most apparent. However, under the influence of humanism, these chairs underwent a change which affected their name as well as their content and pretenses. About the beginning of the fourteenth century poetry appears as a special teaching subject at Italian universities. After that time, the teaching of grammar was considered primarily as the task of elementary instructors, whereas the humanists proper held the more advanced chairs of poetry and of eloquence. For eloquence was the equivalent of prose writing as well as of speech. The teaching of poetry and of eloquence was theoretical and practical at the same time, for the humanist professor instructed his pupils in verse-making and speech-making both through rules and through models. Since classical Latin authors were considered as the chief models for imitation, the reading of these authors was inseparably connected with the theoretical and practical teaching of poetry and of eloquence.

Thus we may understand why the humanists of the fourteenth and fifteenth centuries chose to call their field of study poetry and why they were often styled poets even though they composed no works that would qualify them as poets in the modern sense.[54] Also the coronation of poets in the Renaissance must be understood against this background.[55] It had been originally understood as a kind of academic degree, and it was granted not merely for original poetic compositions, but also for the competent study of classical poets.[56]

History was not taught as a separate subject, but formed a part of the study of rhetoric and poetry since the ancient historians were among the prose writers commonly studied in school. Moral philosophy was always the subject of a separate chair and was commonly studied from the *Ethics* and *Politics* of Aristotle. However, after the beginning of the fifteenth century, the chair of moral philosophy was often held by the humanists, usually in combination with that of rhetoric and poetry.[57] This combination reflects the expansion of humanist learning into the field of moral philosophy. The chairs of Greek language and literature which were an innovation of the fourteenth century were also commonly held by humanists. This teaching was not as closely tied up with the practical concern for writing verses, speeches, or letters as was the study of Latin, and it was therefore more strictly scholarly and philological. On the other hand, since the fifteenth century we find several cases where humanist teachers of Greek offered courses on Greek texts of philosophy and science and thus invaded the territory of rival fields.[58]

Later on, the fields of study cultivated by the humanists were given a new and more ambitious name. Taking up certain expressions found in Cicero and Gellius, the humanists as early as the fourteenth century began to call their field of learning the humane studies or the studies befitting a human being (*studia humanitatis, studia humaniora*).[59] The new name certainly implies a new claim and program, but it covered a content that had existed long before and that had been designated by the more modest names of grammar, rhetoric, and poetry. Although some modern scholars were not aware of this fact, the humanists certainly were, and we have several contemporary testimonies showing that the *studia humanitatis* were considered as the equivalent of grammar, rhetoric, poetry, history, and moral philosophy.[60]

These statements also prove another point that has been confused by most modern historians: the humanists, at least in Italy or before the sixteenth century, did not claim that they were substituting a new encyclopaedia of learning for the medieval one,[61] and they were aware of the fact that their field of study occupied a well defined and limited place within the system of contemporary learning.[62] To be sure, they tended to emphasize the importance of their field in comparison with the other sciences and to encroach upon the latter's territory, but on the whole they did not deny the existence or validity of these other sciences.

This well defined place of the *studia humanitatis* is reflected in the new term *humanista* which apparently was coined during the latter half of the fifteenth century and became increasingly popular during the sixteenth. The term seems to have originated in the slang of university students and gradually penetrated into official usage.[63] It was coined after the model of such medieval terms as *legista, jurista, canonista,* and *artista,* and it designated the professional teacher of the *studia humanitatis.* Thus the term *humanista* in this limited sense was coined during the Renaissance, whereas the term *humanism* was first used by nineteenth century historians.[64] If I am not mistaken, the new term *humanism* reflects the modern and false conception that Renaissance humanism was a basically new philosophical movement, and under the influence of this notion the old term humanist has also been misunderstood as designating the representative of a new *Weltanschauung.* The old term *humanista,* on the other hand, reflects the more modest, but correct, contemporary view that the humanists were the teachers and representatives of a certain branch of learning which at that time was expanding and in vogue, but well limited in its subject matter. Humanism thus did not represent the sum total of learning in the Italian Renaissance.

If we care to look beyond the field of the humanities into the other fields of learning as they were cultivated during the Italian Renaissance, that is, into jurisprudence, medicine, theology, mathematics, and natural philosophy, what we find is evidently a continuation of medieval learning and may hence very well be called scholasticism. Since the term has been subject to controversy, I should like to say that I do not attach any unfavorable connotation to the term scholasticism. As its characteristic, I do not consider any particular doctrine, but rather a specific method, that is, the type of logical argument represented by the form of the *Questio.*

It is well-known that the content of scholastic philosophy, since the thirteenth century, was largely based on the writings of Aristotle, and that the development of this philosophy, since the twelfth century, was closely connected with the schools and universities of France and England, especially with the universities of Paris and Oxford. The place of Italy, however, is less known in the history and development of scholastic philosophy. Several Italians are found among the most famous philosophers and theologians of the twelfth and thirteenth centuries, but practically all of them did their studying and teaching in France. Whereas Italy had flourishing schools of rhetoric, jurisprudence, and medicine during the twelfth and early thirteenth century, she had no native center of philosophical studies during the same period. After 1220 the new mendicant orders established schools of theology and philosophy in many Italian cities, but unlike those in France and England, these schools of the friars for a long time had no links with the Italian universities. Regular chairs of theology were not established at the Italian universities before the middle of the fourteenth century, and even after that period, the university teaching of theology continued to be spotty and irregular.

Aristotelian philosophy, although not entirely unknown at Salerno toward the end of the twelfth century, made its regular appearance at the Italian universities after the middle of the thirteenth century and in close connection with the teaching of medicine.[65] I think it is safe to assume that Aristotelian philosophy was imported at that time from France as were the study of classical authors and many other forms of intellectual activity.[66] After the beginning of the fourteenth century, this Italian Aristotelianism assumed a more definite shape.[67] The teaching of logic and natural philosophy became a well-established part of the university curriculum and even spread to some of the secondary schools. An increasing number of commentaries and questions on the works of Aristotle reflect this teaching tradition, and numerous systematic treatises on philosophical subjects show the same general trend and background. During the fourteenth and fifteenth centuries, further influences were received from Paris in the field of natural philosophy and from Oxford in the field of logic;[68] and from the latter part of the fourteenth century on we can trace an unbroken tradition of Italian Aristotelianism which continued through the fifteenth and sixteenth century and far into the seventeenth century.[69]

The common notion that scholasticism as an old philosophy was superseded by the new philosophy of humanism is thus again disproved by plain facts. For Italian scholasticism originated toward the end of the thirteenth century, that is, about the same time as did Italian humanism, and both traditions developed side by side throughout the period of the Renaissance and even thereafter.

However, the two traditions had their locus and center in two different sectors of learning: humanism in the field of grammar, rhetoric, and poetry and to some extent in moral philosophy, scholasticism in the fields of logic and natural philosophy. Everybody knows the eloquent attacks launched by Petrarch and Bruni against the logicians of their time, and it is generally believed that these attacks represent a vigorous new movement rebelling against an old entrenched habit of thought. Yet actually the English method of dialectic was quite as novel at the Italian schools of that time as were the humanist studies advocated by Petrarch and Bruni,[70] and the humanist attack was as much a matter of departmental rivalry as it was a clash of opposite ideas or philosophies. Bruni even hints at one point that he is not speaking quite in earnest.[71]

Such controversies, interesting as they are, were mere episodes in a long period of peaceful coexistence between humanism and scholasticism. Actually the humanists quarreled as much among each other as they did with the scholastics. Moreover, it would be quite wrong to consider these controversies as serious battles over basic principles whereas many of them were meant to be merely personal feuds, intellectual tournaments, or rhetorical exercises. Finally, any attempt to reduce these controversies to one issue must fail since the discussions were concerned with many diverse and overlapping issues.[72] Therefore, we should no longer be surprised that Italian Aristotelianism quietly and forcefully survived the attacks of Petrarch and his humanist successors.

But the Aristotelianism of the Renaissance did not remain untouched by the new influence of humanism. Philosophers began to make abundant use of the Greek text and the new Latin translations of Aristotle, his ancient commentators, and other Greek thinkers. The revival of ancient philosophies that came in the wake of the humanist movement, especially the revival of Platonism and of Stoicism, left a strong impact upon the Aristotelian philosophers of the Renaissance.[73] Yet in spite of these significant modifications, Renaissance Aristotelianism continued the medieval scholastic tradition without any visible break. It preserved a firm hold on the university chairs of logic, natural philosophy, and metaphysics, whereas even the humanist professors of moral philosophy continued to base their lectures on Aristotle. The literary activity of these Aristotelian philosophers is embodied in a large number of commentaries, questions, and treatises. This literature is difficult of access and arduous to read, but rich in philosophical problems and doctrines. It represents the bulk and kernel of the philosophical thought of the period, but it has been badly neglected by modern historians. Scholars hostile to the Middle Ages considered this literature an unfortunate survival of medieval traditions that may be safely disregarded, whereas the true modern spirit of the Renaissance is expressed in the literature of the humanists. Medievalists, on the other hand, have largely concentrated on the earlier phases of scholastic philosophy and gladly sacrificed the later scholastics to the criticism of the humanists and their modern followers, a tendency that has been further accentuated by the recent habit of identifying scholasticism with Thomism.

Consequently, most modern scholars have condemned the Aristotelian philosophers of the Renaissance without a hearing, labeling them as empty squibblers and as followers of a dead past who failed to understand the living problems of their new times. Recent works on the civilization of the Renaissance thus often repeat the charges made against the Aristotelian philosophers by the humanists of their time, and even give those attacks a much more extreme meaning than they were originally intended to have. Other scholars who are equally unfavorable to the humanists include both scholastics and humanists in a summary sentence that reflects the judgments of seventeenth-century scientists and philosophers. Only a few famous figures such as Pietro Pomponazzi seem to resist the general verdict.

There has been a tendency to present Pomponazzi and a few other thinkers as basically different from the other Aristotelians of their time and as closely related with the humanists or with the later scientists. This is merely an attempt to reconcile the respect for Pomponazzi with modern preconceptions against the Aristotelians of the Renaissance. Actually Pomponazzi does not belong to the humanists or to the later scientists, but to the tradition of medieval and Renaissance Aristotelianism. The number of modern scholars who have actually read some of the works of the Italian Aristotelians is comparatively small. The most influential comprehensive treatment of the group is found in Renan's book on Averroes and Averroism, a book which had considerable merits for its time, but which also contains several errors and confusions which have been repeated ever since.[74] If we want to judge the merits and limitations of Renaissance Aristotelianism we will have to proceed to a new direct investigation of the source materials, instead of repeating antiquated judgments. It will be necessary to study in detail the questions discussed by these thinkers, such as the doctrine of immortality and its demonstrability, the problem of the so-called double truth, and the method of scientific proof.[75] Due consideration should also be given to the contributions made by these Aristotelian philosophers to medicine and natural history, and to the influence they exercised upon such early scientists as Galilei and Harvey.[76] Current notions about the prevalence of Thomism among the Aristotelians, about the controversy of the Averroists and the Alexandrists, about the continuity and uniformity of the school of Padua, and even the very concept of Averroism will have to be reexamined and possibly abandoned. Also the widespread belief that the Italian Aristotelians were atheists and free-thinkers who merely did not dare to say what they thought must be investigated in its origin and validity.[77]

Thus we may conclude that the humanism and the scholasticism of the Renaissance arose in medieval Italy about the same time, that is, about the end of the thirteenth century, and that they coexisted and developed all the way through and beyond the Renaissance period as different branches of learning. Their controversy, much less persistent and violent than usually represented, is merely a phase in the battle of the arts, not a struggle for existence. We may compare it to the debates of the arts in medieval literature, to the rivaling claims of medicine and law at the universities, or to the claims advanced by Leonardo in his *Paragone* for the superiority of painting over the other arts. Humanism certainly had a tendency to influence the other sciences and to expand at their expense, but all kinds of adjustments and combinations between humanism and scholasticism were possible and were successfully accomplished. It is only after the Renaissance, through the rise of modern science and modern philosophy, that Aristotelianism was gradually displaced, whereas humanism became gradually detached from its rhetorical background and evolved into modern philology and history.

Thus humanism and scholasticism both occupy an important place in the civilization of the Italian Renaissance, yet neither represents a unified picture, nor do both together constitute the whole of Renaissance civilization. Just as humanism and scholasticism coexisted as different branches of culture, there were besides them other important, and perhaps even more important branches. I am thinking of the developments in the fine arts, in vernacular literature, in the mathematical sciences, and in religion and theology. Many misunderstandings have resulted from the attempts to interpret or to criticize humanism and scholasticism in the light of these other developments. Too many historians have tried to play up the fine arts, or vernacular poetry, or science, or religion against the "learning of the schools." These attempts must be rejected. The religious and theological problems of the Protestant and Catholic Reformation were hardly related to the issues discussed in the philosophical literature of the same time, and supporters and enemies of humanistic learning and of Aristotelian philosophy were found among the followers of both religious parties. The development of vernacular poetry in Italy was not opposed or delayed by the humanists, as most historians of literature complain. Some humanists stressed the superiority of Latin, to be sure, but few if any of them seriously thought of abolishing the *volgare* in speech or writing. On the other hand, many humanists are found among the advocates of the *volgare,* and a great number of authors continued to write in both languages. Again, modern historians have tried to interpret as a struggle for existence what in fact was merely a rivalry between different forms of expression.[78]

The admirable development of the fine arts which is the chief glory of the Italian Renaissance did not spring from any exaggerated notions about the creative genius of the artist or about his role in society and culture. Such notions are the product of the Romantic movement and its eighteenth-century forerunners, and they were largely foreign to the Italian Renaissance.[79] Renaissance artists were primarily craftsmen, and they often became scientists, not because their superior genius anticipated the modern destinies of science, but because certain branches of scientific knowledge, such as anatomy, perspective, or mechanics were considered as a necessary requirement in the development of their craft. If some of these artist-scientists were able to make considerable contributions to science, this does not mean that they were completely independent or contemptuous of the science and learning available in their time.

Finally, mathematics and astronomy made remarkable progress during the sixteenth century and assumed increasing importance in their practical applications, in the literature of the time, and in the curriculum of the schools and universities. If this development did not immediately affect philosophy, this was due not to the stupidity or inertia of contemporary philosophers, but to the fact that physics or natural philosophy was considered as a part of philosophy and that there was almost no traditional link between the mathematical sciences and philosophy. Galileo was a professional student and teacher of mathematics and astronomy, not of philosophy. His claim that physics should be based on mathematics rather than on logic was not merely a novel idea as far as it went, but it revolutionized the very conceptions on which the curriculum of the schools and universities was based. It is hence quite understandable that he was opposed by the Aristotelian physicists of his time who considered his method as an invasion of their traditional domain by the mathematicians. On the other hand, there is no evidence that Galileo met with any serious resistance within his own field of mathematics and astronomy in which the main chairs were soon occupied by his pupils. If we want to understand and to judge these developments we must know the issues and the professional traditions of the later Middle Ages and of the Renaissance.

Modern scholarship has been far too much influenced by all kinds of prejudices, against the use of Latin, against scholasticism, against the medieval church, and also by the unwarranted effort to read later developments, such as the German Reformation, or French libertinism, or nineteenth-century liberalism or nationalism, back into the Renaissance. The only way to understand the Renaissance is a direct and, possibly, an objective study of the original sources. We have no real justification to take sides in the controversies of the Renaissance, and to play up humanism against scholasticism, or scholasticism against humanism, or modern science against both of them. Instead of trying to reduce everything to one or two issues, which is the privilege and curse of political controversy, we should try to develop a kind of historical pluralism. It is easy to praise everything in the past which happens to resemble certain favorite ideas of our own time, or to ridicule and minimize everything that disagrees with them. This method is neither fair nor helpful for an adequate understanding of the past. It is equally easy to indulge in a sort of worship of success, and to dismiss defeated and refuted ideas with a shrugging of the shoulders, but just as in political history, this method does justice neither to the vanquished nor to the victors. Instead of blaming each century for not having anticipated the achievements of the next, intellectual history must patiently register the errors of the past as well as its truths. Complete objectivity may be impossible to achieve, but it should remain the permanent aim and standard of the historian as well as of the philosopher and scientist.

6.

Renaissance Philosophy and the Medieval Tradition

Although I consider myself a realist in metaphysics, I am a thorough nominalist in reference to several terms employed in historical discourse; therefore, I think it is necessary for me to define the meaning of the terms used in the title of this essay.

The term "Renaissance" has been the topic of many debates and controversies and has been defined in a great variety of ways. As a result, the so-called problem of the Renaissance has become the subject matter of a whole literature.[1] I shall not attempt to enter into this debate here, but merely say that by Renaissance I mean roughly the period of Western European history between 1300 or 1350 and 1600. The controversies concerning the meaning of this period in Western history are partly due to national, religious, and professional ideals and preferences that have influenced the judgment of historians, and partly to the great complexity and diversity that belongs to the period itself and which will necessarily be reflected in the accounts of modern historians, depending upon those aspects which they choose to emphasize. The Renaissance includes many outstanding individuals who were very different from their contemporaries, but I do not think any individual ever can be said to speak for his age. There are great national, regional, and even local differences; and the choice of countries or cities on which to focus our attention will make a great difference in our account of the period. Still it makes some sense to stress the predominant role of Italy and of the Low Countries during the Renaissance[2] and to acknowledge the fact that within the broader framework of European civilization, the cultural centers of gravitation lay in those parts, whereas in earlier or later periods it was located in France or in some other countries.

Moreover, within the larger Renaissance period that extends over several centuries there are different phases with distinct physiognomies; it is certainly true that the fourteenth century with Dante and even with Petrarch and Salutati was more medieval and less modern than the fifteenth with Bruni, Valla, and Alberti, or the sixteenth with Erasmus and Montaigne. Even within the same time and geographical area, different subjects and professions do not present a homogeneous picture. We do not find, and we cannot expect to find a parallel development in political and economic history, in theology, philosophy, and the sciences, in literature and the arts. In the Renaissance, just as in our own time or at any other time, we must be prepared to encounter a number of crosscurrents and conflicting currents even within the same place and time and subject matter. Certainly the spirit of the Renaissance to which some historians like to refer should be defined and demonstrated rather than merely asserted; and it would be wise to treat the unity of the period, not as an established fact, but as a regulative idea in the Kantian sense, something that may guide our investigations and that we hope to attain as a result of our studies, rather than as something we may take for granted at the beginning of our endeavors.

If my last statements may have sounded pleasing to the ears of medievalists, my next remark, I am afraid, will disappoint them. For what I have said about the Renaissance applies to an even larger degree to the Middle Ages, a much longer period of history generally taken to extend from 500 to 1300 or 1350. Although this is not frequently stressed, I cannot help noticing that the medieval period as a whole is as complex as the Renaissance, if not more so. Medieval culture is usually treated as a universal or international phenomenon, yet regional differences are by no means absent from it; the fact is merely concealed when a historian purporting to describe the history of the Middle Ages recounts in effect the medieval history of his own respective country.

Moreover, differences, for example, between the period of the barbaric invasions, the Carolingian age, and the twelfth or thirteenth century may seem even greater than those between the fourteenth and sixteenth centuries; and in the thirteenth century, after the rise of the universities, the specialization of learning and the diverse development of different sectors of civilization was as great, or nearly as great, as during the Renaissance.

In other words, a single medieval tradition does not exist; rather, there are many different medieval traditions, some of them quite opposed to others. We should really speak of medieval traditions, in the plural, or define in each instance which particular medieval tradition we have in mind. If it is true that the Renaissance in many of its aspects may be linked with medieval precedents, as I shall tend to confirm in this essay, it is equally true that those medieval phenomena which seem to foreshadow certain Renaissance developments did not necessarily occupy the center of the stage during their own period, or especially during that phase of the Middle Ages that immediately preceded the early Renaissance.[3] Consequently, when we look for medieval precedents of the Renaissance, we may see the Middle Ages themselves in a different perspective from the one we usually have when we consider the medieval period in its own terms and with reference to its own prevailing trends. Such a different perspective may be instructive as long as we do not pretend that it is the only legitimate one, just as it has been instructive to view classical antiquity occasionally in medieval or Renaissance perspective, as distinct from its own ancient perspective, or from what the nineteenth and twentieth centuries took that perspective to be.[4]

Further, I should say a few words about the term tradition, which has been a favorite with many scholars, including myself. Lately, historians have tended to stress continuity in history and to emphasize the fact that, even after a radical change such as a revolution or conquest, certain features of the previous order were retained. Yet, we should not forget that there are discontinuities in history and that even continuity means continuity in change, not mere stability. Stability is inertia, which belongs to things, to institutions rather than to human beings. Nor is any phase of human history so perfect that it would be worth preserving in all its aspects, even if that were possible. One of the most obvious causes for change, one that is usually forgotten by sociologists, is the fact that human beings are mortal and are inevitably replaced by new persons and new generations. In the long run, it is these new persons who will decide how much of what they receive from their predecessors will be preserved or changed, abandoned or destroyed. Traditions should be preserved whenever they represent genuine values, and not all of them do. But in order to be kept alive, they must be appropriated by new generations; and thus they are inevitably transformed. On the other hand, traditions may be effective, in a sense, even when they are not appropriated or continued, but reacted against.

When we ask what the medieval tradition, or the medieval traditions, meant in relation to the Renaissance, we must try to understand how many of these traditions the Renaissance retained and what it retained. The Renaissance retained some, perhaps many of the medieval traditions, but certainly not all. It made changes; and we must see these changes as well as the continuity. They may be subtle and hard to describe. Yet, in history, as in art and in life, nuances are as important as crude facts. And if they are hard to describe, the need for a penetrating study becomes the more imperative.

When I say the Renaissance made some changes, I do not mean only the original elements introduced by the Renaissance, or those elements in the Renaissance that seem to bring it closer to the modern age. I should like to include also the strengthening of classical influences which had been less effective during the Middle Ages; new approaches to familiar sources, for example, to the works of St. Augustine;[5] a new emphasis given to certain elements of the medieval tradition that had been present but less prominent during the Middle Ages; finally, a recombination and rearrangement of the very same older elements as they appear in a new and different looking whole.

The stability of traditions concerns primarily such general patterns as literary and artistic genres, academic and professional methods and pursuits (although these too are subject to change), whereas within these general patterns there may be considerable changes and differences in style, quality, standing, and prestige, as well as in quantity. Some of the changes that occurred from the Middle Ages to the Renaissance may appear small from our modern perspective although they seemed important in their own time; this may be due to a foreshortening produced by our own distance from both periods. Obviously, the Renaissance must share with the Middle Ages the absence of all those elements of modern civilization that were the result of later developments. If the Renaissance lacks the physical science and philosophy of the seventeenth century, the technology, industrial economy, or political democracy of later periods, this does not make the Renaissance any more medieval than it would make the Middle Ages ancient or prehistoric.

Finally, I do not consider value judgments a part of the historian's task and should like to avoid them as much as possible. When a great medievalist once stated that the Renaissance is the Middle Ages minus God,[6] he pronounced an unfair value judgment in addition to committing a factual mistake. We must record past events as they are attested for us, whether we like them or not. We certainly cannot have it both ways and claim that the Renaissance was no different from the Middle Ages and also that it was inferior to them. Our likes and dislikes are unavoidable and hardly subject to discussion; but they are not relevant to our task as historians, nor will they undo those events which we happen to dislike. Moreover, we should admit that human "progress" has its limitations and that genuine progress is paid for by the loss of something else.

The last term which we should discuss is most difficult of all: philosophy. It is well-known that every philosopher, depending on his philosophy, has given a different definition of his subject. Moreover, philosophy is linked with many other aspects of human endeavor: religion and theology, law and politics, the sciences and scholarship, literature and the arts. These links are themselves subject to historical change. At the same time, philosophy has its own specific and professional tradition which distinguishes it from all those other pursuits with which it has been more or less intimately connected in various phases of its history. If we want to understand the role of philosophy in the Middle Ages and in the Renaissance, we must consider both aspects of philosophy, that is, its close links with other subjects, and its independent place within a broader and more complex system of thought and of culture.

In discussing our subject, I shall not attempt to consider individually the main schools and currents of Renaissance philosophy, describing for each of them its main ideas and its relations with medieval thought. Such a procedure would require much more space than I have at my disposal. I shall choose instead another procedure which may seem to be more ambitious and for which I may be less qualified. That is, I shall try to discuss briefly some of the main intellectual traditions of the Middle Ages and to ascertain what became of them during the Renaissance. In following this approach we shall view the Middle Ages in Renaissance perspective, but also the Renaissance in a medieval perspective. This does not mean that I wish to overlook or underestimate those aspects of Renaissance thought that were unrelated to the medieval tradition or that prepared the way for later, modern developments; but my very task will prompt me to place less explicit emphasis on them. I also fear that my all too broadly formulated topic will lead to an excessive amount of generalization and force me to reduce a great number of thoughts and thinkers to their least common denominator, for too broad a perspective makes everything look alike and appear almost empty. I hope to achieve a greater degree of concreteness by also paying some attention to specific currents and problems. Yet, the very attempt to compare large periods and broad traditions will force us to emphasize the general patterns which characterize them in their entirety and not those specific ideas which may be much more impressive, but which are distinctive of individual thinkers rather than of their school or period.

This survey must begin with the development of grammatical and rhetorical studies, since their development is closely linked, as we shall see, with the most pervasive intellectual movement of the Renaissance, humanism; also, during the Middle Ages they represent the earliest and most continuous tradition. Grammar and rhetoric were the main subjects of ancient Roman school instruction. The study of these subjects included the reading and interpretation of classical Latin poets and prose writers as well as practical exercises in speech and writing.[7] Training in law was available to the future jurist or statesman, but there were no established schools of philosophy, medicine, or mathematics in the Western part of the Empire such as existed in the Greek East; this negative fact is important to remember since the Middle Ages were built upon a Roman and Latin, and not directly upon a Greek foundation.[8] The Christian Latin scholars of late antiquity who became the founders of the Middle Ages had absorbed the grammatical and rhetorical learning of the pagan schools. Some of them, such as Augustine and Boethius, were able to add to this background a thorough acquaintance with important sectors of Greek philosophy, known to them from extensive readings. Through their teaching and example, this heritage was bequeathed to subsequent centuries.[9]

During the early Middle Ages, learning became to a large extent a monopoly of the clergy since the most important schools were those attached to the monasteries of the Benedictine order. Their instruction was based on the scheme of the so-called seven liberal arts which were considered the sum total of secular learning and identified with philosophy.[10] Within this cycle of subjects that included logic and the mathematical disciplines, grammar and rhetoric, and especially grammar, came to occupy the leading position. By then Latin had ceased to be the spoken language of Western Europe, but continued for many more centuries as the language of the Church and of learning, administration, and international diplomacy. Thus the study of the Latin language became the most elementary and also the most important part of grammatical instruction.[11] Yet, medieval grammatical studies at their best included also the reading and interpretation of the classical Latin authors and the composition of Latin prose and verse based on the imitation of these classical models.

The grammatical and rhetorical orientation of early medieval culture has become increasingly evident as the work of Irish and Carolingian scholars and the contribution of the cathedral schools down to the twelfth century has become better known. It appears in the form and content of the writings that have come down to us from the period, in the manuscripts of ancient authors which were copied and often glossed during this period, in the catalogues of its libraries, and in the testimonies about its schools. The rise of the universities and of scholasticism in the thirteenth century brought about a decline of grammatical and classical studies; but after the beginning of the fourteenth century, the tradition was resumed by the prehumanists and humanists of the early Italian Renaissance.

The connection between French grammarians of the twelfth century and Italian humanists seems to be obvious, but the precise nature and extent of this connection has not yet been sufficiently explored. What is needed is a close analysis of the content and sources of the writings of the Italian prehumanists and humanists and especially of their commentaries on classical Latin authors. A comparison between these commentaries and those of the preceding centuries will no doubt go far in showing a certain continuity in the form and content of scholarship, and in the instruction through which this scholarship was transmitted.[12]

Yet, when the formal link between the grammatical studies of the Middle Ages and of Renaissance humanism has been recognized, their differences should not be overlooked. Although some of the formal pattern may seem to be the same, it remains to be seen how the quantity and quality of humanist learning compares with that of the medieval period. It is important to realize, as many students of the Renaissance have failed to do, that in one aspect of their activity Renaissance humanists were the professional successors of medieval grammarians. Yet, it is equally necessary to see, as many medievalists have refused to do, that in their knowledge of Latin and of the Latin classics Renaissance humanists made considerable advances over their medieval predecessors.

The difference between the classical learning of the humanists and that of the medieval grammarians becomes more marked when we pass from the study of Latin to that of Greek. The knowledge of Greek was not completely absent from the Middle Ages, as recent studies have convincingly shown; but it was never as common or as extensive as it was in Roman antiquity or during the Renaissance.[13] Many important texts were translated from Greek into Latin during the Middle Ages, and especially during the twelfth and thirteenth centuries. These translations played an important part in the study of Aristotelian philosophy and of the sciences, as we shall see.[14] Yet the Greek studies of Renaissance humanists went much further. They really mastered the language and its idioms; and their translating activity covered the entire range of ancient Greek literature, filling all the gaps that had been left by the medieval translators, and thus making many important authors and texts available to Western readers for the first time. The number and diffusion of humanist translations from the Greek is now being more fully explored on the basis of the manuscript and printed sources.[15] Moreover, the humanists made new translations of the same texts which had been translated before, for example, of Aristotle and of some of his commentators. It has been shown that in some instances the humanists merely revised some available medieval translations.[16] But, on the whole, we are not yet in a position to judge the relative merits of the medieval and humanist translations, say, of Aristotle, since to my knowledge nobody has yet taken the trouble to compare them with each other or with the Greek text. Under these circumstances, most of the judgments expressed by modern scholars on the subject must be considered gratuitous. There is no doubt that the Renaissance humanists were indebted for many aspects of their Greek learning to the Byzantine tradition; but this is a subject which has not yet been sufficiently studied, and it does not directly concern our topic.[17]

Rhetorical studies were in many ways connected with grammar; but, according to ancient tradition, they were considered more advanced. After the end of antiquity, the practice of public speech for which Roman rhetoric had been especially designed came to an end. Early medieval rhetoric was thus reduced to a theory of prose composition, and as such it occupied an important place in the curriculum. During the eleventh century at the latest, the eminently practical task of writing business letters and documents became the subject matter of a special branch of rhetoric, called *dictamen*, which apparently originated in Montecassino and spread from there to the papal curia and the schools of Italy, France, and other countries.[18] The huge literature of *dictamen*, consisting of theoretical treatises and model collections, has been the subject of considerable study, especially the earlier period. Again, as in the case of commentaries on the Latin classics, there is a formal link between the medieval *dictamen* literature and the epistolography of the humanists. I have found and published a treatise on *dictamen* by one of the leading prehumanists, which seems to confirm this connection.[19] Yet, the persistence of a formal pattern should not prompt us to overlook the considerable differences in style and literary quality that separate the epistolography of the Renaissance humanists from that of their medieval predecessors. The Renaissance humanists were consummate classical scholars, as the medieval *dictatores* were not; and they shaped their letters, as far as possible, after classical models rather than after the business practice of the medieval chanceries.[20] The *dictamen* literature deserves considerable respect and attention for its great practical and cultural importance, but any reader imbued with a moderate amount of classical training can hardly help finding the letters of the humanists more interesting and more enjoyable.

I should like to insist that the core of the medieval rhetorical tradition lies in the *dictamen*, and not in the study of Aristotle's *Rhetoric*, which has received much greater attention from some historians of the subject.[21] Aristotle's *Rhetoric* was studied in the thirteenth and fourteenth centuries by Aristotelian philosphers, rather than by the professional rhetoricians and, for good reasons, in close connection with Aristotle's writings on moral philosophy.[22] Yet, this is a narrow trickle compared with the broad stream of the *dictamen* which leads gradually but directly into the equally broad current of humanist rhetoric and epistolography. It is true that the *dictamen* had no connection with Aristotelian philosophy and that its philosophical content is meager; but it is historically significant that the *dictatores* in their prologues made at least some philosophical claims and pretensions for their discipline.[23] This claim, empty as it may appear to us, links the *dictatores* not only with the early medieval tradition of the *Artes Liberales*, but also with the program of ancient and Renaissance rhetoric.

The practice of public speaking that disappeared at the end of antiquity, along with political and legal institutions on which it depended, came to be revived in late medieval Italy with the rise of city republics and the revival of Roman law during the thirteenth century, if not earlier.[24] It was soon made the subject of theoretical and practical instruction. The treatises on the *ars arengandi* and the surviving model speeches cannot compare in number or diffusion with the vast literature on *dictamen*, but their very existence is sufficient to prove the rise and relative importance of secular oratory as a historical phenomenon which until very recently had been overlooked by most students of medieval rhetoric. The study of this material is still in its early stage, but it can be shown easily that all major types of Renaissance oratory made their first appearance in late medieval Italy and that there is a close and direct formal connection between medieval and humanist oratory. Again we must add that humanist orations are very different from their medieval counterparts and, in my opinion, superior to them in style and learning, if not in historical interest.

The rise of humanistic studies in the Renaissance was not a phenomenon restricted to the area of grammatical and rhetorical studies, as some of my previous remarks might have suggested, but it had a tremendous impact upon all other areas of learning and civilization, including philosophy. Practically all sources of Greek philosophy became known either for the first time or through new and reputedly better translations. Many medievalists fail to appreciate this development or to realize that the sources of ancient thought available to medieval thinkers were quite limited and indirect compared with the actual body of extant Greek literature, although the twelfth and thirteenth centuries exhibited great activity in translation. In the wake of Renaissance humanism, ancient philosophies other than Aristotelianism became much better known and were revived: philosophies such as Stoicism, Epicureanism, and Skepticism, not to speak of Platonism which occupied a place of its own and of which we shall have more to say later on.

Under the influence of their rhetorical and cultural ideals, the humanists brought about a thorough change not only in the sources, but also in the style, terminology, and literary genres of philosophical writing. They coined (after ancient precedents) the term *studia humanitatis* (humanities) for their studies[25] and formulated a new educational and cultural ideal that went a long way to enhance their prestige and influence.[26] They also claimed to accomplish a rebirth of learning and letters and thus were responsible for the name "Renaissance" by which the entire period is known to us.[27]

In making these claims, the humanists were no doubt unfair to their medieval predecessors; but they were trying to assert the importance of their field, the humanities, against the traditional claims of other subjects. This is the meaning of the so-called defense of poetry on the part of early humanists (where poetry stands for humanist learning) and of their repeated attacks on scholasticism.

The humanists were engaged in transforming the entire system of secondary education and in imposing their scholarly and stylistic standards upon the other academic disciplines, and to some extent they succeeded. They did not, however, replace the traditional subject matter of these disciplines, although one of their latest and most brilliant representatives, the Spaniard Vives, also attempted to accomplish that.

As far as philosophy is concerned, the humanists considered moral thought their province. They produced a large literature of moral treatises, dialogues, and essays. The moral ideas of Petrarch and Salutati, Bruni, Valla and Alberti, of Erasmus and Montaigne, and many other scholars constitute the most direct contribution of Renaissance humanism to the history of Western thought.

Leaving aside a number of important specific ideas which are the property of individual humanists rather than of the entire movement, the main contribution of Renaissance humanism seems to lie in the tremendous expansion of secular culture and learning which it brought about in the areas of literature, historiography, and moral thought. This development was not entirely new and to some extent may be traced back to the later Middle Ages; but it did reach its climax during the Renaissance.

There is some justification in the statement that the humanist program and contribution was in its core cultural rather than philosophical. It omitted several problems and areas that form an integral part of philosophy as previously or commonly understood, and it included many subjects such as literature and historical scholarship that are usually not considered a part of philosophy. Yet, in our time, when many people take the praise of the sciences as a substitute for philosophy, we might forgive the humanists for having done the same with the humanities. After all, there are philosophical problems and implications in the humanities as there are in the sciences.

The concern of Renaissance humanists with the classics and secular learning led many contemporary critics and modern historians to label them as pagan, but this charge can hardly be sustained in the light of our present information. If we call Alberti pagan for not referring to Christian sources in his moral writings, we should have to say the same about Boethius. It is fashionable now in certain popular circles to maintain that our entire spiritual and moral heritage is due to what is called the "Judaeo-Christian" tradition. Such a claim reveals an abysmal ignorance of the real history of Western thought. For the roots of many of our basic ideas lie in Greek philosophy; these ideas have never ceased to exert a direct influence and have been themselves assimilated in various ways into the Jewish and Christian traditions.[28]

It is now time for us to say a few words about the medieval tradition of Christian theology and about its transformation during the Renaissance. The origin and rise of the Christian religion, the development of its main theological doctrines, and its synthesis with the literary and philosophical traditions of the Greeks and Romans still belong to the later phases of classical antiquity. This process was almost completed before the beginning of the Middle Ages. Christianity and Catholicism are no more medieval than they are ancient or modern. Whereas nobody would deny that religion and theology played a dominating role in the Middle Ages, it has become increasingly clear that medieval thought and learning were never completely limited to theology. Even in the early Middle Ages grammar and the other liberal arts were studied apart from theology, though usually as a preparation for it.

During the high Middle Ages theology itself underwent important changes.[29] In the eleventh and twelfth centuries, the study of logic and dialectic began to expand at the expense of grammar and rhetoric, especially in the schools of Northern France; the forms of the question and of the commentary became more fully developed; and the new method of logical argument was applied to the subject matter of theology. This is the precise meaning of the term "scholastic theology"; and the attitude of John of Salisbury or of St. Bernard of Clairvaux shows that its rise met with resistance even among scholars of unquestioned intellectual and religious integrity.

Another change that accompanied this development was the effort to transform Christian doctrine from scattered pronouncements of Scripture, the Councils, and the Church Fathers into a coherent and systematic body of statements. This process culminates in Peter Lombard's *Sentences,* the leading theological textbook of the subsequent centuries, and in St. Thomas Aquinas' *Summa Theologiae.*

During the thirteenth and fourteenth centuries, theology came to be taught at Paris and other universities alongside other learned disciplines; it tended to abandon its previous reliance on the writings of St. Augustine and to ally itself to an increasing degree with Aristotelian philosophy. St. Albertus Magnus, St. Thomas Aquinas, Johannes Duns Scotus, William of Ockham, and the Averroist Siger of Brabant represent different types and phases of this Aristotelianizing theology.

When we pass from the late Middle Ages into the Renaissance, we note that the traditions of scholastic or Aristotelian theology were vigorously continued. The theological schools of Thomism, Scotism, and Ockhamism all had numerous followers. It can be shown that during that period Thomism began to exert a much greater influence outside the Dominican order than during the thirteenth or fourteenth century.[30] It has been shown that Luther's theology was influenced by the strong Ockhamism of the German universities of the fifteenth century;[31] and it has now become fashionable to call him a medieval thinker. On the other hand, Catholic theology experienced a strong revival during the sixteenth century after the founding of the Jesuit order and the Council of Trent, especially at the Universities of Spain and Portugal; and this revival is linked in many ways with the ideas and methods of St. Thomas and other medieval theologians.[32]

It would be a mistake, however, to overlook the impact of the humanist movement upon Renaissance theology. Those humanists who were explicitly concerned with theological questions (and we might as well call them Christian humanists) were by no means opposed to religion or theology as such, but they criticized scholastic theology in the name of simple piety and religious scholarship in accordance with their own ideals. They preferred St. Bernard to the scholastics, considered the Church Fathers as the Christian classics, insisted that they were grammarians rather than dialecticians in the medieval sense, and advocated the direct study of Scripture. They also proceeded to apply their new methods of philological and historical scholarship to the textual study and interpretation of Scripture and of the early Church writers.[33]

This humanist approach to theology may be traced from Petrarch to Erasmus, and it left a powerful impact upon Catholics and Protestants alike. Even Luther is not untouched by it, whereas it is easy to discern its influence in Melanchthon and Calvin as well as in some of the Spanish theologians.

The Renaissance may have produced some scholars and thinkers who were indifferent to Christianity or estranged from some of its teachings. But as a whole, the period is far from being un-Christian as it has sometimes been represented. Certainly the term Christian philosophy, which has recently been used to characterize medieval thought,[34] would have been more easily understood by some of the Renaissance humanists than by the medieval scholastics. It is Erasmus who speaks of the Philosophy of Christ, as Justinus Martyr had done in the second century.[35] Thomas Aquinas could not and did not use this phrase. For him theology was Christian, to be sure, but philosophy was Aristotelian; and the question was not to substitute Christian for Aristotelian philosophy, but to determine their relationship and to reconcile them as far as possible.

This problem of the relationship between philosophy and theology continued to preoccupy the thinkers of the Renaissance as it had worried Thomas Aquinas and the other scholastics. The very existence of the problem shows that, contrary to frequent modern claims, philosophy in the thirteenth century, if not before, was distinct from theology, though subordinate and not opposed to it. In the fourteenth century, even at Paris, the teaching of philosophy was more and more divorced from theology; and the prevailing tendency among philosophers was to recognize the basic superiority of theology, but to assert at the same time the relative independence of philosophy within its own domain. It is the position which Siger of Brabant took, and it is usually referred to as "Averroism" or as "the doctrine of the double truth."[36]

The Italian Aristotelians of the Renaissance, such as Pomponazzi, inherited this position from their medieval predecessors.[37] On the other hand, Renaissance Platonists emphasized the harmony between religion and philosophy and thus came closer to the position of St. Thomas, although they tended to grant philosophy more equality and independence than medieval theologians would have done.[38] This is a nice example of the inadequacy of labels usually employed in historical discourse about these subjects and of the fact that there are several medieval traditions and several Renaissance philosophies. Each Renaissance philosophy has different medieval sources and antecedents; and even if we succeed in establishing the right connections, the presence of a link does not mean that a given system of thought occupied the same place within its own time as its predecessor had done within the previous period.

We can touch but briefly upon another branch of learning which had great importance both during the Middle Ages and the Renaissance, but which for a variety of reasons had but tenuous connections with the mainstream of philosophical thought during those periods: jurisprudence. In the earlier Middle Ages, the study of both civil and canon law was somewhat submerged and seems to have been largely carried on within the broader framework of the seven liberal arts. After the eleventh century, the study of canon law underwent a development similar to theology: it was subjected to the new methods of dialectic, and it received a systematic order and arrangement in Gratian's *Decretum* and other great canonist collections.[39] In the case of civil law the main fact, aside from the dialectical method, was the adoption of the Roman *Corpus Iuris* as the authoritative textbook of instruction at Bologna and other law schools and its reception as a valid law code in Italy and elsewhere.[40]

When we pass from the Middle Ages to the Renaissance, we note an unbroken continuity of legal teaching as well as a voluminous body of legal commentaries, questions, and opinions (*consilia*) which for the later period have been hardly sorted, let alone studied, and are sometimes treated by historians as if they did not exist.

Aside from this legal tradition, often referred to as *mos Italicus*, because it was most strongly represented at the Italian law schools, Renaissance humanism had a strong impact on jurisprudence, which culminated in the sixteenth century under the name of *mos Gallicus*. Its main tendency was to replace the abstract dialectical method of the medieval jurists with a philological and historical interpretation of the sources of Roman law. If the ties between legal practice and the Roman law were reportedly weakened as a result of this development, historical understanding of the Roman law certainly made tremendous progress.[41]

The philosophical significance of the legal tradition lies primarily in the area of political thought; and it is significant that some of the leading political thinkers of the sixteenth century, such as Jean Bodin, had received legal training.[42] We may add the concept of natural law, an important notion which originated in Stoic philosophy and was introduced from Stoic sources into the very text of the Roman law.[43] When adopted by St. Augustine, it was reinterpreted in a Neoplatonic fashion[44] and bequeathed in this form to Thomas Aquinas and other medieval theologians. The revival of this doctrine in the seventeenth century owes much to the legal and theological thought of the sixteenth century. It is now fashionable to consider the doctrine of natural law as antiquated, but I do not see how we can ever subject a given positive law to moral criticism unless we maintain a universally valid moral standard by which it may be judged and measured.

The scientific traditions of the Middle Ages which we must mention, at least in passing, have been the subject of many recent studies; they have also played a central role in the often heated controversies about the relation between the Middle Ages and the Renaissance, and about the merits and contributions of these two periods.[45] I should like to stress that in my opinion there is no such thing as Science with a capital S, but there are a variety of different sciences, each with its own tradition and historical development. Only two sciences, or groups of sciences, had from antiquity a separate history that was relatively, if not entirely, independent of philosophy: medicine, and the mathematical disciplines including astronomy.

The early Middle Ages inherited but a small share of the rich heritage of ancient Greek medicine. Medical theory was usually treated as an appendix to the seven liberal arts, and medical practice was often exercised by people without learning or formal theoretical training.[46] The main changes occurred again during the twelfth century. A sizable body of more or less advanced medical treatises were translated from Greek and Arabic and adopted as textbooks for medical instruction. At the same time, medical theory underwent the influence of scholastic logic and found its literary expression in commentaries and questions. The school of Salerno, which in an earlier period had originated as a society of practitioners, shows this transformation in the direction of theory and scholasticism during the course of the twelfth century; and the same is true of Montpellier and the other centers of medical study. At the same time, medicine formed an alliance with Aristotelian philosophy which was to remain characteristic of the Italian universities far into the Renaissance.[47] This alliance accounts, at least in part, for the secular and "Averroistic" character of Italian Aristotelianism, which has been noted by many historians.

In spite of this continuity, Renaissance medicine underwent the influence of humanism no less than did theology or law. Several writings of Hippocrates and Galen were widely known since the twelfth century or even earlier, others since the fourteenth century, but a surprisingly large number of their works were translated for the first time between the fifteenth and sixteenth centuries.[48] The significance of this fact will become fully apparent when the contribution of these newly translated ancient writings to medical knowledge are carefully studied and evaluated, something which has just barely been started.

On the other hand, a subject such as anatomy or surgery, which benefited less from theory than from observation and practice, made steady progress during the sixteenth century. A figure such as Paracelsus illustrates that a real or imagined emancipation from ancient authorities could attain at least a certain measure of success.

Of even greater historical significance was the development of the mathematical disciplines including astronomy. In the early medieval schools they were studied as part of the seven liberal arts and constituted one of the two major subdivisions of the system, the so-called quadrivium. The actual content of this instruction was extremely elementary, however, compared with the achievements of Greek antiquity; this fact is not surprising if we remember that the ancient Romans themselves had but a modest part, if any, in these achievements.[49]

The rise of mathematical and astronomical studies in the West is linked also with the translations of Greek and Arabic scientific writings made during the twelfth and thirteenth centuries. Building on these foundations, the medieval scientists absorbed Euclidean geometry, Arabic algebra, Ptolemaic astronomy, and at least part of Archimedian mechanics, making independent contributions, especially in the field of mechanics, as has been emphasized in recent studies.[50]

Yet, it appears certain that some of the most advanced Greek treatises on mathematics were translated only in the sixteenth century and that the same century witnessed the first marked advances beyond the ancients, such as the solution of cubic equations as well as the new astronomy of Copernicus, Tycho Brahe, and Kepler.[51]

By the end of the sixteenth century, Galileo had taken the crucial step that was to be the foundation for early modern science, that is, the application of mathematical methods to the subject matter of physics, which up to that time had been treated as an integral part of Aristotelian philosophy. If we wish to insist that medieval scholars of the thirteenth and fourteenth centuries had anticipated some of these developments, a claim that has by no means been accepted by all competent students of the subject,[52] we should not blame the humanists for having delayed the progress of science for a hundred years, but rather study the much neglected work of the mathematicians, astronomers, and Aristotelian physicists of the fifteenth century, especially in Italy. Obviously, they must have been the transmitters of fourteenth-century lore to the sixteenth century.[53]

We can merely mention the steady progress made in such fields as technology and geography since they are hardly connected with philosophy and depend largely upon practice and experience. In the case of geography, it is worth noting that the best Greek sources, Ptolemy and Strabo, were translated for the first time by fifteenth-century humanists.[54] These translations were extremely popular and they probably helped to develop the interest in travels and explorations which culminated in the discovery of the New World.

Before we proceed to the other sciences and to the Aristotelian philosophy of which they formed a part, we must discuss briefly the so-called pseudo-sciences, that is, the occult tradition. Long ridiculed as a monument of medieval superstition, these disciplines have now been recognized as close companions of the contemporary sciences. Whatever occasional opposition they met with was based on religious rather than scientific grounds.[55]

The development of the various disciplines, especially astrology, alchemy, and magic, was not identical. Intellectually, astrology was the most respectable and had its precedents in late antiquity, whereas alchemy and magic were more practical and depended largely on Arabic authorities. All these studies may have found fertile soil in the early medieval habit of symbolical and allegorical thought, but they did not develop substantially until the twelfth century, when numerous treatises dealing with these subjects began to be translated from the Arabic. Astrology was allied with astronomy and medicine and became an integral part of cosmology. Although it met opposition during the Middle Ages, as before and after, it received much public recognition and was even taught at various universities. Alchemy and magic never attained such academic status and catered more openly to the material ambitions of princes and private individuals.

During the Renaissance, the occult sciences met with occasional opposition from theologians and humanists rather than from scientists; but, on the whole, their influence and appeal continued and even increased in comparison with the previous period. The cosmology of many Renaissance Platonists and sixteenth-century philosophers of nature posited a universe animated by a world soul and held together by hidden forces of affinity, which the wise and properly trained scholar could detect and control.[56] Thus Arabian occult writings were as popular in many circles during the sixteenth century as they had ever been before.

It was only the physical science of the seventeenth and eighteenth centuries that gradually brought about a neat separation between genuine and false sciences and put an end to the fantastic cosmology of the Middle Ages and Renaissance. Since its disappearance from the realm of science, this cosmology has continued to exercise a nostalgic appeal and to lead a precarious existence in modern poetry and occultism, just as pagan gods and myths survived in the Christian Middle Ages and Renaissance after they had ceased to be the objects of actual religious belief and worship.[57]

Returning from the occult to the genuine sciences, we encounter at the same time one of the two great philosophical traditions, Aristotelianism. For the study of physics as well as biology was pursued during the later Middle Ages as an integral part of Aristotelian philosophy, in the same manner as logic, ethics, or metaphysics.

The greatness of Aristotle as a philosopher was generally recognized throughout later antiquity, yet his most important systematic writings were not widely known for several centuries after his death. He left behind an organized school which flourished for a long period. His chief works were made the subject of detailed commentaries by members of this school and later by the Neoplatonists, who held Aristotle in great respect and tended to combine his teachings with those of Plato and of the Platonist tradition. Yet, it was only among the Arabs that Aristotle acquired a predominant authority to the exclusion of other Greek philosophers. There he became known as "the philosopher."

From antiquity, the earlier Middle Ages had inherited Boethius' translations of the first two treatises of the *Organon* along with Porphyry's introduction to the *Categories*. This group of writings was called *Logica Vetus* and formed the basis of logical study and teaching until the end of the eleventh century. The bulk of Aristotle's writings, along with those of his Arabic commentators and several Greek commentators, was translated into Latin only during the twelfth and thirteenth centuries.[58] When the medieval universities reached their full development during the thirteenth century, the works of Aristotle were adopted as standard textbooks for the philosophical disciplines. Philosophy was thus taught for the first time in the West as an independent discipline distinct from the liberal arts and theology; and it is no coincidence that the modern terms for several philosophical and scientific disciplines correspond to the titles of those works of Aristotle that were used as textbooks: physics, ethics, metaphysics.

Through these works of Aristotle, the West acquired not only a large body of specific problems and specific ideas, but also a developed terminology and a strict method of reasoning as well as a systematic and reasonably complete framework within which all relevant problems could be treated and discussed. The study of biology, and especially the great work done in physics during the thirteenth and fourteenth centuries was due, as we know, to students and interpreters of Aristotle. In many instances they departed from the text and doctrine of Aristotle and developed theories of their own, such as the *impetus* theory of projectile motion.[59] It is now widely agreed that the Paris Aristotelians of the fourteenth century took the first steps in the realm of physics that prepared the way for early modern science, although opinions differ much concerning the extent to which they anticipated the work of Galileo and Newton.[60] If Galileo was partly indebted to the work of the Aristotelian school, as he seems to have been, this was caused by the influence of the Aristotelian tradition which flourished at the Italian universities during the fifteenth and sixteenth centuries.[61] For the Italian Aristotelians of the Renaissance continued and developed the work of their French and English predecessors of the fourteenth century. Instead of blaming the humanists for their failure to contribute to physics (which would be like blaming historians, literary critics, or existentialist philosophers of our time for not promoting our contemporary progress in atomic physics or in technology), we should study the much neglected work of these contemporaries of the humanists who were professionally concerned with the study of physics. Only in this way will it be possible to understand the history of physics before Galileo and to evaluate the contributions made during the entire period.

On the other hand, the Renaissance did not merely witness a continuation of late medieval Aristotelianism. The humanists supplied new translations of Aristotle[62] and translated all Greek commentators of Aristotle, many of them for the first time.[63] Thus a tendency to emphasize the original, Greek Aristotle instead of his medieval Arabic and Latin translators and commentators developed.

Moreover, several waves of anti-Aristotelianism emerged, which tended to reduce Aristotle's authority although they were not immediately successful in overthrowing it. Many humanists attacked the Aristotelian tradition in natural philosophy in the name of man's moral concerns and literary scholarship. The Byzantine debate about the superiority of Plato and Aristotle had its repercussions in the West; and the rise of Platonism in the fifteenth century, though not necessarily anti-Aristotelian, no doubt had a limiting effect upon Aristotle's authority. Finally, in the sixteenth and early seventeenth century, the great philosophers of nature from Cardano and Telesio to Bruno and Campanella consistently opposed the authority and doctrine of Aristotle and attempted to develop new systems of the physical universe to replace that of Aristotle and his school.

Yet, it was Galileo alone who succeeded in placing physics on a firm new foundation which was mathematical and experimental in nature. With him, the Aristotelian tradition in physics came to an end, whatever his partial indebtedness to it may have been.[64] Although we cannot claim Galileo as a representative of the Renaissance, there is no doubt that his work was at least as much indebted to Renaissance thought as to medieval Aristotelianism and more specifically to new developments in mathematics and astronomy that occurred during the sixteenth century, and to the recently increased knowledge of Plato and Archimedes.[65]

Whereas in physics the end of the Renaissance brought about an anti-Aristotelian revolution, the effects of which are still felt to the present day, Aristotle's authority continued to prevail throughout the Renaissance and into the eighteenth century in the field of biology. This does not mean that the Renaissance acquired no new knowledge in this area. It is enough to remember the study of the hitherto unknown flora and fauna of the Western hemisphere, which was described with great care and attention. Yet, leading biologists tried to fit new facts into the familiar pattern of Aristotelian biology, rather than work out new concepts or theories.

After discussing those Aristotelian disciplines that have become independent sciences in modern times and are no longer treated as parts of philosophy, we must consider those subjects which are still considered the proper domain of philosophy. The field of logic, with which we might suitably begin, was the only philosophical discipline of Greek origin that occupied a place in the scheme of the seven liberal arts, which dominated the school curriculum of the earlier Middle Ages. The study of logic was based on the *Logica Vetus*, to which we had occasion to refer, and hence retained a rather elementary character for a long time. Yet, the rise of early scholasticism, which began during the latter part of the eleventh century in the French cathedral schools, was largely due to an increased study of logic and the tendency to apply the more refined methods of logic to other learned disciplines, including theology. With the new translations of the twelfth century, the West acquired the more advanced logical writings of Aristotle, especially the *Prior* and *Posterior Analytics;* and thus a new foundation was laid for logical investigations during the subsequent period.

The thirteenth century saw also the beginnings of a further development beyond Aristotle in logic which was associated with the name of Peter of Spain: terminism.[66] In the fourteenth century advanced logical studies flourished especially in England. The work of what we might call the first Oxford school of logic consisted in a highly technical formal doctrine which centered on forms of inference, on fallacious arguments, and on interesting attempts to develop logical and even quantitative formulas for degrees of quality, and for the gradual transition from one qualitative stage to another.[67]

Usually overlooked is the fact that the Oxford tradition of late medieval logic enjoyed a tremendous vogue at the Italian universities between the late fourteenth and early sixteenth century, at a time when the English school had long ceased to be active. In this field, just as in physics, the Italian Aristotelians continued vigorously the work of their fourteenth century Northern predecessors, as university records, manuscripts, and early editions abundantly show. A more detailed study of these materials would aid us in understanding the impact which fourteenth century logic may have had on later developments in the field of logic and in other philosophical and scientific disciplines.

It would be wrong, however, to attribute all significant developments in Renaissance logic to the traditions of Aristotelian or terminist logic. Anti-Aristotelian tendencies were at work in this area no less than in natural philosophy. Even the humanist critique of Aristotelianism, which in the field of natural philosophy remained largely rhetorical and ineffective, led to influential if not entirely successful attempts at a radical reform and innovation of logic. Valla's treatise on dialectic was the first attempt of this kind to replace the logic of the Aristotelians and he had several followers and successors during the sixteenth century. One of them, Marius Nizolius, attracted the attention of Leibniz.[68] Another of these logical reformers, Peter Ramus, became the fountainhead of a school of logic that exercised wide influence down to the eighteenth century in a number of European countries and in early America.[69] Recently we have learned much about Ramus and his school; and it has become apparent that the main purpose of humanist reforms in logic was characteristically to simplify logic for the purposes of teaching and literary presentation and to relate or even subordinate it to the theory of rhetoric.

Whereas physics and logic were the main philosophical disciplines which every student supposedly studied, metaphysics and ethics were considered elective courses. Hence the impact of Aristotle's work in these fields was less extensive, a fact which is apt to surprise the modern student.

The tradition of Aristotle's metaphysics is closely linked with that of theology, as we might expect; but it would be wrong to consider the two disciplines identical. Since Aristotle himself applies the term theology to at least a portion of the subject matter of this work, it was easy to consider it as a treatise on "natural" theology. Yet, the study of Aristotelian metaphysics was not the same as the study of Christian theology on the basis of Peter Lombard's *Sentences* or of Thomas Aquinas' *Summa*. The difference lay in the subject matter as well as in the method and sources of knowledge. If we wish to show a link between Renaissance thought and the tradition of Aristotelian metaphysics, it is sufficient to point to some of the problems which continued to be discussed, or even acquired a greater importance. The discussion concerning the immortality of the soul, which occupied a central place in the thought of the later fifteenth and of the earlier sixteenth century, involved the interpretation of Aristotle as well as that of Plato; the controversy between Pomponazzi and his opponents illustrates this fact abundantly. The question of the superiority of the intellect and of the will was debated not only by the followers of St. Thomas and of Duns Scotus, but also by several humanists and by the Platonists of the Florentine Academy.[70] If the problems were the same, however, the solutions often differed, and even where solutions sound alike, significant differences exist in the arguments, in the emphasis given to various aspects of a problem, and in the reasons why a given problem is discussed or solved in a certain manner.

The role of Aristotle's *Ethics* was more complex and perhaps more important. Prior to the thirteenth century, writings on moral subjects were largely influenced by Cicero, Seneca, and Boethius; by theological conceptions; and by popular codes of conduct such as those of chivalry. With the rise of scholasticism and of the universities during the thirteenth century, moral philosophy became a formal academic discipline for the first time in the West, based on Aristotle's *Nicomachean Ethics* and *Politics,* and to a lesser extent on his *Rhetoric* and the *Economics* attributed to him.

Since the humanists considered moral philosophy part of their domain, it was in this field, rather than in logic or physics, that the impact of humanism on philosophical thought was felt most immediately. Aristotle's *Ethics, Politics,* and *Economics* were the first of his writings for which the humanists supplied new translations;[71] and it was Bruni's version of the *Ethics* which kindled the first great debate about the relative merits of medieval and humanist translations—a debate in which modern historians have continued to take sides.[72] In his humanist garb, Aristotle as a moral philosopher found many adherents among Renaissance humanists, and it is no coincidence that the humanists continued to use Aristotle's *Ethics* as a textbook in their courses on moral philosophy. Yet, many of them preferred to combine Aristotle's ethical views with those of other ancient philosophers in an eclectic fashion whereas others opposed or ignored Aristotle's ethics in favor of Stoic, Epicurean, or other views.[73]

It has become apparent, I hope, that the influence of Aristotle was not a unified phenomenon. This influence, and the reaction against it, differed greatly between the various philosophical and scientific disciplines which he treated in his various writings. It is interesting to point out that Aristotle's *Poetics* and *Rhetoric,* the former practically unknown during the Middle Ages, the latter largely treated as a work on moral philosophy, became prominent as textbooks of literary theory only during the sixteenth century.[74] They attained a position of authority in the later sixteenth and in the seventeenth century, that is, at the same time when his authority in physics came to be criticized and finally overthrown.

In trying to sum up the rather complex subject of Aristotle in the Renaissance, it might be best to state that the Aristotelian traditions of the later Middle Ages (especially in the fields of physics and of logic) were continued; that there developed, alongside with them, a new humanistic Aristotelianism that was based on new translations and had its center in ethics, rhetoric, and poetics; and finally, that there was a rising tide of anti-Aristotelianism which consisted of several quite different waves, scored a certain amount of success in logic, and gradually prepared the way for the destruction of Aristotelian physics in the seventeenth century.

Before I begin to speak of the other great philosophical tradition of Western thought, Platonism, I must admit that I am partial to it; and that the manner in which I understand and describe it, and even the historical importance I attach to it may be influenced by this partiality. Compared with the humanist or Aristotelian traditions, Platonism cannot be easily described in institutional terms. It is intangible in a sense, but no less important or pervasive.

In classical antiquity Plato's school was the one that had the longest span of life, and his writings were widely read at all times even outside the precincts of that school. The early Middle Ages inherited from the Romans only a fragmentary translation of the *Timaeus*,[75] but a number of Latin writers transmitted in more or less precise form many teachings of Plato and his school: Cicero, Boethius, and above all, St. Augustine, who always spoke with respect of the Platonists and, in spite of his unquestioned piety and originality, was indebted to them for many of his philosophical ideas. The continuity of the Platonic tradition during the Middle Ages, which has been studied and emphasized extensively in recent years,[76] depends to a considerable extent, although not entirely, on the authority and influence of St. Augustine and his writings. This fact acquires additional significance if we remember that in early scholasticism, prior to the introduction of Aristotle, and outside the field of logic, St. Augustine was the chief source and inspiration of philosophical as well as of theological thought for the good reason that he was probably the greatest Latin philosopher of classical antiquity.

There were, however, other factors in addition to the influence of St. Augustine. The writings attributed to Dionysius the Areopagite, composed by a Christian mystic strongly influenced by Neoplatonism, had been repeatedly translated since the eighth century[77] and exercised a continuous influence on medieval theology. The greatest thinker of the Carolingian age, Johannes Scotus Eriugena, was a Neoplatonist in his general orientation. In the school of Chartres, where early scholasticism attained perhaps its highest development, cosmological speculation drew heavily on Plato's *Timaeus* and on his Latin commentator Calcidius. Moreover, the great wave of translations made in the twelfth and thirteenth centuries included at least two more works of Plato, the *Phaedo* and the *Meno,* and several works of Proclus, among them his important *Elements of Theology* and his commentary on Plato's *Parmenides* which incorporates part of Plato's text.[78]

During the thirteenth century, Augustinianism and Platonism receded before the rising tide of Aristotelianism. Yet, the Franciscan school of theology maintained at least in part an Augustinian orientation; and we have recently learned that even St. Thomas Aquinas not only preserved important elements of Augustinianism in his theology, but also borrowed several concepts of his philosophy from the newly translated works of Proclus.[79] In the early fourteenth century, a German Dominican composed a bulky commentary on Proclus' *Elements of Theology;*[80] Master Eckhart, another Dominican whose work inspired all later medieval currents of mysticism in Germany and the Low Countries, derived many of his basic ideas from Proclus and from the Areopagite.

It is against this background that we must understand the Platonism of Cusanus, Ficino, and other Renaissance Platonists. We know that Cusanus read Proclus and Dionysius;[81] and it is quite evident that the writings of St. Augustine were among Ficino's earliest and most important sources of inspiration.[82]

In spite of these tangible elements of continuity, we should not overlook the fact that Renaissance Platonism was in many ways different from medieval Platonism. Obviously, Renaissance thinkers gradually gained access to the entire body of Greek Platonist literature, especially all the works of Plato[83] and Plotinus; surely no one would contend that it makes no difference whether a Platonist has read all of Plato (and of Plotinus), or only a few of his writings in addition to secondary accounts of his doctrine.

Secondly, the Renaissance Platonists were influenced in a complex manner by other intellectual currents which had not affected their medieval predecessors, for example, humanism and even scholastic Aristotelianism.[84]

Finally, the more important Renaissance Platonists were highly original thinkers, and must be judged on the basis of specific ideas as we find them expressed and developed in their writings. The fact that two thinkers are commonly labeled as Platonists, or that they read St. Augustine or some other Platonist source, is not sufficient if we wish to understand or describe their contribution to the history of philosophy. Thus Cusanus, Ficino and Pico, Patrizi and Bruno belong in a broad sense to the Platonic tradition; but in each of them this tradition assumes a different physiognomy. Space does not permit and my topic does not prompt me to discuss or even to mention the philosophical ideas of these thinkers, for which I must refer to the monographic literature on the subject of Renaissance Platonism.

I will, however, discuss one characteristic notion, since it seems to be relevant to the general problem underlying this lecture. For the very concept of a philosophical tradition, subject to many changes and variations but basically uniform and continuous, seems to have been formulated by Renaissance Platonists. The apocryphal writings composed during the later centuries of antiquity and attributed to such venerable authors as Hermes Trismegistus, Zoroaster, Orpheus, and Pythagoras contain many elements of Platonist thought which were absorbed quite naturally from the environment of Alexandria in which several of them originated.[85] The Neoplatonist Proclus and others accepted these attributions at their face value, treating the reputed authors as ancient sages who were the earliest witnesses of Platonic wisdom, prior to Plato himself, and hence his forerunners and sources. Marsilio Ficino borrowed this notion from Proclus and the Byzantine Platonists, developing it even further.[86] For him, the ancient sages were not only forerunners of Plato, but representatives of a venerable pagan philosophy and theology. He was also convinced that Platonic philosophy and theology, which had its basis in human reason, agreed fundamentally with Jewish and Christian religion and theology which rested on faith and revelation. Both traditions were equally old and lasting instruments of divine providence. In this manner, Ficino could consider himself a new link in a philosophical tradition that began with the ancient sages, culminated in Plato, and continued through the Platonic schools of antiquity, through St. Augustine and the medieval Arabic and Latin Platonists down to his own age.[87]

This notion became dear to many Platonists of the sixteenth century, and Ficino's translation of the *Corpus Hermeticum* attained for a while an authority and diffusion equal or even superior to that of his versions of Plato and of Plotinus.[88] It was in this context that Augustinus Steuchus, a Catholic theologian of the sixteenth century strongly committed to the Platonic and pseudo-Platonic tradition in philosophy, coined the term *philosophia perennis* and adopted it for the title of his main work.[89]

I surely do not wish to endorse the fantastic views held by the Renaissance Platonists about Hermes Trismegistus and other ancient sages, but I would suggest that the Platonic tradition deserves the name of a *philosophia perennis* no less than other traditions which have since appropriated this title for themselves. However that may be, the name and its underlying conception show that Renaissance Platonism was fully conscious of being part of a tradition and clearly realized that this tradition, although of ancient origin, had had a more or less continuous life during the Middle Ages. We may thus say that the theme of this chapter receives an explicit confirmation through the historical interpretation which the Renaissance Platonists gave of their own work and achievement.

In summary, we may say that during the Renaissance philosophical thought, without abandoning its theological connections, strengthened its link with the humanities, the sciences, and we may add, with literature and the arts, thus becoming increasingly secular in its outlook. The partial continuity of medieval traditions, the introduction of new sources and problems, and the gradually increasing quest for new solutions and original ideas makes the Renaissance an age of fermentation rather than an age of synthesis in philosophy. When philosophy and the physical sciences made a fresh start in the seventeenth century, they consciously abandoned both the traditions of the Middle Ages and the Renaissance. Yet, it could be easily shown that Renaissance philosophy shared in preparing the way for these changes and that its influence persisted in many areas of European thought until the eighteenth century.[90]

I hope that this very general and wide-ranging essay may offer an example of the continuity of a living tradition which is at the same time in a process of steady transformation. The thought of the Renaissance, considered as a whole, worked with some of the old material supplied to it by medieval thought but produced out of it something new and different which expressed its own insights and aspirations.

The concept of tradition which finds its expression in the idea of a *philosophia perennis* may still serve as a model and guide. Our Western philosophical tradition has a long history; and I hope and believe that it has a future, although this future may be within the framework of a broader and more comprehensive world culture than we have yet known. This *philosophia perennis* will include not only the thought of the Middle Ages but also that of antiquity, the Renaissance, and the best of modern thought—not only because it happens to be there, but because it contains a core of truth which we cannot afford to lose. This *philosophia perennis,* in my view, will include Plato and Aristotle, St. Augustine and St. Thomas, Spinoza and Leibniz, Kant and Hegel, and many others. Some of their ideas may be refuted or forgotten, some of their writings may even be lost. For every idea in its material expression is subject to destruction, just as are works of art or cities. I am deeply distressed as anyone by the amount of destruction that we have experienced in our time or that we may face in the future. Yet, I take comfort in the thought that a valuable portion of past life and experience is preserved by history and by tradition.

If I may be allowed to conclude with a personal confession, I believe that nothing that once was can be completely undone. Even if destroyed in the material world and forgotten by men, it remains and will remain alive in the memory of an infinite being for which the past as well as the future is always present, and that is thus the greatest, the only true historian, and the keeper of the eternal tradition of which even our best human traditions, to use a Platonist phrase, are but shadows and images.

THREE

RENAISSANCE
THOUGHT
AND
BYZANTINE
LEARNING

7.

Italian Humanism and Byzantium

The Italian humanistic movement of the Renaissance has been the subject of many recent studies and discussions, but there seems to be by now a fairly general agreement that it was a broad and pervasive cultural movement that affected at the same time the literature and philosophy, the historiography and philological scholarship of the period and that also had wide repercussions in theology, in the sciences, and in the arts. In their efforts to determine the sources and the originality of Italian and European humanism, historians have mainly compared it with the Latin Middle Ages and have tried to define the affinities and differences between humanistic culture and the Western culture of the preceding age. The question of Byzantine contacts and influences imposes itself for obvious reasons only in one area of humanistic culture, Greek studies. It will thus be necessary for us to limit our attention in this essay almost entirely to this area, whereas the contacts between Byzantium and the Italian Renaissance in the field of philosophy will be the subject of the following chapter.

A discussion of our subject would seem to be most timely since Byzantine studies have been much cultivated during the last few decades. Yet, these studies deal with a period that lasted more than a thousand years, and they have concentrated for the most part on political and economic history, on religious institutions and theological doctrines, on literature, music, and the visual arts but have dealt only to a small extent with classical scholarship and with philosophy. Hence, many questions that from our point of view would be especially important remain to my knowledge still unresolved and are in need of further research.[1]

If we want to understand the state and development of Greek studies in the West during the Middle Ages and the Renaissance, we must go back to classical antiquity, that is, to the Greek culture of the Romans; for the foundation of medieval Western culture was Latin and not Greek. During the later Republic and the first centuries of the Empire most educated Romans knew Greek, and many of them even wrote in Greek, as did Marcus Aurelius. At the same time Latin literature developed under the continuing influence of Greek models, and the small number of Latin writings that dealt with philosophical or scientific subjects is entirely derived from Greek sources.[2] Also Latin Christianity derived its scriptures and its theology from the Greek East.

With the end of antiquity and the beginning of the Middle Ages, the Latin West not only became separated from the Greco-Byzantine East in a political sense, but it also lost the knowledge of the Greek language and thus its direct access to ancient Greek culture.[3] Hence, the first medieval centuries, up to the middle of the eleventh century, were largely restricted to the literary, philosophical, and scientific resources of the Latin tradition. This tradition was rich in concepts and ideas, literary forms, and rhetorical and poetical theory and practice of Greek origin, but it possessed or, at least, preserved but very few translations of Greek texts. The Latins had above all the Bible and many writings of the Greek Fathers, a part of Plato's *Timaeus,* the *Categories* and *De interpretatione* of Aristotle with Porphyry's *Introduction to the Categories,* in the translation of Boethius, and some medical and mathematical writings. That large and important part of classical Greek literature which had not been translated into Latin was not accessible to the first centuries of the Latin Middle Ages, and the significance of this fact seems to have escaped some recent historians of that important period.

This situation changed to some extent, but only to some extent, during the period that extends from the second half of the eleventh century to the end of the thirteenth or the first half of the fourteenth. Historians of that period have rightly emphasized the continued or resumed contacts of the West with Byzantium in the political and economic fields, in church affairs, and in the arts, and they have also stressed the continued presence of the Greek language and culture in Sicily and in some parts of Southern Italy. The Crusades and the Latin conquest of the Byzantine Empire had their repercussions also in the area of intellectual history. This period produced a sizable number of Latin translations of ancient Greek texts that had never been translated at the time of antiquity or of the early Middle Ages. Some of these translations were made from the Arabic, others, directly from the

Greek. The Greco-Latin translations evidently presuppose both some knowledge of Greek on the part of the translators and some access to the Greek texts.[4] There were also several attempts, especially at the time of the Council of Vienne, to introduce the teaching of Greek at some of the major universities.

These facts should be duly considered, but we should also note their limited significance and should not exaggerate their importance. We know from other medieval and modern examples that political and commercial contacts and even artistic influences do not require a close acquaintance with the language or civilization of the country of origin. Hence, they do not always lead to scientific or literary influences since the latter depend on such an acquaintance and also presuppose in him who learns a genuine interest in the characteristic values of a foreign civilization. The fact that Greek was spoken in Sicily and Southern Italy does not indicate by itself a flourishing state of Greek classical studies unless there was also some knowledge of the classical Greek language, some Greek classical texts in the libraries of the region, and some tradition of classical and not only ecclesiastic studies in the monastic or city schools of the area. We have recently learned a good deal about the libraries and the manuscripts and also about the literary production of Greek Italy but so far very little about its schools and studies.[5] At the present state of our knowledge I am not convinced that Greek classical studies in the West were as strongly influenced by Greek Italy as they were by Greece herself, and especially by Constantinople. Greek Italy made, no doubt, its contribution to Byzantine civilization, and not only in the field of theology; but in the case of some of its notable representatives, such as Johannes Italos or Barlaam of Calabria, it is probable that they received their classical education, at least in part, at Constantinople rather than at home. To my knowledge, there is not yet any evidence that Greek Italy had her own indigenous tradition in the field of classical studies, as was the case in ecclesiastic learning or in Byzantine literature.

If we pass from Greek Italy to the rest of Latin Europe, the traces of Greek learning are very scanty indeed.[6] The decrees intended to introduce the study of Greek at the universities remained, for the most part, a dead letter, and we have no clear case of a tradition of Greek studies in the West before the second half of the fourteenth century. In the inventories of medieval libraries Greek manuscripts are extremely rare, and in most instances what we find are bilingual Gospels or psalters. As to the translators from the Greek, we know that they acquired their knowledge of Greek and the Greek books from which they worked either in Sicily or in the East. Their knowledge of Greek was also quite limited, as we can see when we study their translations and collate them with the Greek originals. They translate "ad verbum" and without any feeling for the syntax or phraseology of classical Greek.[7] Also the content of their translations is narrowly limited. The translations cover almost exclusively the fields of theology, the sciences, and philosophy, and among the philosophical writings the works of Aristotle predominate. The other ancient Greek philosophers are represented only to a small extent, and the poets, orators, and historians of ancient Greece are practically omitted.[8] This choice, in what it includes and excludes, reflects in part a strong theological interest and in part a scientific interest of Arabic origin.[9] The interest that inspires these translations is didactic and scholastic. The translators choose treatises full of a content that may be learned and developed. That which was to characterize the humanists is completely absent: an interest for literature and for a thought that is diversified and fluid and a taste for the form and the nuances of language, of style, and of thought.

During the next period, which runs from the middle of the fourteenth to the end of the sixteenth century, the state of Greek studies in Western Europe underwent a profound change. During the sixteenth century, the teaching of the classical Greek language and literature had become firmly established at the major universities and at many secondary schools. The chief Western libraries were full of Greek classical manuscripts, and a large part of the classical Greek texts had by then been widely distributed in printed editions. All these Greek texts were translated into Latin and into the various national languages, either for the first time or in new and more accurate translations, and these translations had an even wider diffusion than the original texts themselves. There also developed a tradition of precise Greek scholarship which constitutes the first phase of Greek philology in the West and which finds expression not only in critical editions and translations of the texts, but also in commentaries and miscellaneous studies and in treatises on history and mythology, grammar and rhetoric, philosophy and theology.

This flourishing state of Greek studies in the West that surpassed anything seen in that part of the world either in Roman antiquity or during the Middle Ages coincides in time with the decline and destruction of the Byzantine Empire and with the emigration of many Byzantine scholars to the West, and especially to Italy. Hence, there arises the question which is the subject of this essay: what was the contribution of the Byzantine tradition to the rich

development of Greek studies that occurred in the West between the fourteenth and the sixteenth centuries and that was due in large part to the work
of the Italian and other Western humanists?

In order to answer this question it would be necessary to study the history
of classical scholarship during the Byzantine Middle Ages, a subject with
which I am not well acquainted and which perhaps has not been sufficiently
explored even by the specialists of Byzantine history. I must limit myself to
a few well-established facts, and perhaps they will be sufficient for our purpose. During the long period that extends from the end of the eighth century
to the fourteenth and fifteenth, classical studies had their shorter or longer
periods of decline, to be sure, but they were never completely abandoned.
We know that many classical texts were lost in the period between the end
of antiquity and the eighth century and many others also after the eighth century. Yet, the greater part of the Greek authors that we now have, with the
exception of the texts recently recovered by papyrologists, have been preserved through the labors of Byzantine scholars. These texts were collected
and kept in their libraries, they were recopied, read, and studied. We also
know that the classical poets and prose writers were read in the schools at
Constantinople and elsewhere at least from the ninth century on, and it
seems to be characteristic of the Byzantine schools that the philosophers,
both Plato and Aristotle, and the Church Fathers were read together with
Homer and the tragedians, historians, and orators. As a matter of fact, we
have Byzantine commentaries and scholia not only on Aristotle and Plato,
but also on Homer, Pindar, and Sophocles, and these commentaries and
scholia that are based in part on the erudition of the scholars of ancient Alexandria have been utilized by modern classical scholars in their work on the
same authors.

We must also keep in mind an important fact concerning the history of the
Greek language. Just as it happened with Latin in the West, the spoken language of the Byzantine Middle Ages for many centuries had moved far away
from classical Greek, whether Attic or Hellenistic, and a student who
wanted to read the classical authors had to learn first the grammar and vocabulary of classical Greek. And just as in the Latin West, there was in the
East a continuous tradition of using as a literary language not the spoken or
popular language but classical Greek, or at least a classicizing Greek resem-
bling that of antiquity. Hence, the study of the classics was not merely
prompted by historical or literary curiosity, but also by the practical requirements of linguistic and literary imitation. Thus, we find handbooks of Greek

grammar composed by Byzantine scholars for the use of students, whose spoken language was no longer classical Greek. It is, therefore, not a mere coincidence if the most important dictionaries of ancient Greek belong to the Byzantine period.

The Byzantine scholars were also critical editors of classical texts in the proper sense of the word, and it is sufficient to cite the *Anthologia Palatina* or the *Bibliotheca* of Photios to remind us that we owe to these editions the preservation and transmission of these texts or at least of their summaries. If we add the textual criticism that is embodied in the Byzantine manuscripts and commentaries, and the historical, mythological, and rhetorical erudition that appears in the encyclopedias, it becomes obvious that Byzantine scholarship, with all its limitations, represents a flourishing and important period in the history of Greek studies and that the West had nothing comparable to offer either at the time of Roman antiquity or during the Latin Middle Ages. Moreover, in spite of its political decline and the continuous losses of important territories, the Byzantine Empire witnessed during its last centuries, and especially during the fourteenth century, a revival rather than a decline of classical studies. A large number of the best-known Byzantine scholars belong precisely to this late period. It is during that same period that we may notice for the first time a Western influence. Several Latin authors such as Cicero, Ovid, St. Augustine, and Boethius were translated into Greek for the first time, and some of these translations were made by authors such as Maximos Planudes, who was also one of the most learned students of classical Greek literature.[10]

If we keep in mind this flourishing state of philological studies in the East, we can easily understand why the Italian humanists, when they began to be interested in ancient Greek literature, had to turn toward Byzantium in order to obtain the texts and also the linguistic and philological knowledge required for reading and understanding them. We know of the first attempts made by Petrarch, who took Greek lessons from Barlaam of Calabria and acquired Greek manuscripts of Homer and Plato,[11] and of Boccaccio, who took Leonzio Pilato into his house and made him teach Greek in Florence and translate Homer into Latin.[12] Even more important was the arrival in Italy of Manuel Chrysoloras and his activity as a teacher in Florence and elsewhere.[13] Among his pupils he counted some of the best humanists and Greek scholars of the early fifteenth century, and in spite of the short duration of his stay, his teaching had a lasting effect. This is attested to by the vast diffusion of the Greek grammar, which he composed for his Italian students, and by the work of his pupils; for example, the translation of Plato's *Republic* made by Uberto Decembrio and suggested and perhaps begun by Chrysoloras himself. With Chrysoloras begins, more than half a century before the fall of Constantinople, the exodus of Byzantine scholars to Italy, a movement that was to continue without interruption for several decades and to increase first with the Council of Ferrara and Florence in 1438 and then with the catastrophe of 1453.[14]

But with Chrysoloras there also begins a movement in the opposite direction. When he returned from Italy to Constantinople, he was accompanied by several Italian pupils, including Guarino. From that time on until the end of the Byzantine Empire and even afterwards under the Turkish rule, there was a steady traveling of Italian humanists to Constantinople and to other Greek cities. We find among them some of the best Greek scholars of the age: Aurispa, Tortelli, and above all Francesco Filelfo, who married the daughter of his Byzantine teacher and who was one of the few Italian humanists capable of writing letters and even poems in classical Greek.[15]

When we speak of the Greek journeys of Guarino, Filelfo, and many others, we usually stress the fact that they learned Greek and brought back an important number of classical Greek manuscripts. We should add that they also learned from their Byzantine masters the philological method that enabled them to read, to understand, and to translate the ancient texts. The same is true of the Byzantine scholars beginning with Chrysoloras himself, who came to teach in Florence, in Padua, and at the other Italian and European universities. They imparted to their Western students not only the Greek classical language that was a learned and not a spoken language, but also the method of interpreting the classical texts as it had been developed in the Byzantine philological tradition. I am convinced that the selection of the Greek authors that were read by the students, and even the choice and sequence of the texts of the preferred authors as they were read, was transmitted in this manner from the Byzantine to the Western schools.[16] To give an example, the reading of Aristophanes always began with the *Plutos* and that of Euripides with the *Hecuba,* and aside from the obvious reasons of facility and decency, there was also an element of school tradition.

There is also a certain conception of learning that is reflected not only in the choice of the authors and texts to be read, but also in the grouping and connection of the subjects taught. The idea that poets and prose writers should form the subjects of different courses is also expressed in the school curriculum of the Latin Middle Ages, but the tendency to treat the philosophers, especially Plato but also Aristotle and the Patristic authors, together with the poets and orators was characteristic of the Byzantine school and seems to have influenced the Greek and perhaps even the Latin scholarship of the Renaissance humanists. I am inclined to think that the learning of the Renaissance humanists, in the extent and limitations of their interests as well as in their attitude toward the texts they studied had closer links with the Byzantine didactic tradition than with that of medieval scholasticism. These are rather minute observations, and at the present state of our knowledge they are hard to prove. Yet, I am convinced that they should and will be investigated as soon as our bibliographical knowledge of manuscripts and printed texts and our documentary knowledge of the universities and other schools will have become more complete than it is at present.

The fourteenth century saw only the first beginnings of Greek scholarship in Italy, whereas the fifteenth and sixteenth centuries brought about the full development of Greek philology in the West, a development that was largely due to the influence of Byzantine philology and of Italian humanism. Let us briefly indicate the diffusion of Greek learning during the Renaissance in its various aspects, and let us begin with the schools.

During the first half of the fifteenth century, the teaching of Greek was still quite sporadic even at the major universities, but during the second half of the century, it became more or less continuous, and during the sixteenth century, it spread also outside of Italy. Among the teachers of Greek we encounter several Byzantine scholars of fame: Theodore Gaza at Ferrara; John Argyropoulos at Florence and Rome; Demetrios Chalcondylas at Padua, Florence, and Pavia; Constantine Lascaris at Messina; and Marcus Musurus at Venice and Padua, to mention only some of the most famous masters. Yet, already during the first half of the fifteenth century, we find also Italian humanists among the teachers of Greek, above all the direct or indirect pupils of the Byzantine masters, for example, Guarino at Venice and Ferrara, Filelfo at Bologna, Florence, and Milan, and Poliziano at Florence. We should add a number of other scholars who have been less studied but probably were quite learned, such as Lianoro Lianori, who taught Greek at Bologna and knew it well enough to write letters in Greek.[17]

Greek instruction obviously began with the elementary study of Greek grammar, and we have numerous manuscript and printed copies of Greek grammars, from the Byzantine grammar of Moschopoulos to the small treatises written by the Greek professors, for example, Chrysoloras, Gaza, and Constantine Lascaris, for their Italian pupils. We are not so well informed about the Greek authors selected for reading since the school documents are usually not explicit enough, whereas the texts of introductory lectures, of courses, and of commentaries are rare and have not yet been much studied. It appears that Homer and Plato, Xenophon, and Demosthenes were among the favorite authors. It is probable, at least for the fifteenth century, that some of the translations from the Greek were school products and also were used to help other beginning students. The introductory lectures given by Chalcondylas at Padua have been preserved by a German student,[18] and we also have some of the introductory lectures given by Argyropoulos in Florence.[19] A manuscript based on the Paduan lectures of Gregoropoulos has been preserved in Germany and has recently been studied, and thus we learn the important fact that he also lectured on Aristophanes and the trage- dians.[20] We may expect further details from Greek manuscripts that carry Latin glosses or translations and from Latin manuscripts that contain Greek notes. For example, I studied some years ago the manuscript of Aristotle's *Ethics* and *Politics,* now preserved in New York, that was used by Ermolao Barbaro for his courses at Padua.[21] I was able to show that he did not work from the Greek text or from Bruni's Latin version, as had often been as- sumed, but from the medieval translations. On the other hand, it is apparent from Ermolao's glosses that he did use the Greek text and Bruni's version to correct the Latin text that he was supposed to explain to his students.

Equally important and perhaps more thoroughly studied are the problems connected with the Greek books and the libraries of the Renaissance period. The fifteenth and sixteenth centuries saw not only the migration of the Byzantine scholars to the West, but also the exodus of many Greek manu- scripts to the Western countries. The Byzantine scholars who went to Italy brought their books with them, and the Italian humanists who went to Greece returned to Italy with Greek manuscripts and sometimes with entire libraries of Greek manuscripts. Italian princes and patrons began to collect Greek manuscripts. They bought the manuscripts brought from Greece by scholars, monks, and merchants, and even sent scholars to Greece for the sole purpose of acquiring manuscripts. The best-known example is the mis- sion of John Lascaris for Lorenzo de' Medici that occurred several decades after the Turkish conquest.[22] Still in the sixteenth century, Francesco Patrizi collected Greek manuscripts in Cyprus and elsewhere and subsequently re- sold them to Philip II of Spain.[23] In other words, the trade in Greek manu- scripts did not stop with the fall of Constantinople, and we should remember that after 1453 several areas of Greek speech and civilization, such as Euboea and Morea, Cyprus, Rhodes, and Crete, remained for shorter or longer periods under Venetian rule.

The core of the great collections of Greek manuscripts in Europe goes back to the fifteenth and sixteenth centuries: the Laurentian and Vatican libraries and the Marciana, which had for its first nucleus the collection of Bessarion, were formed in the fifteenth century; the collections in Paris, the Escorial, Munich, and Vienna in the sixteenth century; those in Oxford and Leyden shortly afterwards. Still at the present time the editor of ancient Greek texts must use the manuscripts in these libraries, as well as those that are still in the libraries of Greece and of the other Eastern countries that have or had close ties with the Greek Church and with Greek culture, such as Russia and Turkey.

The Western collections of Greek manuscripts contain not only manuscripts written in Greece and later brought to the West. There are also some manuscripts written in Greek Italy and Sicily during the Middle Ages and a large number of manuscripts that were copied in the West itself from older manuscripts, as we learn from the dates and colophons of the manuscripts. They were mostly written by exiled Byzantine scholars who made their living as copyists but also often by Western scholars who copied the Greek texts for their own use. We have Greek manuscripts copied or annotated by Poliziano, Ficino, Ermolao Barbaro, and even by Leonardo Bruni.[24] In spite of their relatively recent date, these Greek manuscripts copied by Byzantine or Italian scholars are important for the history and emendation of the texts, and in some instances where we have no older manuscripts these late copies must even serve as the basis for editing the text.

The Greek manuscripts also reflect the influence of the Byzantine tradition in the field of paleography. The majority of our Greek manuscripts were written in Byzantine minuscule, a script that was in general use for literary texts from the ninth century on. This was the script still used by the Byzantine scholars of the fifteenth century and adopted and imitated by the Italian and other Western scholars when they learned to write Greek. This Byzantine minuscule is the basis of the Greek characters used by Aldus and the other printers and publishers of Greek texts in the sixteenth century, just as the Roman and Italic characters used by the early printers are based on the two humanist scripts commonly used in the Latin manuscript books of fifteenth-century Italy. Aside from certain conventional abbreviations and ligatures that have been abandoned in more recent times, the Byzantine minuscule is still the recognizable source for the printed characters used in our modern editions of the Greek classics.

This last observation leads us to another important factor in the diffusion of Greek learning during the Renaissance, that is, to printing. The first Greek classical texts were printed in Florence and Milan, but very soon, through Aldus and other learned printers both Greek and Italian, Venice became the most active center of Greek printing. She later had to share this place with Paris, Antwerp, and Leyden, just as she shared her predominance in the field of Latin printing with Lyons and Basel.[25] Erasmus went to Venice and to the printing shop of Aldus when he wanted to enhance his knowledge of Greek, a very significant episode that has been properly emphasized in recent studies. Within the vast output of the presses during the late fifteenth and sixteenth centuries, Greek books constituted but a small percentage, but their distribution is a decisive element for the history of advanced learning during the period. We may say without exaggeration that in the course of the sixteenth century almost all the important texts of ancient Greece that had been preserved by the Byzantine Middle Ages had become accessible to Western scholars, both through the manuscripts of the major Western libraries and through the printed editions published by the great Hellenists of the period that found their place also in the more modest libraries of schools and of private scholars.

If we want to understand the diffusion of Greek literature during the Renaissance, we must also take into consideration the translations into Western languages, and especially into Latin. Even during the sixteenth century, when Greek learning was more widely diffused in the West than ever before, the scholars who knew Greek and knew it well constituted only a minority, whereas Latin was known more or less well by every person who had received a humanistic or university education. Hence, it is quite understandable that the Latin translations of the Greek authors, either by themselves or along with the Greek text, had a much wider diffusion than the original Greek texts themselves.[26] Whereas the diffusion of the original Greek texts was a completely new fact and never occurred during the Middle Ages, Latin translations from the Greek were by no means unknown during the Middle Ages, as we have seen before.

If we wish to define the difference between the Middle Ages and the Renaissance in this area, we must stress two different facets of the question. In the case of those Greek texts that had been known before through medieval Latin translations, it would be necessary to compare the new humanist translations of the same texts with the earlier ones. Curiously enough, such a comparison between the medieval and humanist translations and the corresponding Greek originals has not yet been attempted; hence, our judgment on the relative merits of these translations must remain rather tentative. We may concede to some admirers of the Middle Ages that some humanist translations, such as Bruni's versions of Aristotle, are rather free and do not sufficiently insist on a precise and consistent terminology. On the other hand, after having examined the medieval versions of Plato and Proclus, I am convinced that the humanists had a more advanced knowledge of classical Greek than had their medieval predecessors, both of its vocabulary and of its syntax, phraseology, and style.[27] We must also note that the vast enterprise of translating the classical Greek authors into Latin was carried out not only by Italian and other Western Hellenists, but also by many Byzantine scholars who had acquired enough Latin learning for the purpose, such as George of Trebisond, Gaza, Argyropoulos, and Bessarion himself to whom we owe some translations of Aristotle and Xenophon.

The rivalry between medieval and humanistic translations poses a number of problems, especially for Aristotle and for some scientific authors such as Hippocrates, Galen, Archimedes, and Ptolemy. We do not yet know precisely to what extent humanist translators utilized earlier translations when available and to what extent they succeeded in replacing the work of their medieval predecessors.[28] We know that in some instances the humanistic and the medieval translations lived far into the late sixteenth century in a kind of coexistence and were used simultaneously by teachers and scholars, but we also know that the medieval translations when copied or printed during the fifteenth and sixteenth centuries were often subjected to more or less extensive revisions. The bibliography and textual history of these translations leaves room for much further study, and it is a subject of great importance. For it is important to know what impact the new translations, with their changed terminology and interpretation, had on the understanding of the basic philosophical and scientific texts and, hence, on the philosophical and scientific thought itself, which was still to a large extent formulated through the interpretation of these texts.[29] The same consideration holds for the new translations of the Bible and of the Greek Church Fathers and for their influence on the theological thought of the period.

Even more obvious and perhaps more important is the humanist contribution in the case of those Greek texts which had never been translated into Latin during the Middle Ages. The volume and importance of these texts seems to have been greatly underestimated by many historians who have studied the problem. They include even a few texts of the *Corpus Aristotelicum,* such as the *Mechanics* (and in a way the *Poetics*) and a large number of Greek commentaries on Aristotle,[30] as well as many writings of the same scientific authors that had been known to the Middle Ages through some of their works, such as Hippocrates, Galen, Archimedes, and Ptolemy.[31] Moreover, there are other ancient philosophers besides Aristotle of whom the Middle Ages knew only some works, such as Plato, Sextus, and Proclus; or nothing at all, such as Epicurus, Epictetus, or Plotinus; and, if we include the more popular and more widely read authors, Xenophon, Plutarch, or Lucian. If we turn to Greek literature in the proper sense of the word, everything was new and unknown from the Western point of view: Lysias, Isocrates, Demosthenes, and the other orators; Herodotus, Thucydides and Polybius; Homer and Hesiod; the tragedians and Aristophanes; Pindar and the other lyrical poets, not to mention the Anthology of the Greek epigrams or many lesser poets and prose writers. In other words, an educated person of the sixteenth century, whether he was able to read Greek or not, had at his disposal the complete patrimony of classical Greek literature and science. For anybody who appreciates Greek literature and non-Aristotelian Greek philosophy, this is a cultural development of the very first order, and it is a fact of which we must remind those numerous historians who insist on the essentially medieval character of humanism and of the Renaissance.

It is to this increased availability of Greek texts brought about under the influence of humanism that we owe at least in part the great literary wealth of the Renaissance and of modern times and the greater variety of modern philosophical ideas as compared to the more rigid and limited alternatives of medieval Aristotelianism. In the scientific disciplines it was necessary to absorb and digest the advanced mathematical, astronomical, and medical texts of ancient Greece before their conclusions could be surpassed. In these fields the quarrel of the ancients and moderns and the idea of progress could not have made their appearance before the sixteenth century.

If the heritage of ancient Greek culture in all its aspects still constitutes an essential part of our present civilization, in spite of the additions and transformations brought about by later centuries, we are indebted for it to the Italian and other Western humanists of the Renaissance and to their Byzantine predecessors. We must also remember another more limited but no less essential contribution that the scholars of the Renaissance have transmitted to later centuries: Greek philology, which includes textual criticism, the method of interpretation, and the method of historical and antiquarian research. This philology passed from the Byzantine scholars to the Italian

humanists and from the latter to the French and Dutch philologists of the
sixteenth century, and to the English and German and finally to the American scholars of more recent times. Each age and country added something
new to the common tradition, and we should like to think that the methods
of research have been steadily improved and refined in the course of the centuries and that they have proved their validity also when applied to the study
of languages and cultures other than those of classical antiquity.

For two reasons, then—for the continuing impact of Greek literature and
culture on modern Western civilization and for the impulse given to classical, philological, and historical studies—Byzantine and Italian humanism,
different and yet connected, have a lasting importance in the history of European civilization. Hence, it should be worthwhile to explore these rich and
interesting movements much further, especially in those aspects that have
not yet been properly investigated or understood.

8.

Byzantine and Western Platonism in the Fifteenth Century

The history of Byzantine and Western Platonism is an important subject
and one that has not been neglected by intellectual historians, but it is somewhat difficult and complicated, and many of its facets have not yet been sufficiently explored. We have a certain number of recent monographs on the
major representatives of Byzantine and Italian Platonism,[1] but several lesser
figures who had a significant part in the intellectual development of the
period remain comparatively unknown. Moreover, we still lack a comprehensive and documented history of Renaissance Platonism, and there is no
modern history of the controversy about the superiority of Plato or Aristotle.[2] In other words, we know to some extent the thought of Plethon and

Bessarion, of Ficino and Pico. But aside from many aspects of the thought of these authors that remain still obscure or doubtful, we do not yet know the precise links that connect them with each other or with other earlier or later thinkers, and their sources and influences are still to a large extent unknown to us. Instead of trying to give a synthesis that would seem premature at this stage, I prefer to admit the preliminary character of our knowledge, and especially of my knowledge of the subject, and to indicate as clearly as possible the problems that are still in need of further investigation.

If we read some of the textbooks of the history of philosophy, we shall usually find them saying (or at least they did so until a few years ago) that the contrast between medieval and Renaissance thought in the West may be roughly described as a contrast between Aristotelianism and Platonism. Medieval scholastic thought was dominated by "the master of those who know,"[3] whereas the Renaissance discovered "Plato who in that group came closest to the goal that may be reached by those whom heaven favors."[4] This simple and pleasant formula has been demolished, as it happens, by the more detailed research of recent historians. We have learned that there was also during the Middle Ages a more or less continuous Platonist current[5] and, on the other hand, that the Aristotelian school remained very strong throughout the sixteenth century and even underwent some of its most characteristic developments during that very period.[6] Yet, in this as in other cases, we should not push revisionism to the utmost extreme. Renaissance Platonism remains, after all, an established fact, and we are still confronted with the task of understanding and explaining it. Cusanus, Ficino, and Pico were the most vigorous thinkers of the fifteenth century, and their influence during their own time and during the subsequent centuries was powerful, although it is somewhat hard to describe, especially if we think exclusively in terms of academic and institutional traditions. Moreover, when we use the term "Platonism," we should not treat it as a fixed and rigid category. We must realize that under this label we may expect to find in each instance a different combination of ideas and doctrines that remains to be identified and explained. We also should admit that the name and authority of Plato covers at the same time the vast tradition of ancient and later Neoplatonism and that for the very reason that people considered Platonism as a kind of perennial philosophy (the term was invented by a Platonizing bishop of the sixteenth century, Agostino Steuco),[7] they were also tempted to associate with it many philosophical, theological, and scientific ideas that had a very different origin.

If we wish to understand the development of Platonism during the Renaissance, we must go back for a moment to Roman antiquity and to the Latin Middle Ages. We find traces of Platonic and Platonist influences in some of the philosophical and rhetorical works of Cicero, who even translated a part of Plato's *Timaeus*.[8] The philosophical treatises of Apuleius are among the most important preserved sources for that school of ancient philosophy which has recently come to be known as Middle Platonism.[9] Apuleius was also the reputed translator of the dialogue *Asclepius*, the only complete source of Hermetism known to Western readers throughout the Middle Ages.[10] In late antiquity, the knowledge of Plato was strengthened by Calcidius' partial translation and commentary of the *Timaeus*, a work whose tremendous influence we can appreciate only now that we have an adequate critical edition of it.[11] The Neoplatonism of Plotinus and his school had its repercussions also in the Latin West. Aside from Victorinus and Macrobius,[12] we must mention especially St. Augustine, whose philosophical thought was much more deeply influenced by Plato and Plotinus than some of his recent theological interpreters are inclined to admit,[13] and Boethius, whose widely read *Consolation of Philosophy* shows the impact of the same school. Compared with these strong elements of Platonism, the traces of Aristotle in the philosophical literature of Latin antiquity are rather meager. We note primarily a certain acquaintance with Aristotelian logic in Cicero and Augustine and, above all, in Boethius, who translated the first two treatises of the *Organon*, along with the Neoplatonist Porphyry's Introduction to the first treatise, and probably also the remaining parts of the same collection.[14]

Thus, we may easily understand why medieval philosophy and theology up to the twelfth century followed a strong Neoplatonic trend, whereas the influence of Aristotle was felt almost exlusively in the field of logic, especially after all treatises of the *Organon* had become generally known. Yet, the twelfth century also saw the beginning of that intellectual revolution that was to bear fruit during the following two centuries. In the vast number of philosophical and scientific texts which were then translated for the first time from Greek and Arabic into Latin,[15] the most important philosophical texts were those of Aristotle and his commentators. Thus, the West acquired the entire, or almost the entire, *Corpus* of Aristotle's preserved writings, along with many of their commentaries. When the new universities in the thirteenth century introduced a systematic instruction in the philosophical disciplines, and especially in logic and natural philosophy, the writings of Aristotle were naturally adopted as the main textbooks, a function for which they were eminently suitable because of the completeness of their coverage and the precision and consistency of their method and terminology. The Aristotelianism of the universities, as it developed in the thirteenth and fourteenth centuries and continued, although with gradually diminishing importance, through the Renaissance down to the eighteenth century, was not so much a compact system of uniform doctrines as a diversified tradition of teaching based on a common terminology and a common set of topics and problems.

The translators of the twelfth and thirteenth centuries did not entirely forget the writings of the Platonist school. There were translations of Plato's *Meno* and *Phaedo* by the Sicilian Henricus Aristippus and several translations of Proclus by the Flemish Dominican William of Moerbeke,[16] translations which had a demonstrable impact on the mystical writers and even on Thomas Aquinas.[17] But without forgetting these exceptions, it remains a basic fact that the academic and scientific philosophy of the Latin West during the later Middle Ages was dominated by the writings of Aristotle in a manner that had its precedent among the Arabs but was entirely different from the traditions of Greek and Roman antiquity and, as we shall see, of the Byzantines.

The preoccupations of the new humanist movement that asserted itself in contrast to the scholastic tradition were in part literary and scholarly, to be sure, but in part also philosophical and, especially, moral. With Petrarch the rebellion against scholasticism took the form of praising Plato above Aristotle, although Plato and his works were still comparatively unknown. This attitude appears not only in the *Triumph of Fame* from which I previously quoted a few lines,[18] but also in the treatise *On His Own and Other People's Ignorance* that was based on a controversy Petrarch had with some friends in Venice.[19] In this, as in so many other ways, we may call Petrarch a prophet of the later Renaissance who opened the way, as it were, that was to lead to the Plato translations of Bruni and of other humanists and to Ficino's first complete translation of Plato's works.[20]

But this new interest in Plato and his works did not turn toward the Latin traditions of antiquity or the early Middle Ages, but rather toward Byzantium, where the original texts of Plato and of his school had been preserved and studied during those long centuries when they had remained largely unknown in the West. Petrarch already received from the Orient a Greek manuscript containing some dialogues of Plato, and this was probably the first Greek manuscript of Plato that came to the West since ancient Roman times.[21] When the teaching of Greek in the West received its first lasting impetus from Manuel Chrysoloras,[22] some of its first fruits were the Plato translations made by his pupils, especially that of the *Republic* by Uberto Decembrio and that of the *Apology, Crito, Gorgias,* and other works by Leonardo Bruni.[23] When the Byzantine Platonist Gemistos Plethon came to the Council of Ferrara and Florence in 1438 and 1439, he aroused so much interest for Platonic philosophy among the Italian humanists whom he met that Marsilio Ficino was able to say several decades afterwards that it was the impression made by Plethon on Cosimo de' Medici that led to the founding of his own Platonic Academy and to the revival of Platonism brought about by the activities of that Academy.[24]

These well-known facts prompt us to enquire about the fate of the Platonic writings and of the Platonic and Neoplatonic tradition in medieval Byzantium. Many details of the history of this tradition are still obscure, but a few facts may be easily summed up. When the Neoplatonic school of Athens, one of the last intellectual centers of ancient paganism, was closed by Justinian in 529, Simplicius and some of his colleagues went to Persia. Yet, it would be wrong to assume that these events marked the end of Platonism in the Byzantine world.[25] Simplicius returned after a short while to Greece, and most of his extant writings were composed after his return. Moreover, the Christian writers of the Greek East had absorbed for several centuries a strong dose of Platonist thought, as may be easily shown in the writings of Clement and Origen, Gregory of Nyssa, and the so-called Dionysius the Areopagite. We also know for sure that at least from the ninth century on Plato's works were copied, read, and studied in Constantinople and in the other cultural centers of the oriental empire. From that period on, the study of Plato and also of Aristotle remained an integral part of the Byzantine scholarly or, if we wish, humanist tradition. That is, Plato was read and studied together with the poets and prose writers of classical antiquity. This seems to have been the type of scholarship that characterized the work of Archbishop Arethas for whom one of the earliest extant manuscripts of Plato was copied.[26]

A Platonism of a more philosophical and speculative kind appears in the eleventh century with Michael Psellos, a man of considerable learning and influence.[27] He attempted a kind of synthesis between Neoplatonic philosophy and Christian theology that found many successors among the Byzantine scholars of subsequent centuries. Following the precedent of Proclus, Psellos included as a part of the Platonic tradition the writings attributed to

Hermes Trismegistus and the *Chaldaic Oracles*. The *Corpus Hermeticum*, as it has come down to us in Greek, is perhaps an edition or anthology due to Psellos, and also the collection of *Chaldaic Oracles* as we have it goes back to Psellos, who added a commentary to it.[28] This commentary was known to Ficino, who also translated part of Psellos' treatise *On Demons*, and to Francesco Patrizi, and it was printed in the sixteenth century.[29]

Among the Byzantine theologians we encounter a strong anti-Platonist current, yet the detailed polemic against Plotinus and Proclus, as we find it in the writings of Isaac Sebastocrator, Nicolaus of Methone, and Nicephoros Chumnos, presupposes a certain popularity of the Neoplatonic doctrines among their contemporaries. Chumnos' work against Plotinus was still copied in the fifteenth century, although the name of the author was usually distorted.[30] Nicolaus of Methone's critical notes on Proclus were known to Ficino, and Ficino's manuscript of this work, with his Latin translation, has been rediscovered recently.[31] Finally, the writings of Isaac Sebastocrator against Proclus have been recently utilized to recover some important fragments of three lost theological works of Proclus that had been known up to that moment only through the Latin versions of William of Moerbeke.[32]

On the other hand, it would be quite wrong to assume that the Aristotelian tradition was lacking in strength among the Byzantines. The vast diffusion of Aristotle's writings among the Byzantines has been recently illustrated by a census of his Greek manuscripts.[33] There were important Byzantine commentators on Aristotle, such as Michael of Ephesus, Eustratius of Nicaea, and others,[34] and some of these Byzantine commentaries were translated into Latin during the Middle Ages or the Renaissance and thus exercised some influence on Western scholastic Aristotelianism.[35] Yet, Byzantine Aristotelianism, unlike its Arabic and Western counterparts, was never separated from the study of rhetoric or of the ancient poets and orators, and in most instances it was not even opposed to Platonism. If we consider the major Byzantine philosophers from Johannes Italos to the scholars of the fourteenth century, we encounter in most instances a combination of Aristotelian logic and physics with Platonist metaphysics, a combination that goes back to the ancient Neoplatonists and their Aristotelian commentaries.[36]

It is often asserted that the philosophical and theological tradition of the Byzantine East was predominantly Aristotelian or anti-Platonist, but I have the impression that these statements are based to a large extent either on Western analogies or on certain polemical positions that appeared among the

Byzantines only in the fifteenth century. I am inclined to think that the exclusive Aristotelianism of some Byzantine thinkers of the fourteenth and fifteenth centuries was due to Western influences which began to become important during that very period. Among the Latin authors translated into Greek at that time, we find not only Cicero and Ovid, Augustine and Boethius, but also Thomas Aquinas.[37]

It is against this background that we must understand the work of a thinker who was celebrated by his pupils and contemporaries as another Plato and who occupied in relation to the mature Platonism of the Western Renaissance a position similar to that of the last Byzantine philologists in relation to the Italian humanists: Georgios Gemistos Plethon.[38] He lived approximately from 1360 to 1452 and spent the greater part of his later life in Mistra, the capital of the despots of Morea, where he served as a counselor to the reigning princes and also gave instruction to some private pupils. He tried to strengthen the Byzantine Empire by a political reform based on ancient Greek models. According to the testimony of several contemporary enemies, which has been accepted by most recent scholars, Plethon also planned to restore the pagan religion of Greek antiquity. In the preserved fragments of his chief work, the Laws, he speaks at length of the ancient deities and their worship.[39] Yet, the work was destroyed after Plethon's death by his enemy Scholarios, who preserved only these paganizing passages in order to justify his action, and I suspect that the complete text of the work might have suggested an allegorical and less crude interpretation of the same passages. The part Plethon took in the Council of Florence, his theological opposition to the Union of the Greek and Latin Churches, and, finally, the unqualified admiration shown for Plethon by his pupil Cardinal Bessarion tend to cast some doubt on the supposed paganism of Plethon.

On the other hand, Plethon always maintained a strict separation between his philosophy and Christian theology and never tried to harmonize them. In his extant writings he professes to be a convinced follower of Plato and his philosophy, and he often praises the Neoplatonic philosophers, especially Proclus by whom he was much influenced. He also likes to cite the early Oriental and Greek sages, especially, the writings attributed to the Pythagoreans, and the so-called Chaldaic Oracles, which he apparently was the first to attribute to Zoroaster and on which he wrote a commentary.[40] His knowledge of the Orphic and Hermetic writings seems to be established, although it appears less prominently in his writings, and the precedent of Proclus and Psellos would be sufficient to make such a knowledge plausible.

Plethon cites the Stoics with favor but is strongly opposed to the Skeptics and especially to Aristotle. This anti-Aristotelianism is by no means typical of the Byzantine tradition; and since Plethon's famous treatise on the difference between Aristotle and Plato was composed during his stay in Italy and for his Italian friends,[41] I am inclined to interpret Plethon's anti-Aristotelianism as a reaction against the exclusive Aristotelianism which he encountered among the Latin theologians and which to him must have appeared excessive.

Among the many characteristic points on which Plethon considers Plato to be superior to Aristotle, he insists on the reality of universals and ideas, on the divine origin of the world, and on the immortality of the soul. He also criticizes Aristotle's description of the moral virtues as means between two opposite vices, and he finally insists that all events are due to necessary causes, defending also in his treatise *On Fate* an extreme determinism that sounds more Stoic than Platonic.[42] We may note in Plethon's Platonism a strongly rationalistic character and the apparent absence of that mystical or spiritualistic element that is so prominent and central in the thought of the ancient Neoplatonists and of many Renaissance Platonists.

Plethon's treatise on the differences of Plato and Aristotle inaugurated the famous controversy on the relative superiority of Plato and Aristotle that continued for several decades among the Byzantine and later among some Western scholars, a controversy that has been given an almost exaggerated importance in some historical accounts of the fifteenth century. However, the significance of this controversy should not be denied. If we disregard for the moment some discussions of special problems involved in the controversy, the first frontal attack against Plethon's treatise was composed by Scholarios around 1443.[43] It is a point by point defense of Aristotle against Plethon that shows a very detailed knowledge of the Aristotelian writings and emphasizes the agreement between Aristotelian philosophy and Christian theology. I am not inclined to attribute this exclusive and theological Aristotelianism of Scholarios to a supposed Byzantine theological tradition, as some historians have done, but rather to his obvious dependence on Western thought, and especially on Thomism. We know that Scholarios was more learned in Latin theology than in the Byzantine traditions of philosophy and philology, and his great admiration for Aquinas is documented by his numerous translations of his writings.[44] These facts are easily overlooked because in his later years Scholarios adopted a theological position hostile to the union with the Latin Church. This typically scholastic and

Western attitude of Scholarios appears in the beginning pages of Scholarios' treatise, where he speaks with contempt of Plethon's Italian friends who are interested in Homer and Vergil, Cicero and Demosthenes and who hence admire Plato for his literary talent and are unable to judge the philosophical merit of Aristotle.[45] In this passage we find the typical Italian contrast between scholasticism and humanism translated into Greek. Plethon replied to Scholarios about 1449 in a treatise in which we note, among other things, the interesting remark that the basic agreement between Plato and Aristotle which Scholarios had attributed to the ancients appears only in Simplicius, who attempted to combine the doctrine of the two philosophers against that of the Christian Church.[46]

Aside from the controversy between Plethon and Scholarios, there was before and after the death of Plethon a discussion of more specific points of doctrine, such as the concept of substance or the doctrine of fate. In addition to Plethon and Bessarion, Theodore Gaza, Michael Apostolis, Andronicus Callistus, and several other Greek scholars participated in this discussion.[47] Most of their treatises were written in Italy but in the Greek language. They can now be read in recent editions, but no detailed history of the debate has yet been written, and I cannot enter into any further details.

We must mention the treatise by George of Trebisond, *Comparationes philosophorum Platonis et Aristotelis,* which was written in Latin after Plethon's death, perhaps in 1455, and printed in the sixteenth century.[48] This work was much more violent than that of Scholarios in its doctrinal and personal attacks against Plethon and Plato himself, and it defended the superiority of Aristotle over Plato on all points, and especially his agreement with Christian theology. This attitude of Trapezuntius is rather strange when we consider his life and training.[49] He came at an early age from Crete to Italy, attended the school of Vittorino da Feltre in Mantua, and thus combined a Latin humanist education with his Byzantine background. He became a bilingual scholar, taught Greek in Venice for some time, made Latin translations from the Greek, especially of Aristotle, Ptolemy, Cyril, and Eusebius, but also of Plato's *Laws* and *Parmenides,* and composed letters and treatises in Latin, including influential handbooks of logic and of rhetoric.[50] His translations and treatises show a certain amount of interest in philosophy, to be sure, but his preparation was by no means theological or scholastic. Since he was involved in many controversies with other scholars, we might look for the motivation of his anti-Platonic treatise in his personal relations with Plethon's school. Perhaps he was also displeased with Plato's hostile attitude towards rhetoric and poetry, an attitude that for a humanist with a rhetorical training must have been difficult to swallow.

Trapezuntius' treatise provoked several answers, and it provided the occasion for Cardinal Bessarion to compose his great treatise *In calumniatorem Platonis*. This work, which was repeatedly revised by its author, was probably written between 1458 and 1469, first in Greek and then in a Latin version that was printed in 1469.[51] Bessarion not only defends Plato's life and doctrine against the attacks of Trapezuntius, but he also describes Plato's contributions to the various fields of learning and then presents Plato's metaphysical doctrines with an emphasis both on their intrinsic merits and on their agreement with Christian theology. Bessarion treats Aristotle with great respect and tends to harmonize him with Plato rather than to criticize him. He often cites the Latin theologians, especially Augustine, Aquinas, and Duns Scotus. The general character of the work is apologetic rather than philosophical, but it had the great merit of presenting to Latin scholars for the first time a broad and balanced, although not always accurate, picture of Plato's doctrine, based on a thorough knowledge of his writings and of his ancient commentators. The work had a wide circulation, being among the first books printed in Italy,[52] and was enthusiastically received by several Greek, Italian, and French scholars whose letters have been preserved.[53] Like Trapezuntius, Bessarion combined a Latin humanist culture with a Byzantine training; and since he was a Cardinal of the Roman Church, his published opinions were bound to carry great weight and authority. Moreover, he was a patron of numerous Greek and Italian scholars who were ready to defend and support his work.

The famous controversy on Plato and Aristotle did not quite end with Bessarion's work but continued for some time even after its publication. Bessarion's influence may be felt not only in Giovanni Andrea de' Bussi's preface to Apuleius[54] and in Perotti's rebuttal of another lost work of Trapezuntius,[55] but also in a series of treatises that are still unknown and unpublished by Domizio Calderini, Fernando of Cordoba, and Andreas Contrarius. In another treatise that is still largely unpublished, Trapezuntius' son Andreas tries to defend his father's position against Fernando of Cordoba.[56] To the sixteenth century already belongs the unpublished treatise against Trapezuntius by the Augustinian Hermit Ambrosius Flandinus,[57] a prolific author who also composed polemical treatises against Pomponazzi and Luther and voluminous commentaries on several works of Plato. We may find a last repercussion of the controversy, and even of Plethon's work, in the anti-Aristotelian polemic of an influential philosopher of the late six-teenth century who had received an excellent training in Greek and who spent a part of his life in Padua, in Venice, and in the Greek territories of Venice: Francesco Patrizi.[58]

In conclusion, I should like to discuss briefly the chief representatives of Western Platonism during the fifteenth century—Cusanus, Ficino, and Pico. They took no active part in the debate on Plato and Aristotle of which we have spoken, and a large part of their thought was either original, or may be traced to classical or medieval Western sources. Yet, we cannot conclude our discussion without mentioning the more or less obvious connections that link these Western Platonists with their Byzantine predecessors and contem-poraries, and especially with Plethon and Bessarion.

It is not possible to reduce the thought of Cusanus, complex and original as it is, under the simple label of Platonism, but it is evident from his doc-trines and quotations and from the content of his library that he was much attracted by Plato and his school.[59] The influence of Augustine and also that of the Areopagite and of Proclus on Cusanus' thought was decisive, and he stated explicitly that he discovered his doctrine of learned ignorance during his return from Constantinople. It now appears, however, that his knowl-edge of Greek was rather limited. We know little about his personal rela-tions with Byzantine scholars except for his friendship with Bessarion, of which we have several testimonies, and the fact that other Byzantine scholars such as Athanasius of Constantinople dedicated to him a few trans-lations of Greek works into Latin.[60] Yet, Cusanus was surrounded by Italian humanists who were Greek scholars, especially Giovanni Andrea de' Bussi, Bishop of Aleria, and Pietro Balbo, Bishop of Tropea, who belonged to his inner circle. We have learned rather recently that Plato's *Parmenides* and Proclus' *Platonic Theology* were translated for Cusanus, the former by Tra-pezuntius and the latter by Pietro Balbo,[61] and I discovered a Latin transla-tion of Plethon's *De fato* by Johannes Sophianos that was made for Cusanus and apparently formed a part of his personal library.[62]

Whereas for Cusanus Platonism was an important part of his background, it constituted for Marsilio Ficino the very center of his work and thought. His Latin translation of Plato made the entire *Corpus* of Plato's dialogues available to Western readers for the first time, and hence it must be recorded as a major event in the history of Platonism and of Western thought. To this translation we must add his introductions and commentaries, among which the commentary on the *Symposium* was especially famous and influential;

his translation and interpretation of Plotinus, which introduced this important thinker to the Western world; and his translations of various writings of other Neoplatonists such as Porphyry, Jamblichus, and Proclus, and of several pseudo-Platonic writers such as Hermes Trismegistus, Zoroaster, Orpheus, and Pythagoras. Ficino also presented Platonic philosophy, as he understood it, in his *Platonic Theology* and in his letters, and he taught it in the courses and discussions of his Platonic Academy. We know from several statements in his writings that he considered the revival of Platonism as a task assigned to him by divine providence.[63]

If we ask what part, if any, Byzantine influences had in this revival of Platonism, we may give at least a partial answer to this question. Ficino himself states in the preface to his version of Plotinus (1492) that Cosimo de' Medici during the Council of Florence had heard some lectures by Plethon and was so deeply impressed by them that he conceived the idea of founding a Platonic Academy in Florence, a task for which he later chose Ficino when the latter was still young.[64] Knowing Ficino's manner of speaking, I hesitate to accept this story in as literal a sense as has been done by many historians, but there is a nucleus of truth in it, and Ficino surely intended to establish a historical link between his own work and that of Plethon. As a matter of fact, the passage is not completely isolated in the work of Ficino. He mentions Plethon in at least four other places, and one of them is of special interest since it says that Averroes misunderstood the thought of Aristotle because he did not know any Greek.[65] In an early preface of ten Platonic dialogues to Cosimo (1464), Ficino states that Plato's spirit flew from Byzantium to Florence.[66] We have recently learned that Ficino owned and partly copied in his own hand the Greek text of some of Plethon's writings.[67] I also found in a manuscript an anonymous Latin translation of Plethon's commentary on the *Chaldaic Oracles* and have some reason for attributing this translation to Ficino.[68] There are other traces of Byzantine influence in the work of Ficino. He copied with his own hand Traversari's translation of Aeneas of Gaza[69] and later translated a work of Psellos.[70] He corresponded with Bessarion and may have visited him, highly praised his work *In calumniatorem Platonis,* and included this work in a list of Platonist writings that he sent to his German friend Martin Prenninger.[71]

When we compare the works of Ficino with those of Plethon and Bessarion, however, we find few close similarities and a great discrepancy in their sources, problems, and intellectual interests. Ficino certainly agrees with Plethon in his historical conception that there was an ancient tradition of pagan theology that goes back beyond Plato to Pythagoras and the Chaldaeans, but Ficino may have derived this conception directly from Proclus rather than from Plethon. Yet, if it is true that Plethon was the first to attribute the *Chaldaic Oracles* to Zoroaster, Ficino would show in this matter his dependence on Plethon, for he often cites the *Oracles* with great respect and always treats them as the work of Zoroaster. Ficino's Platonism agrees with that of Plethon in the theory of ideas and in the doctrine of immortality, but I am inclined to think that these concepts are more central and more elaborate in Ficino than in Plethon. Ficino certainly rejects Plethon's fatalism, and since he emphasized the harmony between Platonic philosophy and Christian theology, he was far removed from the pagan tendencies attributed to Plethon. On this point, as well as in his comparatively tolerant attitude toward Aristotle, Ficino rather agreed with Bessarion. But unlike Bessarion, Ficino was not interested in attributing to Plato the specific doctrines of the various elementary and philosophical disciplines or of dogmatic theology. Vice versa, some of the fundamental teachings of Ficino's Platonism, such as the central position of man in the hierarchy of the universe, the spiritual experience of the contemplative life, or the doctrine of Platonic love, apparently did not occupy a significant place in the Platonism of his Byzantine predecessors.

If we pass from Ficino to Pico, the links with Byzantine Platonism become far less direct; for certainly Pico's scholastic training, which he received at Padua and Paris, his Averroism, and his enthusiasm for Hebrew theology and for the Cabala separate him much more decidedly than Ficino from the humanist tradition of Byzantine Platonism, and especially from Plethon.[72] But the famous project to establish a harmony between Plato and Aristotle as well as between their schools may be compared to a certain extent with the attitude of Bessarion.

When we proceed from the fifteenth to the sixteenth century, we notice some strongly anti-Aristotelian tendencies that come to a climax in the work of Francesco Patrizi and that may be connected more or less directly with the work of Plethon. Yet, the prevalent form in which the sixteenth century received the heritage of Platonism was that of Ficino and of Pico. The function of that Platonism consisted in establishing a kind of rational metaphysics beside, rather than against, dogmatic theology and empirical science. The Platonist conceptions that were most popular in the sixteenth century were the doctrines of the contemplative life, of immortality, of the dignity of man, and of Platonic love. The historical conception of ancient theology found expression in the perennial philosophy of Augustinus Steuchus, which continued a notion derived from Proclus and Plethon and more directly from Ficino and Pico. Yet, Steuco's attempt to harmonize Platonism with Christian theology and even with Aristotelian science was closer to the attitude of Bessarion. It is the same attitude which we encounter in Raphael's Stanze, where the School of Athens is placed in front of the Disputation on the Sacrament and where Plato and Aristotle together occupy the center in a symbolic representation of secular philosophy.

Before concluding, I should like to correct a misunderstanding to which my position has sometimes given rise. I am convinced that the Platonism of the fifteenth century, as well as its humanism, were intellectual movements of great importance and some originality, but I never meant to give the impression that the intellectual life of the fifteenth century, or of the Renaissance in general, can be understood exclusively in terms of humanism and Platonism. There were also the powerful traditions of Aristotelian philosophy, of theology, of law, and of the various scientific disciplines, not to speak of the popular literature, the arts, and the religious, political, and economic life of the period. On the other hand, if we focus our attention on humanism and on Platonism alone, we notice in them a great variety of original and traditional elements. And among the traditional elements, great importance must be attributed to the influence of ancient and medieval Latin authors. I do not wish to deny any of these points even by implication. I have merely tried in this paper, according to its chosen topic, to emphasize the fact which I believe cannot be denied, that the Italian Platonism of the Renaissance, just as Renaissance humanism, received some important impulses from the Byzantine tradition. It was fortunate that Byzantine culture at the moment of its tragic end was able to transmit to the modern Western world the heritage of its thought, as well as of its scholarship and of its books, along with the ideas and texts which it had received from ancient Greece and which it had preserved for the future through a period of nearly a thousand years.

FOUR

RENAISSANCE
CONCEPTS
OF
MAN

Introduction

If we think or hear of such a topic as "renaissance concepts of man," we are immediately reminded of a view of the Renaissance period that is widespread and has often been repeated: the Renaissance, according to this view, had a special interest in, and concern with, man and his problems. Very often, and in my view mistakenly, this notion is associated with the phenomenon called Renaissance humanism, and in stressing the difference which distinguishes the Renaissance from the period preceding it, it has been pointedly asserted that the thought of the Renaissance was man-centered, whereas medieval thought was God-centered. Many historians have praised the Renaissance for this so-called humanist tendency and have seen in it the first step in an intellectual development that was to lead toward the Enlightenment and toward modern secular thought. Other historians, more sympathetic to the Middle Ages and less enthusiastic about modern secular thought, have held the same factual view while reversing the value judgment, stating, as one of them put it, that the Renaissance was the Middle Ages minus God.[1]

Yet the view of the Renaissance which we have indicated is subject to certain difficulties and, hence, has often been questioned in recent years. On the one hand, it is quite clear that the emphasis which Renaissance thought placed on man, and the manner in which it conceived of his place in the world, was not entirely new and that similar views can be found in ancient and medieval writers, views which in some instances were demonstrably known to Renaissance thinkers and even cited or used by them.[2] On the other hand, Renaissance thought, when seen in its entire range, say, from 1350 to 1600, presents a very complex picture. Different schools and thinkers expressed a great variety of views, on problems related to the conception of man as on others, and it would be extremely difficult if not impossible to reduce all of them to a single common denominator.

In spite of these difficulties, I believe that there is at least a core of truth in the view that Renaissance thought was more "human" and more secular, although not necessarily less religious, than medieval thought and that it was more concerned with human problems—a tendency that has recently been branded as antiscientific by some historians of science. But when we try to answer the question of what the Renaissance concept of man really was, we face several grave difficulties. Not only do we have to consider a great variety of views on the same problem, but the problem itself is far too broad and complex to permit any simple answer. One of the secrets of the so-called scientific method, which applies not only to the disciplines usually called sciences, but also to such fields as philosophy and history that are not commonly known by that honorific designation, consists in asking very specific questions which may permit us to find specific answers. Now the concept of man is not such a specific problem. It involves a great variety of moral, political, and religious questions with which we can hardly deal in these essays. The problems of free will, fate, and predestination are in a broad sense human problems that are intimately connected with the concept of man, and these problems were widely discussed by the thinkers of the Renaissance and the Reformation. The theological doctrine of sin and salvation is, broadly speaking, a human question, and it was no less debated during the Renaissance than during the Middle Ages; or even more so, if we consider the Reformation of the sixteenth century as a part of the Renaissance period. Another distinctly human problem is the more or less optimistic or pessimistic view of life held by Renaissance writers, a problem that has been treated by several scholars. Whereas the older view tended to describe the Renaissance as an optimistic age, Charles Trinkaus has shown us how deep and widespread a pessimistic view of life was present even among the leading humanists of the period, and more recently Eugenio Garin has pointedly asserted that the Renaissance was a splendid but not a happy age.[3]

All these questions, and a number of others, are rather important and quite relevant to our topic, but they are far too broad and complex for a short discussion such as this. Instead, we shall focus attention on three specific problems related to this topic—the dignity of man, the immortality of the soul, and the unity of truth—and shall limit our discussion on the whole to the thought of a few specific thinkers whom I happen to know best, but whom I should like to consider sufficiently important and influential to justify their selection.

9.

The Dignity of Man

In discussing the Renaissance notion of man's dignity and his place in the universe, we shall treat mainly the views of Petrarch, Ficino, Pico, and Pomponazzi, four authors who together may be considered representative of the early Italian Renaissance, if not of the entire period or of all Europe and who have at least this much in common that they do assign an important place to man in their scheme of things.[1] These are by no means the only voices that have come down to us from the period. Many important thinkers seem to pay much less attention to this particular problem, and others, even among the Italians, would express quite different views on the matter. To the doctrines which we are going to discuss we may not only oppose those of Luther or Calvin, who insist on the depravity of man after Adam's fall, perhaps in conscious reaction against the humanist emphasis on his dignity, but also Montaigne who stresses man's weakness and the modest place he occupies in the universe, and who is yet, in many other respects, a typical representative of Renaissance humanism.[2] In other words, the glorification of man, which we are going to discuss, was not approved by all Renaissance thinkers, but only by some of them.

This glorification of man was by no means a new discovery of the Renaissance. The praise of man as inventor of the arts is common in Greek literature where the myth of Prometheus and the second chorus of Sophocles' *Antigone* may be cited as famous examples. The notion of man as a lesser world, a microcosm, is widespread in the popular thought of late antiquity, and the phrase that man is a great miracle which occurs in one of the so-called Hermetic treatises, was eagerly cited by Pico and other Renaissance thinkers.[3] In a way, classical Greek thought might be called man-centered. This is what Cicero meant when he said of Socrates that he brought philoso-

phy down from heaven to earth.[4] Man and his soul, his excellence and ultimate happiness occupy a central place in the philosophy of Plato and Aristotle. Plato actually placed the human soul in the middle between the
corporeal world and the transcendent world of pure forms,[5] and this notion
was to be adopted and further developed by the Neoplatonists and by many
medieval thinkers. The early Stoics treated the universe as a community of
gods and men, and this view, as well as their notions of natural law and the
solidarity of mankind, had a wide influence on later thought through Cicero
and the Roman jurists, the Neoplatonists, and St. Augustine.

  On the other hand, the superiority of man over other creatures is clearly
indicated in Genesis and in several other passages of the Old Testament,
whereas early Christian thought with its emphasis on the salvation of mankind and the incarnation of Christ gave at least implicit recognition to man's
dignity. This notion was further developed by some of the Church Fathers,
especially Lactantius and Augustine. In the medieval Christian tradition in
which all these ideas were repeated and developed, the dignity of man rested
primarily on his status as a creature made in the image of God and capable
of attaining salvation, and less on his worth as a natural being. This natural
worth was often recognized in terms suggested by ancient philosophy, but no
medieval thinker could avoid stressing the fact that man, on account of
Adam's fall, had lost much of his natural dignity. In many ways a pessimistic view of man and his state is typical of medieval thought. The treatise on
the contempt of the world by Lotharius (who was to become one of the most
powerful popes, Innocent III) is not only a good example of this outlook,
but also an influential one.[6] It seems significant that the humanists Facio and
Manetti wrote their treatises on the dignity and excellence of man as supplements or criticisms of Innocent III, drawing for their arguments not only on
classical sources such as Cicero, but also on the Church Fathers, especially
Lactantius.[7]

  In spite of these earlier precedents, we cannot escape the impression that
after the beginnings of Renaissance humanism, the emphasis on man and his
dignity becomes more persistent, more exclusive, and ultimately more systematic than it had ever been during the preceding centuries and even during
classical antiquity. Petrarch, who in his unsystematic way so often expresses
ideas which were to be elaborated by his successors, seems to have led the
way in this respect also. In his treatise *On His Own and Other People's Ignorance,* Petrarch stresses the point that our knowledge of nature and of the
animals, even if true, is useless unless we also know the nature of man, the

end for which we are born, whence we come and where we go.[8] And when he describes in a famous letter his climbing of Mont Ventoux, he tells us that, overwhelmed by the marvelous view, he took his copy of Augustine's *Confessions* out of his pocket, opened it at random, and came upon the following passage: "Men go to admire the heights of mountains, the great floods of the sea, the courses of rivers, the shores of the ocean, and the orbits of the stars, and neglect themselves." "I was stunned," Petrarch continues, "closed the book and was angry at myself since I was still admiring earthly things although I should have learned long ago from pagan philosophers that nothing is admirable but the soul in comparison with which, if it is great, nothing is great." Petrarch thus expressed his conviction that man and his soul are the truly important subjects of our thought, and in doing so—and this is significant—he quotes Augustine and Seneca.[9]

Later in the fourteenth century and during the fifteenth century, Renaissance scholars began to use the term "humanities" (*studia humanitatis*) for the disciplines they studied, taught, and liked. The term, borrowed from Cicero and other ancient writers, was taken up by Salutati and Bruni and came to signify, as we know from many sources, the fields of grammar, rhetoric, poetry, history, and moral philosophy.[10] The fact that the term "humanities" was applied to these subjects (and even for this there was some ancient precedent) expresses the claim that these studies are especially suitable for the education of a decent human being and, hence, are, or should be, of vital concern for man as such. By the use of this very term, the humanists expressed their basic and, as it were, professional concern for man and his dignity, and this aspiration becomes quite explicit in many of their writings. It appears as a passing notion in their orations, moral treatises, and dialogues, as we have seen in the case of Petrarch, and it even came to constitute the subject matter for some special treatises.

The earliest one, written by Bartolomeo Facio, treats the subject in a strongly religious and theological context, as has been noticed by most historians.[11] What they have failed to notice is the curious fact, indicated by one of Facio's biographers many years ago, that he was encouraged to write this treatise by a Benedictine monk of his acquaintance, Antonio da Barga, who not only sent Facio a letter, urging him to write a supplement to the treatise of Pope Innocent III but even attached to his letter an outline of the treatise, which Facio seems to have followed to a certain degree.[12] It would be easy to draw the amusing inference from this episode that the first humanist treatise on the dignity of man was really of monastic, and hence of medieval inspiration. However, it would be more correct to say that an Italian monk of the fifteenth century, who happened to be also a friend of Manetti and of other humanists and the author of treatises that we may call humanistic, was himself affected by the humanistic culture of his age and hence able to make direct and indirect contributions to it.[13]

More important and more substantial than Facio's treatise on the dignity of man is the treatise composed shortly afterwards by Giannozzo Manetti, another noted humanist famous for his philosophical and theological interests, his biblical translations, and his Hebrew studies whose work has not yet received sufficient scholarly attention.[14] Manetti never questions or challenges the theological doctrines of sin and salvation or of man as an image of God, but in his treatise on man's dignity, man is primarily praised for his reason, for his arts and skills, on account of his natural condition, and his secular knowledge.

When we enter the second half of the fifteenth century, the philosophical scene in Italy, and especially in Florence, came to be dominated increasingly by a new Platonic current which had its center in the so-called Florentine Academy and found expression in the writings of its founder Marsilio Ficino, his younger friend and associate, Giovanni Pico, and some other members of their circle. Unlike the earlier humanists, whose interests and concerns were largely literary and scholarly and whose philosophical ideas were on the whole limited to the field of moral philosophy and expressed in a loose and unsystematic fashion, Ficino and Pico, in spite of their wide knowledge and interests, were primarily professional philosophers and metaphysicians, well-grounded in the texts and doctrines, terminology and methodology of ancient and medieval philosophy. Hence, I am disinclined to treat Renaissance Platonism merely as a part or offshoot of Renaissance humanism, as many historians of philosophy have done, and prefer to assign to it a distinctive place within the framework of Renaissance thought.[15]

I do not wish to deny that Ficino and Pico were linked rather closely with earlier and contemporary humanism. These ties are strong, and they do not merely affect the scholarly methods and literary style of the two thinkers, but also their historical orientation and some of their central ideas and problems. In the treatment of the problem with which we are concerned in this essay, the relation of Ficino and Pico to the earlier humanists is quite clear: they share with their humanist predecessors and take over from them a profound concern with man and his dignity; but they develop this notion within a framework that was completely absent in the earlier humanists, that is, they assign to man a distinctive position within a well-developed metaphysical system of the universe, and they define and justify man's dignity in terms of his metaphysical position.

Ficino did not dedicate a special treatise to the subject of man and his dignity, as Manetti had done, but he discusses the problem rather prominently in his major philosophical work, the *Platonic Theology,* which contains a number of striking passages on the subject. In trying to illustrate the divinity of the human soul, Ficino describes at length man's skill in the arts and in government, as Manetti had done before him.[16] He also stresses the intermediary position of the human soul between the incorporeal and the corporeal worlds, and if I am not mistaken, he reconstructs the Neoplatonic hierarchy of being in such a way that the rational soul which stands for man comes to occupy the place in the center, below God and the angels and above qualities and bodies.[17] Moreover, Ficino insists on the universality of the human mind and sees in this its basic affinity with God. The soul tends to know all truth and to attain all goodness; it tries to become all things and is capable of living the life of all beings higher and lower. In this way the soul tries to become God, and this is its divinity.[18] It is, however, inferior to God, since God actually is all things, whereas the soul merely tends to become all things.[19] Thus centrality and universality are the chief grounds and aspects of man's excellence according to Ficino. The human soul is praised as the bond and juncture of the universe that contributes in a unique way to its unity.[20]

Two other ideas which occur in Ficino are worth mentioning because they were to be developed by later thinkers more fully than by him: man's end is to dominate all elements and all animals, and thus he is the natural lord and ruler of nature;[21] and man the astronomer, who can understand the motions of the celestial spheres and construct a model of them on a smaller scale, is virtually endowed with a mind similar to that of God who constructed the spheres themselves.[22]

When we pass to the doctrine of man in Pico della Mirandola, we see that he follows in several respects the doctrine of his older friend Ficino, but he modifies that doctrine in a number of significant points. Pico's treatment of the question is best known from his so-called Oration on the Dignity of Man. I say so-called, for the phrase "on the dignity of man" was not used by the author but was added only by later editors. As a matter of fact, this phrase suits only the first half of the work, whereas the other half deals with entirely different questions. The original title of the work is merely "Oration,'' and this title is perfectly sufficient since Pico wrote no other oration besides this one. The oration was composed in 1486 to serve as an introductory speech for a public disputation on his 900 theses that Pico planned to hold in Rome.[23] Pico wrote the speech at least in two versions, and the text of the earlier version has been recently discovered and published by Eugenio Garin.[24] This earlier version is shorter than the final one, and it contains a few striking phrases of its own but does not differ from the final version in its basic content. When a papal commission found that some of the 900 theses were heretical or subject to a heretical interpretation, Pope Innocent VIII condemned the theses and prohibited the disputation. The speech thus was never delivered, and it was never published during Pico's lifetime. However, Pico used some parts of it in a defense of his theses which he published in 1487,[25] and the original oration was printed shortly after his death in the collection of his works edited by his nephew.[26]

In beginning his oration, Pico takes the dignity of man as his point of departure. He starts with two quotations, one of which is the passage on man as a miracle found in the Hermetic *Asclepius* and quoted already by Ficino for the same purpose.[27] Asking what really constitutes the superiority of man over other beings, Pico rejects some traditional answers as insufficient, among them the view that man is the intermediary between stable eternity and fluid time and, as the Persians say, the bond of the world.[28] The last point evidently contains a critique of Ficino, and Pico's subsequent remarks show the reasons for this divergence. In order to explain man's position and peculiar character, Pico describes the moment of his creation. When the creation of the whole universe had been completed, the Creator decided to add a being capable of meditating on the reasons of the world, loving its beauty, and admiring its greatness. Thus He undertook the creation of man. All gifts had by then been distributed among the other creatures, Pico continues, with a clear allusion to the myth of Plato's *Protagoras*.[29] Hence, the Creator decided that the being for which nothing had been left as its peculiar property might in turn have a share of all the gifts that had first been assigned singly to the various other beings. Man, therefore, has no clearly determined essence or nature. He is neither celestial nor earthly, neither mortal nor immortal. On the contrary, he may become all of this through his own will. The Creator gave him the germs of every sort of life. Depending on whatever potentiality he develops, he may become a plant, an animal, a celestial being, an angel, or he may even be unified with God Himself.[30] Man therefore possesses all possibilities within himself. It is his task to overcome the lower forms of life and to elevate himself toward God.

The famous passage which we have just summarized requires some further comment. It has been argued quite often that Pico seems to attribute to man an unlimited freedom, and thus to deny, at least by implication, the Christian doctrines of grace and predestination. This view may easily be exaggerated, for Pico never denies these doctrines, and even in this passage we should not overlook a significant detail: the often quoted words about man's freedom are addressed by God to Adam upon his creation, that is, before his fall. Hence, we might stretch the point and insist that Pico describes man's dignity before the fall, and somehow leaves it undetermined to what extent this dignity has been affected by the fall and by original sin. Nothing in what Pico says excludes the view that man in his present state needs the help of divine grace in order to make the best choice among those that are open to him on account of his nature.

If we compare Pico's position on purely philosophical grounds with that of Ficino, it is evident that Pico follows Ficino in his insistence on man's universal nature and on his share in the gifts of all other beings. This conception is based on the ancient idea of man the microcosm, and it constitutes for Pico, as for Ficino, one of the basic reasons for man's privileged place in the universe. On the other hand, Pico differs from Ficino at the point where the latter assigns to man and his soul a central but fixed place in the universal hierarchy of things. For Pico, man has no determined nature and no fixed place in the hierarchy of beings, but he is somehow placed outside this hierarchy. This fact is closely connected with the greater emphasis Pico gives to man's freedom of choice between the different natures or ways of life all of which are equally possible for him. I should like to go even further and suggest that it was Pico's passionate concern with freedom (which is also apparent in several other aspects of his thought) which made the notion of a fixed though central position of man unacceptable to him and compelled him to place man outside the hierarchy. This is a rather bold view, and it may be considered as one of the first steps in dissolving the notion of the great chain of being that had dominated Western thought for so many centuries.[31]

Pico's position is noteworthy for one additional point. His insistence on man's freedom to choose his own nature among many potentialities does not mean that all choices are equally good or desirable. On the contrary, there is a clear order and rank among these possibilities, and it is man's task and duty to choose the highest form of life that is accessible to him. Man's dignity consists in his freedom of choice because the different possibilities open to him include the highest; his dignity is fully realized only when this highest possibility is chosen. Even if we disregard the theological background of Pico's thought and consider only his secular emphasis on man's unlimited freedom, he does not mean to suggest that human nature in any of its given forms, or human choice in any of its varieties is equally good or dignified. Pico rather thinks in terms of moral and intellectual alternatives. Man's excellence is realized only when he chooses the higher forms of moral and intellectual life that are open to him, and this excellence belongs to his given nature only in so far as this nature includes among its potentialities those higher forms of life.

One of the recent interpreters of Pico, who made a valuable contribution by exploring some of the medieval sources of Pico's thought, dismissed the Oration as a mere rhetorical exercise and believed that the doctrine of the dignity of man as it appears in the Oration is nothing but a piece of oratory and, hence, should not be taken too seriously in a philosophical account of Pico's thought.[32] I cannot agree with his view. First of all, the fact that an author uses the genre of the oration in presenting some of his ideas does not prove in itself that he fails to believe in the validity of these ideas. It is certainly true that an orator will adapt his words and thoughts to a given occasion. But the question whether a particular piece of oratory does or does not reflect the considered thought of its author must be examined in each case on the basis of available evidence, and the answer will vary according to the character of the author and the oration that are being examined. Pico was not the kind of rhetorician who would readily lend emphatic expression to ideas which he did not believe in. The very care he took in writing and revising his speech and the way in which he refers to it in his letters tend to prove, on the contrary, that he felt very strongly about the ideas contained in it.

Moreover, there is an even stronger argument against a merely rhetorical interpretation of the speech and in favor of its positive philosophical meaning. Several of the main ideas contained in the Oration are repeated by Pico in other works which cannot be dismissed as rhetorical. For example, the idea which dominates the second part of the Oration, that is, that the opposed views of different philosophical schools may be reconciled and that there is some truth in the teachings of all major philosophers that theologians, is repeated verbatim in the *Apologia*, the treatise with which Pico tried to defend his theses against the charges of the papal commission and which is otherwise quite doctrinal and even scholastic in its style and character.[33] And the doctrine of the dignity of man which occupies the center of attention in the first part of the speech is repeated, at least in some of its features, in one of Pico's main doctrinal works, the *Heptaplus*, a commentary on the first section of Genesis, which he wrote and published in 1489. In this work Pico begins his exposition by distinguishing three different worlds—the elementary, the celestial, and the invisible—which form a kind of ascending hierarchy of being and constitute together, as it were, the universe of things. After having discussed this hierarchy of three worlds, Pico introduces man as a fourth part of the world, thus indicating once more that man does not occupy a fixed place in the hierarchy of things, but, rather, a place of his own outside that hierarchy.[34] In discussing the relation between these different worlds, Pico says explicitly that man is the connection and juncture of the three other worlds and thus echoes to some extent Ficino's notion of man as a center of the universe and as the intermediary between the other parts of the world.[35] Pico goes on to say, and here he obviously refers to the Oration, that God after the creation of the world placed man as His image in the center of that world, just as a prince places his monument in the center of a newly built city, where it may be seen by all the people.[36] The question of what the dignity of man is based on and what his affinity with God consists in occurs again, and it is answered in terms which differ but slightly from those of the Oration. Emphasis is given to the fact that man combines and unites all things, not only through his thought, but also in reality (*re ipsa*). He shares this power with God alone, and the only difference is that God contains all things because He is the cause of all, and man combines all things because he is the center of all.[37] Pico then describes in detail how man contains all substances: his body corresponds to the animals, and so forth.[38] This enumeration is very similar to the text of the Oration, and Pico concludes it with the same quotation from the Hermetic *Asclepius*, which we encountered already in Ficino and in the Oration.[39] Thus, there is a close relationship between the passage in Pico's Oration from which we started and a passage in one of his later doctrinal works, and apart from minor differences mainly of emphasis, the relationship is close enough to prove that the passage in the Oration, in spite of its eloquence, must be taken to express Pico's considered opinion. It is one of the most famous and influential passages in Renaissance literature, and there is no reason whatsoever to minimize its significance as a representative document of Renaissance thought.

The last philosopher whom we shall consider in this essay, Pietro Pomponazzi, belongs to an entirely different intellectual tradition. He was trained at Padua and taught philosophy at that university and later at Bologna. He belongs to the professional tradition of scholastic Aristotelianism that had been identified with the European universities ever since their origin in the twelfth and thirteenth centuries.[40] The professional philosophers of this school were engaged in the detailed interpretation of the writings of Aristotle, basing themselves on Latin translations of the text and on earlier Greek, Arabic, and Latin commentaries and applying to the text a logical rather than a philological or historical method. Being interested in the subject matter of logic and physics, and to a lesser extent of ethics and metaphysics, these philosophers carried on the development of logic and of physical science during the later Middle Ages. For a long time they remained untouched by Renaissance humanism, which began as a literary, scholarly, and ethical movement and was from its start strongly opposed to the scholasticism of the Aristotelians. For the understanding of Renaissance thought, Pomponazzi is important because he shows that the Aristotelian tradition remained strong and vigorous in spite of the humanist attacks directed against it. At the same time it is significant to see that Pomponazzi, without ever abandoning the Aristotelian tradition, was affected in an indirect way by the new currents of humanism and Platonism. This latter fact becomes quite apparent when we focus our attention on his conception of man's dignity and his place in the universe.

I shall largely limit my discussion of Pomponazzi to his famous treatise on the immortality of the soul which was published in 1516 and immediately became the subject of a heated controversy among philosophers and theologians. Pomponazzi holds a "naturalistic" view of the human soul and does not believe that its immortality can be proven on rational grounds, as we shall see in the next chapter. Nevertheless, he endorses the traditional medieval and Neoplatonic doctrine that the human soul occupies a middle position in the universe, and he formulates this notion in terms that are quite reminiscent of Ficino and of Pico. "Man is not of simple but of multiple, not of a fixed, but of an ambiguous nature, and he is placed in the middle between mortal and immortal things. . . . Hence the ancients rightly placed him between eternal and temporal things, since he is neither purely eternal nor purely temporal, because he participates in both natures. Thus existing in the middle, he has the power to assume either nature."[41]

Man occupies an intermediary place between the pure intelligences of the angels and the irrational souls of the animals. Yet, whereas the Platonists had taught that the goal of human life is contemplation and that this goal is fully attained only in a future life, Pomponazzi formulates the ideal of a moral virtue which can be attained during the present life. In this manner the dignity of man is not merely maintained, but man's present earthly life is credited with an intrinsic significance that does not depend on any hopes or fears for the future. The peculiar excellence of man consists in his moral virtue, according to Pomponazzi, and this excellence can and should be attained by every person, whereas contemplation is attainable only for a few privileged persons.[42] This view of human life is the more remarkable since it is at variance with the position held by Aristotle in his *Nicomachean Ethics* and elsewhere. In concise statements that are reminiscent of Plato and the Stoics, rather than of Aristotle, and resemble Spinoza and Kant, Pomponazzi states that virtue is essentially its own reward, and vice, its own punishment and that a good deed done without the hope of an external reward is superior to one done with such a hope.[43]

The same notion that human virtue has its intrinsic value and that this constitutes the peculiar dignity of man, as compared with other beings, is forcefully expressed in a shorter "Question on Immortality" which Pomponazzi wrote in 1504 and which I discovered and edited some years ago. "To last for a long time does not imply perfection. . . . An oak lasts for a thousand years, but for that reason it still does not have the thousandth part of that perfection which belongs to man. It is rather more perfect to be a man for one year, than to be an oak for ten thousand years."[44]

I hope it has become apparent that the Renaissance thinkers whom we have mentioned and who represent at least three different intellectual and philosophical traditions were all very much concerned with the dignity of man and with his place in the universe. The humanistic movement which in its origin was moral, scholarly, and literary rather than philosophical in a technical sense provided the general and still vague ideas and aspirations as well as the ancient source materials. The Platonists and Aristotelians, who were professional philosophers and metaphysicians with speculative interests and training, took up these vague ideas, developed them into definite philosophical doctrines, and assigned to them an important place in their elaborate metaphysical systems.

These ideas are not only interesting in their own right, but they also exercised a wide influence on later thinkers. The notion that man rules the elements and all of nature, which we find in Ficino, has something in common with Francis Bacon's concept of man's dominion over nature that contains, as it were, the entire program of modern science and technology. Ficino's idea that man is endowed with a god-like mind because he can understand the heavenly spheres and construct them on a smaller scale has rightly been compared with Galileo's claim that man's knowledge of mathematics is different in quantity but not in kind from that of God Himself.[45] On the other hand, Pico's tendency to abandon the rigid hierarchy of being had its counterpart in Nicholas of Cusa and was to find its fuller development in the cosmology of Bruno and in the astronomy of Kepler and Galileo. In this way some of the ideas we have discussed are linked with the main currents of modern thought and exercised at least an indirect influence on later science and philosophy.

As I stated in the beginning, the notion of the dignity of man found prominent expression in several representative thinkers of the Renaissance period, and we have tried to discuss and understand some of the main forms of this expression, but the concept was not universally emphasized even during the Renaissance, but rather strongly opposed by some other thinkers, for example, by the reformers and by Montaigne. This fact should not cause us too much surprise. I think it would be somewhat naïve to assume that such an idea as that of the dignity of man should ever completely dominate the thought of a given period, let alone ever attain a final victory that would assure its permanent predominance over other competing ideas in the history of thought. The notion that man occupies an exalted place in the universe, and the opposite idea that he is a small and powerless creature at the mercy of far stronger divine, natural, or historical forces, are not only contrary to each other but also complementary. Both of them are too well grounded in obvious facts of human experience and, hence, supply more or less permanent themes for human thought and discourse at any time, in the Renaissance as well as in our own time. These ideas will always be debated, and whether one of them is emphasized at a given moment depends very much on the mood of the period or even of an individual thinker or writer. The notion of man's dignity may be easily exaggerated, and perhaps it was exaggerated in the Renaissance by the thinkers we have discussed. But in our time when the notion seems to be out of fashion, and opposite ideas tend to be exaggerated, there might be some good reason for emphasizing again the dignity of man in order to restore the balance.

Human thought, we might say with Hegel, always tends to move from one extreme to another before attaining a balanced synthesis. Yet, when we try to make sense out of the idea of human dignity, we should not settle for too cheap and easy a solution, as we might be tempted to do. Man's dignity is not merely something that is given him with his birth, according to Pico, but rather something he has to attain and to realize through his own effort. What is given is merely the ability to strive toward this end. We assert our dignity as human beings not simply by being what we happen to be but by choosing the best among our potentialities, by cultivating reason rather than blind feeling, and by identifying ourselves with tasks that are morally and intellectually worthwhile and that lead us beyond the narrow confines of our personal interests and ambitions.

10.

The Immortality of the Soul

Among the many problems and concepts that have occupied the thinkers of the past, and especially those of the Renaissance, the doctrine of immortality seems especially remote from the discussions and concerns of our time. In spite of a widespread talk about religion and a persistent concern with death and its significance, our outlook is very much confined to the problems of this world, and we seem to worry very little about what may happen to us or to the world after we are dead. Everything is measured by the present and its needs, and the present seems to live at the expense of the past and the future. People who have ambition eagerly seek a publicity that is quickly forgotten, and the quest for everlasting fame, once a powerful incentive for political or cultural achievement, is no longer felt or, at least, no longer admitted to be a living impulse for human endeavor.

The reasons for the recent disappearance of this once strong human concern would form an important and interesting subject of historical investigation but cannot detain us in this essay. I suspect that the quest for fame presupposes a firm belief in the lasting continuity of a tradition, political or religious, philosophical or cultural, of which we wish to be a part and that this belief has been undermined for many people in a variety of ways. Yet, the deep desire to extend our perspective and our aspirations beyond the short and narrow limits of our personal life has by no means disappeared, but has found expression in other forms of thought and belief that are subtler and less tangible than the compact theories of fame and immortality that were formulated in the past. I wonder whether the widespread curiosity now felt about distant places, times, and civilizations may not be due to an instinctive desire to extend the boundaries of our personal life, as it were, by a kind of vicarious participation. Perhaps this residual feeling may enable us to grasp the significance of those strong beliefs about the future that have sustained other times and cultures.

In many religions and civilizations, primitive or more advanced, the spirits of the dead are thought to continue to live and to demand the attention of their descendants, if not of strangers. The belief that our moral conduct in this life will be followed by rewards and punishments after death was until recently, and in a sense still is, an essential part of Christian doctrine, and had been held, long before the rise of Christianity, by Greek religious and philosophical teachers. Everlasting fame was an admired and frequently asserted goal of human efforts through classical antiquity and again in modern times. It is against this background, and not only from the perspective of our present indifference to eternity, that we must try to understand the speculations of Renaissance thinkers about the immortality of the soul.

As compared with the otherworldliness of the Middle Ages, the Renaissance has often been characterized as a "this-worldly" age, and not entirely without reason. For it is true that Renaissance writers pay much greater attention to the problems and experiences of the present life than their predecessors, and it is much easier for the modern reader to gain from their writings a concrete and almost visual impression of their daily thoughts and activities. Yet, the Renaissance was also an age in which the desire for everlasting fame was more vocal and widespread than at any time since classical antiquity, and Jacob Burckhardt has rightly given an important place to this cult of fame in his still suggestive and largely valid picture of the early Italian Renaissance.[1] As in many other instances, Renaissance humanists were prone to repeat what the ancients had said about the desirability of lasting fame, but they surely had a spontaneous desire to perpetuate their own work and reputation through fame. In a sense, the humanists knew that by their very cult of antiquity they were reviving or keeping alive the fame of the ancients whom they admired, and they must have hoped that through their own labors they would come to share in the fame of the ancients and that their students and readers and successors would do for their own fame what they themselves had done for that of the ancients. In dedicating their works to the princes and notables of their time, and in carrying out their commissions, the writers and artists of the Renaissance thought they were insuring the fame of their patrons, and it is quite evident that the patronage extended to the arts and to learning during the Renaissance was partly motivated by this hope for fame and that in some, though by no means in all instances, this hope has been fulfilled by the judgment of posterity.

The cult of fame was linked with the belief in the dignity of man and certainly with the pervasive individualism of the period, a phenomenon admirably described by Burckhardt and often misunderstood by his critics.[2] When we speak about Renaissance individualism, we do not mean the actual presence of great individuals who may be found at any period of history, or the metaphysical emphasis on individual objects as against universals, as we find it in nominalism, which applies to stones no less than to human beings and, hence, is as far removed from "humanism" as is the so-called existentialism of Thomas Aquinas from that of Kierkegaard and his successors. We rather mean the importance attached to the personal experiences, thoughts, and opinions of an individual person, and the eager or, if you wish, uninhibited expression given to them in the literature and art of the period. Behind the endless display of gossip and invective, of description and subtle reflection there is the firm belief that the personal experience of the individual writer is worth recording for the future, preserving his fame and, as it were, prolonging his life. I cannot help feeling that the widespread and prominent concern of Renaissance thinkers with the immortality of the soul was on the metaphysical level another expression of the same kind of individualism. For in his immortal soul, the individual person continues to live more effectively than in his fame and to extend his experience into eternity.

The concern for immortality and the concern for fame are effectively combined in Dante's great poem which in this way proves to be a creation, not of the high Middle Ages, but of the period of transition from the Middle Ages to the Renaissance. Because the immortality of the soul was felt to be a metaphysical projection of that individual life and experience which was the center of attention for Renaissance writers and scholars, we can understand why this doctrine, though often expressed in other times and contexts, attained in the Renaissance a greater philosophical prominence than it had at any earlier or later period and why the discussion of this problem became one of the most important and characteristic themes of Renaissance philosophy.[3]

There is also a conscious link between the immortality of the soul and the dignity of man. More than once Ficino stresses the fact that the immortality of the soul is an essential part of its dignity and divinity, and he argues suggestively that without the immortality of his soul man would be inferior to the animals.[4] In the earliest humanist treatise on the dignity of man, that of Bartolomeo Facio, the immortality of the soul is even presented as the chief argument for man's excellence.[5] But unlike the dignity of man and the other notions which we have just discussed, the immortality of the soul became a prominent topic of philosophical discussion during the fifteenth and sixteenth centuries.

As in many other instances, the Renaissance discussion of immortality depended in many ways on ancient and medieval sources, and the novel and distinctive traits of that discussion must be sought in matters of detail and of emphasis. In order to understand the issues, it is necessary not merely to enumerate previous doctrines that are roughly relevant to the problem under discussion, but also to pay attention to some precise distinctions.

In Greek popular and religious thought, as expressed by Homer, there was something called the soul which survived as a shadow after the death of the body, but it did not possess a life or substance that would give it an immortality comparable to that of the gods.[6] In a later phase of Greek religion that is associated with the name of Orpheus, the soul was capable of religious and moral purification and was subject to rewards and punishments after death.

Among the early philosophers the soul was mainly conceived as the animating principle of the body. It was Plato who in a sense combined the religious and philosophical notions of the soul, conceiving it both as the animating principle of the body and as a moral and metaphysical agent capable of more or less perfect moral status. In his myths which have been connected with Orphic sources, Plato describes the rewards and punishments of the soul after death and also accepts the transmigration of the soul into other human and animal bodies as taught by the Pythagoreans. In the doctrinal sections of his dialogues, and especially in the *Phaedo*, Plato asserts and tries to demonstrate the immortality of the soul. He conceives this immortality as the natural attribute of an incorporeal substance that extends into the past as well as into the future. Among his chief arguments appears that from affinity. The soul is capable of knowing the pure intelligible forms or ideas; hence, it must be incorporeal and eternal like them.[7]

This Platonic doctrine of immortality was preserved and further developed by Plato's pupils and followers, and especially by the Neoplatonists. For them, not only the natural immortality of the soul as an incorporeal substance is an accepted doctrine confirmed by further arguments, but also the mythical notions of the rewards, punishments, and transmigration of the soul assume a literal significance and are made an integral part of the metaphysical system.[8] This position is not shared by the other leading schools of later Greek philosophy. Aristotle in his early writings seems to have followed Plato, but in his extant works his attitude towards immortality is, at least, ambiguous. He nowhere asserts that the soul is immortal, and whereas he does say that the intellect is incorruptible, he does not state explicitly that this incorruptible intellect is a part of the individual human soul; and thus he left room for a wide area of debate among his followers and interpreters.[9] Some of his most important ancient commentators, such as Alexander of Aphrodisias, explicitly placed the active intellect outside the individual human soul and thus tended to consider the latter as mortal. The Stoics did not consistently uphold individual immortality. They either restricted it to the sages or denied it altogether, and the doctrine of recurrent conflagrations would limit even the immortality of the sages to the present world period. Finally the Epicureans denied immortality altogether and had the soul perish together with its body, aside from considering the soul as a corporeal substance, a doctrine also held by the Stoics.

Whereas the history of the doctrine of immortality in classical antiquity is pretty clear, its vicissitudes within the religious traditions of Judaism and Christianity are far less easily described. There has been a good deal of controversy on the matter, and I must say that my own view differs from that of many other scholars and may be shocking to some. It is clear that some notions of a future life appear in the Old Testament and that the New Testament speaks very explicitly about the kingdom of God, eternal life, and resurrection. It is also true that body and soul are repeatedly distinguished in the New Testament and that at least one passage speaks of the future life of the soul.[10] However, the writers of the Bible were no professional philosophers and had a very slight, if any, acquaintance with Greek philosophy and its terminology. There is an occasional, but not a consistent distinction between body and soul and no hard and fast statement that the soul (or even

God) is incorporeal, or that the soul is immortal, let alone by nature. The majority of recent theologians have been led to admit that there is no scriptural basis for the natural immortality of the soul,[11] and those who refused to go that far have been forced to rely on implications or on later interpretations or on the dubious confusion of immortality with resurrection or eternal life.

The Christian doctrine of immortality is not found in Scripture, but in the work of the early apologists and Church Fathers, from Justinus Martyr to St. Augustine. These writers were familiar with Greek philosophy, as the biblical authors were not, and for them it was as vital a task to reconcile Christian doctrine with Greek philosophy as it is for modern theologians to reconcile it with modern science. The Christian notion of the immortality of the soul, as it was finally formulated by St. Augustine, is clearly derived from that of Plato and the Neoplatonists. The soul is incorporeal and by nature immortal, and one of the chief arguments of its immortality is again its affinity with God and the eternal ideas inherent in Him which the soul is able to know.[12] Of the Neoplatonic doctrine of immortality, Augustine merely rejected what was incompatible with Christian doctrine: transmigration and preexistence. Thus modified, the concept of immortality without preexistence lost some of its consistency, and the argument from affinity, some of its force, but it became a part of standard medieval doctrine, more or less taken for granted by everybody, and especially by the followers of Augustine, but it was rarely challenged or discussed in detail.

When Aristotle instead of Plato became the chief philosophical authority in the thirteenth century, the doctrine of the immortality of the soul did not gain in prominence. Thomas Aquinas duly defends the incorruptibility and future beatitude of the rational soul, but he seems to avoid the term "immortality," and he does not attach special importance to the subject.[13] Duns Scotus explicitly states that the traditional arguments for the immortality of the soul are weak and inconclusive and adds that the belief in resurrection and eternal life should be based on faith alone.[14] Whether also immortality is based on faith he does not state with equal clarity, and I tend to doubt he held this view since in his time the immortality of the soul had not yet been declared to be an article of faith. Instead the Council of Vienne declared the Aristotelian definition of the soul as form of the body to be an article of faith, a striking instance of the impact which a hundred years of Aristotelian speculation at Paris and elsewhere were to have even on theology and church dogma. The scriptural grounds for this dogma might be even harder to find than for immortality, but this is no serious objection when tradition and church authority are given equal power with Scripture in establishing official doctrine.

A much more serious threat to the doctrine of immortality than the indifference of Aquinas or the fideism of Scotus was the doctrine of the unity of the intellect taught by Averroes and his Latin followers. In interpreting the third book of Aristotle's *De anima*, Averroes went beyond Alexander and maintained that both the active and the passive intellect are but one for all men and exist outside the individual human souls, and that the latter merely participate momentarily through their thinking faculties in this universal intellect whenever they perform an act of knowledge.[15] In thus asserting the immortality of the universal intellect, Averroes removed at the same time the basis for the immortality of the individual human souls which are outside this intellect and merely have a temporary connection with it. Averroes' authority as a commentator on Aristotle was great, and his doctrine of the unity of the intellect exerted a great influence on all Aristotelian philosophers of the Middle Ages and the Renaissance. While the so-called Averroists accepted the doctrine on purely philosophical grounds and thought it to be in accordance with Aristotle, all other Aristotelians who did not accept it still gave it careful consideration, including Thomas Aquinas, who wrote a special treatise on the subject in which (and this is characteristic) the issue of immortality is not prominently discussed.[16]

If we take all these facts into consideration, we arrive at the curious and unexpected conclusion that the doctrine of immortality did not play a major role in medieval thought, especially not during the thirteenth and fourteenth centuries when the teachings of Aristotle and his commentators tended to prevail. The central importance which the doctrine came to assume during the Renaissance thus appears in a new perspective, that is, as a conscious reaction against later medieval thought, a reaction that would quite properly claim to be a fight in the name of Plato (and of Augustine) against Aristotle or, at least, against his commentators. The link between immortality and some other favorite notions of Renaissance thought might actually have been a factor in the growing vogue and appeal of Plato that we may observe from the fourteenth to the sixteenth centuries.

It has often been thought that the prominence of immortality in the Renaissance is due to the activity of the Florentine Academy and of its leader Marsilio Ficino. Yet, while it is true that Ficino was responsible for the full philosophical development of the doctrine and for much of its subsequent diffusion, we have learned more recently that the concern for immortality, just as the interest in Plato, predated the rise of Florentine Platonism. Attention has been called to a sizable number of special treatises on the immortality of the soul written by many more- or less-known humanists and theologians of the fifteenth century.[17] They vary greatly in length and diffusion and also in their sources, the orientation of their thought, and the quality of their reasoning. These treatises do not represent a unified group, and their authors do not form a school. While it is still too early to assess the contribution of these treatises, some of which have not yet been analyzed or even edited, their very existence and number prove the fact that the problem was of considerable interest at the time, as it had not been during the preceding period. Among the authors we find eclectic humanists like Pier Candido Decembrio, who relies heavily on a twelfth-century treatise attributed to St. Augustine, or Agostino Dati; humanist theologians like Antonio degli Agli, who in his treatise does not yet betray the influence of Ficino to whose circle he later belonged; and Franciscan and Dominican friars such as John of Ferrara, Philippus de Barberiis, and above all, Jacopo Camfora, who wrote a treatise in the vernacular that had a considerable diffusion in both manuscripts and printed editions.

This literature is significant because it indicates a background and a climate of opinion that was receptive for a detailed discussion of the immortality of the soul such as we encounter it in the work of Marsilio Ficino. His major philosophical work, which consists of eighteen books and is entitled *Theologia Platonica de immortalitate animorum,* deals mainly with the problem of immortality and might be described as a *Summa* on the immortality of the soul.[18] Whereas the first four books deal with the hierarchy of being, the attributes of God, and the distribution of the souls in the universe, thus providing a general metaphysical background for the discussion, the remainder of the work consists technically of a series of arguments for immortality, although there are many digressions, and many arguments serve as an occasion, and perhaps as a pretext, for discussing other philosophical problems that are intrinsically important apart from their close or remote connection with immortality. While drawing freely on the arguments formulated by Plato, Plotinus, Augustine, and other thinkers, Ficino adds many of his own and also revises and recombines the thoughts derived from his predecessors. While it is true that in his presentation of the doctrine he bases himself on a long and venerable tradition and that in dedicating a special treatise to the problem he has the precedent of some of his favorite predecessors, it is also worth noticing that Ficino's *Platonic Theology* greatly exceeds the immortality treatises of Plato, Plotinus, Augustine, or other writers, both in its bulk and in the relative importance it has within the framework of his own work and thought.

Ficino became in a sense the philosopher of immortality, and it is legitimate to ask not only what he had to say about the subject, but also why it came to occupy such a place in his doctrine. We have indicated as one factor that the problem was of wide interest to other writers and thinkers of the fifteenth century. Other factors must be considered that are connected with Ficino's own thought and orientation. I do not think that Ficino focused from the very beginning on the problem of immortality, if we may judge his development from his preserved early writings. His prevalent interest in the problem seems to begin with the *Platonic Theology,* a work which he first composed between 1469 and 1474 and published in 1482. His intent may have been in part polemical. He was dissatisfied with the tendency of contemporary Aristotelians to separate philosophy and theology, and he considered it his task to establish a basic harmony between the two, that is, between Platonism and Christianity. He was convinced that the Averroist doctrine of the unity of the intellect undermined the immortality of the soul and thus the whole of Christian theology, since he thought, though perhaps wrongly, as many theologians before and after him, that the immortality of the soul was a pillar of Christian theological doctrine. Important for this polemical purpose of the work is the fifteenth book, which consists entirely of a series of arguments against the unity of the intellect. It is the most detailed refutation of Averroism after that of Aquinas, and a close comparison between them might lead to interesting conclusions. However, Ficino's critique was concerned primarily, and even exclusively, with the defense of immortality, as that of Thomas had not been.

Aside from this negative consideration, there are also positive elements in Ficino's thought that may explain his prevalent concern with immortality. As some of his humanist predecessors, he clearly links immortality with the divinity of the soul and of man. Even more crucial, in my opinion, is another factor. Ficino's entire analysis of man, of his life and ultimate purpose, is based on the view that the true aim of man, and especially of the philosopher, is the ascent through contemplation toward the direct vision of God. The contemplative life is for Ficino a matter of direct spiritual experience to which he constantly points and which he actually uses as evidence for the existence of God and the divine ideas, the incorporeality and divinity of the soul, and for the claim that the human soul was actually created with the task of knowing and attaining God through contemplation. Like some of his Neoplatonic and mystical predecessors, Ficino even hints that some privileged thinkers, perhaps even himself, were able to attain a direct vision of God during their earthly life, although but for a short moment.[19] However, this is not enough. If the human soul was created with the task of attaining God and has an inborn natural appetite for God, we must postulate, unless this appetite were thought to be vain, that a large number of human beings will attain this goal in a permanent fashion. Hence, we must posit the immortality of the soul and a future life in which it will forever attain its goal, provided it has duly prepared itself for it during the present life through moral conduct, and above all, through contemplation.[20]

This line of argument, which appears in a number of different versions, constitutes a recurrent theme throughout the *Platonic Theology* and is occasionally repeated in other works of Ficino. It is so closely linked with the central motive of Ficino's philosophy that I am inclined to consider it as the main argument that in his own mind was not only the most persuasive one, but the one that actually prompted him to undertake his great effort to prove immortality. The argument is not entirely original, and some of its versions may be easily traced to medieval sources or to St. Augustine, but the peculiar formulation given to it by Ficino seems to be his own, as is its predominant function and the attempt to link it with some of his other basic ideas.

Aside from this argument, which we might call the argument from the natural appetite of the soul, the most important argument is that from affinity, that is, the notion that the soul is able to attain direct knowledge of incorporeal entities such as God and the ideas and must hence be itself incorporeal, incorruptible, immortal, as are its objects. This argument occurs in one of its versions already in Plato, and it has been repeated throughout the Platonic and medieval tradition. It is, of course, hard to reconcile with the position of many Aristotelians who deny that the soul during the present life can know anything except sense objects. Moreover, it proves too much since it applies to preexistence as well as to future immortality, once we assume a direct present knowledge of incorporeal objects and assign to it more than an a priori meaning. Yet, Ficino considered the argument valid and made an effort to elaborate it with great detail. He could not accept preexistence any more than St. Augustine had done, but he did not attempt to demonstrate the creation of the soul as he tried to prove immortality. Rather, he seems to have considered it as an article of faith, confirmed, as it were, by one of the interpretations that may be given to Plato's *Timaeus*.

Ficino's massive work established a firm connection between the doctrine of immortality and Renaissance Platonism and also served as an arsenal of arguments for those who were interested in defending immortality on philosophical or theological grounds. The traces of its influence may be found throughout the sixteenth century and afterwards. Even in the controversy aroused by Pomponazzi to which we shall turn immediately, it is quite evident that the position identified and criticized by Pomponazzi as that of Plato is the one represented by Ficino and his *Platonic Theology*, with which Pomponazzi was clearly acquainted. On the other hand, some of Pomponazzi's opponents clearly draw on Ficino's arguments in trying to defend immortality against Pomponazzi. This is especially apparent in Agostino Nifo, as was recognized by Pomponazzi and other contemporaries,[21] and in the Augustinian hermit Ambrogio Fiandino, whose Platonic orientation and dependence on Ficino appears in a number of his other writings.[22] Historians of Averroism and of Paduan Aristotelianism are too much inclined to identify the opponents of that school in the fifteenth and sixteenth centuries with Thomism or traditional theology and fail to see or to appreciate the fact that the resistance to Averroism drew fresh strength from the humanist dislike of Aristotle, and from the Platonist critique of Averroism. It is significant that Pico della Mirandola, in his attempt to reconcile the views of different thinkers and traditions, intended to prove that the unity of the intellect was compatible with the immortality of the soul, a position that Ficino would have rejected; but we do not know the arguments with which Pico planned to defend this position.[23]

The wide impact of the Platonism of the Florentine Academy on Renaissance theology appears in the writings of many sixteenth-century theologians and may even be seen in the decree by which the Lateran Council of 1513 condemned the unity of the intellect and formulated the immortality of the soul as a dogma of the Church.[24] The fact that the decree was opposed by Cajetan and that Giles of Viterbo played a prominent role at the Council tend to confirm the conclusion that this decree is as much the echo of Renaissance Platonism as the decree of Vienne about the soul as form of the body had been the echo of thirteenth-century Aristotelianism. The Lateran decree also confirms the suspicion that the immortality of the soul had to be officially promulgated as a church dogma at that late date because it was considered indispensable for other theological doctrines but had no clear or explicit support in Scripture or other valid theological authorities.

In a strict sense, the immortality of the soul as a Catholic dogma owes its authority and its status as an article of faith to the Lateran decree, which is still most commonly cited by Catholic authors when they discuss the problem. When it is now so widely believed that all of our convictions, especially in ethics and metaphysics, that are not derived from modern science stem from the religious traditions of Judaism and Christianity, we may point in reply not only to the recurrent influence of Greek thought on secular philosophy and literature, but also to the numerous instances, of which the Lateran decree is but one, in which ideas first derived from Greek philosophy were actually absorbed and inextricably assimilated into the very heart of Christian, and to a lesser extent of Jewish doctrine.

A few years after the publication of the Lateran decree, the problem of immortality became again the center of philosophical and theological attention. In 1516 Pietro Pomponazzi, the Aristotelian philosopher trained at Padua and teaching at Bologna published his treatise on the immortality of the soul, in which he argues at great length that immortality cannot be demonstrated on purely natural or Aristotelian grounds, but must be accepted as an article of faith. The treatise immediately aroused violent opposition, and although Pomponazzi's opponents did not succeed in having his work officially condemned, an entire sequence of treatises was published against him, both by theologians and philosophers, including the later Cardinal Gasparo Contarini, the Augustinian hermit Ambrogio Fiandino, the Dominican Bartolomeo Spina, and the fellow Aristotelian Agostino Nifo. Pomponazzi tried to answer some of his opponents with two other works that are much longer than his original treatise—the *Apologia* and the *Defensorium*—but the controversy continued for many years, even after his death, and its repercussions may be seen as late as the eighteenth century and, if you wish, in the partisan views of many modern historians.[25]

The statement often repeated in textbooks and other popular accounts that Pomponazzi completely denied the immortality of the soul is obviously incorrect. He merely denied that it can be demonstrated on rational or Aristotelian grounds, and he even asserted that the reasons against immortality were stronger than the reasons for it but insisted that it was true as an article of faith.[26] This is what he persistently and explicitly stated, and the claim of some historians that he was not serious about it, but really meant to deny immortality altogether is merely an inference based on no textual or factual evidence. The question whether Pomponazzi was sincere in thus separating, or even opposing, reason and faith, philosophy and theology, is part of a much broader problem with which I deal in my next essay. On the other hand, it has been claimed that Duns Scotus and other medieval thinkers had argued that the proofs proposed for the immortality of the soul are not valid and that hence Pomponazzi was by no means original. The answer is that Duns Scotus was far less explicit in discussing these proofs or in asserting that immortality was an article of faith and that in his time immortality had not yet been declared to be an article of faith. Moreover, Duns Scotus' remarks did not arouse much public controversy whereas Pomponazzi's did, partly on account of the Lateran decree, but also because of the much wider interest and stake Renaissance thinkers had in the problem and of the much more explicit challenge offered to it by Pomponazzi.

We cannot here go into the details of the controversy, which has received much more detailed attention recently than in the past. I merely wish to emphasize that Pomponazzi explicitly sets his own opinions against three others which he attributes to Averroes, Plato, and Thomas Aquinas, respectively.[27] This presentation of the problem means that Pomponazzi is not merely setting up his own view against those of Averroes and St. Thomas, whom he recognizes as prominent authorities within his own Aristotelian tradition, but he also meant to deal with the Platonic position as recently restated by Marsilio Ficino whom he knows and respects. Considering the central place of immortality in Ficino's thought and the wide influence his work had exercised in this as in many other respects, we should not be surprised to see Pomponazzi offer an attack or a counterattack against the Platonic doctrine of immortality; and the fact that he also criticizes the Thomist and Averroist position might mean that he considers them adequate interpretations of the Aristotelian view, as against that of the Platonists. The point is of some importance because Gilson, in his recent treatment of the controversy, which is extremely subtle and fair as far as Pomponazzi is considered, interprets Pomponazzi's view exclusively against the background of Thomism and Averroism and completely ignores the Platonist position, although it had played such a prominent role in the decades preceding Pomponazzi's treatise, is explicitly discussed by Pomponazzi, and was explicitly used and restated by some, at least, of his opponents.

Pomponazzi's arguments against immortality and against the specific proofs offered in its support are numerous and complex. However, I am inclined to think that the central argument, which is often repeated in slightly different form, is the one based on the relationship of the soul to the body. The statement that the soul during the present life depends on the body, especially for its knowing activity, must be clarified by an important distinction. The statement may mean that the soul needs the body for its subject, that is, that the soul, and even the intellect, has a material substratum and may be called material in this sense. The statement may also mean that the soul needs the body for its object, that is, that it cannot attain any knowledge except through data supplied by the body through sense perception and imagination. While denying the assertion in the former sense, Pomponazzi keeps insisting on the validity of the second meaning. The result is that we have no knowledge whatsoever that is not based on bodily objects, and in this way the Platonist claim of pure intelligible knowledge during the present life is rejected.[28] It is this claim on which the argument from affinity and also the argument from natural appetite rested, as well as the constant appeal to contemplative experience.

In the claim that all human knowledge rests on sense objects, Pomponazzi goes beyond the position of Aristotle, but we still may say that his basic argument against the proofs for immortality reflects the Aristotelian position, interpreted in an empiricist or naturalist sense, as against the basic Platonist position represented by Ficino. This confrontation between Pomponazzi's Aristotelianism and Ficino's Platonism as expressed in their discussion of immortality is very instructive, and it also throws much light on the subsequent controversy, in addition to the fact that Pomponazzi, within the Aristotelian tradition, tends to criticize the interpretations offered by Averroes and by Thomas.

It might be argued that Pomponazzi's attempt to refute immortality, at least on purely natural and philosophical grounds, would show an indifference to immortality on his part and thus throw doubt on our initial claim that the problem of immortality occupied a central position in Renaissance thought. I do not think that this argument is valid. First of all, the strong and widespread reaction to Pomponazzi's treatise is sufficient to show that the problem remained at the center of philosophical and theological attention during the first half of the sixteenth century. Second, the fact that Pomponazzi devoted three of his chief works, not to mention an early question, to the problem of immortality shows that he is seriously concerned with it, and the fact that he arrives at the conclusion that it cannot be demonstrated merely indicates the great honesty of his thought, which appears also in his other writings. Finally, and this seems to me most important, Pomponazzi does not reject immortality altogether, even within the realm of philosophy, but holds on to a limited concept of immortality, while admitting that the more comprehensive traditional concept is philosophically untenable. In beginning his treatise, he asserts in a manner reminiscent of the Platonists that man occupies an intermediary position between mortal and immortal things, and shares through the faculties of his soul both in mortality and immortality.[29] In the course of his work, where he formulates his own position as distinct from that of Plato, Averroes, and Thomas, he states that man is absolutely speaking (*simpliciter*) mortal, but relatively speaking (*secundum quid*) immortal, and in defending this view he states that the human intellect, though mortal, participates in immortality.[30] In other words, even within purely natural considerations, Pomponazzi expresses his basic concern for eternity by admitting a kind of residual immortality, one that does not depend on an infinite extension in time, but is fully realized in the actual experience of the present moment.

Thus the Renaissance left more than one heritage to later thought, on immortality as well as on many other issues. Ficino's concept of immortality as a postulate foreshadows Kant's treatment of the problem in his moral philosophy, although Kant would agree with Pomponazzi that the traditional proofs cannot be accepted as theoretically valid. On the other hand, Pomponazzi's residual immortality as a participation of the present in the eternal anticipates Spinoza and, perhaps, Hegel.

In recent thought the problem of immortality has been much neglected under the impact of positivism. Philosophers have tended to treat it as a theological problem that is of no concern to them, completely forgetting the philosophical origin of the theory. No attempt to revive the doctrine of immortality on the basis of linguistic analysis has yet come to my attention, although I should not be surprised if this were to be done. Theologians, on the other hand, have been so eager to come to terms with modern science that some of them have been quite ready to sacrifice that part of their heritage that is derived from Greek philosophy, even if that meant to undo the work of the apologists and Church Fathers to an extent that goes far beyond the intentions or practice of the sixteenth-century reformers.

I am not sure whether we can revive the metaphysical doctrine of individual immortality, and I do not feel committed to such an enterprise. Yet, I strongly believe that our individual life, every part and every moment of it, belongs to the universe of nature and of history and is, as such, eternal. Our life is immortal insofar as in the comprehensive reality of the universe or, if you wish, of God, everything that once was or will be is eternally present. I find this view not only necessary as a comfort in the face of constant change and destruction, but also as an indispensable counterpart of death. Some residual notion of immortality seems to correspond to a basic and ineradicable need and desire of human nature and to be irrefutable by facts or reasons. I should like to think that the teachings of Renaissance and other thinkers concerning the immortality of the soul, though expressed in crude and often untenable forms, may be interpreted as respectable attempts to deal with one of the permanent problems of human life and thought. The problem is still with us, and we may hope that it may yet lead to new answers that are more in accordance with our knowledge and our sensibilities than those transmitted to us by the thinkers of the past, especially those of the fifteenth and sixteenth centuries.

11.

The Unity of Truth

Unlike the dignity of man and the immortality of the soul, the unity of truth has been discussed by recent thinkers no less than by those of the Renaissance or other periods of the past. Naturally, the terms of this discussion have varied at different times and places. The conflict or harmony between religion and the sciences has been a problem for many thoughtful writers for a long time, and the most thoughtful of them have tried to reconcile their religious beliefs not only with the findings of the natural sciences, but also with historical scholarship, with philosophical reasoning, and with all of secular learning. The increasing acquaintance of Western scholars with other cultures, and especially with the old civilizations of Asia, has led to a demand for reconciling the traditions and the thought of East and West.

In the last few years we have heard a good deal about the two cultures, the sciences and the humanities, and the need for harmonizing them, and it would not be difficult to show that there are, in fact, more than two cultures that make a claim on our time and attention, on our curiosity and intellectual allegiance. The unity of science has been proclaimed as an immediate goal by a group of influential philosophers, and in the current chaos of philosophical opinion where different schools seem to ignore rather than to refute each other, at least one lonely voice has advocated their reunion.[1] Our time, no less and perhaps even more than other times, has been puzzled by the actual diversity and competing claims of different philosophical positions, cultural orientations, and intellectual or professional traditions. The desire to attain a kind of harmony or synthesis seems natural enough, and the attempts to satisfy this desire are numerous, but they vary in scope and persuasiveness; and in their very effort to achieve a unity, they often produce new divisions.

These attempts have always taken a number of typical forms. One way out of the confusion is always to assert one's own position in a dogmatic fashion and to impose it on others by propaganda or force, if not by strength of argument, while rejecting all other alternatives as false or irrelevant. Another attempt is the position known as skepticism in ancient, and as relativism in modern times. This position treats all philosophical and other opinions as erroneous, and leads us to a state of resignation in which we quietly accept the fact that we cannot know anything for certain and that all the claims made upon our intellectual assent are basically unfounded. This relativism may be given a slightly positive turn, and it becomes a kind of perspectivism that admits all different views, not as simply false, but as partly true. Hegel made the ambitious attempt to construct a system in which each position, however conflicting with others, is assigned its place as a particular moment of truth.

If we look at the confusing multiplicity of opinions and insights, of cultures, and traditions, we are impelled to admit that the desire to transform this multiplicity into unity, the conflict into harmony or synthesis, is as natural and inevitable as it is difficult or impossible to achieve. The unity of truth is in my view a regulative idea in the Kantian sense. It imposes on us the task of bringing together into a single system the scattered and apparently irreconcilable insights we derive from different sources, but this task is never ending not only because the elements of knowledge now given to us cannot be reconciled, but because the quest and discovery of new insights will always continue as long as there will be human beings.

The problem of the unity of truth had a comparable, though not identical, significance for the Renaissance as it has had for modern times. In the history of philosophical thought, of science and learning, the Renaissance was an age of fermentation rather than of synthesis. It inherited from the Middle Ages the problem of reconciling philosophy, and especially Aristotelian philosophy, with Christian theology. With the revived interest in ancient literature and thought, Renaissance thinkers and scholars again were confronted with the problem that the Church Fathers had faced: how the substance of classical literature and of ancient philosophies other than Aristotelian could be absorbed and amalgamated, although this problem assumed quite different forms and dimensions from those of late antiquity. The thought of the fifteenth and sixteenth centuries is full of varied attempts to restate specific ancient or medieval positions or to arrive at new combinations or original solutions. The variety of new sources and of old and new opinions and positions brought many thinkers face to face with the question of how this diversity of purported truths could be brought to a unity.

In facing this task Renaissance thinkers were able to draw on a variety of ancient and medieval precedents, which they tended to adapt to their own problems and ideas. Late ancient thought, confronted with the conflicting claims and results of different schools and traditions, offered to the attentive reader several fully developed forms of skepticism, both the Academic skepticism known from the writings of Cicero and the Pyrrhonian skepticism preserved by Sextus Empiricus.[2] Cicero and other writers presented the example of that eclecticism that had prevailed among the Middle Stoics and the Middle Platonists. Finally, the writings of the Neoplatonists and, in a sense, also those of Aristotle provided the model for a philosophical synthesis that tried to comprehend all that was valid in the thought of previous thinkers while rejecting their errors.

Medieval thought, on the other hand, provided the Renaissance with a large arsenal of arguments, formulated in terms of many different issues, for the discussion of the relationship between faith and reason, philosophy and theology, as well as with a few general attempts to define this relationship: the harmony between faith and reason or the confirmation of faith by reason, as proposed by Aquinas; the gradual withdrawal of reason from the area of faith and the tendency to base theological doctrine on faith and authority alone, which we may notice in the schools of Duns Scotus and William of Ockham; and finally the coexistence of faith and reason that grants to faith a superior validity, but not the right to interfere in the domain of reason, a position known under the crude label, "double truth theory," and usually associated with Latin Averroism but actually found in the work of many thinkers who cannot be considered followers of Averroes in any precisely definable sense. We shall try to describe as best we can how some of the Renaissance thinkers dealt with the same insistent and elusive problem, and what use, if any, they made of the various solutions placed at their disposal by their ancient and medieval predecessors.

In discussing the views of some Renaissance thinkers on this subject, I shall begin this time with Pomponazzi, the representative of the Aristotelian school, since his attitude is most closely connected with the medieval tradition, at least on this particular issue. In his famous treatise on the Immortality of the Soul, Pomponazzi carefully distinguishes, both at the beginning and at the end, between that which is true and most certain in itself and must be accepted as such on the basis of faith and that which can be proven within natural limits and in accordance with the teachings of Aristotle.[3] The immortality of the soul must be accepted as an article of faith, as we saw in the preceding essay, but it cannot be demonstrated on natural or Aristotelian grounds. In other words, although Pomponazzi rejects in his treatise the specific position of Averroes according to which there is only one intellect both active and passive for all men, on the question of the relation of faith and reason, theology and philosophy, he adopts a view that has been crudely labeled the double truth theory, and that had been associated during the preceding centuries, primarily if not exclusively, with the tradition of Latin Averroism.

This doctrine, which we might more fairly describe as a separation or dualism of faith and reason, has been much discussed by modern historians and has received from them a varied interpretation. Since the position evidently considers the teachings of faith and of reason incompatible in a plain and simple sense and since thinkers such as Pomponazzi display a great deal of acumen and persistence in setting forth the arguments of reason, many scholars have inferred that Pomponazzi, and other thinkers using the same line of reasoning, were not sincere, but merely adopted the dualistic theory as a protective device to cover their real but secret disbelief against ecclesiastic censure. Among the historians who have adopted this view, those who themselves held strong convictions of a secular and anticlerical, if not outright atheistic nature, praised Pomponazzi and the Averroists as the standard-bearers of modern free thought in a period otherwise oppressed by religious conformism; whereas some others, who favored the medieval Catholic view of the world, concurred in the assumption that the double truth theory was hypocritical but reversed the value judgment and condemned the hypocrisy, as well as the underlying disbelief, in no uncertain terms.[4]

Leaving aside the question whether and to what extent it is the business of the historian, and especially of the historian of philosophy, to heap praise or blame on the victims of his interpretation, I am inclined to doubt the basic assumption that Pomponazzi wrote his statements on faith and reason in bad faith. I find no textual evidence for such a view, and I do not purport to possess special devices, chemical or intuitive, that bring forth the secret thoughts which an author wrote with invisible ink between his lines or kept in his mind without committing them to writing. I rather leave the burden of proof to those who make such claims, and stand for the time being on the written record as I think the historian, not unlike the judge, is obliged to do. If we make the contrary assumption, namely that an author meant to say what he said, an assumption which is not always wrong, we will come out with the conclusion that Pomponazzi, one of the most honest and acute thinkers of the Renaissance, found himself in a genuine dilemma when he was forced to admit, as in the case of immortality, that there was a discrepancy between the conclusions of reason and Aristotle and the teachings of the Church.

I am inclined to admit that the dualistic theory, unsatisfactory as it may seem to us, is one of the possible attempts to deal with a genuine dilemma, and specifically with a case where there is an insoluble discrepancy between philosophy and theology, between reason and faith. I should even say that for a thinker who wanted to hold on to both reason and faith and found himself confronted with such a discrepancy, this is the most plausible manner in which he can face, if not solve, the dilemma. For somebody who is willing to do either without reason or without faith or without both, the dilemma ceases to exist, and the theory loses its purpose and meaning. But we have no basis to assume that this was the case of Pomponazzi or of his predecessors or contemporaries who adopted the same or a similar position.

It is interesting to note that the different interpretations of Pomponazzi's view which we have encountered in modern historians were expressed already in his own time and shortly afterwards by his friends and opponents, but this is a subject which we cannot pursue in this essay. Instead, I should like to emphasize the contribution made by Pomponazzi's dualism to the discussion of the problem with which we are concerned. Faced with the competing claims of religion and philosophy and committed to uphold both of them, Pomponazzi in substance defends the view that faith and reason are each master in its own domain, and thus he opens the way for a genuine dualism or even pluralism that makes allowance for different sources of truth. I am convinced that his position still deserves examination on the part of theologians conscious of the competing claims of the sciences and of secular learning and on the part of scientists and philosophers tolerant of the claims that religion or art or other areas of human experience may make upon our thought. Perhaps this might be a way for us to deal with the "two cultures," or rather with the many cultures that are contained in the complex texture of our life and knowledge.

If we pass from the Aristotelians to the typical humanist scholars of the Renaissance, our problem appears in less precise outlines, as might have been expected, but still is felt to be present in several distinct ways. One type of discussion that seems to be relevant to our topic is the widespread debate about the relative superiority of the various arts and sciences. There is a whole literature on the merits of medicine and law that has received some recent attention.[5] There is a similar discussion on arms and letters,[6] and the superior claims of different arts and sciences found eloquent defenders, frequently, and by pure coincidence, among their own professional representatives. A famous example is Leonardo's *Paragone,* in which the superiority of painting over other arts and sciences is argued in some detail.[7] This kind of literature is merely a part of a broader humanist tendency to indulge in the praise or blame of different pursuits and in the comparison of those thought to be in competition with each other. It is a manner of reasoning that is also found in some areas of medieval literature but which goes back, as a general pattern, to ancient rhetorical theory and literature which became much better known during the Renaissance.

Especially important for the humanists was, of course, the defense of their own studies against the claims of other disciplines, most frequently against theology but occasionally also against medicine or other fields. This literature is best known under the label "the defense of poetry," and we find it in the work of Petrarch and before him in Mussato and again in Boccaccio and Salutati and in some writers of the later fifteenth century.[8] The label should not deceive us, for by "poetry" these authors do not understand, as a modern reader might suspect, the composition of vernacular verse, but rather the composition of Latin poetry, and above all, the study and interpretation of the ancient poets and of other classical writers and even the entire cycle of learning, the *studia humanitatis,* with which the humanists were concerned and from which they derived their own name. In defending the study of the classical poets against their theological critics, the humanists used some of the arguments advanced by the Church Fathers and often insisted that the pagan poems and the myths contained in them had an allegorical meaning that was compatible and in fundamental agreement with the truth of Christian religion. The faith in allegory and in the harmony or parallelism of ancient and Christian wisdom had a very great importance in the thought, literature, and art of the Renaissance and of the subsequent period down to the eighteenth century.[9] Allegory has gone out of fashion since, and its somewhat crude application to the defense of ancient literature is no longer to our taste. But the claim that poetry and the other arts reveal their own truths, compatible with those of religion and of the sciences, or even superior to them, has found many defenders among romantic and later literary critics, as well as in modern philosophical thought.

In another sense, the humanists had to face the problem of truth in their discussion of straight philosophical and especially of moral problems which they considered to be a part of their legitimate domain. Uninterested as most of them were in a precise method or terminology, in a systematic presentation of their thought, or even in the content of cosmology or metaphysics, they were encouraged by the example of Cicero, their favorite ancient author, to borrow individual ideas or sentences from a great variety of ancient authors and to adapt them rather freely and flexibly to their own thought and writing. Ciceronianism in thought, as distinct from mere style or rhetorical doctrine, is the equivalent of eclecticism, and the moral writings of the humanists, from Petrarch to Montaigne, are full of quotations or adapted ideas taken from the most diverse ancient writers—technical philosophers as well as moralists, orators, poets, or historians. Not the authors whom modern scholarship considers as the greatest thinkers of antiquity were favored, but rather Cicero and Seneca among the Latins, Isocrates, Plutarch, and Lucian among the Greeks, authors whom modern scholarship studies for the information they contain on earlier and more original thinkers rather than for their own sake but who appealed to the humanists through their terse sentences and striking anecdotes. Ancient quotations were treated as authorities, that is, as a special kind of rhetorical argument, and each humanist kept his own commonplace book as fruit of his readings for later writing, doubly important at a time when there were no dictionaries or indices to speak of. Finally, Erasmus with his *Adagia* earned the gratitude of posterity by supplying his successors with a systematic collection of anecdotes and sentences ready for use, the real quotation book of the early modern period that everybody used but few cared to mention. Superficial as humanist eclecticism tended to be, much more superficial than its ancient counterpart, it still had the merit of broadening the sources of thought and information that an individual moralist was ready to use. It reflects the wide curiosity of the age, more eager to draw freely upon a vast range of undigested ideas than to submit a narrow body of authoritative texts to minute logical analysis, as the preceding period had tended to do.

Aside from the eclectic use of ancient ideas, especially in the area of moral thought, the chief impact of classical humanism on Renaissance philosophy was the revival of ancient philosophical doctrines other than Aristotelianism. Of special relevance to our problem is the revival of ancient skepticism that we may observe in several thinkers and writers of the fifteenth, and especially of the sixteenth century.[10] The skeptical position insists that all philosophical doctrines may be refuted and is, on the face of it, quite negative with reference to the attainment of truth. But ever since antiquity, skepticism has proclaimed itself to be bringing about intellectual freedom, since it liberates its adherents from the narrow restraints of fixed doctrines.[11] Moreover, the skeptical doctrine enabled its followers to approve any number of specific thoughts in an eclectic fashion, provided they admitted that these thoughts were merely probable and not strictly certain or demonstrable. Occasionally, a skeptic such as Montaigne would even grant that there is a single and immutable truth but add that this truth cannot be grasped by any human being, at least not in its entirety.[12] In the Renaissance skepticism often entered an alliance with a kind of fideism, as in the thought of Gianfrancesco Pico or in Montaigne, in a manner that had a precedent in Augustine but was, of course, quite unknown to the Greek skeptics.[13] That is, whereas it is possible to refute and thus to discard any definite statement in the field of philosophy and of secular learning, religious doctrine, based on faith and authority alone, would be exempt from this rule of uncertainty and thus provide us with a firm belief that cannot be shaken by any rational arguments.

Another ancient philosophical school that was revived in the wake of humanism was Platonism, and it was Renaissance Platonism that, in my opinion, made the most interesting contributions to our problem. Here we find the tendency not only to establish a harmony between religion and philosophy, thus overcoming the dualism of the Aristotelians and the Skeptics, and in a sense returning on a different level to the Thomist position, but also to recognize that there is a comprehensive universal truth in which the doctrines of each school or individual thinker merely participated, thus reasserting in a more positive fashion the intellectual variety and liberty at which the eclectics and skeptics had aimed.

The general view is clearly implied in the thought of Nicolaus Cusanus.

In his metaphysics each particular being is nothing but a particular manifestation or contraction of the one infinite and divine principle, and, in the same way, each human doctrine is but a special expression of the universal truth that can never be expressed in any one particular statement. On this basis, it is possible for Cusanus to find a partial truth in a variety of philosophical and religious doctrines, including Mohammedanism.[14]

What in Cusanus is a pervasive conception closely linked with the center of his metaphysics, appears in the Florentine Academy and its followers as a series of articulate, though not always fully developed statements. In the work of its leader, Marsilio Ficino, we find several concepts pointing toward the idea of a universal truth. First of all, he insists on a basic harmony between Platonic philosophy and Christian theology. In trying to defend the immortality of the soul, which he considered essential for religion and theology, and to refute the Averroist doctrine of the unity of the intellect, which he considered incompatible with immortality, he insisted that his opponents had destroyed the harmony between religion and philosophy and that he himself had been destined by providence to restore that unity.[15] Yet, in his attempt to establish the harmony between philosophy and theology, he goes a long way toward putting them on the same level, calling religion and philosophy sisters and claiming that they are different expressions of the same basic truth.[16] In thus raising philosophy to the level of theology (and he called his chief philosophical work *Platonic Theology*), Ficino goes not only beyond his Thomist predecessors, but also beyond his Aristotelian opponents. Moreover, although Ficino often speaks exclusively in terms of Platonic philosophy and Christian theology, his horizon of truth is somewhat larger than we might expect. Not only does he consider ancient Judaism as the true predecessor of Christian doctrine, as orthodoxy required, but he also asserts that all other religions are based on man's fundamental desire for God, that they all aim, though unconsciously, at the one true God, and that they are all species of the same genus religion of which Christianity constitutes the most perfect species.[17]

A similar tendency toward a broader tolerance may be noticed in Ficino's view of the history of philosophy. Following the precedent of his Neoplatonic and Byzantine predecessors, Ficino considers the works attributed to Hermes Trismegistus, Zoroaster, Orpheus, and Pythagoras, which modern scholarship has recognized as forgeries of late antiquity, to be genuine monuments of ancient pagan wisdom, Oriental and Greek. Ficino insists on the doctrinal affinity between these writings and those of Plato and his school and treats the ancient sages, reputed authors of these writings, as predecessors and teachers of Plato. In his view, they form an ancient tradition of pagan theology and philosophy that is as old as that of the Hebrew and Christian religion, going back to Mercurius Trismegistus, a contemporary of Moses. Thus there arises in his view a more or less continuous tradition in two different but parallel branches, philosophical or pagan and religious or Hebrew and Christian that extends in a nearly continuous line from the early days of Moses and Trismegistus down to his own day.[18]

In the history of philosophy proper, there are a good many schools and doctrines which he rejects, but he is obviously eager to absorb as many authors as possible into his synthesis, as we may see from the variety of writers whom he quotes as authorities for specific ideas he endorses. Apart from the Platonic tradition, Ficino respects and utilizes Aristotle and his commentators, and even Epicurus and Lucretius, much more frequently and openly than we might expect, and it is apparent that his Platonism, rightly so called since he admires Plato and his school above all, tends to be inclusive rather than exclusive as far as other schools and thinkers are concerned.

Ficino's younger friend and associate, Giovanni Pico della Mirandola, went much further than his teacher in his conception of universal truth, and he gave the doctrine of universal truth a classical formulation that is most representative of the Renaissance period and has remained most famous ever since. In emphasizing the similar elements in the work of Ficino, I did not intend to diminish Pico's merit, but rather tried to show how and to what extent Ficino had prepared the ground for Pico's much more developed ideas on the subject.

For Pico, the idea that truth is universal and that thinkers of all philosophical and religious traditions have a part in it is one of his most pervasive and fundamental assumptions. And it is closely connected with his idea of liberty, for he keeps telling us that we should not be limited to the teachings of a single thinker or school but should study all thinkers of the past to discover the truth contained in their writings. It is this conviction that a share of truth may be found in the works of thinkers of all times, places, and religions that motivates and justifies the vast scholarly curiosity for which Pico has rightly become famous.

This universal curiosity is reflected in Pico's training and in his library. He had a humanist education that comprised a solid knowledge of classical Greek and Latin literature, and he had also a scholastic training acquired both at Padua and Paris that gave him an unusual familiarity with the philosophical and theological writers of the Middle Ages. This combination of humanistic and scholastic training was unusual, at least in its extent, and it explains why Pico, though recognized as a consummate humanist by his friends and contemporaries, went out of his way to defend the scholastics against Ermolao Barbaro. Through his contact with Ficino, he acquired a thorough familiarity with the authentic and apocryphal sources of Platonism. But his curiosity went further. Pico learned Hebrew, Aramaic, and Arabic, and he had the works of many Arabic and Hebrew writers that had been unknown to Western scholars explained or translated for his use. This applies to Averroes and other Arabic thinkers, to the Jewish commentators on the Old Testament, and to the Jewish Cabalists. Pico's conviction that the Cabalists were in basic agreement with Christian theology gave rise to a whole current of Christian Cabalism that remained alive for several centuries and has attracted much scholarly attention in recent years. The vast variety of sources used by Pico appears not only in his library, but also in his writings.[19]

The most direct expression of Pico's belief that truth may be discovered in the writings of many authors and schools is found in the 900 theses, which Pico put together in 1486 for a public disputation he intended to hold in Rome during the following year and which was subsequently prohibited by Pope Innocent VIII, after a papal commission had examined the theses and found some of them to be heretical or dubious. The theses cover philosophy, theology, and several other fields, and some of them are presented as expressing Pico's own opinion. Yet a large number are explicitly taken from the writings of a great variety of thinkers. Among the authors used we find not only Albert, Thomas, and Duns Scotus, but also several other medieval scholastics, then Averroes, Avicenna, and several other Arabic and Jewish thinkers, then a number of Greek Aristotelian and Neoplatonic philosophers, the ancient theologians such as Pythagoras and Trismegistus, and finally the Cabalists.[20] The combination of so many authors whose views had given rise to competing schools clearly implies Pico's conviction that their teachings, or at least some of them, may be reconciled in a comprehensive doctrine, and this tendency becomes curiously evident in another thesis where Pico claims that the unity of the intellect may be reconciled with the immortality of the soul, a view to which neither Ficino nor Pomponazzi would have subscribed.[21]

Yet, the notion that all thinkers have a share in truth is not merely implied by the choice of authors cited in the theses, but it is explicitly set forth in the

Oration Pico composed for the disputation. This Oration, which has been preserved for us in an early draft (discovered by Garin) and in a posthumous edition, as eloquently treats in its second part the universality of truth as its first part deals with the dignity of man. It also is apparent that the universality of truth constitutes the theme which is meant to announce and justify the disputation of the theses, and hence this section was repeated with but minor changes in the *Apologia,* which Pico published in 1487 after the condemnation of some of his theses. "Pledged to the doctrines of no man," Pico says, "I have ranged through all the masters of philosophy, investigated all books, and come to know all schools." He adds that each school, and each philosopher, has some distinctive merit, and he praises in turn the philosophers whose doctrines he is going to defend. "This has been my reason for wishing to bring before the public the opinions not of a single school alone . . . but rather of every school to the end that the light of truth. . . . through this comparison of several sects and this discussion of manifold philosophies might dawn more brightly on our minds."[22] But not content with repeating the truths discovered by others, Pico claims to add some of his own and proceeds to justify some of his own teachings set forth in the remainder of the theses. Still more concisely, the underlying idea appears in the early version of the speech: "There has been nobody in the past, and there will be nobody after us, to whom truth has given itself to be understood in its entirety. Its immensity is too great for human capacity to be equal to it."[23]

Pico's notion of truth shares with the skeptics the rejection of the dogmatic claims of any particular master or school and with the eclectics the intellectual freedom to choose from the writings of any philosopher what seems to be true or useful. Yet, unlike the eclectics, he does not choose at random what he pleases, but he seems to be guided by an intuitive certainty of what is true (and this he derives from the Platonist tradition); and unlike the skeptics he does not stress the inadequacy that separates all human opinion from the absolute truth, but rather the positive share it derives from that truth. Pico does not believe with Hegel that every philosophical position as a whole constitutes, as it were, a form of truth. He rather thinks (and this idea he derives from the scholastic tradition) that the work of every thinker is made up of a great number of specific statements and that the truth or falsity of any one of them does not stand or fall with that of all others. He feels perfectly free to reject the views of any past thinker on any particular point, but he is convinced that the work of every philosopher worthy of the name contains some true statements and that the presence of these true statements makes the philosopher worth studying and justifies the effort we may have to make to study his language and to read his writings.

At the same time, Pico does not think that the study of past opinions leaves us no room for new or original thoughts. In combining or recombining the views expressed by our predecessors, we already give them a form and synthesis that differs from any one of them, and in adopting or criticizing their opinions, we clear the ground for advancing new and more valid opinions of our own. Thus, Pico voices a supreme confidence in the value of both learning and originality, and the only reservation we may have to make about it is that while what he offers us is, to be sure, a magnificent program, he was prevented, and perhaps not only through his early death, from working it out in a concrete and viable system. Yet, if we take his view of universal truth not as an established doctrine, but as a regulative idea, it is still as suggestive as it was in Pico's own time. Only the specific ideas and traditions and elements of knowledge that are given to us and that we must try to harmonize are different from those of the Renaissance.

Before we leave our subject, we must briefly discuss another Renaissance author who belonged to the school of Ficino and Pico and who was much less famous or distinguished than either of them. This author is Agostino Steuco, a liberal Catholic theologian of the mid-sixteenth century. Restating and developing with great learning the views of the Renaissance Platonists, he chose for his main work a title that summed up their aspirations in a new way and that was to have a persistent appeal through subsequent centuries up to the present: the perennial philosophy.[24] The notion of a perennial philosophy, of a wisdom that pervades the entire history of human thought, although it may be obscured in each instance by false or irrelevant ideas, has been expressed a number of times even in our century; although, in effect, many different systems of thought have claimed, each for itself, to represent this perennial philosophy. Most frequently the term has been used in connection with Thomism, and hence some scholars, who knew the title but not the content of Steuco's work, have thought that he was a Thomist. Actually, Steuco was a Renaissance Platonist, and the perennial philosophy which he had in mind was the doctrine of Platonism, represented by Plato and his ancient and early modern followers but also by his supposed early predecessors. Steuco, in effect, conceived a Plato who was in basic agreement with Aristotle and other ancient philosophers on a number of points and, above all, with Jewish and Christian theology.

The label "perennial philosophy" turned out to be fortunate, and the term was taken up by many later thinkers, whether or not they shared Steuco's philosophical position or even were aware of it. It is a term that may be used for the claims of a special school, but in its original intent it reflects the idea, best expressed by Pico, of a universal truth that is beyond any particular human doctrine but in which each doctrine, if worthy of that name, has a share. The idea of the perennial philosophy imposes upon us the task of keeping it alive by trying to grasp and synthesize every element of truth given to us by the earlier thinkers and traditions which are accessible to us and by adding to it whatever we may be able to discover for ourselves by the resources of our thought or experience.

We have reached the conclusion of our rapid and somewhat superficial discussion of three major themes of Renaissance thought: the dignity of man, the immortality of the soul, and the unity of truth. We have not tried to exhaust the numerous philosophical and theological doctrines that may be said to add up to such a thing as the Renaissance conception of man. We have merely touched on three aspects of that conception. The praise of man's dignity reflects some of the aspirations of the period and leads to an attempt to assign to man a privileged place in the scheme of things. The doctrine of immortality is, in a way, an extension of man's dignity and individuality beyond the limits of his present life, and, thus, the emphasis on immortality provides, in turn, a horizon for this life itself. The problem of truth may be conceived and treated in different terms, but the angle of it which we have stressed, the quest for the unity of truth in the face of divergent and apparently incompatible doctrines, is again related to man and his concerns. In a moment such as ours when there is so much talk about commitment, it might not be amiss to point out that one of the basic human commitments, and for a philosopher or theologian, scientist or scholar the only legitimate commitment, is the commitment to truth and that there is even some existentialist authority for this statement. But I gladly admit that the problems discussed here represent but a small and arbitrary selection among the philosophical ideas expressed by Renaissance thinkers on man or on any other subject. I have selected them merely because they have impressed me as interesting and characteristic among the ideas found in the work of some Renaissance authors whom I have read most frequently and most attentively, although even in the case of these authors, my knowledge and my understanding obviously have their limitations.

I do not wish to suggest that Renaissance thought, on the matters we have discussed or on any others, supplies us with ready-made solutions that we could accept as valid answers to our own problems. Every period, every generation, every thinking person must find its own answers, and if we study the history of philosophy or of civilization in search of such ready answers, we are bound to be disappointed. Past thought is intrinsically interesting, I believe, because it shows us precedents and analogies for our problems, and it may enlarge our perspective by putting before us alternatives of which we had not thought. We should neither uncritically admire nor imitate the past but neither can we afford to completely ignore it. We must know it first before we can take from it what we can use and approve, while rejecting the rest.

I often hear responsible, or rather irresponsible, educators say that the knowledge of the past, or even our present knowledge, should be adapted to the needs and interests of our time, and especially of our younger generation. We should rather stand by our conviction that some, if not all, of this knowledge is intrinsically true and valid and that the younger generation will have to absorb it before it can make any significant contribution of its own. In the long run, it is not the past that is measured by us, but we ourselves will be measured by it and judged by it since we have to prove to the future whether we have lived up to the standards of the past. As it has been said that nobody can command who has not first learned to obey, so I should like to say that nobody can create or build who has not first learned what there is to be learned.

Human civilization is a cumulative process, and any part of it is more easily and more quickly destroyed than rebuilt. No single generation can hope to build or rebuild it from the bottom, and hence we should gratefully accept and appreciate the building materials which past periods no less creative than ours have left to us. It is an inheritance each generation is called upon to hand on to its successor. It cannot help neglecting and destroying a part of this heritage, but it should always try to preserve what is worth preserving and to add something that is better in the place of what has been destroyed.

FIVE

PHILOSOPHY AND RHETORIC FROM ANTIQUITY TO THE RENAISSANCE

Introduction

The relationship between rhetoric and philosophy is a very complex phenomenon, and it has had in the Western world a long and complicated history that extends from Greek and Roman antiquity through the Byzantine and Latin Middle Ages, and through the Renaissance at least to the eighteenth century, and in a modified form even to the present day. This relationship may be characterized, depending on the period or trend under discussion, as one of coexistence or rivalry, overlapping or mutual influence. As a historian of philosophy, I tend to take the definition and basic history of philosophy for granted, and to worry about the definition and history of rhetoric, a subject that seems to have had a less continuous tradition, and that has been less thoroughly explored, although it has attracted increasing scholarly attention in recent years.

If we want to arrive at a clear notion of rhetoric, we have to contend with a number of current confusions that tend to obscure the subject. Recent thought has been much concerned and even obsessed with the problem of language. For many thinkers of our time, philosophy has been reduced to the analysis of language, and the problems of language are central to such diverse disciplines as logic, linguistics, anthropology, and literary criticism, to mention but a few. Yet strangely enough, few attempts seem to have been made to coordinate these diverse approaches to language, or to relate them to such past treatments of language as grammar or rhetoric.

Another source of confusion is the current popular use of the term rhetoric. Rhetoric is considered the equivalent of empty rhetoric, and it is widely held that an ornate speech, in most cases laudatory, does not reflect the facts of the case or the real opinion of the speaker, but is merely a pretense. Behind this popular notion is the view that goes back to Romanticism and that doubts whether there are any valid rules for speaking or writing well. More recently, there has been much talk about "radical rhetoric," a phrase used to excuse the excesses of irresponsible popular propaganda and to conceal its dangers, as if these had not been obvious during the last fifty years or so.

I should like us to forget about these clichés, and to go back to the original and traditional meanings of rhetoric as they were current before the nineteenth century. Even at that time, and already in classical antiquity, the term rhetoric had several meanings, connotations, and associations. As a theory of speech, it was an instrument of politics and legal practice. As a theory of arguing, it was related to logic and dialectic. As a theory of prose composition, it had close links with poetics and literary criticism. Rhetoric touched on grammar and on the theory and practice of historiography. Because it aroused passions and made use of moral sentences, rhetoric was related to ethics and often claimed to be a philosophy. As a program of advanced instruction, rhetoric was for many centuries a rival, and often a successful rival, of philosophy and the sciences. Its concerns are by no means dead, in spite of Romanticism and of current ignorance. There are still chairs and courses of rhetoric in American universities and periodicals dedicated to its theory and history, and where the name of rhetoric has disappeared, the subject survives under different labels such as composition or criticism or even English literature, the most widely taught academic subject in this country.

In studying the history of rhetoric, in antiquity and in later periods, we must keep in mind several aspects that are connected but distinct: the actual practice of speaking and writing; the theories that attempt to describe or regulate it; the teaching of the subject in schools and universities; and the extant literature in which practice, theory, and instruction are reflected and remain available to a later age. This literature consists of speeches and other compositions, of models and exercises, of theoretical treatises and textbooks. In the case of some of the more authoritative texts, their diffusion in manuscripts and printed editions, their actual use in the schools, and the commentaries written on them constitute an important aspect of our subject. Yet the available evidence, though rather large, is far from being complete. Much literature, especially from classical antiquity, has been lost, and its significance must be inferred and reconstructed from fragments and testimonies; and even when we come to the Middle Ages and Renaissance, many texts have not survived, and many more that have been preserved in manuscripts have remained unedited, unstudied, or even unnoticed.

If we try to distinguish between rhetoric, as the art of speaking well, and philosophy, as the science of knowing and describing the truth (at least in a general sense, as distinct from the special sciences), the two enterprises, in antiquity as at other times, not only coexisted and often competed with each other, but they also overlapped, encroached on each other's territory, and influenced each other. We must always keep in mind that there is not only a philosophy practiced by and for philosophers, but also a philosophy implicit in rhetoric and claimed as their domain by the rhetoricians. Vice versa, there is not only a rhetorical theory taught by philosophers as a part of philosophy, but also a rhetoric developed by and for professional rhetoricians who were often quite unconcerned with philosophy and who have often been overlooked by historians of philosophy.

12.

Classical
Antiquity

In talking about ancient Greek and Roman rhetoric, we cannot help noticing the enormous influence which it had on later periods, and hence must be attentive to those texts and doctrines that played a central role in this influence. On the other hand, the influence of ancient rhetoric in the Middle Ages and in the Renaissance involved a continuing process of selection and transformation, and thus there are many aspects peculiar to ancient rhetoric that did not survive antiquity and that should not be overlooked.[1]

Whereas Greek philosophy originated in Asia Minor early in the sixth century B.C. with the natural philosophers known to us as the Presocratics, rhetoric appeared in Sicily after the middle of the fifth century. The first textbooks of rhetoric, written by Corax and Tisias, apparently attempted to formulate rules for the judiciary speeches commonly delivered by lawyers before the courts of the Greek cities in Sicily, and as a result of this origin, ancient rhetorical theory down to the very end emphasized the spoken rather than the written word, and especially the judiciary speech. Soon, two other genres of speech were added to the practice and theory of the rhetorician, the deliberative speech before a public assembly, and the epideictic oration, the speech given for display before a public audience.

When Gorgias, who came from Sicily, and other Sophists taught rhetoric in Athens and other cities during the second half of the fifth century, both by rules and by models, they developed all three genres of classical oratory. They promised to educate future lawyers and statesmen for their tasks, but although the art of speech occupied a central part in their program, they were also concerned with a variety of other subjects, such as grammar and logic, ethics, and literary criticism.[2] Their theory and practice influenced Euripides and other poets, and the historians Herodotus and Thucydides show the strong influence of contemporary rhetoric in their prose style and in the composition of their fictitious speeches, a practice that influenced later historiography down to early modern times. As we learn from Aristophanes, Socrates was confused by many contemporaries with the Sophists, but if we may believe his pupils, Plato and Xenophon, he was concerned with logic and ethics, but not with rhetoric.[3] Plato, especially in his *Gorgias* and other works of his early and mature period, was a bitter critic of the Sophists and of their rhetoric, and branded it as a fake knowledge that produced opinions but no firm knowledge.[4]

Fourth-century Athens, which witnessed the activities of Plato and Aristotle, also produced the most famous orators whose works have come down to us from Greek antiquity, the Attic orators, and especially Lysias, Isocrates, Demosthenes, and Aeschines.[5] Lysias, who began his activity in the fifth century, excelled especially in his judiciary speeches, but he also wrote declamations and was a successful teacher. Plato in the *Phaedrus* gives us a caricature of Lysias as a teacher, and a parody of a declamation written in his style.[6] In the *Menexenus*, Plato gives his own version of a funeral speech in honor of the Athenian soldiers who had died during the war.[7] It is a genre based on actual practice, and invites comparison with similar pieces attributed to Lysias and Demosthenes, and above all with the famous speech of Pericles in Thucydides.[8]

Plato's *Phaedrus*, one of his later writings, is also important for another reason. Differently from the *Gorgias*, where rhetoric is condemned altogether, the *Phaedrus* leaves room for a rhetoric disciplined by philosophical and ethical considerations and thus capable of serving as an instrument of truth.[9]

Isocrates composed judiciary and especially epideictic speeches, and also founded a school of rhetoric that competed for many years with Plato's Academy as a center of higher education. He offered a curriculum that was not limited to formal rhetoric, but included a broad literary, moral, and political instruction. He also claimed to teach philosophy, using the term in a wider sense that was not limited to professional philosophy. He is the prototype of the humanist concerned with literature and with ethics but not with the sciences or technical philosophy.[10]

With Demosthenes and his contemporaries, Athenian and Greek oratory reached its highest point in the area of political eloquence. As a statesman, Demosthenes was ultimately unsuccessful, but his speeches have been always admired and imitated as unmatched models of classical prose style and composition.

Whereas Plato in his later years had come to recognize the limited value of rhetoric, his pupil Aristotle went further and actually taught rhetoric in his own school, the Lyceum. Aristotle's *Rhetoric,* the text of his lectures on the subject, is one of the most important rhetorical treatises that have come down to us from antiquity.[11] The work tends to show that the philosophers were better equipped to teach rhetoric than were the professional rhetoricians themselves. On the other hand, Aristotle does not treat rhetoric as the core subject of higher education, but as a limited and even subordinate part of the philosophical curriculum. In the Aristotelian *Corpus,* the *Rhetoric* follows after the *Politics* (and *Oeconomics*) and precedes the *Poetics,* indicating two links that are traceable to the Sophists. The work also contains a detailed theory of the passions that links it with the *Ethics,* and a detailed theory of argument that links it with logic and dialectic, a link also expressed in its first sentence.[12] These links are significant, and reappear in all later classifications of the sciences down to early modern times.

It is evident that Aristotle in his *Rhetoric,* while adding and clarifying many concepts, borrowed a good deal of his subject matter from earlier treatises written by professional rhetoricians. On the other hand, in spite of its excellence, this work did not exercise as great an influence on later professional rhetoricians as is often assumed. However, Aristotle set the precedent for later professional philosophers who included rhetoric among their subjects. Aristotle's pupil, Theophrastus, made significant contributions to rhetorical theory,[13] and the Stoics taught rhetoric as a part of logic.[14] Panaetius, the founder of Middle Stoicism, transferred the category of the *decorum* from rhetoric to ethics,[15] and Philo of Larissa, an Academic philosopher and one of Cicero's teachers, lectured on rhetoric as well as on philosophy, thus competing with the professional rhetoricians on their own ground. On the other hand, Plato's critique of rhetoric was taken up by Epicurus and his school, and later by the Peripatetic philosopher Critolaus, and by the sceptic Sextus Empiricus.[16] Among the Neoplatonic philosophers, we find at least some who showed an interest in problems of rhetoric and literary criticism, and others that even taught the subject and left some writings on it.[17] Thus we might say that the attitude of the Greek professional philosophers towards rhetoric, from Plato and Aristotle to the end of antiquity, moves between two poles: they either reject rhetoric altogether, or they treat it as a subordinate part of philosophy, claiming to treat the subject with greater competence than the professional rhetoricians were able to do.

The history of rhetoric after Isocrates and the last Attic orators is rather obscure. We know that the art of public oratory continued to be practiced and taught, not only in the old Greek cities, but also in the new Hellenistic cities founded all over Asia by Alexander and his successors. This oratory was later criticized and labeled as Asianism because it flourished in Asia and indulged according to its critics in a tasteless and artificial style. No texts and only a few names survive, and allegedly these orators neglected all theory as well as the study of earlier models. Most modern historians think that during the third century rhetoric ceased, at least temporarily, to compete with philosophy in higher education. Many orators were active in Greece and in Asia at that time, and there is reason to believe that they received and imparted rhetorical training of a sort and that there were schools of rhetoric in all major cities of the Greek-speaking world. Hermagoras who flourished in the second century B.C. proposed important and influential new rhetorical theories, and it seems unlikely that he operated in a vacuum or had no predecessors. The testimonies abound from the second and later centuries for widespread rhetorical instruction throughout the Hellenistic world.

In the first century B.C. there began a strong classicist reaction known as Atticism which added to the theory and practice of rhetoric the ideal of the imitation of classical models, and especially of the Attic orators, but also of Plato, Xenophon, and Thucydides. Distinguished specimens of Atticist theory and literary criticism are the writings of Dionysius of Halicarnassus and the treatise *De sublimitate* attributed to Longinus which date from the beginning of our era. Shortly thereafter, the so-called Second Sophistic began to flourish, excelling primarily in the epideictic oratory of traveling orators, exemplified for us in the writings of Dio of Prusa, Aristides, and Libanius.[18] This oratory presupposed a widespread and intensive rhetorical instruction based on theories and on models, and is reflected in a number of treatises and exercises that have come down to us from that period. One of the leading rhetorical theorists, Hermogenes, who was active in the later second century A.D., composed a group of textbooks that consolidated many earlier theories and added several new ones. The influence of his treatises is shown by the number of commentaries that were written on them, for the commentary as a literary genre usually reflects a course of lectures based on a textbook.[19]

Apart from oratory proper and the theoretical treatises on rhetoric, we should remember that much of ancient prose literature, especially on history and popular philosophy, and a good deal of later ancient poetry, reflects the influence of rhetorical training and theory. On the other hand, the political conditions of later antiquity brought it about that the emphasis in both rhetorical practice and theory switched from judiciary and political to epideictic oratory. To my knowledge, classical antiquity never developed a comprehensive or systematic theory of prose composition as such, but later rhetorical theory often dealt with historiography, and occasionally with epistolography.[20] Attention was paid to the poets at least in the theory of imitation, and there was a literature on poetics that had many analogies with rhetoric, that was influenced on many points by rhetoric, and that in turn helped to shape the style of later Greek poetry.

The rise and later the predominance of Christianity introduced many new doctrines, a new model for imitation, namely Scripture, and a new literary genre, the homily.[21] Yet Christian scholars soon began to receive and to impart rhetorical instruction and began to excel in rhetorical theory and practice. The Cappadocian Fathers of the fourth century soon became admired models of Christian oratory and literature, and the tradition of sacred and secular oratory continued without interruption from late antiquity through the Byzantine period down to the fifteenth century.[22] This continuity also appears in the commentaries on Hermogenes and Aphthonius, many of which date from the Byzantine period.[23]

We should also note that both in theory and practice epistolography occupied a very important place during the Byzantine period. The precedents must be sought in late antiquity, if not during the classical period. The letters attributed to classical philosophers are for the most part apocryphal, but at least one of Plato's letters is accepted by many scholars, and several of Epicurus' are considered authentic. From the later centuries we have many letters written with a literary intent, including the letters forged under the names of earlier authors, and the letters of Synesius and Libanius are an important part of their literary work. Some later rhetorical treatises also dedicate a section to the composition of letters, and there are at least a few collections of form letters from late antiquity,[24] as there are collections of form speeches or form introductions from earlier times. The Epistles of Paul and those attributed to other Apostles constitute an important part of the New Testament, and hence it is not surprising that the Greek Fathers and many of their Byzantine successors composed and preserved numerous letters, and edited and collected them as a part of their literary work.

Let us now turn from Greece to Rome and consider very briefly the role and history of Latin rhetoric.[25] In rhetorical theory, as in all theoretical subjects such as philosophy and the sciences, the Romans were completely dependent on the Greeks, their teachings and writings, their doctrines and terminology. However, the Romans contributed a new language and a native tradition of oratory that included the political speech and the funeral oration. In the area of rhetorical teaching and writing, they turned out to be much more active pupils of the Greeks than they were in philosophy or the sciences.

Roman acquaintance with Greek rhetoric and oratory seems to date from the second century B.C., when Greek ambassadors came to address the senate, as did the three philosophers from Athens in 155, and when educated Romans including the elder Cato and the younger Scipio began to study Greek literature. Early in the first century B.C., the Athenian philosopher Philo of Larissa and the Rhodian orator Molo taught for a while in Rome and were heard by the young Cicero. The earliest attempts to give regular rhetorical instruction in Rome were at first opposed by the authorities, but later in the same century oratory and rhetoric achieved their first great triumphs in Rome.

As a public orator, both judicial and political, Cicero surpassed all his predecessors and contemporaries who are known to us only by name and through later testimonies. Cicero's orations were to remain through many centuries the chief models of Latin speech and prose style, although they met with occasional criticism. In his youth, Cicero was still exposed to the influence of the so-called Asian oratory, and his speeches are said to retain some traces of that style which came increasingly under attack on the part of Atticist critics. Besides being a practicing orator and writer, however, Cicero was also deeply imbued with the theories of Greek rhetoric, and he wrote important and influential treatises on the subject. His early treatise *De inventione,* along with the *Rhetorica ad Herennium* often attributed to Cicero but actually composed by an older contemporary, constitutes the first Latin *Corpus* of rhetorical theory. These two works went a long way to make most of the earlier doctrines of Greek rhetoric available to Latin readers and to create a fairly complete terminology for Latin rhetoric by transliterating or translating the major Greek terms.

Yet Cicero was not merely an orator and a trained rhetorician, but also a student of Greek philosophy, and even had learned some of his rhetoric from Greek philosophers, that is, from the writings of Aristotle and from his own teachers in the Athenian Academy. For this reason, Cicero was more inclined than any other Roman rhetorician or any Greek professional rhetorician to combine rhetoric with philosophy and to consider rhetoric as part of a broader scheme of education and learning. His later rhetorical writings, especially *De oratore, Brutus,* and *Orator,* are not textbooks for students of rhetoric, as the *De inventione* (and the *Ad Herennium*) had been, but rather cultural programs that present the orator as a broadly educated person, and rhetoric and oratory as the center of the liberal studies (he actually uses that word) that include literature and that are at least allied with philosophy.[26] Cicero thus revived the Isocratean ideal of the widely educated and "philosophical" orator, and even went beyond it since he had a much deeper and more diversified acquaintance with genuine Greek philosophy than Isocrates or any of his successors had ever had. Cicero's mature rhetorical writings, and especially the *Orator,* are full of philosophical ideas such as the *decorum* in both its rhetorical and ethical meaning.

When Cicero, in the famous opening chapters of the *Orator,* introduces the perfect orator as an ideal present in our mind and never fully realized, comparing it with Plato's ideas and with the ideas in the mind of the artist,[27] he is in my opinion adapting to the orator and to rhetoric a notion that one of his favorite sources, the Stoic philosopher Panaetius, seems to have formulated for philosophy and especially for ethics, and for the sage or wise man. Panaetius granted to the Academic critics of Stoicism that the Stoic sage was not to be found anywhere in the real world, and retorted that he was an ideal in our mind.[28] Since the Stoics considered ethics as the art or technique of living and the wise man as the practitioner of that art,[29] it was easy for a philosophical rhetorician like Cicero to transfer these notions from ethics and the sage to rhetoric and the perfect orator.

Cicero's philosophical writings have been criticized for their lack of original ideas and for their occasional lack of conceptual precision, but they show a considerable knowledge of Greek philosophical literature, some of it known to us only through him, and they have the great merit of being among the earliest attempts to discuss philosophical problems in Latin and to create a Latin philosophical terminology.[30] The ideal of the broadly educated, literary, and philosophical orator as Cicero tried to promote it in his mature rhetorical writings found an echo in later Roman rhetorical writers, and especially in Quintilian and Tacitus.

Cicero's death coincides with the end of the Roman Republic, and the change in the political climate under the Empire, just as in Greece after Alexander, had the effect that judiciary and political oratory were restricted in their freedom, and that epideictic or ceremonial oratory became prevalent. Most of the speeches that have come down to us from the Roman Empire are panegyrics, whereas the speeches contained in the works of the Roman historians, fictitious in their wording but often authentic in their general content, continue to the very end the old genres of Greek oratory. I once had occasion to study the first hortatory speech of Pericles in Thucydides and was able to trace its general pattern all the way back to Homer and forward to Procopius and Ammianus Marcellinus.[31]

The imperial period left us also a large body of rhetorical literature that includes such ambitious works as Tacitus' *Dialogus* and Quintilian's *Institutio,* as well as collections of rhetorical exercises such as those of the elder Seneca and those attributed to Quintilian. There are also many modest textbooks that perpetuate for Latin students the old doctrines of Greek rhetoric: the parts of speech, the genres of style, the rhetorical figures, the rhythmic clauses, and many more. There are late commentaries on Cicero's *De inventione* by Marius Victorinus and by Grillius which show that this work was used as a school text even in antiquity.[32]

The Romans, just as the Greeks, developed also the art of letter-writing. We have literary collections of letters by Cicero, Pliny, and others, and doctrinal letters by Seneca, and this example was followed by the great Latin Church Fathers: Cyprian, Ambrose, Jerome, and Augustine. We know little of the official letters composed in the chancery of the emperors and early popes, but the extant register of Pope Gregory I would seem to presuppose a long tradition.[33] Some of the rhetorical treatises of the later period begin to pay attention to the letter, although they continued to focus on the composition of speeches.[34]

The rhetorical literature as well as the widespread application of rhetorical precepts in later Roman prose literature and poetry confirms what we know from the historical and literary sources. There was, not only in Rome and in Italy but throughout the Western, Latin-speaking provinces of the Roman Empire, a dense network of more or less advanced schools of rhetoric. They supplied the only form of higher education available beyond the level of the grammar school, and they offered a rhetorical and literary education that was considered an appropriate training for future lawyers, administrators, and public officials. There were no permanent schools of philosophy, or for that matter of medicine or mathematics, in Rome as there were in Athens, in Alexandria, and perhaps in Antioch and other large cities of the East, and later in Constantinople, and there were no such schools at all in the Western provinces outside of Rome. Rhetorical training was easily available in Latin and in the West, whereas philosophical training existed only in Greek and in the East. In the East, there was a coexistence and at times a rivalry between rhetoricians and philosophers. In the West, the rhetoricians completely dominated education and culture, and there was no philosophical tradition at all that might have competed with them. This explains why ancient philosophical literature in Latin is so scanty and unoriginal, and for the most part popular and amateurish. Only a few works of Greek philosophical literature were translated into Latin since they were not needed for popular use, and the development of a philosophical terminology in Latin, although begun by Cicero and Lucretius and continued by Seneca and Boethius, did not progress very far. A person who wanted to study philosophy learned Greek and studied in Greece or under Greek tutors, and some Roman philosophers even wrote in Greek, for example, the emperors Marcus and Julian.

When the Latin world became Christianized, the consequences were in many ways comparable to what happened in the Greek East. The Latin Christian writers absorbed and continued the grammatical and rhetorical education that had preceded them, and added the study of Scripture and Christian theology, and the literary genre of the homily or sermon. There was the additional problem of translating Scripture and Christian theology from Greek into Latin, a language that had a much more limited abstract and especially philosophical vocabulary. When Cicero translated *Logos,* he used both *Ratio* and *Oratio,* and when St. Jerome, and perhaps an earlier translator, translated the first line of the Gospel of St. John into Latin, he rendered *Logos* as *Verbum* which gave a distinctly more concrete and linguistic twist to the term than it had in Greek. I often wonder what course Western thought might have taken if the standard biblical text had been *In principio erat ratio*—although I do not wish to blame St. Jerome for the recent obsession of philosophers with language and linguistics. When the Council of Nicea tried to define the doctrine of the Trinity, it used the subtle distinction between *Usia* and *Hypostasis,* two similar terms for substance rooted in Greek philosophy and especially in Neoplatonism. When the Latins substituted *Substantia* and *Persona,* they relinquished philosophical finesse for a more tangible and legal terminology with which they were familiar. These are instances where the choice of words has a broad historical importance and appears to determine the course of thought for centuries and even millennia.

I should like to conclude with a few later Roman authors who are not only important in their own right but also were influential as founders of the Middle Ages, to use the title of a famous book.[35] For it should always be clear that the Middle Ages were the direct successors, not of Greek, but of Roman and Latin antiquity, and not of pagan and Republican, but of Imperial and Christian Rome.

The last Roman author of significance, Boethius, was not a rhetorician, though he had surely received a rhetorical education, but a trained philosopher thoroughly familiar with Greek philosophy and literature. He was a Christian and wrote a few treatises on theology, but his philosophical works show no Christian influence. The *Consolation of Philosophy* is a highly personal and original work imbued with Stoic and Neoplatonic conceptions that has continued to impress its readers to the present day although it is no longer as widely read as it was in former centuries. For the Middle Ages, Boethius was equally important as a translator of Greek textbooks on arithmetic and music, and above all on logic. His translation and interpretation of Aristotle's *Categories* and *De interpretatione,* with Porphyry's *Introduction,* remained the basis for elementary logic down to the twelfth century and beyond. He planned to translate all of Plato and Aristotle into Latin, and we may again speculate on the course that Western thought might have taken if he had been allowed to carry out his project. As it stands, two short logical works of Aristotle translated by Boethius and half of Plato's *Timaeus* translated by Calcidius were about the only texts of classical Greek philosophy that Roman antiquity at its very end cared to translate and thus bequeathed to the following centuries that lost the knowledge of Greek which Roman antiquity still possessed.

Going back from Boethius to an earlier thinker, St. Augustine, we may characterize him as the greatest theologian and philosopher among the Latin Christians, and perhaps as the greatest Latin thinker of antiquity. His interest in philosophy is not unique among the Latin Fathers, for it is shared by Tertullian, Lactantius, and Ambrose, but it goes deeper, and we may say that most of the Latin Fathers, in good Roman fashion, were versed in rhetoric and jurisprudence but not in philosophy. Even Augustine himself is a case in point. He was trained as a professional rhetorician, and was active as a professor of rhetoric until the time of his conversion. His interest in philosophy was deep and original, but it was not professional. He had no instruction in philosophy, and he derived his knowledge of the subject, and most of his ideas, from private reading. The texts he read were partly in Latin, for we know that he read Cicero's philosophical works, some of them now lost, and a Latin version of Plotinus that is also no longer extant. I am convinced that he also read some philosophical texts in Greek, for his knowledge of

Greek, though limited, must have been sufficient for that purpose, and there was not enough philosophical literature that he could have read in Latin. Augustine's own writings turned out to be an important theological and philosophical source for many centuries.

Two other Latin authors of late antiquity must be mentioned because of their influence on the subsequent period. One is Cassiodorus, the adviser and chancellor of Theodoric, who founded a monastic community with an important library in Vivarium and who wrote his *Institutions* to provide a program of instruction for its school. The other is Martianus Capella who gave in his strange treatise, *The Marriage of Mercury and Philology,* an elementary account of the seven liberal arts that were to dominate the school curriculum of the early Middle Ages.[36] The seven liberal arts constitute a scheme of subjects of primary or secondary education that among the Greeks had been considered preliminary to philosophy.[37] Some of its features may be traced back to the Pythagoreans, the Sophists, and Plato. Sextus Empiricus who seems to express the consensus of later Greek antiquity discusses six liberal arts (*mathemata*) that are separate from the three parts of philosophy, that is, logic, physics, and ethics.[38] For Sextus, and for most Greek philosophers, logic is one of the parts of philosophy, and not one of the elementary disciplines introductory to philosophy. It is quite understandable that in the West where instruction in philosophy was unknown elementary logic would be added to the other six elementary disciplines to form a complete curriculum. At the end of the Roman Empire when most of its political and educational institutions were destroyed by the Germanic and other invaders, education remained in most areas and for the most part a monopoly of the clergy, and especially of the monks. The schools of rhetoric that had flourished in the Latin West even after its Christianization disappeared. The only schools that were left were those of the monasteries, and their curriculum was based on the seven liberal arts. This curriculum included the mathematical disciplines as well as some rhetoric and elementary logic, but its dominant part was for some time to come the study of grammar.

I hope this very brief survey may have helped to clarify at least some features of ancient rhetoric and of its relation to philosophy. Rhetoric, the theory of good speech, originated as a theory of the judiciary and political speech and gradually developed into an elaborate system of rules and doctrines that came more and more to serve also epideictic oratory, prose composition, and literary criticism. The subject was taught in numerous schools that occupied a dominant place in secondary and higher education, produced a large literature, and exercised a deep influence on all branches of literature, including historiography, popular philosophy, and poetry. The philosophers either rejected rhetoric, as did the early Plato and Epicurus, or tried to teach it as a part of philosophy, as did Aristotle and the Stoics. The rivalry between philosophy and rhetoric remained a persistent feature of Greek education and learning down to Christian and Byzantine times.

When the Romans began to assimilate Greek culture, they fully adopted the rhetorical theory and practice of the Greeks and created their own network of rhetorical schools that flourished throughout the Latin West down to the end of the Empire. Interest in philosophy was much more sporadic among the Romans. There were no schools of philosophy in the West, and hence no rivalry between philosophy and rhetoric. Yet a smattering of philosophy was added to the Latin tradition, and the first attempts were made to develop a philosophical terminology in Latin, thanks to a small number of important Latin writers who had a deep and genuine interest in Greek philosophy: they include Cicero and Lucretius, Seneca, Augustine, and Boethius. With the exception of Lucretius, they all served as transmitters of ancient philosophy to the Middle Ages, at a time when the knowledge of Greek declined and for a while almost disappeared in Western Europe.

13.

The
Middle
Ages

Medieval rhetoric, as compared with ancient rhetoric, presents a number of different and perhaps greater problems. Over a period of time that lasted almost as long as classical antiquity including the late Roman Empire, the Middle Ages may seem to have been less productive, both in the variety and originality of its rhetorical theories and in the volume of its rhetorical literature. Rhetoric apparently played a lesser role in teaching and scholarship; it was less influenced by philosophy or other learned disciplines; and in turn it had less influence on them. The rhetorical elements found in medieval philosophy and theology by McKeon and others are all derived from ancient rather than from medieval rhetoric. On the other hand, far less scholarly work has been devoted to medieval than to ancient rhetoric, because medieval studies developed more slowly than classical studies, and a much larger proportion of the extant sources remains unpublished and even unstudied, so that any attempt at a synthesis must remain more tentative.[1]

We shall for our purpose define the Middle Ages as the period that goes roughly from A.D. 600 to 1350, excluding at its beginning the later Roman and early Christian writers, and including at the end some of the followers of the scholastic tradition that were contemporary with the earliest phases of Renaissance humanism. This long period falls in turn into several subdivisions whose limits may be roughly assigned to the late eighth, the late eleventh, and the early thirteenth century.[2]

The earliest Middle Ages can be separated from late antiquity only in a rather artificial manner, and at least certain theories and texts of classical Latin rhetoric were known and accessible to medieval scholars from the beginning to the end. However, the manner and extent to which this ancient heritage was studied and utilized varied from time to time and also from place to place and depended on the scholarly interests prevailing in various schools and circles. There are periods of scholarly decline, especially during the earlier centuries, followed by various renaissances, in rhetoric as well as in other fields and in general learning. Moreover, even where ancient doctrines were studied and restated, they were not necessarily understood, emphasized, or used in the same way as they had been in antiquity, and were often combined with different notions or adapted to different, contemporary purposes. We should constantly keep in mind the fact that there was almost no knowledge of Greek, and hence no direct acquaintance with the original Greek literature of rhetoric or oratory. Whatever ancient sources the Middle Ages possessed and used were Roman and Latin. In the field of rhetoric, these sources were not as meagre as in philosophy or the sciences, for they included such inportant rhetorical texts as those of Cicero and Quintilian. Yet the wealth and finesse of the Greek rhetorical tradition as it was available to the Byzantine East, as it gradually became known to the Renaissance, and as it has been studied by modern classical scholars, was unknown to the Middle Ages, except through the selective filter of Roman antiquity.

During the centuries following the sixth, classical learning flourished mainly in Ireland and England, but there is reason to assume that elementary instruction in the seven liberal arts including rhetoric was offered in all the schools of Western Europe. These schools were for the most part monastic, but they had at least some lay pupils, and there seems to have been an unbroken tradition of lay instruction in parts of Italy.

The so-called Carolingian Renaissance of the eighth and ninth century brought about a reform of script and an increase in libraries, and also a revival of school instruction and of literature. Alcuin, one of the leading scholars of the age, wrote on rhetoric as on the other liberal arts,[3] and authors such as Rabanus Maurus covered rhetoric in their encyclopedic works. Yet throughout this period, the dominating field among the liberal arts was grammar. In many of the Carolingian schools the teaching of the liberal arts was based on the work of Martianus Capella as we can see from the extant commentaries on that work which date from this period.[4] Several of these commentaries are due to Irish scholars active in France, and one of them is attributed to Johannes Scotus Eriugena, the greatest scholar of the age, who was unique as a Greek scholar capable of translating philosophical and theological writings into Latin, and as an original philosopher.[5] Martianus Capella deals in one of his books with rhetoric, and the glosses on the book represent for us the main body of rhetorical theory from this period. These glosses reflect an elementary knowledge of ancient Roman sources, but not any general or philosophical background.

The tenth century is usually considered as a period of decline, but to this century belongs a document that is of great interest for our purpose, the letter of Gunzo of Novara to the monks of Reichenau.[6] This letter is clearly composed according to the later rhetorical precepts on the parts of the letter, and it thus seems to supply clear evidence that the practice, if not the theory, of *dictamen* antedates Alberic of Monte Cassino who is usually considered as the founder of that tradition.[7] To the eleventh century belongs Anselm of Besate ''the Peripatetic'' who wrote a Retorimachia and was trained in both rhetoric and dialectic.[8] He is an isolated figure, especially in Italy, but significant for the unusual connection between the two fields and as a witness of what must have been a broader tradition that preceded the rise of scholasticism.

The late eleventh century and all of the twelfth witnessed another renaissance of learning that is associated with such centers as Chartres and Laon, Paris and Oxford, Montpellier, Salerno, and Bologna, and that in many of its areas may be identified with early scholasticism. The liberal arts flourished as never before in the preceding centuries, but among them it was the study of logic that now received the greatest impetus and left the other arts far behind. Moreover, thanks to an expanding intellectual curiosity, to a wave of new translations from the Arabic and Greek, and to the rise of new educational institutions, the traditional pattern of the seven liberal arts proved to be too narrow, and new disciplines such as philosophy and theology, civil and canon law, and medicine were now developed as advanced subjects of study for which the liberal arts of grammar and rhetoric and even of logic were merely preparatory.

The form of the commentary became the most important genre of scholarly literature, for it reflected the teaching practice of the *lectura*. The ancient Roman models of the commentary had been largely grammatical (for example, Servius and Donatus), but within the scheme of the liberal arts, Boethius' commentary on the logical works of Porphyry and Aristotle was also used, and since Boethius followed the model of the Greek commentators on Aristotle, we can understand why the medieval commentators on any text began their introductions or *accessus* with a set of questions that included the question *cui parti philosophie supponatur*.[9] The answer was usually ethics when a poet was the subject of the commentary, since the early Middle Ages, with the exception of Eriugena, had no conception of philosophy in the Greek and technical sense of the word, but equated philosophy with the sum total of their own secular learning, that is, with the seven liberal arts. They knew through Isidore that there were three parts of philosophy, namely logic, physics, and ethics.[10] The schemes for the classification of learning that have come down to us in numerous commentaries and other sources from the eleventh century on vary a great deal among each other, but they are best explained by the persistent effort to harmonize the seven liberal arts and the three parts of philosophy.[11]

As a consequence of the new expansion of learning, the traditional scheme broke apart. An author, i.e., a poet, does not belong to philosophy according to Bernard of Chartres, says William of Conches in his commentary on Juvenal,[12] and a century later Thomas Aquinas was to state that the seven liberal arts do not constitute philosophy.[13] The new fields, especially philosophy, law, and medicine, were gradually detached from their common matrix, the liberal arts and especially grammar.

The scholastic commentaries of the twelfth and later centuries followed a different course in each field, yet they continued some of the patterns which they had inherited from the earlier grammatical and encyclopedic tradition. The schools of the twelfth century, especially Chartres and Orléans, produced several commentaries on ancient poets such as Vergil, Ovid, and

Lucan.[14] It is important for our purpose that we also have commentaries on the *De inventione* and the *Ad Herennium* that originated in the Northern schools of the twelfth century, one of them by one of the leading masters, Thierry of Chartres, another by Alanus who may be identical with the author of the *Anticlaudianus*.[15]

It is interesting to observe that in the developing conflict between the *artes* and the *auctores* which was to be won in the thirteenth century by the *artes* (though not by the liberal arts as previously understood),[16] the *De inventione* and the *Ad Herennium* occupy a kind of middle position. They are theoretical textbooks of one of the arts, rhetoric, but their real or reputed author is also one of the greatest *authores, Cicero*. Certainly a commentator on these two works was to acquire and to transmit a much larger body of ancient Roman rhetorical theory than was the case with a glossator of Martianus Capella. The body of these rhetorical commentaries, many of them anonymous and hard to date, is large and complex, and the task of studying them and of assigning to them some kind of order has been undertaken but recently. Only when this study has been further advanced shall we be able to see how the interpretation of ancient rhetorical theory as it is found in these commentaries may be related to the work done in other fields of learning and also to contemporary rhetorical practice.

Some scholars have stressed the fact that in medieval and later classifications rhetoric along with dialectic is subordinated to logic, but I am inclined to interpret this in a different way. The common denominator of these classifications is the attempt to harmonize the seven liberal arts and the three parts of philosophy. Just as the *quadrivium* was equated with physics at a time when physics as a separate field of study was unknown, so it was convenient to equate the *trivium* with logic, understanding logic in the broader sense of *philosophia rationalis* or *sermocinalis,* while reserving for logic in the narrower sense the term dialectic.

From the theoretical rhetoric that had such complicated relations with logic and philosophy and found its expression in the commentaries on Cicero's *De inventione* and on the *Rhetorica ad Herennium,* we must now turn our attention to a more practical branch of medieval rhetoric that is represented by a much larger body of literature. I am referring to the vast literature of medieval epistolography known as *ars dictaminis,*[17] and to a few other branches closely allied with it, such as the *ars notaria,* the *ars poetica,* the *ars praedicandi,* and the *ars arengandi.*

Throughout Roman antiquity, the notarial profession had the important task, not merely to stamp documents written and signed by others, as is now the case in this country, but to compose them according to legally valid forms, to write them down for clients who were often illiterate, to validate them, and to deposit them in some public registers or archives. The notarial profession survived the fall of the Roman Empire and the following centuries, and it retained and even increased its social and cultural importance since it required literacy and some elementary legal knowledge that were both in short supply, and since it was, at least in Italy, a lay profession that maintained its continuity through its own specialized instruction and training.[18] Apart from legal documents, the notaries composed the letters needed for administration and business. In order to exercise their profession, they needed forms or models for the letters and documents they composed, and we may assume that collections of such forms or models circulated at all times for the benefit of notaries and scribes. Some of them have survived even from Merovingian and Longobard times.[19]

There must also have been some oral transmission of the rules for composing letters, even before the appearance of theoretical textbooks at the end of the eleventh century.[20] Gunzo of Novara in the tenth century composed his letter according to the rule that a letter consists of five parts, as we find it in later treatises.[21] The fact cannot merely be explained by his acquaintance with the *Ad Herennium*. The *Ad Herennium,* in accordance with Greek rhetorical theory and practice, prescribes six parts for an oration: *exordium, narratio, divisio, confirmatio, confutatio,* and *conclusio,* whereas other ancient treatises omit the *divisio* and substitute *argumentatio* for *confirmatio* and *confutatio*. Apart from minor fluctuations of the doctrine, the following steps are needed in order to pass from the parts of the oration in the *Ad Herennium* to the parts of the letter in Gunzo's practice and in later *dictamen* theory: the principle must be asserted that the parts of an oration should also be applied to the letter, a notion that is by no means obvious; and the *salutatio* which has no place in the oration but is an essential and in a way the most important part of the letter must be added at the beginning of the scheme. I am inclined to infer from Gunzo's practice that there was in the tenth century, and perhaps much earlier, a tradition of regular instruction in letter-writing that included, as one of its features, the later doctrine of the parts of the letter, as adapted from the ancient rhetorical doctrine of the parts of the oration.

The earliest extant author who deals with the theory of *dictamen* is Alberic of Monte Cassino who was active towards the end of the eleventh century.[22] The fact that he was from Monte Cassino, a leading monastic school, is significant, and so is the fact that he treated *dictamen,* not as an isolated subject, but as part of a broader scheme of learning that included grammar and the other liberal arts. When his immediate successors in the twelfth century treat *dictamen* as a separate field, this means that *dictamen,* a special branch of rhetoric, has become detached from the common matrix of the seven liberal arts, in the same way as it happened at about the same time to other specialized fields of learning, including law and medicine.

The twelfth century produced a large body of *dictamen* literature, much of it anonymous, and some of it assignable to specific authors, places, and dates. The identifiable authors are all Italian or French, but their texts spread to other countries that contributed to this literature at a later date.[23] A prominent role during the first half of the twelfth century and for at least two more centuries belongs to Bologna, which was then emerging as a leading university, especially in the fields of civil and canon law. The instruction in *dictamen,* if not a part of the university curriculum proper, was obviously considered a useful preparation for students of the notarial art, and for future or actual students of law. The extant literature consists of rules and models for the composition of letters, whereas the related *ars notaria* supplied the rules and models for the composition of legal documents.

The model letters, partly historical and partly fictitious, are usually concerned with church and state affairs, but they soon came to include the affairs of cities and of private citizens, including love letters and family letters, and the letters of students to their friends and relatives, describing their life or asking for money. These letters provide a fairly comprehensive view of the political and private life of the period, including many details for which we have no other sources. Obviously, the person who had received this kind of training was well equipped to serve as a chancellor or secretary to popes and bishops, emperors and kings, but also to feudal lords and city officials. Some of the chanceries, and especially the papal Curia, adopted their own specific rules of composition, and some of the collections originated with them or were written for their benefit.

The collections of model letters represent an older type of literature, and they often circulated separately. The *dictamen* literature proper, which is of more direct interest for the history of rhetoric, consists of theoretical treatises which give the rules for writing letters, often with inserted or appended models. They contain a number of standard rules that are repeated with minor variations from one treatise to the other. They usually begin with a prologue in which the author praises his subject and often claims to provide an introduction to all the liberal arts and even to philosophy. Near the beginning of the treatise, it is usually stated that there are three kinds of *dictamen: prosaicum, metricum,* and *rhythmicum.* The author then proceeds to state that he will limit himself to the *dictamen prosaicum* and especially to the letter. The scheme is interesting since it suggests a parallel treatment of poetry, as we find it in the *artes poeticae* or *poetriae* of the same period, and since it indicates a clear distinction between metrical and rhythmical poetry.

We have mentioned before the doctrine of the parts of the letter. We may add that the *salutatio* is always treated in great detail, and it is this topic that had no precedent in the ancient treatments of the oration. At a slightly later date, we even find separate treatises on *salutatio,* and entire collections of *salutationes,* form addresses. Other sections of the *dictamen* treatises deal with punctuation (a subject that also was later discussed in separate treatises [24]), with figures of speech, evidently taken over from ancient rhetoric, and finally with the *cursus,* the rhythmical forms prescribed for the end of a sentence, and especially of the entire letter. The *cursus* has been much studied by modern scholars,[25] but they do not always emphasize a point that seems important: ancient rhetoric prescribed metrical *clausulae* for the end of sentences and sections of a speech, and the *cursus* rules of the *dictamen* are to a large extent an adaptation of the ancient metrical clauses to the rhythmical practices of medieval Latin, just as many schemes of ancient metrics were adapted to the rhythmical and accented verse of medieval Latin poetry.

The *ars dictaminis* as it had developed during the twelfth century continued to flourish through the thirteenth and well into the fourteenth century.[26] Throughout this period, Bologna retained an important role, but many treatises and collections were also produced in other schools, and in monasteries and chanceries both in Italy and in other countries. The demand for models and rules of letter-writing was great and even expanding. The leading Bolognese masters of the thirteenth century were Boncompagno and Guido Faba, and they were followed by many others, including Matteo de'Libri, Giovanni di Bonandrea, Mino da Colle, Pietro de'Boattieri, and Giovanni del Virgilio.[27] There has been a good deal of recent scholarship on the *dictamen,* but much of it remains to be sorted, studied, and edited.[28]

The later literature follows in many ways the earlier pattern, but there are also a few new features. We find many models of *exordia* rather than of complete form letters, indicating that the beginning phrases of a letter demanded special stylistic attention. There also seems to be an increasing tendency to define and distinguish special categories of letters that were of special interest, such as letters of recommendation or consolation, letters of praise and letters of blame (*invectivae*).[29]

The *ars notaria* which served for the composition of legal documents had a literature of its own, especially in the thirteenth century.[30] Its most famous product was Rolandino Passeggeri's *Summa artis notariae* which again originated at Bologna and dominated the field in Italy down to the eighteenth century.[31] The medieval *artes poeticae,* much less numerous than the treatises on dictamen, originated for the most part in France, but the famous *Poetria nova* of the Englishman Geoffrey of Vinsauf shows some connection with Bologna and was often copied and commented upon in Italy and elsewhere.[32]

There is one fundamental distinction between the *dictamen* and ancient rhetoric, apart from its narrow scope and its scanty relation to other fields except law: ancient rhetoric was concerned with the oration and the spoken word, the *dictamen* with the letter and the written word. One of the reasons ancient rhetoric was considered impractical by the *dictatores* was the fact that the public oratory for which the precepts of ancient rhetoric had been intended actually disappeared from the scene after the end of Roman antiquity. It is for this reason that Boncompagno could say that he had not read Cicero, that is, that he had not lectured on him.[33]

In classical antiquity, and especially in later Rome, the letter undoubtedly occupied an important place, but it did not leave a large trace in extant literature or in rhetorical theory. In the High Middle Ages, the letter became more important, it occupies a large place in the body of extant literature, and thanks to the *dictamen,* it also conquered a leading place in rhetorical theory such as it had never obtained in antiquity. The difference between the written and the spoken word is significant but not decisive, for the letter was often dictated when written and read aloud when received. Yet the function of the letter as a message from the sender to the recipient is quite different from that of a speech delivered before a law court, a political assembly, or a public audience. The practice of having a public audience, and of addressing it aloud, did not exist between the end of the Roman Empire and the twelfth century.

The only spoken composition known to this period was the sermon delivered in church, and there was a continuous tradition of preaching from early Roman Christianity through the medieval centuries and down to modern times, although the practice of preaching underwent many changes during that long period. Many sermons have been preserved from different centuries, and it is quite evident that they were copied and read as models for later preachers, and that they served a literary as well as a religious function.[34] In the twelfth and thirteenth century, theoretical handbooks for preachers were composed in increasing numbers, the *artes praedicandi*.[35] They are real textbooks for preachers, and their prescriptions show many analogies with ancient and medieval textbooks of secular rhetoric. A characteristic feature of the medieval sermon is the practice of beginning with a passage from Scripture as a theme, and with a *divisio* of that passage. The main body of the sermon follows precise structural rules as described in the handbooks. There are also occasional specimens of lay sermons, composed and delivered by laymen rather than by priests or friars, which follow the same general pattern.[36]

Yet the view that the Middle Ages had no secular eloquence, and that medieval rhetoric was geared only to the letter and the sermon, although widely held until recent times,[37] ceases to be true, especially for Italy, as we approach the later part of the twelfth century. The rise of the city-states with their independent political and legal institutions generated the practice of publicly addressing popular assemblies, councils, and law courts, and the same was true of the universities that shared their status as corporations with the cities and the guilds. Italian popular oratory is noticed by foreign observers at the time of the Emperor Barbarossa,[38] although no actual speeches have come down to us from that early period. We may very well assume that in this as in other cases practice preceded theory, and that it took a few decades, if not longer, before model speeches were recorded, let alone collected or composed.

From the thirteenth century on, we have model speeches as well as model letters, all of them from Italy, and it is evident that the *ars arengandi,* the art of composing speeches, was taught by the same persons who also taught the art of writing letters. One of Boncompagno's works, the *Rhetorica novissima,* has nothing to do with *dictamen,* but it is a textbook, with models, for the benefit of lawyers, teaching them how to compose pleas and forensic speeches.[39]

There are many collections of form speeches, some of them in the vernacular, and whereas many of them remain anonymous, others were composed by such well-known *dictatores* as Guido Faba and Matteo de'Libri.[40] In a group of treatises written for the instruction of the *podestà,* the public official called from the outside to govern a city, we find rules and models for speeches that he was supposed to deliver on certain public occasions, including the funerals of prominent citizens.[41] In a few instances, speeches actually delivered on specific occasions have been preserved from the thirteenth century, such as the speech given by Franciscus Accursius in the name of the English King to the pope.[42] From these sources we learn that there were certain types of speeches that were commonly practiced and for which models and rules were needed and provided with increasing frequency: funeral speeches, wedding speeches, assembly speeches, ambassador's speeches, and university orations, to list only some of the most common types. We are thus led to the conclusion that in Italy, in the thirteenth and perhaps even in the twelfth century, all genres of secular speech that were to be cultivated by the Renaissance humanists had come into being out of the legal, political, and social institutions of the later Middle Ages, and that they were composed in the rhetorical style of the time, that of the *dictatores*, long before the humanists had a chance to apply to them their own different standards of style.[43] The specimens of prehumanist oratory that have survived represent only a small part of what was actually composed.

We may also note that secular oratory was in some instances influenced by the older traditions of sacred eloquence. When Petrus de Vineis addressed the citizens of Padua in the name of the Emperor Frederick II, so we are told by a chronist, he began his speech with a line from Ovid as his theme.[44] In the same way, Petrarch began his coronation speech with a line from Vergil.[45] Obviously this was an attempt to imitate the practice of contemporary preachers, by substituting a line from a pagan poet for a line from Scripture to serve as a theme for the oration. On the other hand, we know that mendicant preachers living in the Italian cities, such as Remigio de'Girolami, would deliver sermons, not only on holidays and at other religious functions, but also on the occasions that had been recently embellished with secular oratory, such as funerals, weddings, and civic gatherings.[46]

Before we discuss Renaissance rhetoric, which will be the subject of our next chapter, we must ask again what happened to classical rhetoric during the later Middle Ages when contemporary rhetorical concern was centered on letters and sermons, and also on public speeches. First of all, the tradition of giving courses on the *De inventione* and the *Ad Herennium* was continued or resumed. Commentaries on these works were composed in France during the twelfth century, as we have seen, but the first half of the thirteenth century seems to mark a gap in this tradition. When we reach the late thirteenth and the fourteenth century, such commentaries appear again, this time in Italy, and we have also documentary evidence that courses on these texts were given at Bologna. Giovanni di Bonandrea seems to have lectured on the *Ad Herennium*, and we know for sure that his successor Bertolinus de Canulis did. In his case, we have not only the university document, but also the commentary itself is extant, in two redactions, and in about twenty copies, some of them written in the fifteenth century and spread all over Europe.[47] We may suspect Northern influence, for one commentary is attributed to Jacques de Dinant who was active at Bologna,[48] and the commentary of Alanus was cited by Bertolinus.[49]

The production and manuscript diffusion of these commentaries seems to speak for itself, and we may interpret them as a sign of a return to the classics, in line with the *preumanesimo* of an Albertino Mussato and a Giovanni del Virgilio. We also note that the study of *dictamen* was now combined with classical studies, that is, with the study of Cicero's rhetoric in Bertolinus, and with the study of Ovid and other poets in Giovanni del Virgilio. Again we are approaching the threshold of Renaissance humanism, and may even have crossed it.

In order to complete our survey of medieval rhetoric, we must finally discuss the appearance of Greek rhetorical texts during the later centuries. The twelfth and thirteenth centuries produced a large number of new Latin translations from the Greek and Arabic, most of them in philosophy and the sciences. These translations greatly enlarged the sources available in these fields, far beyond the heritage of ancient Roman times, enriched the medieval Latin terminology, and broadened the range of problems discussed by teachers, students, and writers. We may well ask to what extent the field of rhetoric benefited from this development.

There were actually four rhetorical texts that were translated for the first time from Greek into Latin during the twelfth and thirteenth century: Aristotle's *Rhetoric*,[50] the pseudo-Aristotelian *Rhetorica ad Alexandrum*,[51] Demetrius' *De elocutione*,[52] and pseudo-Isocrates' *Ad Demonicum*.[53] The appearance of all these texts is of considerable interest and should be duly noted. However, the last three of these texts each survive in only a few manuscripts and do not seem to have exercised any tangible influence on medieval rhetoric.

Aristotle's *Rhetoric*, on the other hand, represents quite a different case. This important work was diffused in a fairly large number of manuscripts, and even was made the subject of several commentaries, which shows that it was used as a textbook in schools or universities. Thus there is no doubt that Aristotle's *Rhetoric* had a certain influence on the thought of the thirteenth and fourteenth century. However, this influence did not affect the professional rhetoricians but rather the scholastic philosophers. In the medieval lists of Aristotle's writings, the *Rhetoric* is grouped among the *Libri morales,* along with the *Ethics, Politics,* and *Economics,* and wherever the *Rhetoric* appears in medieval manuscripts together with other works of Aristotle, it is in the company of these same texts.[54] This fact is doubly significant because it has no analogy in the Byzantine manuscript tradition of Aristotle's Greek writings,[55] but is peculiar to the medieval Latin tradition. It is not surprising, for even in ancient classifications and groupings rhetoric is associated with politics as often as it is with logic. Moreover, Aristotle's *Rhetoric* includes an important section on the passions, a doctrine which is not treated explicitly in his *Ethics* and which constitutes in other philosophical systems, especially in that of the Stoics, an integral part of ethics. In other words, the medieval philosophers grouped the *Rhetoric* with the moral writings of Aristotle because they used it as a supplement of his *Ethics* for the theory of the passions,[56] and they found this procedure justified by the traditional link between rhetoric and politics.

This same pattern is confirmed when we look at the commentaries on Aristotle's *Rhetoric.* A complete listing of Aristotelian commentaries is in progress and is not yet completed,[57] but it is safe to say that the best-known medieval commentaries on Aristotle's *Rhetoric* were written, not by professional rhetoricians, but by scholastic philosophers who commented also on Aristotle's *Ethics* and some of his other philosophical writings and who had no connection with the professional rhetoric of their own time: Giles of Rome, Guido Vernani, the critic of Dante's *De monarchia,* John of Jandun, and John Buridan.[58] It would be an interesting task for further study to see whether Aristotle's *Rhetoric* influenced these philosophical commentators in their understanding of other writings of Aristotle or of other philosophical doctrines. I am not sure this question has yet been raised, but it would help to clarify the mutual influence of rhetoric and philosophy during the Middle Ages. On the other hand, although the *dictatores* and the other professional rhetoricians were not immune to Aristotelian influences, there is to my knowledge no evidence that they were especially interested in or influenced by Aristotle's *Rhetoric.* The fact is significant, for in the sixteenth century Aristotle's *Rhetoric,* along with his *Poetics,* was studied and commented upon by professional rhetoricians and humanists and did exercise an influence on rhetorical as well as on poetical theory and practice. However, this did not happen in the Middle Ages, not even during its last phase when the text as such had become widely available.

I hope our brief survey has illustrated some of the characteristics of medieval rhetoric, and some of the features that link it with, or distinguish it from, both ancient and Renaissance rhetoric. The basis of medieval rhetoric is ancient Roman, not Greek rhetoric, and especially Roman rhetoric as it appears in Cicero's *De inventione,* in the *Rhetorica ad Herennium,* and in Martianus Capella, was studied and appropriated more or less thoroughly at different times. Greek rhetoric was inaccessible before the thirteenth century, and when some of its texts, and especially Aristotle's *Rhetoric,* became known through Latin translations, it circulated among the students of Aristotelian philosophy, and especially of his *Ethics* and *Politics,* and was commented on by them, whereas the professional rhetoricians took little or no notice of it.

The professional rhetoricians had turned more and more to those branches of prose composition that were of practical importance after the end of antiquity when the public speech, the main theme of ancient rhetoric, had disappeared. The largest number of medieval professional rhetoricians were interested in the composition of letters (*ars dictaminis*) and of documents (*ars notaria*) whereas the theory and practice of preaching (*ars praedicandi*) was cultivated by members of the clergy. It was only after the twelfth century, with the reappearance of public oratory in the Italian city-states, that a new branch of rhetoric began to deal with secular oratory (*ars arengandi*), composing models and rules for speaking, paying attention to the chief genres of speech then in use, and extending its interest at times from Latin to vernacular oratory.

The body of literature that belongs to the *dictamen* and its related enterprises is very large indeed, and exceeds by far in bulk anything comparable that has been preserved from classical antiquity, and anything else remotely rhetorical, such as the rhetorical commentaries on Cicero, produced in the Middle Ages. This literature makes up not only in bulk but also in "relevance" and historical interest for what it may lack in finesse or conceptual depth, and it should hence be studied as an integral part of medieval literature and culture. It is this literature on *dictamen* and related subjects, and to a lesser extent the commentaries on Cicero's rhetoric, that constitute the core of medieval rhetoric, and not the rhetorical terms and implications, most of them ancient, that may be found in the writings of medieval logicians, philosophers, and theologians.

14.

The
Renaissance

If we understand by the Renaissance the period that runs roughly from 1350 to 1600, we find that rhetoric during this era occupied a broader and more important place than during the Middle Ages. In the Renaissance, rhetoric expanded and developed greatly, and came to pervade all areas of civilization, as it had not been the case during the preceding centuries. The rule of rhetoric during the Renaissance was not as complete as it had been in Roman antiquity or in certain periods of Greek antiquity, for Renaissance rhetoric always had to compete with scholastic philosophy and theology and with the professional disciplines of law, medicine, and mathematics, with the arts and popular literature, and with many other activities. Yet the study, imitation, and cult of classical antiquity that was one of the characteristic traits of the Renaissance had in turn the effect of strengthening and promoting rhetoric.

However, Renaissance rhetoric was in many ways different from ancient rhetoric and influenced by medieval as well as by new, contemporary patterns. Unlike ancient rhetoric, Renaissance rhetoric was not primarily concerned with the political and even less with the judiciary speech. It cultivated the letter as much as the oration, and it tended to include all forms of prose composition, and to enter a close alliance with poetics, since prose and verse composition were considered as alternating forms of the same enterprise. The ancient view that rhetoric and oratory aimed at persuasion was often repeated, but it did not dominate the prevailing conception of rhetoric.[1]

The close alliance of rhetoric and poetics and their mutual influence can be traced back from the Renaissance through the Middle Ages to late and even classical antiquity. It has been uniformly deplored by modern historians, but its consequences have not been uniformly harmful. For example, the rhyme originated in oratory long before it was adopted in poetry. The subject obviously needs further investigation, as does the reverse influence of poetry and poetics on prose and rhetoric.

During the Renaissance, rhetoric belonged to the domain of the humanists, and it occupied an important and perhaps central, though by no means exclusive place in their work. For the *studia humanitatis* included grammar and poetry, history and moral philosophy, as well as rhetoric. As a humanist enterprise, rhetoric was thus closely connected with all these other subjects, and the rhetoric of the humanists must be understood as an integral part of their widespread interests and activities. These activities included the study of ancient literature, involved the copying, editing, translating, and interpreting of classical Greek and Latin texts, and led to an impressive development of classical scholarship and philology. The humanists also produced a vast amount of literary works in prose and verse, mostly in Latin, and hence they were usually labeled as orators and poets before the term *humanista* came into use. They also claimed philosophy, and especially moral philosophy, as a part of their domain, and proposed to combine eloquence and wisdom, that is, rhetoric and philosophy, thus reviving an ideal formulated by Cicero.[2]

The quantity and quality of the works produced by the humanists, the level of their literary and scholarly achievement, their success and prestige greatly enhanced the role of the studies which they cultivated, and of rhetoric in particular. They soon began to dominate secondary education, and to play a significant, though not a dominant role in the universities.[3] As chancellors and secretaries of princes and republics, as teachers and tutors of noblemen, patricians, and professionals, the humanists acquired a formative influence on the upper classes of Renaissance society. The term "civic humanism" has been used to designate the ideal of an educated citizen in a free republic, especially in Florence during the early fifteenth century.[4] The concept has its validity within its well-defined limits of place and time. Yet I should hesitate to identify civic humanism with humanism as a whole, even in Italy, let alone with the whole of Renaissance civilization. There was a good deal of humanism other than civic during the early fifteenth century, in Florence and elsewhere, and even more of it before and after the half-century that marks the high point of the alliance between humanism and Florentine political thought and propaganda. For humanism included at all times a number of moral and other ideas that were not political or social,[5] and many literary and scholarly pursuits that had nothing to do with thought in any sense of the word. On the other hand, the Renaissance, in Italy and else-where, always cultivated many professional, scholarly, and intellectual tra-ditions that were not rooted in humanism, although they may at one time or another have been influenced or affected by humanism.[6]

To understand Renaissance rhetoric, and that means largely humanist rhetoric, it is useful to start from the classifications of the arts and sciences and from the place rhetoric occupied in them. In the scheme of the seven liberal arts which dominated from late antiquity to the high Middle Ages, rhetoric was allied with the mathematical disciplines, that is, with the *qua-drivium* of arithmetic, geometry, astronomy, and music, and more inti-mately with grammar and dialectic which together with rhetoric formed the *trivium*. When rhetoric was treated as a part of logic, the term logic was not taken in the specific sense, but was merely used as a label to identify the *trivium* with one of the three traditional parts of philosophy. After the rise of the universities in the twelfth and thirteenth century, it became apparent that the seven arts no longer represented the sum total of secular learning or of philosophy, and that the new university subjects, that is, theology, philoso-phy, medicine, and jurisprudence, were different from the liberal arts and were more advanced subjects of study and instruction. Among the arts of the *trivium*, grammar and rhetoric were now confined to elementary and prelimi-nary instruction, whereas logic or dialectic left them far behind and became closely connected with natural philosophy and with other philosophical and scientific disciplines.

The fourteenth century witnessed a rise of grammar and rhetoric, espe-cially in Italy, and this is reflected in the new scheme of the *studia hu-manitatis* which we encounter in the course of the fifteenth century. This scheme, as we saw before, includes grammar, rhetoric, poetry, history, and moral philosophy. It means, when compared with the older scheme of the seven arts, that rhetoric and grammar have now lost their connections with dialectic and with the *quadrivium;* that poetry and history, previously treated as parts of grammar and rhetoric, are now explicitly recognized as related but independent pursuits; and that moral philosophy, one of the three main parts of ancient philosophy, is now reclaimed as a part of the humanities and detached from the other more technical parts of philosophy, following the ancient model of Isocrates and Cicero.

The scholar who mastered these *studia humanitatis,* who had been called *orator et poeta* since the time of Petrarch, finally became known as *human-ista,* a term that originated late in the fifteenth century in the slang of university students and gradually found its way into official documents if not into literature—it was after all a word unknown to Cicero and other ancient writers.[7] We might add that during the eighteenth century the scheme of the humanities gave way to that of the fine arts where poetry and eloquence were grouped together with music and the visual arts, and sometimes with dancing and gardening.[8] With the rise of Romanticism, eloquence was driven out from the illustrious company of the creative arts, whereas poetry, along with the others, was raised to such awesome heights as it had rarely, if ever, reached in previous centuries.

Before we pursue the rhetorical theory and practice of the Renaissance, and the links between its rhetoric and other fields, I should like to discuss briefly the ancient sources of Renaissance rhetoric.

If we begin with the Latin sources, we should remember that the *Rhetorica ad Herennium* and Cicero's *De inventione* had been available through the Middle Ages and were interpreted at different times by a number of commentators. Also some of Cicero's speeches and philosophical writings were more or less widely known during the Middle Ages. On the other hand, Cicero's letters, some of his orations and philosophical writings, and his more mature rhetorical works such as *De oratore, Orator,* and *Brutus* were either rediscovered by the humanists or more widely read than before. This was also true of Asconius, the ancient commentator of Cicero's orations. The other great Roman rhetorician, Quintilian, was known during the Middle Ages only in a truncated version, and his complete text was recovered only during the early fifteenth century. Also the declamations of the elder Seneca and those attributed to Quintilian began to attract greater attention in the fourteenth century.[9] The textual history of these writings in manuscripts and early printed editions and the commentaries written on them still await further investigation. Yet Renaissance Ciceronianism, beginning with Gasparino Barzizza, if not with Petrarch, had a much broader textual basis than had been available to the preceding centuries, and humanists like Loschi and Polenton were encouraged by the model of Asconius to undertake the interpretation of some of Cicero's orations.[10]

The difference between medieval and Renaissance rhetoric is even more striking when we look at the available sources of Greek rhetoric. As we remember, only one Greek oration and three rhetorical treatises had been translated during the thirteenth century, and three of these texts had practically no circulation, whereas the fourth, Aristotle's *Rhetoric,* was treated as a work on moral philosophy and ignored by the professional rhetoricians of the period.[11] During the Renaissance, these texts were retranslated and more widely circulated, and Aristotle's *Rhetoric* was at last studied and utilized by the professional rhetoricians, along with his *Poetics* which became widely known and influential after the end of the fifteenth century, whereas it had been almost, though not entirely, unknown during the preceding centuries.[12] Moreover, the fifteenth and sixteenth centuries produced a large number of Latin translations from the Greek and gradually introduced the entire patrimony of Greek literature, as far as it had survived, into the mainstream of Western learning. In the field of rhetoric, the Attic orators now became completely known, and especially Lysias, Isocrates, and Demosthenes were widely read and admired. To this we must add the later orators such as Dio of Prusa and Libanius, and especially the large body of Greek rhetorical literature: Demetrius and Dionysius of Halicarnassus, ps. Longinus and Menander, Aphthonius, and Hermogenes.[13] The bibliographical information concerning these authors is now being investigated, and this will for the first time provide a firm foundation for exploring their influence.

It is in this area where we may also look for Byzantine influence in Renaissance rhetoric. The history of Byzantine rhetoric and its influence on Italian humanism have recently attracted some scholarly attention,[14] but the subject seems to be in need of much more detailed study than it has received so far. As far as rhetorical theory is concerned, the study of the ancient Greek orators and rhetoricians and their wide diffusion in Latin and vernacular translations, as we find it in the Renaissance, presupposes the Byzantine transmission of these texts and is a part of the general appropriation of the Greek and Byzantine heritage that characterizes the Italian and European Renaissance of the fifteenth and sixteenth century. More specifically, the works of Aphthonius and Hermogenes had dominated Byzantine rhetorical theory before they became known and influential in the West. It is characteristic that an author who combined Byzantine and Western learning, George of Trebisond, and who wrote one of the new and influential rhetorical textbooks of rhetoric in the fifteenth century, was also the first who made extensive use of Hermogenes.[15]

In the field of epistolography, there was a large Byzantine literature, but its influence in the West is not known, except for the Greek Church Fathers and for Libanius. The large literature of Byzantine homilies does not seem to have interested Western scholars, except for the Greek Church Fathers, and the same is apparently true of the large Byzantine literature of panegyrics and encomia. It is important to realize that epistolography and oratory flourished in the East as well as in the West during the medieval centuries, but direct links, if they exist, have not yet been investigated. In the case of secular oratory, we may very well argue that it was based in the East and West on different institutional traditions.

Let us now turn to the rhetorical literature produced by the Renaissance humanists. The general treatises on rhetoric, intended to serve as manuals of instruction, were not as numerous as we might expect, at least during the fifteenth century. We may assume that most of the instruction was based on ancient or even on medieval treatises, and on the use of classical and contemporary models. The best known rhetorical treatises of the fifteenth century are those by Gasparino Barzizza, George of Trebisond, Giorgio Valla, Guillaume Fichet, and Philippus Callimachus.[16] The question to what extent they repeated ancient theories and models and in what way they were influenced by modern practice remains to be clarified in most instances. I had occasion to examine Fichet's treatise which introduces a new terminology of its own, and a sermon composed by Fichet and accompanied by a gloss that is based on his own rhetorical textbook and terminology.[17]

There is a whole literature on imitation which takes up the theme of the Atticists of later antiquity, and in which the merits and demerits of imitating Cicero or other ancient writers are discussed. This literature includes a correspondence between Poliziano and Paolo Cortesi, and treatises by Bembo and Gianfrancesco Pico, and later by Erasmus and others.[18] Valla's *Elegantiae* is strictly speaking a grammatical rather than a rhetorical treatise, but it serves stylistic and rhetorical purposes and it was read and used for centuries for that reason. Rhetorical theory was contained in the commentaries on the works of Cicero and Quintilian, and in the commentaries on Aristotle's *Rhetoric* which in the sixteenth century, unlike the medieval commentaries on that work, were written by humanist rhetoricians and not by Aristotelian philosophers.[19]

The teaching of rhetoric was served, as in antiquity and the Middle Ages, not only by theoretical treatises, but also by collections of models. Numerous speeches and letters, both by ancient and contemporary authors, were copied and collected for the purpose of imitation. There are collections of form speeches, and especially of form letters, form introductions (*exordia*), and form addresses (*salutationes*).[20] It is a humble type of literature, and scholars have been rightly unimpressed by its literary and intellectual level, but its mere existence and frequency helps to remind us of an area of activity that we might otherwise ignore.

Even more significant than the treatises and models intended for rhetorical instruction is the very large literature that reflects the activity of the humanists as trained and self-conscious orators. Orations and letters are probably the most numerous products of humanist prose that have come down to us in manuscripts and early editions, and they evidently constitute only a part of what was actually spoken and written during our period.[21] This literature has usually been despised or ignored by modern historians, and it needs much further study. It does contain a good deal of empty rhetoric and of insincere praise or exaggerated blame. However, much of it is well-written and by classical standards more elegant than the average products of the medieval *dictatores*. Moreover, this literature is full of interesting historical information, and it contains many ideas that are not necessarily false or insincere because they are expressed with eloquence.

In the field of oratory, Renaissance society provided many occasions for which a speech was demanded and where in later times the speech was accompanied or replaced by a play or show or by a recital of poetry or music. Many of these conventions go back to the late Middle Ages, as we have seen, but the fifteenth century left us a much larger number of actual specimens, and they compare favorably in style and content with the earlier products: funeral and wedding speeches; speeches by ambassadors; speeches addressed to popes, princes, or magistrates upon their accession to office or upon their visit to a city; and, less frequently, deliberative speeches to an assembly or council, or lawyers' speeches before a law court. Very frequent are the speeches connected with the universities: orations held at the beginning of the academic year or of a course of lectures, or speeches held by the candidate and his professor upon the conferral of a degree. There were speeches given at the beginning of a public disputation,[22] or before gatherings such as the general chapter of a religious order. There were speeches before an academic or religious assembly in praise of specific saints, especially Augustine, Jerome, St. Catherine of Alexandria, or Thomas Aquinas.[23] Many of these speeches, though addressed to an assembly of friars, were given by secular clerics or by laymen, apparently upon invitation. Vice versa, we find friars and clergymen appearing as orators on secular as well as on religious occasions.

As a further step, humanist rhetorical style began to influence the practice of sacred eloquence. After the middle of the fifteenth century, more and more priests and friars who had enjoyed a humanist education adopted the pattern of secular, humanist eloquence for their sermons, depart from the precepts of the *artes praedicandi,* and preach sermons that begin with a *prooemium,* instead of, or in addition to, a verse from Scripture, and follow the rules for the composition of a secular speech while retaining the theological content pertaining to their subject. Northern listeners such as Luther and Erasmus professed to be shocked by this mundane appearance of sacred oratory, and modern historians have often repeated their criticism, not realizing that they are in fact condemning in the religious literature the same features that they are accustomed to admiring in the religious art of the same period, namely a combination of classical or Renaissance form with religious content. This subject has just begun to attract scholarly attention, but it requires much further study.[24]

I should like to add that humanist oratory also penetrated the vernacular speech, especially in Florence.[25] The orations addressed to incoming officials (*protesti*) follow a rhetorical pattern, and since their content was fixed, namely the praise of justice, the tendency to provide pleasant and interesting variations on the theme is quite understandable. The same was true of contemporary sermons, many of them given by laymen, such as the ones delivered in the lay religious associations (*compagnie*) of Florence.[26] I sometimes wonder whether the greater finesse of literature and art before the nineteenth century may be due to the very fact that the writers and artists had to find new variations on given themes that were well-known to themselves and to their audiences.

No less extensive than the humanist literature of orations was that of letters.[27] We must distinguish between state and private letters. The state letters were composed and copied for rhetorical purposes, and served as an instrument of public propaganda when circulated and published. It is no coincidence that many chancellors and secretaries of princes and republics were noted humanists, who were able to compose the well-phrased letters that satisfied the taste of the senders and recipients. The private letters of the humanists also served a literary and rhetorical purpose, as we can see from the fact that they were often edited and collected by their authors. These letters often read very well, and they also are important sources of biographical, historical, and scholarly information. They are also vehicles of an author's opinions and ideas, and hence the letters of Petrarch, Salutati, Ficino, and others have rightly been utilized for an interpretation and reconstruction of their thought. The large poetical output of the humanists does not directly concern our subject and can only be mentioned in passing. On the other hand, their historical works and their moral treatises and dialogues were conscious prose compositions and clearly intended for a public that would read them not only for their content but also for their linguistic and stylistic elegance of expression.

After a brief description of the rhetorical theory and practice of the humanists, I should like to discuss even more briefly the links that connect the rhetoric of the humanists with their other interests and activities. The humanist study of grammar was closely allied with rhetoric and even subordinate to it, for the purpose of studying grammar was to acquire the mastery of correct Latin that was the prerequisite for any literary composition. The humanist contribution to grammar still remains to be explored, including such fields as orthography and prosody or metrics, which then as before were considered as parts of grammar.[28] Valla's *Elegantiae*, as we saw before, was a contribution to grammar because it attempted to establish a correct Latin phraseology on the basis of classical sources. The work had a strong influence down to the early nineteenth century. It was a great merit of the humanists that they did restore correct Latin usage according to classical standards. The statement made by a distinguished scholar that they thus transformed the living language of medieval Latin into a dead language is belied by the flourishing state of written and spoken Latin for several more centuries.[29]

Valla took a further step that is interesting and should appeal to current philosophers; he considered the linguistic usage of classical Latin as a source and standard of philosophical truth.[30] Yet I cannot see at all that Valla or other humanists formulated a philosophy of language as was done at a later time by Giambattista Vico. Nor do I see any textual evidence for the view that humanist rhetoric and nominalist or terminist logic were closely related on the ground that they were both concerned with language or with individual facts. The humanists were firmly opposed to scholasticism, and especially to nominalism.

The relation between humanist rhetoric and historiography follows in part a pattern that had its precedents in antiquity and to a lesser extent in the Middle Ages. History was a recognized branch of prose literature, and the ancient historians were among the preferred prose writers studied in courses on Greek and Latin literature. The writing of historical works according to the standards of good style and of the ancient historians was a part of the literary activity of the humanists, and in many cases their main occupation.[31] We find many of them employed as official historiographers of princes or cities, and often they combined this assignment with a position of chancellor or teacher. The inserted fictitious speeches were an inheritance from ancient historiography, and it was here that the rhetorical rules were applied with special care. But the "rhetorical" style was no more an obstacle to the practice and refinement of historical criticism for the humanists than it had been for Thucydides. In the late sixteenth century, a new genre of *artes historicae* developed that evidently grew out of the *laudes historiae* in humanist courses and that tried to do for history what rhetoric and poetics had always done for oratory and poetry. This literature which has received some recent attention was intended to guide the reading and teaching as well as the writing of history.[32]

The relation between rhetoric and poetics has been repeatedly mentioned. In the Renaissance, as often before, it was a relation of mutual influence and of parallelism. The less the rhetoricians stressed persuasion and political action, and the more they emphasized the task of speaking and writing well, the more oratory and poetry became the sister arts of writing well in prose and in verse, just as the medieval *dictatores* had conceived them before. In the sixteenth century, this attitude was further encouraged by the pairing of Aristotle's *Rhetoric* and *Poetics*.[33] The emphasis in rhetoric had shifted from persuasion to style and imitation, and to literary criticism, and if we wish to have a complete picture of the literary theory and criticism of the period, we need a detailed study of the rhetorical treatises, including the commentaries on Aristotle's *Rhetoric*, to supplement Weinberg's work on the poetical treatises and on the commentaries on Aristotle's *Poetics*.[34] Even in Renaissance poetics, the influence of Aristotle's *Poetics* was combined with that of his *Rhetoric*, as well as with that of Plato and Horace.[35] There is at least one full-fledged treatise on poetics from the fifteenth century that antedates the influence of Aristotle's *Poetics*,[36] and there is a long work on poetics by a major philosopher that is entirely based on Platonist and not on Aristotelian principles.[37]

We might add that Renaissance poetics, no less than its rhetoric, was applied to the vernacular, and this was only natural. For the vernacular had created new genres of poetry, but no new critical theories comparable to those of antiquity, and as far as vocabulary, grammar, and style are concerned, Italian and the other vernacular languages had to be educated and developed after the model of Latin before they were able to take over all the functions of literary Latin. This can be clearly seen in Dante and Boccaccio, and even more in the writers of the sixteenth century. The view that the humanists tried to abolish the vernacular is plainly wrong. It is refuted by ample evidence, and especially by the vernacular compositions and translations due to the leading humanists themselves.[38]

Of even greater importance, at least for the problem we are pursuing, is the relation between humanist rhetoric and philosophy, and the contribution of the humanists to philosophy, and especially to ethics.[39] As we have seen before, the humanists claimed moral philosophy as a part of their domain, and they proposed, after the model of Cicero, to combine eloquence and wisdom. They often dealt with moral questions in their speeches and letters, and composed numerous treatises and dialogues in which they discussed questions of moral philosophy as well as of politics, religion, and education. This literature contains a great number and variety of ideas, and it has been amply explored and discussed by several scholars. I gladly agree that this literature is interesting and significant, and that it constitutes an important contribution to Renaissance thought and philosophy, but I must qualify this statement in more than one way.

The humanists were not professional philosophers, and their writings on moral subjects lack the terminological precision and logical consistency that we have a right to expect of professional philosophers. Secondly, the opinions held by a humanist in a given passage may be contradicted by his opinions in another work or even in another passage of the same work, and even more by the opinions of other humanists. In other words, even if we were able to construct a coherent philosophy for individual humanists, we cannot discover a common philosophy for all humanists, and hence it is not possible to define their contribution in terms of a specific set of philosophical doctrines. Finally, the opinions voiced by the humanists may at times be original in content or detail, but in many instances they are mere repetitions or variations of ancient philosophical ideas. Hence any attempt to construct the thought of a humanist without reference to the classical sources that determined it and of which he was fully conscious must be highly misleading and is often wrong.

The humanists were as eclectic in philosophy as their admired master Cicero had been, and many of their more consistent philosophical efforts were restatements of ancient doctrines. As a matter of fact, thanks to humanist efforts, the Renaissance witnessed a revival of such ancient systems as Stoicism, Epicureanism, and Scepticism.[40] Some of the best contributions the humanists made to philosophy consisted in translating or retranslating the sources of Greek philosophy, and in restating and popularizing Greek philosophical ideas and doctrines that were not connected with the Aristotelian and Neoplatonic traditions—which were the only ones known to the medieval philosophers. In providing new alternatives for philosophical and scientific thought, the humanists created a kind of intellectual fermentation, and thus they prepared the ground for the philosophers of the seventeenth century who were far more original than the humanists themselves.

Finally, we must mention the impact of humanist rhetoric on a field that was not a part of the *studia humanitatis* but had belonged to the *trivium* and more recently to philosophy: logic or dialectic.[41] There is a whole series of humanist attempts to reform logic that began with Lorenzo Valla and ended with Nizolius and with Peter Ramus and his school.[42] These authors were trained humanists and tried to replace Aristotelian and scholastic logic with a logic subordinated to rhetoric. Their aim was clarity rather than precision, two qualities that are by no means always identical. When Ramus assigned invention and disposition to dialectic, he split traditional rhetoric into two parts and called the first part dialectic, putting it into the place previously occupied by scholastic logic.

It remains for us to consider briefly the professional philosophers who were concerned with the problems of natural philosophy and metaphysics, subjects that never belonged to the domain of the humanists and that were based on the traditions of medieval and ultimately of ancient Greek philosophy. The humanists had often attacked the scholastic philosophers and their Aristotelianism, but this tradition remained very strong throughout the Renaissance period, and especially in Italy, it dominated the teaching of philosophy at the universities and influenced large sectors of popular thought and literature.[43] These Aristotelian philosophers were not interested in rhetoric or poetics, and many of them were quite insensitive to the charge that their Latin terminology and style were ''barbarous.''

However, Renaissance Aristotelianism was in several ways exposed to the influence of humanism and transformed by this influence. The humanists supplied new translations of Aristotle that competed with the medieval versions and often led to interesting comparisons. They translated the works of the ancient Greek commentators on Aristotle, including Alexander and Simplicius, many of them for the first time, and thus supplied new and authoritative alternatives to the commentaries of Averroes and Thomas Aquinas.[44] They insisted on the study of the Greek text of Aristotle. There were also several humanists who favored Aristotle over other ancient thinkers and claimed to understand him better than his scholastic interpreters were able to do. This attitude appears first in Petrarch, and it was adopted by Leonardo Bruni, Ermolao Barbaro, Jacques Lefèvre d'Etaples, Philip Melanchthon, and many others.[45] We may add that during the fifteenth and sixteenth century, not only Aristotle's *Rhetoric* and *Poetics*, but also his *Ethics*, *Politics*,

and other moral writings were largely, if not entirely, left to the humanists.[46] Yet in the fields of logic, natural philosophy, and metaphysics, the
scholastic tradition held firm, except for the use of new translations, the
newly translated Greek commentators, and the Greek text, which led to a
better understanding of Aristotle than the scholastics had reached, for example in the case of Jacopo Zabarella.[47]

The Renaissance Platonists are often treated as a part of the humanist
movement, but I think they deserve a place of their own, apart from humanism proper to which they were clearly indebted, and from Aristotelian scholasticism by which they were also more deeply influenced than is commonly
known.[48] Ficino and others supplied the first complete translations of Plato
and of the Neoplatonists, thus continuing the work of the humanists.[49] Yet
they were interested in philosophical doctrine rather than in literary form,
and they inherited Plato's critique of the rhetoricians and the poets. They
tended, however, to tone down this critique, for they harmonized Plato's critique of the rhetoricians in the *Gorgias* with his defense of a philosophical
rhetoric in the *Phaedrus;* they attached great importance to the doctrine of
poetic madness, disregarding the ironic overtones of the *Ion;* and they practically ignored Plato's critique of Homer and the other poets. Pico's defense
of the scholastic philosophers against Ermolao Barbaro reflects his tendency
to stress content rather than form and to separate philosophy from rhetoric,
whereas Melanchthon, although sympathetic to Aristotle, wrote a posthumous defense of Ermolao against Pico, restating the typical humanist alliance of wisdom and eloquence.[50]

The natural philosophers of the sixteenth century attempted to develop
new and original positions beyond the customary alternatives of scholasticism and humanism, Aristotelianism and Platonism. Their contribution to
our problem seems to have been marginal, and it has not yet received sufficient scholarly attention. Girolamo Fracastoro wrote a dialogue on poetics
that reflects his humanist background rather than his contributions to natural
philosophy.[51] Tommaso Campanella composed treatises on rhetoric, poetics, and historiography that have not yet been studied in detail.[52] Francesco Patrizi composed treatises on rhetoric, the theory of history, and poetics.[53] His extensive work on poetics which has recently been published for
the first time in a complete text deserves further study. As all of Patrizi's
works, it is markedly anti-Aristotelian and attempts to construct a new
theory of poetics, drawing on Plato and the Neoplatonists.[54]

On the whole, Renaissance philosophers, whether Aristotelians, Platonists, or natural philosophers, showed comparatively little interest in rhetoric and poetics and left these fields to the humanists and literary critics.

Before concluding, I should like to add a few words about the history of our subject after the Renaissance, including our own time. The seventeenth century was the great age in which the mathematical and physical sciences were placed on a new foundation, one that has remained valid to the present day in spite of later additions and transformations. The attempts to compete with the new sciences and to emulate their methods and achievements also led with Descartes, Spinoza, and others to a new philosophy that abandoned in principle, though not always in practice, the traditions of medieval as well as Renaissance philosophy. These momentous changes did not for a while affect the fields of rhetoric and poetics, or the theory and practice of the arts in general. The place of rhetoric among the humanities and the basic notions of traditional rhetoric remained unchanged through the seventeenth and part of the eighteenth century. When the new system of the fine arts began to take shape in the course of the eighteenth century, eloquence at first retained its place alongside poetry, as may be seen in the work of Baumgarten who coined the term aesthetics and established it as a philosophical theory of the arts.[55]

However, the eighteenth century brought about a radical change in the theory and practice of the arts that reached its high point in the early nineteenth century and that in many ways is still with us.[56] I am speaking of Romanticism, a movement which has greatly contributed to our conception and understanding of history and the arts, but which is also responsible for many ideas that are wrong and harmful and that were exaggerated and carried *ad adsurdum* long after the original Romantic movement had passed away. I have often thought that it was the task of my generation of scholars to liquidate the remnants of Romantic misconceptions in our respective fields, but I am now forced to observe that in recent years some of the worst excesses of Romanticism have been revived and seem to be immune to factual or rational refutation, at least among laymen if not among professional scholars—although I find that also professional scholars often bow to popular fashions against their own better judgment and knowledge.

The aesthetics of Romanticism rejected all rules in the arts and extolled the genius and his power of original expression. In early Romanticism, this was a highly elitist conception that was applied only to the outstanding artist, but in our egalitarian age we have now reached the point where every

activity, artistic or otherwise, is considered creative, and where every person, whether gifted or not, is considered original and free from any rules
and restrictions, aesthetical or ethical. Modern writers find it difficult to
believe that God created the world out of nothing, but they see no difficulty
in assuming that a human artist, even a minor artist, creates his art out of
nothing. They should know from classical and modern psychology that our
productive imagination does not produce anything out of nothing, but works
by freely recombining past impressions and experiences, with each other and
with the basic concepts inherent in our mind.

An early consequence of the Romantic movement was the complete rejection of rhetoric as a system of rules. The cult of the original and the spontaneous led to the emphasis on poetry, and to a lesser extent, on prose fiction,
as the exclusive domain of literary criticism and of literary history, leaving
out entirely the area of doctrinal prose that earlier literary historians of literature had still included, and relinquishing it in a sense to the reign of formless
pedantry uninhibited by any literary discipline. The term "rhetoric" in a
positive sense tended to disappear, although it has been continued or revived
as a teaching subject in a few universities. The traditional content of rhetoric
was split up among several disciplines that differ from each other in their
goals and assumptions and do not even seem to be related to each other: aesthetics, which is a part of philosophy; literary scholarship and composition,
which constitute different sectors of English literature and of other literatures; and literary criticism, which is an enterprise shared by scholars with
writers and journalists.

The old *ars dictaminis* and *ars arengandi* have sunk to philistine depths:
there are courses and handbooks of business correspondence for future secretaries, and I have seen a manual for college officials that contains form
letters soliciting donations from different types of alumni. There are, or at
least there were until recently, letter-writers with models for love letters, and
with typical letters of condolence, congratulation, and recommendation. I
bought for fun a book containing models for after-dinner addresses, featur-
ing jokes and stories with which a contemporary speech begins as invariably
as a medieval sermon begins with a verse from Scripture—a veritable *ars
dictaminis* or *ars arengandi Americana*.[57] We have a flourishing tradition of
political oratory, in this country as in England and other countries, but although we often hear of speeches written by ghost writers, I am not aware of
any conscious theory concerning the form and delivery of a speech, as
against its content which is of course dictated by the political circumstances,

the opinions of the speaker and his advisers, and the emotions and preconceptions of the expected audience.

What we have left of the glorious and ancient tradition of rhetoric are
some broken pieces without the name, of varying quality and pretense, but
sometimes sufficient to kindle a renewed interest in the history of rhetoric.[58]
With the recent progress of vulgarized Romanticism, even the teaching of
composition has been replaced by an emphasis on self-expression, a part of
the general tendency among educators to teach the unteachable and to refuse
to teach the teachable. I remember a distinguished friend and fellow scholar
who took a course in creative writing and was ready to apply the flashback
technique to a historical paper until I successfully advised him against this
experiment.

The heirs of rhetoric in modern times have usually refrained from competing with philosophy in the manner attempted more or less successfully by
their ancient predecessors. Yet there have been literary critics who claim
that they are better students and historians of philosophy than the professional philosophers, and that also the poets of the past were better philosophers than their philosophical contemporaries. In our age when so many professional philosophers are anti-historical and omit from their consideration
many important problems of traditional philosophy, the literary critics have
an easy time, and we should even be grateful to them if they take up the history of past philosophy abandoned by the philosophers. I gladly agree that
there is a good deal of philosophy in the great poets and writers of the past,
if we take philosophy in the broad rather than in the strict professional sense
of the term. However, the literary critics spoil their game when they first insist on the philosophical importance of past writers and then refuse to apply
to their thought the standards of conceptual precision and consistency that
are the earmarks of a philosopher, avoiding their intellectual responsibility
with such phrases as intellectual play or deliberate ambiguity. There are
plenty of ambiguities and inconsistencies even in the greatest professional
philosophers, but the task of understanding and interpreting them just
begins, and does not end, with the awareness of these inconsistencies. For I
venture to think and to say that the only safe way for a philosopher who tries
to avoid inconsistencies altogether is to have and express only one single
idea.

I am afraid we are left in a chaos, in rhetoric as in other areas of our civilization. The old formulas have ceased to satisfy, and the new ones that may
satisfy have not yet appeared. I am no prophet and do not claim to know the

answers to our grave educational and other problems. At present, everybody has to find his own way, and by lucky chance or providence, there seem to be enough people around, old and young, who have found a decent solution for themselves and for their friends and pupils. My political sympathies are democratic as I understand that word, and although I admire Plato for many reasons, I should not like to see my ideas or opinions imposed on others by force. The ideas that I have seen imposed on people in various places during the present century are neither true nor adequate, and I do not hope to see the day when the truth of ideas, political or otherwise, is measured by the number of divisions or airplanes that may be mobilized in their support.

What we as teachers can do is to transmit and spread knowledge—even information, which is now considered to be a bad word, but which is a very important thing and which certainly is the basis of any original ideas that have validity. I also think that we must try to extend the area of our knowledge, as best we can, and thus limit the range of mere opinion, and originality. I see no value in ideas that are original but false.

We also should encourage in all areas an effort to aim at clarity and consistency which seem to be the basic concern of rhetoric and philosophy. Rules are not sufficient, and talent is needed, as the ancient rhetoricians knew very well, although I am afraid talent is not as widely diffused as people now like to believe. Knowledge is needed, for I do not think originality can or should be based on ignorance. To be sure, not everything is known or can be known, and thus the range of opinion and of taste will always remain large enough to satisfy our desire for intellectual freedom. Many people now seem to feel that submitting to the truth, factual or rational, and to valid standards of conduct and of taste, is a restriction of their freedom, and that the best defense of this freedom is to deny that there is any valid truth or standard. Such views were expressed more subtly by the sceptical philosophers of antiquity and of later times. I do not share them, and rather believe with many respectable philosophers that the submission to truth and to valid norms is what constitutes our true intellectual and moral freedom.

I must profess in the end something that may have been inferred from my previous statements. I am at heart a Platonist, on the issue of rhetoric as on many, though not on all, others. Rhetoric in all its forms is based on mere opinion, and therefore it should be subordinated to philosophy, that is, to all forms of valid knowledge where such knowledge is available. Our ability to write and to speak well must be disciplined by the acquisition of knowledge and the refutation of error, and used as an effective tool for expressing and conveying knowledge and insight. Rhetoric is important, as it always was, as a technique of expression, for we wish and try to write and speak well and clearly. Yet in our universe of discourse, and in our system of education that should reflect this universe, rhetoric should not occupy the center, but be subordinated, not only to philosophy, but also to the sciences as well as to poetry and the other arts.

Notes

Part One: Renaissance Thought and Classical Antiquity

INTRODUCTION

1. Jacob Burckhardt, *Die Cultur der Renaissance in Italien* (Basel, 1860), trans. by S. G. C. Middlemore as *The Civilization of the Renaissance in Italy* (London, 1878), and many subsequent editions in both languages. Johan Huizinga, *The Waning of the Middle Ages* (London, 1924). Wallace K. Ferguson, *The Renaissance in Historical Thought* (Boston, 1948). Symposium on the Renaissance by Dana B. Durand, Hans Baron, et al., in *Journal of the History of Ideas* 4 (1943): 1–74. Erwin Panofsky, *Renaissance and Renascences in Western Art* (Stockholm, 1960). August Buck, ed., *Zu Begriff und Problem der Renaissance* (Darmstadt, 1969). François Masai, "La notion de Renaissance," in *Les catégories en histoire* (Brussels, 1968), pp. 57–86.

2. *The Battle of the Seven Arts . . . by Henri d'Andeli*, ed. L. J. Paetow (Berkeley, 1914). Eduard Norden, *Die antike Kunstprosa vom VI. Jahrhundert v. Chr. bis in die Zeit der Renaissance,* 2 vols. (Leipzig, 1898), 2: 688ff., 724ff.

1. THE HUMANIST MOVEMENT

1. For some influential definitions of humanism, with which I happen to disagree, see Étienne Gilson, *Saint Thomas d'Aquin* (Paris, 1925), pp. 6–7; *id.,* "Humanisme médiéval et Renaissance," *Les idées et les lettres* (Paris, 1932), p. 189ff.; Douglas Bush, *The Renaissance and English Humanism* (Toronto, 1939), p. 39ff.; *id., Classical Influences in Renaissance Literature* (Cambridge, Mass., 1952), p. 48ff.; Gerald G. Walsh, *Medieval Humanism* (New York, 1942), p. 1: "Humanism, in general, I take to be the idea that a human being is meant to achieve, during life, a fair measure of human happiness" (by this definition Aristotle is a humanist, but Petrarch is not); Paul Renucci, *L'Aventure de l'humanisme européen au Moyen Age* (Paris, 1953), p. 9.

2. Walter Rüegg, *Cicero und der Humanismus* (Zurich, 1946), p. 1ff.

3. See essay 5. Augusto Campana, "The Origin of the Word 'Humanist,' " *Journal of the Warburg and Courtauld Institutes* 9 (1946): 60–73.

4. Werner Jaeger, *Humanism and Theology* (Milwaukee, 1943), pp. 20ff., 72ff. Rudolf Pfeiffer, *Humanitas Erasmiana* (Leipzig-Berlin, 1931).

5. See essay 5.

6. This has been done, to a certain extent, by Eugenio Garin, *Der italienische Humanismus* (Bern, 1947).

7. Hans von Arnim, *Leben und Werke des Dio von Prusa* (Berlin, 1898), pp. 4–114. Heinrich Gomperz, *Sophistik und Rhetorik* (Leipzig, 1912). Werner Jaeger, *Paideia: The Ideals of Greek Culture*, trans. Gilbert Highet, 3 vols. (Oxford, 1939–44), 1: 286–331 and 3: 46–70, 132–55. See chapter 12.

8. Richard McKeon, "Rhetoric in the Middle Ages," *Speculum* 17 (1942): 1–32.

9. Alfredo Galletti, *L'Eloquenza dalle origini al XVI secolo* [*Storia dei generi letterari italiani*] (Milan, 1904–38).

10. Remigio Sabbadini, *Le scoperte dei codici latini e greci ne'secoli XIV e XV*, 2 vols. (Florence, 1905–14). Maximilian Manitius, *Handschriften antiker Autoren in mittelalterlichen Bibliothekskatalogen* (Leipzig, 1935). Giuseppe Billanovich, "Petrarch and the Textual Tradition of Livy," *Journal of the Warburg and Courtauld Institutes* 14 (1951): 137–208. *Catalogus Translationum et Commentariorum*, 3 vols., ed. P. O. Kristeller and F. Edward Cranz (Washington, D.C., 1960–76), especially the articles on Juvenal by Eva M. Sanford (vol. 1) and on Persius by Dorothy M. Robathan and F. Edward Cranz (vol. 3). *Der Kommentar in der Renaissance*, ed. August Buck and Otto Herding (Boppard, 1975).

11. Louise R. Loomis, *Medieval Hellenism* (Lancaster, Pa., 1906). Valuable recent studies by Roberto Weiss and others do not fundamentally alter this picture. Yet Sicily and Southern Italy in this respect occupy a place of their own. See Weiss, "The Greek Culture of South Italy in the Later Middle Ages," *British Academy, Proceedings* 37 (1951): 23–50. Robert Devreesse, *Les manuscrits grecs de l'Italie méridionale* [Biblioteca Vaticana, *Studi e Testi* 183] (Vatican City, 1955). Kenneth M. Setton, "The Byzantine Background to the Italian Renaissance," *Proceedings of the American Philosophical Society* 199 (1956): 1–76.

12. Karl Krumbacher, *Geschichte der byzantinischen Literatur*, 2d ed. (Munich, 1897). Louis Bréhier, *La civilisation byzantine* (Paris, 1950). Aleksandr Aleksandrovich Vasiliev, *History of the Byzantine Empire* (Madison, Wis., 1952), pp. 713–22. Jean Verpeaux, "Byzance et l'humanisme," *Bulletin de l'Association Guillaume Budé*, 3d ser., no. 3 (October 1952): 25–38. See essay 7.

13. Maurice De Wulf, *Histoire de la philosophie médiévale*, 6th ed., 3 vols. (Louvain, 1934–47), 1: 64–80 and 2: 25–58 (these valuable sections by Auguste Pelzer have not been completely included in the American translation). George Sarton, *Introduction to the History of Science*, 3 vols. (Baltimore, Md., 1927–48). Joseph Thomas Muckle, "Greek Works Translated Directly Into Latin Before 1350," *Mediaeval Studies* 4 (1942): 33–42 and 5 (1943): 102–14. George Lacombe et al., *Aristoteles Latinus, Codices*, 3 vols. (Rome, 1939; Cambridge, 1955; Bruges and Paris, 1961). Eugenio Garin, "Le traduzioni umanistiche di Aristotele nel secolo XV," *Atti e Memorie dell'Accademia Fiorentina di Scienze Morali "La Colombaria"* 16 [n.s. 2] (1947–50, published 1951): 55–104. *Catalogus Translationum*, ed. Kristeller and Cranz, especially the article on Alexander of Aphrodisias by F. Edward Cranz (vol. 1).

14. Giovanni Gentile, *La filosofia* [*Storia dei generi letterari italiani*] (Milan, 1904–15), reprinted as vol. 11 of his *Opere* under the title *Storia della filosofia italiana* (*fino a Lorenzo Valla*), 2d ed., ed. Vito A. Bellezza (Florence, 1962), and under the same title as part of *Storia della filosofia italiana*, ed. Eugenio Garin, 2 vols. (Florence, 1969), 1: 3–216; Eugenio Garin, *Der italienische Humanismus; id., La filosofia* [*Storia dei generi letterari italiani*], 2 vols. (Milan, 1947). Giuseppe Saitta, *Il pensiero italiano nell'Umanesimo e nel Rinascimento*, 3 vols. (Bologna, 1949–51). Charles Trinkaus, *Adversity's Noblemen* (New York, 1940); *id., In Our Image and Likeness*, 2 vols. (Chicago, 1970).

15. Charles Lenient, *De Ciceroniano bello apud recentiores* (Paris, 1855). Remigio Sabbadini, *Storia del ciceronianismo* (Turin, 1885). Tadeusz Zielinski, *Cicero im Wandel der Jahrhunderte*, 3d ed. (Leipzig, 1912). Hans Baron, "Cicero and the Roman Civic Spirit in the Middle Ages and Early Renaissance," *Bulletin of the John Rylands Library* 22 (1938): 72–97. Rüegg, *Cicero und der Humanismus*. Izora Scott, *Controversies Over the Imitation of Cicero* (New York, 1910).

16. Alamanno Rinuccini, *Lettere ed Orazioni*, ed. Vito R. Giustiniani (Florence, 1953), p. 97.

17. P. O. Kristeller, "Florentine Platonism and Its Relations with Humanism and Scholasticism," *Church History* 8 (1939): 201–11.

18. Giovanni Gentile, "Il concetto dell'uomo nel Rinascimento," *Il pensiero italiano del Rinascimento*, 3d ed. (Florence, 1940), pp. 47–113. See also essay 9.

19. Cf. "Du repentir," *Essais* III, 2.

2. THE ARISTOTELIAN TRADITION

1. Werner Jaeger, *Aristotle*, 2d ed. (Oxford, 1948). Ingemar Düring, *Aristotle in the Ancient Biographical Tradition* (Göteborg, 1957). Paul Moraux, *Der Aristotelismus bei den Griechen von Andronikos bis Alexander von Aphrodisias*, vol. 1 (Berlin, 1973).

2. Cf. Raymond Klibansky, *The Continuity of the Platonic Tradition during the Middle Ages* (Oxford, 1939), p. 13.

3. Basile Tatakis, *La philosophie byzantine* [Émile Bréhier, *Histoire de la philosophie*, deuxième fascicle supplémentaire] (Paris, 1940). Klaus Oehler, "Aristoteles in Byzanz," *Antike Philosophie und byzantinisches Mittelalter* (Munich, 1969), pp. 272–86. André Wartelle, *Inventaire des manuscrits grecs d'Aristote et de ses commentaires* (Paris, 1963).

4. Moritz Steinschneider, *Die arabischen Übersetzungen aus dem Griechischen* [*Beihefte zum Centralblatt für Bibliothekswesen*, no. 5] (Leipzig, 1890), pp. 51–82 and [no. 12] (Leipzig, 1893; reprint ed., Graz, 1960), pp. 129–240. Richard Walzer, "Arabic Transmission of Greek Thought to Medieval Europe," *Bulletin of the John Rylands Library* 29 (1945–46): 160–83; *id., Greek into Arabic* (Oxford, 1963). 'Abd al-Rahmān Badawī, *La transmission de la philosophie grecque au monde arabe* (Paris, 1968).

5. See essay 1, note 13. Moritz Steinschneider, "Die europäischen Übersetzungen aus dem Arabischen," *Sitzungsberichte der kaiserlichen Akademie der Wissenschaf-*

ten in Wien, Philosophisch-Historische Klasse, 149, no. 4 (1904) and 151, no. 1 (1906; reprint ed. Graz, 1956).

6. Hastings Rashdall, *The Universities of Europe in the Middle Ages,* 2d ed., 3 vols., ed. Frederick Powicke and Alfred B. Emden (Oxford, 1936). Heinrich S. Denifle and Émile Chatelain, *Chartularium Universitatis Parisiensis,* 4 vols. (Paris, 1889–97).

7. For some curious examples, see Ernest A. Moody, "Galileo and Avempace," *Journal of the History of Ideas* 12 (1951): 163–93, 375–422.

8. Ernest Renan, *Averroès et l'averroïsme,* 3d ed. (Paris, 1867). Pierre Mandonnet, *Siger de Brabant et l'averroïsme latin au XIIIe siècle,* 2d ed. (Louvain, 1908–11). Fernand Van Steenberghen, *Les oeuvres et la doctrine de Siger de Brabant* (Brussels, 1938); *id., Siger de Brabant d'après ses oeuvres inédites,* 2 vols. (Louvain, 1931–42). Bruno Nardi, *Sigieri di Brabante nel pensiero del Rinascimento italiano* (Rome, 1945); *id.,* "Averroismo," *Enciclopedia Cattolica* 2 (Vatican City, 1949): 524–30. Anneliese Maier, "Eine italienische Averroistenschule aus der ersten Hälfte des 14. Jahrhunderts," *Die Vorläufer Galileis im 14. Jahrhundert* (Rome, 1949), pp. 251–78. P. O. Kristeller, "Petrarch's 'Averroists,' " *Bibliothèque d'Humanisme et Renaissance* 14 (1952): 59–65. Zdzislaw Kuksewicz, *Averroïsme Bolonais au XIVe siècle* (Wroclaw, 1965); *id., De Siger de Brabant à Jacques de Plaisance* (Wroclaw, 1968).

9. Ricardo Garcia Villoslada, *La Universidad de Paris durante los estudios de Francisco de Vitoria* (Rome, 1938).

10. William T. Costello, *The Scholastic Curriculum at Early Seventeenth-Century Cambridge* (Cambridge, Mass., 1958). Mark H. Curtis, *Oxford and Cambridge in Transition* (Oxford, 1959).

11. Carlo Giacon, *La seconda scolastica,* 3 vols. (Milan, 1944–50).

12. Peter Peterson, *Geschichte der aristotelischen Philosophie im protestantischen Deutschland* (Leipzig, 1921). Max Wundt, *Die deutsche Schulmetaphysik des 17. Jahrhunderts* (Tübingen, 1939).

13. Étienne Gilson, *Etudes sur le rôle de la pensée médiévale dans la formation du systemè cartésien* (Paris, 1930). Matthias Meier, *Descartes und die Renaissance* (Muenster, 1914). Léon Blanchet, *Les antecédents historiques du "Je pense, donc je suis"* (Paris, 1920). Harry Austryn Wolfson, *The Philosophy of Spinoza,* 2 vols. (Cambridge, Mass., 1934). Joseph Politella, *Platonism, Aristotelianism, and Cabalism in the Philosophy of Leibniz* (Philadelphia, 1938).

14. Martin Grabmann, *Mittelalterliches Geistesleben,* vol. 2 (Munich, 1936), pp. 239–71; *id.,* "Gentile da Cingoli," *Sitzungsberichte der bayerischen Akademie der Wissenschaften,* Philosophisch-Historische Abteilung, Jahrgang 1940, no. 9 (Munich, 1941); *id.,* "L'Averroismo italiano al tempo di Dante," *Rivista di filosofia neo-scolastica* 38 (1946): 260–77. Bruno Nardi, "L'averroismo bolognese nel secolo XIII e Taddeo Alderotto," *Rivista di storia della filosofia* 23 (1931): 504–17. P. O. Kristeller, "A Philosophical Treatise from Bologna Dedicated to Guido Cavalcanti," in *Medioevo e Rinascimento, Studi in Onore di Bruno Nardi,* 2 vols. (Florence, 1955), 1: 425–63. See also note 8.

15. Marshall Clagett, *Giovanni Marliani and Late Medieval Physics* (New York,

1941). Silvestro da Valsanzibio, *Vita e dottrina di Gaetano di Thiene,* 2d ed. (Padua, 1949). Curtis Wilson, *William Heytesbury* (Madison, Wis., 1956). Theodore E. James, "De primo et ultimo instanti Petri Alboini Mantuani" (Ph.D. diss., Columbia University, 1968).

16. John Herman Randall, Jr., "The Development of Scientific Method in the School of Padua," *Journal of the History of Ideas* 1 (1940): 177–206, reprinted in his *The School of Padua and the Emergence of Modern Science* (Padua, 1961), pp. 13–68. William F. Edwards, "The Logic of Jacopo Zabarella" (Ph.D. diss., Columbia University, 1960). P. O. Kristeller, "Renaissance Aristotelianism," *Greek, Roman, and Byzantine Studies* 6 (1965): 157–74. Edward P. Mahoney, "The Early Psychology of Agostino Nifo" (Ph.D. diss., Columbia University, 1966). Charles B. Schmitt, *A Critical Survey and Bibliography of Renaissance Aristotelianism* (Padua, 1971). Herbert S. Matsen, *Alessandro Achillini (1463–1512) and His Doctrine of "Universals" and "Transcendentals"* (Lewisburgh, Pa., 1974). See also, Charles H. Lohr, "Renaissance Latin Aristotle Commentaries," *Studies in the Renaissance* 21 (1974), *Renaissance Quarterly* 28 (1975), *ibid.,* 29 (1976), *ibid.,* 30 (1977), to be continued. F. Edward Cranz, *A Bibliography of Aristotle Editions 1501–1600* (Baden-Baden, 1971).

17. Franz Ehrle, *Der Sentenzenkommentar Peters von Candia* (Muenster, 1925), p. 114ff. Ricardo Garcia Villoslada, *La Universidad de Paris durante los estudios de Francisco de Vitoria,* pp. 279–307. P. O. Kristeller, *Medieval Aspects of Renaissance Learning,* ed. and trans. Edward P. Mahoney (Durham, N.C., 1974), pp. 29–91.

18. P. O. Kristeller, *Studies in Renaissance Thought and Letters* (Rome, 1956), pp. 337–53.

19. Francesco Patrizi, *Discussiones Peripateticae* (Basel, 1581).

20. See essays 13 and 14.

21. Aristotle, *De arte poetica* Guillelmo de Moerbeke interprete, ed. Erse Valgimigli, Ezio Franceschini, and Lorenzo Minio-Paluello [*Aristoteles Latinus,* vol. 33] (Bruges and Paris, 1953).

22. Joel Elias Spingarn, *A History of Literary Criticism in the Renaissance,* 2d ed. (New York, 1908). Giuseppe Toffanin, *La fine dell' umanesimo* (Turin, 1920). Bernard Weinberg, *A History of Literary Criticism in the Italian Renaissance,* 2 vols. (Chicago, 1961).

23. For example, in the work of Ulisse Aldrovandi.

24. Léontine Zanta, *La renaissance du stoïcisme au XVIe siècle* (Paris, 1914). P. O. Kristeller, *Studies in Renaissance Thought and Letters,* pp. 279–86; *id.,* "A New Manuscript Source for Pomponazzi's Theory of the Soul . . . ," *Revue Internationale de Philosophie,* vol. 2, fasc. 2 [16 of the series] (1951): 144–57; *id.,* "Two Unpublished Questions on the Soul by Pietro Pomponazzi," *Medievalia et Humanistica* 9 (1955): 76–101 and 10 (1956): 151. John Herman Randall, Jr., "Pietro Pomponazzi: Introduction," in *The Renaissance Philosophy of Man,* ed. Ernst Cassirer, P. O. Kristeller, and J. H. Randall, Jr. (Chicago, 1948), pp. 257–79.

25. For Bruni, see Eugenio Garin, *Prosatori latini del Quattrocento* (Milan, 1952), p. 41ff. For Ermolao, see Quirinus Breen, "Giovanni Pico della Mirandola

on the Conflict of Philosophy and Rhetoric . . . ," *Journal of the History of Ideas* 13 (1952): 384–426, reprinted in his *Christianity and Humanism* (Grand Rapids, Mich., 1968), pp. 1–68.

26. *The Battle of the Seven Arts . . . by Henri d'Andeli*, ed. L. J. Paetow (Berkeley, 1914). Lynn Thorndike, *Science and Thought in the Fifteenth Century* (New York, 1929), pp. 24–58. Eugenio Garin, *La disputa delle arti nel Quattrocento* (Florence, 1947).

27. Perry Miller, *The New England Mind* (New York, 1939). Walter J. Ong, *Ramus, Method, and the Decay of Dialogue* (Cambridge, Mass., 1958); *id., Ramus and Talon Inventory* (Cambridge, Mass., 1958).

28. P. O. Kristeller, "Florentine Platonism and Its Relations with Humanism and Scholasticism," *Church History* 8 (1939): 201–11; *id.*, "The Scholastic Background of Marsilio Ficino," *Studies in Renaissance Thought and Letters*, pp. 35–97. Eugenio Garin, *Giovanni Pico della Mirandola* (Florence, 1937). Avery Dulles, *Princeps Concordiae* (Cambridge, Mass., 1941); Breen, "Giovanni Pico della Mirandola. . . ."

29. Ernst Cassirer, *Das Erkenntnisproblem*, vol. 1 (Berlin, 1922).

30. Edward W. Strong, *Procedures and Metaphysics* (Berkeley, 1936).

31. Moody, "Galileo and Avempace."

32. Alexandre Koyré, *Etudes Galiléennes*, 3 vols. (Paris, 1939).

3. RENAISSANCE PLATONISM

1. Alfred N. Whitehead, *Process and Reality* (New York, 1941), p. 63.

2. Philip Merlan, *From Platonism to Neoplatonism* (The Hague, 1953).

3. Harold Cherniss, *The Riddle of the Early Academy* (Berkeley, 1945).

4. Willy Theiler, *Die Vorbereitung des Neuplatonismus* (Berlin, 1930).

5. A.-J. Festugière, *La révélation d'Hermès Trismégiste*, 4 vols. (Paris, 1944–54).

6. Proclus, *The Elements of Theology*, ed. and trans. E. R. Dodds (Oxford, 1933).

7. Raymond Klibansky, *The Continuity of the Platonic Tradition during the Middle Ages* (London, 1939, 1950). This little book is the most important single, though not the only, source of this essay down to the fifteenth century. Cf. also Paul Shorey, *Platonism Ancient and Modern* (Berkeley, 1938).

8. See essay 1, note 12, and essay 2, note 3.

9. Milton V. Anastos, "Pletho's Calendar and Liturgy," *Dumbarton Oaks Papers* 4 (1948): 183–305. François Masai, *Pléthon et le Platonisme de Mistra* (Paris, 1956). For the conception of pagan theology, Plethon (like Ficino) was obviously indebted to Proclus. Cf. H. D. Saffrey, "'Notes platoniciennes de Marsile Ficin dans un manuscrit de Proclus," *Bibliothèque d'Humanisme et Renaissance* 21 (1959): 161–84.

10. Ludwig Mohler, *Kardinal Bessarion*, 3 vols. (Paderborn, 1923–42). John Monfasani, *Georges of Trebisond* (Leyden, 1976).

11. See essay 2, note 4. Franz Rosenthal, "On the Knowledge of Plato's Philosophy in the Islamic World," *Islamic Culture* 14 (1940): 387–422.

12. Gershom Scholem, *Major Trends in Jewish Mysticism* (Jerusalem, 1941).

13. *De Civitate Dei* VIII, 5 and 9ff.; IX, 1; X, 1. See also, Pierre Courcelle, *Recherches sur les Confessions de Saint Augustin* (Paris, 1950).

14. Gabriel Théry, *Etudes Dionysiennes*, 2 vols. (Paris, 1932–37).

15. Toni Schmid, "Ein Timaioskommentar in Sigtuna," *Classica et Mediaevalia* 10 (1948): 220–66.

16. Eugenio Garin, "Una fonte ermetica poco nota," *La Rinascita* 13 (1940): 202–66.

17. *Corpus Platonicum Medii Aevi, Plato Latinus*, ed. Raymond Klibansky, 4 vols. (London, 1940–62)—vol. 1: *Meno interprete Henrico Aristippo*, ed. Victor Kordeuter and Carlotta Labowsky (1940); vol. 2: *Phaedo interprete Henrico Aristippo*, ed. Lorenzo Minio-Paluello (1950); vol. 3: *Parmenides . . . nec non Procli Commentarium in Parmenidem, pars ultima adhuc inedita interprete Guillelmo de Moerbeka*, ed. Raymond Klibansky and Carlotta Lobowsky (1953); and vol. 4: *Timaeus, a Calcidio translatus commentarioque instructus*, ed. J. H. Waszink (1962). See also, Proclus, *Elementatio Theologica*, ed. C. Vansteenkiste, *Tijdschrift voor Philosophie* 13 (1951): 263–302, 491–531. Proclus, *Elementatio physica*, ed. Helmut Boese (Berlin, 1958). Proclus, *Tria opuscula*, ed. Helmut Boese (Berlin, 1960).

18. Albert Hyma, *The Christian Renaissance* (Grand Rapids, Mich., 1924).

19. Ludwig Mohler, *Kardinal Bessarion*, 3 vols. (Paderborn, 1923–42).

20. Giovanni Gentile, "Le traduzioni medievali di Platone e Francesco Petrarca," *Studi sul Rinascimento*, 2d ed. (Florence, 1936), pp. 23–88. Lorenzo Minio-Paluello, "Il Fedone latino con note autografe del Petrarca," *Accademia Nazionale dei Lincei, Rendiconti della Classe di Scienze morali, storiche e filologiche*, ser. 8, no. 4 (1949): 107–13.

21. For a list of humanist versions of Plato, see P. O. Kristeller, *Supplementum Ficinianum*, vol. 1 (Florence, 1937), pp. CLVI–CLVII. Eugenio Garin, "Ricerche sulle traduzioni di Platone nella prima metà del sec. XV," in *Medioevo e Rinascimento, Studi in Onore di Bruno Nardi* (Florence, 1955), vol. 1, pp. 339–74. P. O. Kristeller, "Marsilio Ficino as a Beginning Student of Plato," *Scriptorium* 20 (1966): 41–54. For the versions of Bruni, see Leonardo Bruni Aretino, *Humanistisch-Philosophische Schriften*, ed. Hans Baron (Leipzig-Berlin, 1928), pp. 161, 163, 172–74. Ludwig Bertalot, "Zur Bibliographie der Übersetzungen des Leonardus Brunus Aretinus," *Quellen und Forschungen aus italienischen Archiven und Bibliotheken* 27 (1937): 180–84. For Trapezuntius' version of the Parmenides, see Raymond Klibansky, "Plato's Parmenides in the Middle Ages and the Renaissance," *Mediaeval and Renaissance Studies* 2 (1943): 289–304.

22. Edmond Vansteenberghe, *Le Cardinal Nicolas de Cues* (Paris, 1920). P. O. Kristeller, "A Latin Transation of Gemistos Plethon's De fato by Johannes Sophianos dedicated to Nicholas of Cusa," in *Nicolò Cusano agli inizi del mondo moderno* (Florence, 1970), pp. 175–93.

23. P. O. Kristeller, *The Philosophy of Marsilio Ficino* (New York, 1943); *id., Il*

Pensiero filosofico di Marsilio Ficino (Florence, 1953). Giuseppe Saitta, *Marsilio Ficino e la filosofia dell'umanesimo,* 3d ed. (Bologna, 1954). Michele Schiavone, *Problemi filosofici in Marsilio Ficino* (Milan, 1957). Daniel Pickering Walker, *Spiritual and Demonic Magic from Ficino to Campanella* (London, 1958). Raymond Marcel, *Marsile Ficin* (Paris, 1958).

24. Eugenio Garin, *Giovanni Pico della Mirandola* (Florence, 1937). Eugenio Anagnine, *Giovanni Pico della Mirandola* (Bari, 1937). *L'opera e il pensiero di Giovanni Pico della Mirandola nella storia dell'Umanesimo,* 2 vols. [Mirandola, Convegno internazionale, September 15–18, 1963] (Florence, Istituto nazionale di studi sul Rinascimento, 1965).

25. Joannes Picus, *Oratio de hominis dignitate,* with English translation by Elizabeth L. Forbes (Lexington, Ky., 1953). See essay 9.

26. P. O. Kristeller, *Studies in Renaissance Thought and Letters* (Rome, 1956), pp. 287–336. Nesca A. Robb, *Neoplatonism of the Italian Renaissance* (London, 1935). John C. Nelson, *Renaissance Theory of Love* (New York, 1958).

27. Sidney Greenberg, *The Infinite in Giordano Bruno* (New York, 1950). Dorothy W. Singer, *Giordano Bruno* (New York, 1950). John C. Nelson, *Renaissance Theory of Love* (New York, 1958). P. O. Kristeller, *Eight Philosophers of the Italian Renaissance* (Stanford, Calif., 1964). Frederick Purnell, "Jacopo Mazzoni and his Comparison of Plato and Aristotle," (Ph.D. diss., Columbia University, 1971).

28. Raymond Marcel, "Les 'découvertes' d'Erasme en Angleterre," *Bibliothèque d'Humanisme et Renaissance* 14 (1952): 117–23. Sears R. Jayne, *John Colet and Marsilio Ficino* (Oxford, 1963).

29. Jack H. Hexter, *More's Utopia* (Princeton, N.J., 1952). Thomas I. White, "A Study of the Influence of Plato and Aristotle on Thomas More's *Utopia,*" (Ph.D. diss., Columbia University, 1974); *id.,* "Aristotle and Utopia," *Renaissance Quarterly* 29 (1976): 635–75.

30. Augustin Renaudet, *Préréforme et Humanisme à Paris* (Paris, 1916). *The Prefatory Epistles of Jacques Lefèvre d'Etaples and Related Texts,* ed. Eugene F. Rice (New York, 1972). Joseph Victor, *Charles de Bouelles* (Geneva, 1978).

31. Christoph von Sigwart, *Ulrich Zwingli, Der Charakter seiner Theologie mit besonderer Rücksicht auf Picus von Mirandola dargestellt* (Stuttgart, 1855).

32. Joseph L. Blau, *The Christian Interpretation of the Cabala in the Renaissance* (New York, 1944). François Secret, *Les kabbalistes chrétiens de la renaissance* (Paris, 1964).

33. Roy W. Battenhouse, "The Doctrine of Man in Calvin and in Renaissance Platonism," *Journal of the History of Ideas* 9 (1948): 447–71.

34. Eugenio Massa, "L'anima e l'uomo in Egidio di Viterbo e nelle fonti classiche e medievali," in *Testi umanistici inediti sul 'De anima' [Archivio di Filosofia]* (Padua, 1951), pp. 37–86. John W. O'Malley, *Giles of Viterbo on Church and Reform* (Leyden, 1968).

35. J. D. Mansi, *Sacrorum Conciliorum Nova et Amplissima Collectio,* vol. 32 (Paris, 1902), pp. 842–43.

36. Walter Mönch, *Die italienische Platonrenaissance und ihre Bedeutung für Frankreichs Literatur- und Geistesgeschichte* (Berlin, 1936). A.-J. Festugière, *La*

philosophie de l'amour de Marsile Ficin et son influence sur la littérature française au XVIe siècle, 2d ed. (Paris, 1941). August Buck, *Der Platonismus in den Dichtungen Lorenzo de' Medicis* (Berlin, 1936). Kristeller, *Studies in Renaissance Thought and Letters,* pp. 213–19.

37. Sears R. Jayne, "Ficino and the Platonism of the English Renaissance," *Comparative Literature* 4 (1952): 214–38. P. O. Kristeller, "The European Significance of Florentine Platonism," in *Medieval and Renaissance Studies, Proceedings of the Southeastern Institute of Medieval and Renaissance Studies,* Summer 1967, ed. John M. Headley (Chapel Hill, N.C., 1968), pp. 206–29.

38. Nesca A. Robb, *Neoplatonism of the Italian Renaissance* (London, 1935), p. 177f. Luigi Tonelli, *L'amore nella poesia e nel pensiero del Rinascimento* (Florence, 1933). John C. Nelson, *Renaissance Theory of Love* (New York, 1958).

39. Francesco Patrizi da Cherso, *Della Poetica,* ed. D. Aguzzi Barbagli, 3 vols. (Florence, 1969–71).

40. P. O. Kristeller, "The Modern System of the Arts," *Journal of the History of Ideas* 12 (1951): 496–527 and 13 (1952): 17–46, reprinted in his *Renaissance Thought II* (New York, 1965), pp. 163–227.

41. Erwin Panofsky, *Idea* (Leipzig-Berlin, 1924).

42. E. H. Gombrich, "Botticelli's Mythologies," *Journal of the Warburg and Courtauld Institutes* 8 (1945): 7–60. Deoclecio Redig de Campos, "Il concetto platonico-cristiano della Stanza della Segnatura," *Raffaello e Michelangelo* (Rome, 1946), pp. 9–27. Erwin Panofsky, *Studies in Iconology* (New York, 1939), p. 171ff. André Chastel, *Marsile Ficin et l'Art* (Paris, 1954).

43. Otto Kinkeldey, "Franchino Gafori and Marsilio Ficino," *Harvard Library Bulletin* 1 (1947): 379–82. Kristeller, *Studies in Renaissance Thought and Letters,* pp. 451–70. Walker, *Spiritual and Demonic Magic,* p. 3ff.

44. Leonardo da Vinci's attitude towards humanism and Platonism has been a subject of controversy. For a more positive opinion, see André Chastel, "Léonard et la culture," in *Léonard de Vinci et l'expérience scientifique au seizième siècle* (Paris, 1953), pp. 251–63.

45. Ernst Cassirer, *Das Erkenntnisproblem,* vol. 1 (Berlin, 1922). E. A. Burtt, *The Metaphysical Foundations of Modern Physical Science* (New York, 1951).

46. Benjamin Brickman, *An Introduction to Francesco Patrizi's Nova de Universis philosophia* (New York, 1941). Frederick Purnell, "Jacopo Mazzoni and Galileo," *Physis* 14 (1972): 273–94.

47. John Herman Randall, Jr., "The Development of Scientific Method in the School of Padua," *Journal of the History of Ideas* 1 (1940): 177–206, reprinted in his *The School of Padua and the Emergence of Modern Science* (Padua, 1961), pp. 13–68. Ernest A. Moody, "Galileo and Avempace," *Journal of the History of Ideas* 12 (1951): 163–93, 375–422. Alexandre Koyré, "Galileo and Plato," *Journal of the History of Ideas* 4 (1943): 400–28. Ernst Cassirer, "Galileo's Platonism," in *Studies and Essays in the History of Science and Learning in Honor of George Sarton* (New York, 1946), pp. 279–97. On the use of Jesuit commentaries on Aristotle in Galileo's early notebooks, see William A. Wallace, *Galileo's Early Notebooks* (Notre Dame, Ind., 1977).

48. "[Q]uando uno non sa la verita da per sè, è impossibile che altri glie ne faccia

sapere. . . . [L]e vere [cose], cioè le necessarie, cioè quelle che è impossibile ad essere altrimenti, ogni mediocre discorso o le sa da sè o è impossibile che ei le sappia mai. . . .": *Dialogo sopra i due massimi sistemi del mondo,* Seconda giornata, in Galileo Galilei, *Le Opere* VII (Florence, 1933), p. 183. Galileo Galilei, *Dialogue Concerning the Two Chief World Systems,* trans. Stillman Drake (Berkeley, Calif., 1953), pp. 157–58. Galileo Galilei, *Dialogue on the Great World Systems,* trans. Thomas Salusbury, ed. Giorgio de Santillana (Chicago, 1953), p. 172.

49. See essay 2, note 13.

50. Ernst Cassirer, *Die platonische Renaissance in England und die Schule von Cambridge* (Leipzig, 1932), trans. by J. P. Pettegrove as *The Platonic Renaissance in England* (Austin, Tex., 1953).

4. PAGANISM AND CHRISTIANITY

1. Similar views on the Renaissance are expressed by Reinhold Niebuhr, *The Nature and Destiny of Man,* 2 vols. (New York, 1941–42), 1: 61ff. and 2: 157ff.

2. J.-R. Charbonnel, *La pensée italienne au XVIe siècle et le courant libertin* (Paris, 1919).

3. P. O. Kristeller, "The Myth of Renaissance Atheism and the French Tradition of Free Thought," *Journal of the History of Philosophy* 6 (1968): 233–43.

4. Ernst Walser, *Gesammelte Studien zur Geistesgeschichte der Renaissance* (Basel, 1952), especially pp. 48–63 ("Christentum und Antike in der Auffassung der italienischen Frührenaissance") and pp. 96–128 ("Studien zur Weltanschauung der Renaissance").

5. The term Pantheist was coined by John Toland in 1705. Cf. *The Oxford English Dictionary,* vol. 7 (Oxford, 1933), p. 430.

6. Charbonnel, *La pensée italienne.*

7. Albert Hyma, *The Christian Renaissance* (Grand Rapids, Mich., 1924).

8. This point is duly emphasized by Jacob Burckhardt, *The Civilization of the Renaissance in Italy* (London, 1878), pt. VI, ch. 2.

9. Gennaro Maria Monti, *Le confraternite medievali dell'alta e media Italia,* 2 vols. (Venice, 1927).

10. Wallace K. Ferguson, "The Revival of Classical Antiquity or the First Century of Humanism," *The Canadian Historical Association, Report of the Annual Meeting Held at Ottawa, June 12–15, 1957,* pp. 13–30: "[I]t is sometimes necessary to point out that Christianity was not a medieval invention and that the Middle Ages have not had a monopoly of Christian faith" (p. 24).

11. Konrad Burdach, *Reformation, Renaissance, Humanismus,* 2d ed. (Berlin-Leipzig, 1926).

12. Giuseppe Toffanin, *Storia dell'umanesimo,* 3 vols. (Bologna, 1950); *id., Che cosa fu l'umanesimo* (Florence, 1929); *id., History of Humanism,* trans. Elio Gianturco (New York, 1954).

13. Siro A. Nulli, *Erasmo e il Rinascimento* (Turin, 1955), p. 445: "[P]arlare di *umanesimo cristiano* ha lo stesso senso che parlare di geometria cattolica o di chi-

mica cristiana: è una cattiva espressione invece di dire: attività filologica e culturale esercitata da individui che si professano seguaci del cattolicismo circa argomenti che appartengono alla storia delle Chiese.''

14. H.-I. Marrou, *Saint Augustin et la fin de la culture antique* (Paris, 1938). Paul Renucci, *L'Aventure de l'Humanisme européen au Moyen Ages* (Paris, 1953). Martin R. P. McGuire, "Medieval Humanism," *The Catholic Historical Review* 38 (1953): 397–409.

15. Charles N. Cochrane, *Christianity and Classical Culture* (London, 1944)—cf. my review in the *Journal of Philosophy* 41 (1944): 576–81. Harry A. Wolfson, *Philo,* 2 vols. (Cambridge, Mass., 1947)—cf. my review in the *Journal of Philosophy* 46 (1949): 359–63. One may also compare the manner in which Étienne Gilson, *Les Métamorphoses de la cité de Dieu* (Louvain-Paris, 1952), p. 6ff., tries to evade the obvious contribution of Stoicism to the notion of human solidarity.

16. Martin Grabmann, *Die Geschichte der katholischen Theologie* (Freiburg, 1933), p. 15ff. Joseph de Ghellinck, *Le mouvement théologique du XIIe siècle,* 2d ed. (Brussels-Paris, 1948). Artur M. Landgraf, *Einführung in die Geschichte der theologischen Literatur der Frühscholastik* (Regensburg, 1948).

17. P. O. Kristeller, *Studies in Renaissance Thought and Letters* (Rome, 1956), pp. 355–72.

18. Pierre de Nolhac, *Pétrarque et l'humanisme,* 2d ed. (Paris, 1907).

19. Quirinus Breen, *John Calvin: A Study in French Humanism* (Grand Rapids, Mich., 1931). Paul Wernle, *Die Renaissance des Christentums im 16. Jahrhundert* (Tübingen-Leipzig, 1904), who stresses this aspect especially in Erasmus and Zwingli.

20. Kristeller, *Studies in Renaissance Thought and Letters,* pp. 355–72. Pontien Polman, *L'élément historique dans la controverse religieuse du XVIe siècle* (Gembloux, 1932).

21. Umberto Cassuto, *Gli Ebrei a Firenze nell'età del rinascimento* (Florence, 1918), p. 275ff. Salvatore Garofalo, "Gli umanisti italiani del secolo XV e la Bibbia," *Biblica* 27 (1946): 338–75, reprinted in *La Bibbia e il Concilio di Trento* (Rome, 1947), pp. 38–75. Apart from the Vatican manuscripts cited by Garofalo, Manetti's version of the Psalms occurs also in two other contemporary manuscripts, which shows that it attained a certain diffusion: Florence, Biblioteca Marucelliana, ms. C 336; Brussels, Bibliothèque Royale, ms. 10745.

22. Grabmann, *Die Geschichte der katholischen Theologie,* p. 155. Ludwig von Pastor, *Geschichte der Päpste,* vol. 10 (Freiburg, 1926), pp. 147ff., 560ff.

23. Polman, *L'élément historique.*

24. Grabmann, *Die Geschichte der katholischen Theologie,* p. 185ff. Albert Siegmund, *Die Überlieferung der griechischen christlichen Literatur in der lateinischen Kirche bis zum zwölften Jahrhundert* (Munich-Pasing, 1949). Sister Agnes Clare Way, "S. Gregorius Nazianzenus," *Catalogus Translationum et Commentariorum,* ed. P. O. Kristeller and F. Edward Cranz, vol. 2 (Washington, D.C., 1971), pp. 43–192. Charles L. Stinger, *Humanism and the Church Fathers: Ambrosio Traversari (1386–1439) and Christian Antiquity in the Italian Renaissance* (Albany, N.Y., 1977).

25. Leonardo Bruni Aretino, *Humanistisch-Philosophische Schriften*, ed. Hans Baron (Leipzig-Berlin, 1928), pp. 99ff., 160ff. Luzi Schucan, *Das Nachleben von Basilius Magnus "ad adolescentes"* (Geneva, 1973).

26. Remigio Sabbadini, *La scuola e gli studi di Guarino Guarini Veronese* (Catania, 1896), p. 138ff. William Harrison Woodward, *Vittorino da Feltre and Other Humanist Educators* (Cambridge, 1897); id., *Studies in Education during the Age of the Renaissance* (Cambridge, 1906).

27. von Pastor, *Geschichte der Päpste*, vol. 10, p. 189. Polman, *L'élément historique*, p. 392ff.

28. Polman, *L'élément historique*, p. 539ff.: "À la considerer dans son orientation historique, la controverse historique du XVIe siècle se rattache à l'humanisme." Eduard Fueter, *Geschichte der neueren Historiographie* (Munich, 1911), p. 246ff., misses the problem by stating that humanism ignored the church and that ecclesiastic historiography, as a child of the Reformation, was independent of humanism.

29. Frederic Seebohm, *The Oxford Reformers* (London, 1887). Walter Dress, *Die Mystik des Marsilio Ficino* (Berlin-Leipzig, 1929). P. A. Duhamel, "The Oxford Lectures of John Colet," *Journal of the History of Ideas* 14 (1953): 493–510.

30. Kristeller, *Studies in Renaissance Thought and Letters*, pp. 355–72.

31. See essay 1, note 1.

32. J. B. Bury, *The Idea of Progress* (London, 1920). Richard F. Jones, *Ancients and Moderns* (St. Louis, 1936).

33. Jacob Burckhardt, *Weltgeschichtliche Betrachtungen* (Leipzig, 1935), p. 10; id., *Force and Freedom*, trans. James H. Nichols (New York, 1943), p. 86.

34. "[D]uo praecipue paranda sunt arma cui sit . . . cum universa vitiorum cohorte pugnandum . . . precatio et scientia. . . . Sed precatio quidem potior, ut quae cum Deo sermones misceat, at scientia non minus necessaria tamen": Desiderius Erasmus, "Enchiridion militis Christiani" (1503), *Ausgewählte Werke*, ed. Hajo and Annemarie Holborn (Munich, 1933), p. 29.

Part Two: Renaissance Thought and the Middle Ages

5. HUMANISM AND SCHOLASTICISM IN THE ITALIAN RENAISSANCE

1. *Die Cultur der Renaissance in Italien* (Basel, 1860), trans. by S. G. C. Middlemore as *The Civilization of the Renaissance in Italy* (London, 1878), with many subsequent editions in both languages.

2. Hans Baron, "Renaissance in Italien," *Archiv für Kulturgeschichte* 17 (1927):

226–52 and 21 (1931): 95–119. Johan Huizinga, "Das Problem der Renaissance," *Wege der Kulturgeschichte*, trans. Werner Kaegi (Munich, 1930), pp. 89–139. See also the discussion in the *Journal of the History of Ideas* 4 (1943): 1–74. Wallace K. Ferguson, *The Renaissance in Historical Thought* (Boston, 1948). See Part 1, Introduction, note 1.

3. Konrad Burdach, *Reformation, Renaissance, Humanismus*, 2d ed. (Berlin-Leipzig, 1926). Wallace K. Ferguson, "Humanist Views of the Renaissance," *American Historical Review* 45 (1939–40): 1–28; *id., The Renaissance in Historical Thought*, p. 1ff. See also, Herbert Weisinger, "The Self-Awareness of the Renaissance," *Papers of the Michigan Academy of Science, Arts, and Letters* 29 (1944): 561–67; *id.*, "Who began the Revival of Learning," *ibid.*, 30 (1945), 625–38; *id.*, "Renaissance Accounts of the Revival of Learning," *Studies in Philology* 45 (1948): 105–18; *id.*, "The Renaissance Theory of the Reaction against the Middle Ages . . . ," *Speculum* 20 (1945): 461–67; *id.*, "Ideas of History during the Renaissance," *Journal of the History of Ideas* 6 (1945): 415–35. Franco Simone, *La coscienza della Rinascita negli Umanisti francesi* (Rome, 1949). Eugenio Garin, "Umanesimo e Rinascimento," in *Problemi ed orientamenti critici di lingua e di letteratura italiana*, ed. Attilio Momigliano, vol. 3: *Questioni e correnti di storia letteraria* (Milan, 1949), pp. 349–404. Most of the passages quoted by these scholars are later than the beginning of the fifteenth century. Yet Frate Guido da Pisa in his commentary on Dante wrote as early as 1330: "Per istum enim poetam resuscitata est mortua poesis. . . . Ipse vero poeticam scientiam suscitavit et antiquos poetas in mentibus nostris reviviscere fecit" (Orazio Bacci, *La Critica letteraria* [Milan, 1910], p. 163). "Ipse enim mortuam poesiam de tenebris reduxit ad lucem, et in hoc fuit imitatus Boetium, qui philosophiam mortuam suo tempore suscitavit" (Guido da Pisa, *Expositiones et glose super Comediam Dantis*, ed. Vincenzo Cioffari [Albany, N.Y., 1974], p. 4).

4. Burdach's attempts to derive the concept of the Renaissance from religious or mystical traditions no longer convince me. However, a Carolingian poet has the following line: "Aurea Roma iterum renovata renascitur orbi" (E. K. Rand, "Renaissance, why not?" *Renaissance* 1 [1943]: 34). Milo Crispinus says in his biography of Lanfranc: "quem Latinitas in antiquum scientiae statum ab eo restituta tota supremum debito cum amore agnoscit magistrum" (Migne, *P.L.*, CL, 29). For the political aspect of the concept, see P. E. Schramm, *Kaiser, Rom und Renovatio*, 2 vols. (Leipzig, 1929). See also Augustine's judgment on Ambrose (*Soliloquia*, II, 14, 26): "ille in quo ipsam eloquentiam quam mortuam dolebamus perfectam revixisse cognovimus."

5. Erwin Panofsky, *Renaissance and Renascences in Western Art* (Stockholm, 1960).

6. Étienne Gilson, "Humanisme médiéval et Renaissance," *Les Idées et les lettres* (Paris, 1932), pp. 171–96. E. R. Curtius, *Europäische Literatur und lateinisches Mittelalter* (Bern, 1948), pp. 41ff. and 387ff., trans. by Willard R. Trask as *European Literature and the Latin Middle Ages* (New York, 1953).

7. The isolation of Italy in the Middle Ages and the comparative scantiness of Italian antecedents for Dante has been noted by Karl Vossler, *Mediaeval Culture,*

trans. W. C. Lawton, vol. 2 (New York, 1929, 1960), p. 4ff. Cf. Vossler, *Die göttliche Komödie*, vol. II, pt. I (Heidelberg, 1908), pp. 582ff.

8. There are notable exceptions, such as Guido of Arezzo, Alfanus of Salerno, and Henricus of Settimello, but they do not change the general picture. For the share of Italy in medieval Latin culture prior to the thirteenth century, see Francesco Novati and Angelo Monteverdi, *Le Origini* (Milan, 1926). Antonio Viscardi, *Le Origini* (Milan, 1939). Maximilian Manitius, *Geschichte der lateinischen Literatur des Mittelalters*, 3 vols. (Munich, 1911–31).

9. Although several of the most famous representatives of scholastic theology were Italians, such as Lanfranc, Anselm, Peter Lombard, Thomas Aquinas, and Bonaventura, they did most of their studying and teaching in France. For Lanfranc, see Francesco Novati, "Rapports littéraires de l'Italie et de la France au XIe siècle," *Académie des Inscriptions et Belles-Lettres, Comptes Rendus des Séances de l'année 1910*, pp. 169–84. A typical representative of Italian theology in the eleventh century was Peter Damiani, and his background was juristic and rhetorical rather than philosophical; see J. A. Endres, *Petrus Damiani und die weltliche Wissenschaft* (Münster, 1910).

10. For the history of education in Italy, see Giuseppe Manacorda, *Storia della scuola in Italia*, 2 pts. (Milan, n.d.). Typical representatives of Italian rhetoric in the tenth and eleventh century are Gunzo of Novara and Anselm the Peripatetic. It should be noted that the library of Bobbio in the tenth century was rich in grammatical treatises, but possessed few classical poets (Gustav Becker, *Catalogi Bibliothecarum antiqui* [Bonn, 1885], p. 64ff).

11. Charles H. Haskins, *The Renaissance of the Twelfth Century* (Cambridge, Mass., 1927).

12. For French influences in the thirteenth century, see Giulio Bertoni, *Il Duecento*, 3d ed. (Milan, 1939). Many poems and prose works by Italian authors were written in French, and much of the early vernacular poetry and prose in Italian is derived from French models.

13. After having praised Dante and Petrarch as the restorers of poetry, Boccaccio continues: "inspice quo Romanum corruerit imperium . . . quid insuper philosophorum celebres titulos et poetarum myrthea laureaque serta meditari . . . quid in memoriam revocare militarem disciplinam . . . quid legum auctoritatem . . . quid morum conspicuum specimen. Haec omnia . . . una cum Italia reliqua et libertate caelesti a maioribus nostris . . . neglecta sunt et a nationibus exteris aut sublata aut turpi conquinata labe sordescunt . . . et si omnia resarciri nequeant, hoc saltem poetici nominis fulgore . . . inter barbaras nationes Roma saltem aliquid veteris maiestatis possit ostendere" (letter to Jacopo Pizzinghe in *Le Lettere edite e inedite di Messer Giovanni Boccaccio*, ed. Francesco Corazzini [Florence, 1877], p. 197). See Konrad Burdach, *Rienzo und die geistige Wandlung seiner Zeit* [*Vom Mittelalter zur Reformation*, vol. 2] (Berlin, 1913–28), p. 510ff. Also Salutati, in his letter to Peter of Mantua, after admitting that Rome now has lost her military power, says that there is no excuse for her being excelled by other nations in literary distinction. "Gaudebam igitur apud nos emergere qui barbaris illis quondam gentibus saltem in hoc palmam eriperet, qualem me tibi (read: te mihi) fama et multorum relatio promittit,"

alluding to the achievements of Peter of Mantua in the field of logic (*Epistolario di Coluccio Salutati*, ed. Francesco Novati, vol. 3 [Rome, 1896], p. 319ff).

14. For the classical studies of the humanists, see Georg Voigt, *Die Wiederbelebung des classischen Alterthums*, 3d ed., vol. 2 (Berlin, 1893), p. 373ff. Sir J. E. Sandys, *A History of Classical Scholarship*, vol. 2 (Cambridge, 1908), p. 1ff.

15. These discoveries included Lucretius, Tacitus, Manilius, several plays of Plautus, and several orations and rhetorical works of Cicero. See Remigio Sabbadini, *Le scoperte dei codici latini e greci ne' secoli XIV e XIV*, 2 vols. (Florence, 1905–14). Maximilian Manitius, *Handschriften antiker Autoren in mittelalterlichen Bibliothekskatalogen* (Leipzig, 1935).

16. It is not generally realized that fifteenth-century manuscripts of the Latin classics are probably more numerous than those of all previous centuries taken together. These manuscripts are disregarded by most modern editors, and their value for establishing a critical text may be small. However, their existence is an important phenomenon since it reflects the wide diffusion of the classical authors during the Renaissance.

17. Louise R. Loomis, *Medieval Hellenism* (Lancaster, Pa., 1906).

18. For the translations of the twelfth century, see Charles H. Haskins, *Studies in the History of Mediaeval Science*, 2d ed. (Cambridge, Mass., 1927). For the thirteenth century, see Maurice De Wulf, *Histoire de la philosophie médiévale*, 6th ed., vol. 2 (Louvain, 1936). A bibliography of Latin translations from the Greek is still a major desideratum, even though some partial contributions have been made recently. See esp. J. T. Muckle, "Greek Works translated directly into Latin before 1350," *Mediaeval Studies* 4 (1942): 33–42 and 5 (1943): 102–14. *Catalogus Translationum et Commentariorum*, ed. P. O. Kristeller and F. Edward Cranz, 3 vols. (Washington, D.C., 1960–76). For the study of Greek in the Middle Ages, see the articles by Roberto Weiss cited in essay 1, note 11.

19. For the study of Greek classical literature in medieval Constantinople, see Karl Krumbacher, *Geschichte der byzantinischen Literatur*, 2d ed. (Munich, 1897), p. 499ff. The direct influence of this Byzantine tradition on the Greek studies of the Italian humanists is beyond any question. There may also have been some indirect Byzantine influence on the Latin studies of the humanists. The range of interest of the humanists resembles that of many Byzantine scholars. See essay 7.

20. For the literary production of the humanists, see Voigt, *Die Wiederbelebung des classischen Alterthums*, vol. 2, p. 394ff. Vittorio Rossi, *Il Quattrocento*, 2d ed. (Milan, 1933).

21. The link between the humanists and the medieval rhetoricians has been recognized by only very few scholars, such as Francesco Novati, Helene Wieruszowski, and Ernst Kantorowicz. These scholars, however, chiefly noticed that the medieval rhetoricians show some of the personal characteristics commonly attributed to the humanists. I should like to go further and assume a direct professional and literary connection of which the personal similarities are merely a symptom. The common opinion is quite different, and most historians speak of the *ars dictaminis* as if there were no humanist rhetoric, and vice versa. See note 38 and essay 13.

22. For the contributions of the humanists to philosophy, see Friedrich Ueberweg,

Grundriss der Geschichte der Philosophie, 12th ed. vol. 3 (Berlin, 1924), p. 6ff. Guido De Ruggiero, *Storia della filosofia,* pt. 3, 2d ed., 2 vols. (Bari, 1937). Giovanni Gentile, *Storia della filosofia italiana,* ed. Eugenio Garin, 2 vols. (Florence, 1969), 1: 111–216. Ernst Cassirer, *Individuum und Kosmos in der Philosophie der Renaissance* (Berlin-Leipzig, 1927). For further literature on the entire subject of Renaissance philosophy, see P. O. Kristeller and J. H. Randall Jr., "The Study of the Philosophies of the Renaissance," *Journal of the History of Ideas* 2 (1941): 449–96. Eugenio Garin, *La filosofia* [*Storia dei generi letterari italiani*], vol. 1 (Milan, 1947), pp. 169–274; *id., Der italienische Humanismus* (Bern, 1947); *id., Filosofi italiani del Quattrocento* (Florence, 1942). Cleto Carbonara, *Il secolo XV* (Milan, 1943). Giuseppe Saitta, *Il pensiero italiano nell'umanesimo e nel rinascimento,* vol. 1: *L'Umanesimo* (Bologna, 1949). See also, Charles Trinkaus, *Adversity's Noblemen* (New York, 1940); *id., In Our Image and Likeness,* 2 vols. (Chicago, 1970).

23. This statement does not mean, as Eugenio Garin implies (*Giornale critico* [1952], p. 99) that I deny the philosophical significance of the Renaissance period. See essay 1.

24. This point has been rightly indicated by Richard McKeon, "Renaissance and Method in Philosophy," *Studies in the History of Ideas* 3 (1935): 37–114: "That shift in the emphasis in the three arts, that subversion of dialectic to grammar, is in itself sufficient to account for the changes which the Renaissance is reputed to have made" (p. 87). I am not convinced by McKeon's attempt to distinguish within the Renaissance, as two separate trends, an emphasis on grammar represented by Erasmus, and one on rhetoric represented by Nizolius. The grammatical character of early Italian humanism and its rise before the time of Petrarch have been illustrated in the studies of Roberto Weiss, *The Dawn of Humanism in Italy* (London, 1947); *id.,* "Lineamenti per una storia del primo umanesimo fiorentino," *Rivista storica italiana* 60 (1948): 349–66; *id., Il primo secolo dell'umanesimo* (Rome, 1949).

25. For Pico's defense of the medieval philosophers against Ermolao Barbaro, see P. O. Kristeller, "Florentine Platonism and its Relations with Humanism and Scholasticism," *Church History* 8 (1939): 203ff. Quirinus Breen, "Giovanni Pico della Mirandola on the Conflict of Philosophy and Rhetoric," *Journal of the History of Ideas* 13 (1952): 384–426, reprinted in his *Christianity and Humanism* (Grand Rapids, Mich., 1968), pp. 1–92. For Alciato's defense of the medieval jurists against Valla, see Remigio Sabbadini, *Storia del ciceronianismo* (Turin, 1885), pp. 88–92. Biagio Brugi, *Per la storia della giurisprudenza e delle università italiane: Nuovi saggi* (Turin, 1921), p. 111ff.

26. This humanist logic is represented by Valla, Agricola, Nizolius, and Ramus. For Nizolius, see Richard McKeon, "Renaissance and Method in Philosophy," *Studies in the History of Ideas* 3 (1935): 105ff. Mario Nizolio, *De veris principiis,* ed. Quirinus Breen, 2 vols. (Rome, 1956). For Ramus, see Perry Miller, *The New England Mind* (New York, 1939), p. 154ff. Walter J. Ong, *Ramus, Method, and the Decay of Dialogue* (Cambridge, Mass., 1958).

27. For the battle of the arts, see *The Battle of the Seven Arts . . . by Henri d'Andeli,* ed. L. J. Paetow (Berkeley, 1914). There was a rivalry between medicine

and law, in which the humanists were not directly concerned. See Lynn Thorndike, "Medicine versus Law at Florence," *Science and Thought in the Fifteenth Century* (New York, 1929), pp. 24–58. Behind this kind of literature is the rivalry of the various faculties and sciences at the universities, a rivalry that found its expression in the opening lectures delivered every year by each professor in praise of his own field. One such lecture by the humanist Philippus Beroaldus the Elder, professor at Bologna, is entitled "Declamatio philosophi, medici et oratoris" (in his *Varia Opuscula* [Basel, 1513]). Of course, the prize is given to the orator. See also Coluccio Salutati, *De nobilitate legum et medicinae,* ed. Eugenio Garin (Florence, 1947), p. xlvi ff.; *id., La Disputa delle Arti nel Quattrocento* (Florence, 1947).

28. Jacob Burckhardt, *Die Kultur der Renaissance in Italien,* 13th ed. (Stuttgart, 1921), p. 151.

29. For the careers of the humanists, see Voigt, *Die Wiederbelebung des classischen Alterthums,* and Rossi, *Il Quattrocento.*

30. For the connection of Salutati with the medieval tradition of the *ars dictaminis* and *ars notaria,* see Francesco Novati, *La giovinèzza di Coluccio Salutati* (Turin, 1888), p. 66ff. This chapter was reprinted with important omissions in his *Freschi e minii del Dugento* (Milan, 1908), pp. 299–328. There is at Naples a manuscript of the early fifteenth century transcribed for a young student of rhetoric, which contains the letters of Petrus de Vineis, together with those of Salutati, and of the latter's contemporary Pellegrino Zambeccari (Ludovico Frati, "L'epistolario inedito di Pellegrino Zambeccari," *Atti e Memorie della R. Deputazione di Storia patria per le provincie di Romagna,* 4th ser., 13 [1923]: 169ff.). Another manuscript with the same content is in The Hague (*Epistolario di Pellegrino Zambeccari,* ed. Ludovico Frati [Rome, 1929], p. xviiff.). I am indebted for this information to Ludwig Bertalot. Although Burdach's attempt to make Cola di Rienzo the central figure of the Italian Renaissance must be rejected, it should be noticed that Cola was a notary by profession and owed a good deal of his reputation to the style of his letters and speeches. Burdach, who emphasized the influence of Joachimite ideas on Cola, fails to meet the objection that Cola became familiar with these ideas only after his flight from Rome (*Rienzo und die geistige Wandlung seiner Zeit* [Berlin, 1923–28], p. 10).

31. For the literary production of the humanists, see Voigt, *Die Wiederbelebung des classischen Alterthums,* and Rossi, *Il Quattrocento.* For their historiography, see Eduard Fueter, *Geschichte der neueren Historiographie,* 3d ed. (Munich, 1936).

32. For the grammatical studies of the humanists in their relation to the Middle Ages, see Remigio Sabbadini, *La scuola e gli studi di Guarino Guarini Veronese* (Catania, 1896), p. 38ff.

33. There are many humanist treatises on epistolography, and many collections of "salutations" in humanist manuscripts. The letters of most major humanists were collected and reprinted primarily as models for literary imitation.

34. Charles S. Baldwin, *Medieval Rhetoric and Poetic* (New York, 1928), pp. 206ff. and 228ff., especially p. 230. Richard McKeon, "Rhetoric in the Middle Ages," *Speculum* 17 (1942): 27ff. For the *ars dictaminis* in Italy, especially during the twelfth century, see Charles H. Haskins, *Studies in Medieval Culture* (Oxford, 1929), pp. 170–92. See also Ernst Kantorowicz, "An 'Autobiography' of Guido

Faba," *Medieval and Renaissance Studies* 1 (1943): 253–80; *id.*, "Anonymi 'Aurea Gemma,' " *Medievalia et Humanistica* 1 (1943): 41–57. Helene Wieruszowski, *"Ars dictaminis* in the time of Dante," *ibid.*, 95–108. For the *ars praedicandi*, see Harry Caplan, *Medieval Artes Praedicandi*, 2 vols. (Ithaca, N.Y., 1934–36). Thomas M. Charland, *Artes Praedicandi* (Paris-Ottawa, 1936). Italy's contribution to the literature on preaching seems to have been small and belated.

35. Voigt, *Die Wiederbelebung des classischen Alterthums*, p. 436ff. For a typical collection of humanist orations, see Ludwig Bertalot, "Eine Sammlung Paduaner Reden des XV. Jahrhunderts," *Quellen und Forschungen aus italienischen Archiven und Bibliotheken* 26 (1936): 245–67.

36. See the studies of Ernst Kantorowicz and Helene Wieruszowski, and especailly Alfredo Galletti, *L'eloquenza dalle origini al XVI secolo* [*Storia dei generi litterari italiani*] (Milan, 1904–38), p. 430ff.

37. Galletti, *L'eloquenza*.

38. Some of the rhetorical treatises and models of the thirteenth century are discussed by Galletti, *L'eloquenza*, p. 454ff. Guido Faba's *Parlamenti ed epistole*, ed. Augusto Gaudenzi, *I suoni, le forme e le parole dell'odierno dialetto della città di Bologna* (Turin, 1889), include several model speeches. Models for political and funeral speeches are inserted in the anonymous "Oculus Pastoralis" and in other treatises written for the instruction of city officials (Fritz Hertter, *Die Podestàliteratur Italiens im 12. und 13. Jahrhundert* [Leipzig-Berlin, 1910]). For an example of early academic oratory, see Hermann Kantorowicz, "The Poetical Sermon of a Mediaeval Jurist," *Journal of the Warburg Institute* 2 (1938–39): 22–41. For the speech of an ambassador, see G. L. Haskins and Ernst Kantorowicz, "A Diplomatic Mission of Francis Accursius and his Oration before Pope Nicholas III," *English Historical Review* 58 (1943): 424–47. The medieval legal background of the wedding speeches of the humanists has been studied by Francesco Brandileone, *Saggi sulla storia della celebrazione del matrimonio in Italia* (Milan, 1906), but he does not mention any pre-humanist wedding speeches. Rhetorical rules and samples are included in some of the early instructions for advocates; see M. A. von Bethmann-Hollweg, *Der Civilprozess des gemeinen Rechts in geschichtlicher Entwicklung*, vol. 6 (Bonn, 1874), pp. 148–59. Boncompagno's *Rhetorica Novissima* (ed. Augusto Gaudenzi, *Bibliotheca iuridica medii aevi: Scripta Anecdota glossatorum*, vol. 2 [Bologna, 1892]) is not a treatise on *dictamen*, as most scholars seem to assume, but a rhetorical instruction for advocates. Also the treatise of Jacques de Dinant, published by André Wilmart, *Analecta Reginensia* (Vatican City, 1933), pp. 113–51, covers judicial oratory.

It is often asserted that the humanists did not cultivate judicial oratory (Rossi, *Il Quattrocento*, p. 154), yet this is contradicted by a passage of Jovius (Burckhardt, *Die Kultur der Renaissance*, p. 176), and there are at least a few examples of judicial speeches composed by humanists (Leonardo Bruni Aretino, *Humanistisch-Philosophische Schriften*, ed. Hans Baron [Leipzig, 1928], p. 179; Jules Paquier, *De Philippi Beroaldi Junioris vita et scriptis* [Paris, 1900], pp. 96–113). A systematic investigation of the various types of humanist oratory and of their medieval antecedents has not yet been undertaken. It ought to include a study of the mutual relations between sacred and secular eloquence, and of possible Byzantine influences. See Krumbacher, *Die Geschichte der byzantinischen Literatur*, pp. 454ff. and 470ff. The legal background of the wedding orations appears sometimes in their titles, e.g., "contractus matrimonialis compillatus per Manfredum de Justis Veronensem" (cod. Laur. Ashb. 271; cf. Cesare Paoli, *I codici Ashburnhamiani della R. Biblioteca Mediceo-Laurenziana di Firenze* [Rome, 1887–1917], p. 296 n. 195); "contractus Guarini Veronensis pro comite Jacopino" (Ricc, 421 f. 43). The title of another form speech shows that also Pico's famous oration belonged to an established formal type: "ad colligendos audientium animos in disputatione fienda" (Ricc, 421 f. 28).

39. Fueter fails to discuss the relations between medieval and humanist historiography.

40. I should like to mention Carolus Sigonius for his masterful discussion of the forged charter of Theodosius II for Bologna university (*Opera Omnia*, vol. 6 [Milan, 1787], p. 985ff.). His remark on the task of history, made in connection with the donation of Constantine, is a quotation from Cicero: "primam legem historiae esse ut ne quid falsi audeat, ne quid veri non audeat" (*ibid.*, p. 985; cf. *De Oratore*, II, 15, 62).

41. For example, Boncompagno of Signa (*Liber de obsidione Anconae*, ed. G. C. Zimolo [Bologna, 1937]) and Rolandinus of Padua (*Cronica*, ed. Antonio Bonardi [Città di Castello, 1905–8]).

42. Giulio Bertoni, *Il Duecento*, p. 263. Machiavelli was on the payroll of the university of Pisa for writing his Florentine history.

43. Allan H. Gilbert, *Machiavelli's Prince and Its Forerunners* (Durham, N.C., 1938). The question *De nobilitate*, dear to the humanists of the fifteenth century, was already discussed in the thirteenth (Giulio Bertoni, "Una lettera amatoria di Pier della Vigna," *Giornale storico della letteratura italiana* 58 [1911]: 33ff.). The humanist treatises on the dignity and happiness of man also continued medieval discussions (Giovanni Gentile, "Il concetto dell'uomo nel Rinascimento," *Il pensiero italiano del rinascimento*, 3d ed. [Florence, 1940], pp. 47–113).

44. Boncompagno of Signa wrote two moral treatises: *Amicitia*, ed. Sarina Nathan (Rome, 1909), and *De malo senectutis et senii*, ed. Francesco Novati, *Rendiconti della Reale Accademia dei Lincei, Classe di Scienze Morali, Storiche e Filologiche*, 5th ser., 1 (1892): 50–59.

45. Novati and Monteverdi, *Le Origini*. Francesco Novati, *L'influsso del pensiero latino sopra la civiltà italiana nel Medio Evo*, 2d ed. (Milan, 1899). Umberto Ronca, *Cultura medioevale e poesia latina d'Italia nei secoli XI e XII*, 2 vols. (Rome, 1892). F. J. E. Raby, *A History of Secular Latin Poetry in the Middle Ages*, 2 vols. (Oxford, 1934).

46. The rise of Latin poetry in Italy begins with the Paduan group of "prehumanists." See Bertoni, *Il Duecento*, p. 272ff. Natalino Sapegno, *Il Trecento* (Milan, 1934), p. 149ff.

47. A comprehensive study of the literature of medieval and Renaissance commentaries on the classical authors is a major desideratum. Much scattered information may be found concerning the commentaries on individual authors. The commentaries written before 1200 are listed in Manitius, *Geschichte der lateinischen Literatur des*

Mittelalters. An interesting survey of such commentaries up to 1300, by B. H. (Hauréau), is hidden in the *Histoire littéraire de la France* 29 (1885): 568–83. Hauréau lists only one commentary which he believes to be from Italy. Of Italian origin are also certain legal glosses on Seneca, written in the twelfth century (Carlo Pascal, *Letteratura latina medievale* [Catania, 1909], pp. 150–54). There are also some Italian commentaries on Martianus Capella, but this refers to the teaching of the "artes" rather than that of the "authores." The Paduans began to study Seneca's tragedies, and after the end of the thirteenth century, the number of classical commentaries begins to increase. That these early Italian commentators were acquainted with the work of their French predecessors has been shown in the case of Giovanni del Virgilio by Fausto Ghisalberti ("Giovanni del Virgilio espositore delle 'Metamorfosi,' " *Giornale Dantesco* 34 [1933]: 31ff.). Relations between medieval and humanistic commentaries are also noticed by Eva M. Sanford ("The Manuscripts of Lucan: Accessus and Marginalia," *Speculum* 9 [1934]: 278–95). For the history and form of medieval commentaries, see E. A. Quain, "The Medieval Accessus ad auctores," *Traditio* 3 (1945): 215–64. R. W. Hunt, "The Introductions to the "Artes' in the Twelfth Century," *Studia Mediaevalia in honorem admodum Reverendi Patris Raymundi Josephi Martin* (Brugis, c. 1949), pp. 85–112. R. B. C. Huygens, "Accessus ad Auctores," *Latomus* 12 (1953): 296–311, 460–84. Cf. also Ludwig Bertalot, *Deutsche Literaturzeitung* 32 (1911): 3166–69.

An important exception which seems to deserve further study is the manuscript 404 of the Pierpont Morgan Library in New York which was written in Italy in the twelfth century and contains the complete works of Horace with early glosses (Meta Harrsen and George K. Boyce, *Italian Manuscripts in the Pierpont Morgan Library* [New York, 1953], p. 6, no. 7). The dating of the manuscript has been confirmed to me by Luisa Banti. See also *Catalogus Translationum et Commentariorum,* ed. P. O. Kristeller and F. Edward Cranz, 3 vols. (Washington, D.C., 1960–76). *Der Kommentar in der Renaissance,* ed. August Buck and Otto Herding (Boppard, 1975).

48. See Sabbadini, *Le scoperie.*

49. Jules Alexandre Clerval, *Les écoles de Chartres au moyen âge* (Paris, 1895). Leopold Delisle, "Les écoles d'Orléans au douzième et au treizième siècle," *Annuaire-Bulletin de la Société de l'histoire de France* 7 (1869): 139–54. See also *The Battle of the Seven Arts,* ed. Paetow. For the contrast of "artes" and "authores," see Eduard Norden, *Die antike Kunstprosa,* vol. 2 (Leipzig, 1898), pp. 688ff. and 724ff. To the well-known material on the study of the "authores" in medieval France, I should like to add the following passage from the chronist Landulphus Junior, which seems to have remained unnoticed: "revocare Yordanum de Clivi a provincia que dicitur Sancti Egidii in qua ipse Yordanus legebat lectionem auctorum non divinorum sed paganorum" (*Historia Mediolanensis,* ed. Carlo Castiglioni [Bologna, 1934], p. 18). The event must be dated shortly after A.D. 1100.

50. Perhaps the earliest dated evidence of the reading of classical authors in an Italian school of the Middle Ages is the criminal record of the theft of "three books of Ovid" from a teacher of grammar in Bologna (1294), see O. Mazzoni Toselli, *Racconti storici estratti dall'archivio criminale di Bologna,* vol. 3 (Bologna, 1870), p. 39ff.

51. In 1321, Giovanni del Virgilio was appointed to lecture at Bologna on versification and on Vergil, Statius, Lucan, and Ovid (Ghisalberti, "Giovanni del Virgilio," p. 4ff.). L. J. Paetow comments on this document as follows: "This was a good beginning . . . but the fair promise had no fulfillment" (*The Arts Course at Medieval Universities* [Urbana-Champaign, 1910], p. 60). Actually, the promise did find its fulfillment in the development of Italian humanism. The teaching of classical authors never ceased in Italy after that memorable date which coincides with the approximate time when Petrarch was a student at Bologna.

52. For French influences on Italian humanism in the fourteenth century, see also B. L. Ullman, "Some Aspects of the Origin of Italian Humanism," *Philological Quarterly* 20 (1941): 20–31. Even earlier (1277) is the correspondence between two notaries concerning the loan of a manuscript of Ovid's *Metamorphoses* (*Il Notariato a Perugia,* ed. Roberto Abbondanza [Rome, 1973], pp. 252–54, no. 199).

53. Burckhardt, *Die Kultur der Renaissance in Italien,* p. 154.

54. Karl Vossler, *Poetische Theorien in der italienischen Frührenaissance* (Berlin, 1900). August Buck, *Italienische Dichtungslehren vom Mittelalter bis zum Ausgang der Renaissance* (Tübingen, 1958).

55. The work by Vincenzo Lancetti, *Memorie intorno ai poeti laureati d'ogni tempo e d'ogni nazione* (Milan, 1839), is antiquated, but has not been replaced. Important contributions were made by Francesco Novati, "La suprema aspirazione di Dante," *Indagini e postille dantesche* (Bologna, 1899), p. 83ff., and by E. H. Wilkins, "The Coronation of Petrarch," *Speculum* 18 (1943): 155–97. I believe that the coronation ceremony developed from the public recitals and approbations of books at the medieval universities (on such approbations, see Lynn Thorndike, "Public Readings of New Works in Mediaeval Universities," *Speculum* 1 [1926]: 101–3, and the additional notes by Haskins and Thorndike, *ibid.,* pp. 221 and 445ff.). The intermediary link is the coronation of the approved book, as in the case of Boncompagno at Bologna 1215 (Novati, *Indagini,* p. 86f.). There is definite evidence that Mussato was crowned not only for his tragedy *Eccerinis,* but also for his historical work on Henry VII. Also the diploma of Petrarch's coronation refers to him repeatedly as a poet and historian (*Opera Omnia* [Basel, 1581], IV, pp. 6–7), and there are later cases of persons crowned as poets and orators.

56. Petrarch was examined by King Robert of Naples and took the king's testimonial letters to Rome, that is, followed much of the procedure that was used for academic degrees in the kingdom of Naples. His diploma resembles doctoral diplomas and grants him the authorization "tam in dicta arte poetica quam in dicta historica arte . . . legendi, disputandi atque interpretandi veterum scripturas et novas (read: novos) a seipso . . . libros et poemata componendi. . . ." (*Opera Omnia,* IV, 6–7).

57. The chair of moral philosophy was held, for example, by Barzizza and by Filelfo.

58. Lectures on the Greek or Latin text of Aristotle and other philosophical authors were given at Florence by Marsuppini, Argyropulos, Politian, at Bologna by Codrus Urceus, and at Padua by Leonicus Thomaeus.

59. On *humanitas* in Roman antiquity, see Werner Jaeger, *Humanism and Theol-*

ogy (Milwaukee, 1943), pp. 20ff. and 72f. Max Schneidewin, *Die antike Humanität* (Berlin, 1897), p. 31ff. Richard Reitzenstein, *Werden und Wesen der Humanität im Altertum* (Strassburg, 1907). I. Heinemann, "Humanitas," in Pauly-Wissowa, *Real-Encyclopädie der classischen Altertumswissenschaft, Supplementband* 5 (Stuttgart, 1931), col. 282–310. Joseph Niedermann, *Kultur* (Florence, 1941), p. 29ff.

60. The clearest statement is found in the famous library canon composed by Nicholas V in his youth for Cosimo de' Medici. After having listed many books on theology, then the works of Aristotle in *logicis,* in *physicis,* in *metaphysica,* and in *moralibus,* the Arabic and Greek commentators on Aristotle, other philosophical works translated from the Greek, and works on mathematics, he continued as follows: "de studiis autem humanitatis quantum ad grammaticam, rhetoricam, historicam et poeticam spectat ac moralem . . ." (Giovanni Sforza, "La patria, la famiglia ed i parenti di papa Niccolò V," *Atti della Reale Accademia Lucchese di Scienze, Lettere ed Arti* 23 [1884]: 1–400, at 380).

An educational charter of the Jesuits of 1591 speaks of "studia humanitatis, hoc est grammaticae, historiae, poeticae et rhetoricae" (quoted by Karl Borinski, *Die Antike in Poetik und Kunsttheorie,* vol. 2 [Leipzig, 1924], p. 327). Pierre Bersuire calls Petrarch "poetam utique et oratorem egregium in omni morali philosophia nec non et historica et poetica disciplina eruditum" (Fausto Ghisalberti, "L'Ovidius moralizatus di Pierre Bersuire," *Studi Romanzi* 23 [1933]: 90). After Leonardo Bruni's death, according to his epitaph in S. Croce, "historia luget, eloquentia muta est, ferturque Musas tum Graecas tum Latinas lacrimas tenere non potuisse." Peter Luder announced at Heidelberg in 1456 public courses on "studia humanitatis id est poetarum oratorum ac hystoriographorum libros," and at Leipzig in 1462 on "studia humanitatis, hystoriographos, oratores scilicet et poetas" (Ludwig Bertalot, "Humanistische Vorlesungsankündigungen in Deutschland im 15. Jahrhundert," *Zeitschrift für Geschichte der Erziehung und des Unterrichts* 5 [1915]: 3–4).

Giovanni Sforza's manuscript source for the "Inventarium Nicolai pape V quod ipse composuit ad instantiam Cosme de Medicis ut ab ipso Cosma audivi die XII novembr. 1463 ego frater Leonardus Ser Uberti de Florentia O. P. presente R. o patre fratre Sante de Florentia priore Sancti Marci Flor(entini) eiusdem ord(inis)" is cod. Conv. Soppressi J VII 30 (S. Marco) of the Biblioteca Nazionale in Florence, f. 180–185v (the reference given by Sforza, "La patria, . . . ," p. 359, is misleading). Characteristic is also the title of one of Filelfo's orations: "oratio de laudibus historie poetice philosophie et que hasce complectitur eloquentie" (cod. Vallicell. F 20 f. 213v). Charles Trinkaus, "A Humanist's Image of Humanism: The Inaugural Orations of Bartolommeo della Fonte," *Studies in the Renaissance* 7 (1960): 90–147.

61. This was attempted, however, in the sixteenth century by Vives in his work *De tradendis disciplinis.*

62. The humanist Leonardo Bruni, when comparing Dante and Petrarch, attributes greater knowledge in philosophy and mathematics to Dante, "'perocchè nella scienza delle lettere e nella cognizione della lingua latina Dante fu molto inferiore al Petrarca" (*Le Vite di Dante, Petrarca et Boccaccio,* ed. Angelo Solerti [Milan, n.d.], p. 292ff.). For Bruni, the learning of Petrarch is not universal and does not include

philosophy. In his early letter to Antonio da S. Miniato, Ficino proposes to abandon his previous rhetorical style and to speak instead as a philosopher ("deinceps philosophorum more loquamur verba ubique contempnentes et gravissimas in medium sententias adducentes," Forlì, Biblioteca Comunale, Autografo Piancastelli no. 907: see P. O. Kristeller, *Studies in Renaissance Thought and Letters* [Rome, 1956], p. 146).

In the preface of his *De regimine sanitatis,* Antonio Benivieni relates that he turned from "oratorie artis studia" to philosophy and medicine (ed. Luigi Belloni [Turin, 1951], p. 19). Alamanno Rinuccini, in the letter to his son Filippo, which is a tract on education, insists that it is necessary to proceed from the study of grammar and rhetoric ("ubi nostrorum hominum plerique gradum sistere consueverunt") to that of philosophy (*Lettere ed Orazioni,* ed. Vito R. Giustiniani [Florence, 1953], p. 97). Pontanus in his dialogue *Aegidius* speaks of the decline of eloquence after the end of the Roman Empire, "cum tamen disciplinae ipsae in honore essent habitae, id quod physicorum theologorumque multitudo quae post Boetium extitit plane declarat, tum in Hispania, tum in Galliis Britaniisque ipsaque in Germania" (*I dialoghi,* ed. Carmelo Previtera [Florence, 1943], p. 259).

63. Rossi, *Il Quattrocento,* pp. 6 and 15, cites a poem of Ariosto (1523) for the earliest appearance of the term *umanista* in Italian, and an epigram of the late fifteenth century for the earliest appearance of the term *humanista* in Latin. I have not been able to verify the latter passage, but I found the following passage in a vernacular letter written in 1490 by the rector of Pisa university to the officials in Florence: "avendo le S. V. condocto quello Humanista che non è venuto," this will be a disappointment for many foreign students who have come "per udire humanità" (Angelus Fabronius, *Historia Academiae Pisanae,* I [Pisa, 1791], pp. 369f.). The original letter (Archivio di Stato, Florence, *Studio Fiorentino e Pisano,* XI, f. 14) was sent by Andreas dal Campo notarius studii to the Officiali dello Studio on December 4, 1490. The original has "non essendo venuto" and some other variants not relevant to our discussion.

During the sixteenth century, the Latin term *humanista* appears in the university documents of Bologna and Ferrara. John Florio in his Italian-English dictionary has the following entry: "Humanista, a humanist or professor of humanitie" (*A Worlde of Wordes* [London, 1598], p. 164). Other examples of this usage are given by Augusto Campana ("The Origin of the Word 'Humanist,' " *Journal of the Warburg and Courtauld Institutes* 9 [1946]: 60–73) who arrives at the same conclusion as to the origin and meaning of the term. The term occurs repeatedly in the *Epistolae obscurorum viorum* (Karl Brandi, *Das Werden der Renaissance* [Göttingen, 1908], p. 23). The original meaning was still alive in the eighteenth century. Salvino Salvini (*Fasti Consolari dell'Accademia Fiorentina* [Florence, 1717], p. xiv) mentions Francesco da Buti as a "dottore in grammatica, come allora si dicevano gli Umanisti"; and Leibniz states of Valla, "qu'il n'étoit pas moins Philosophe, qu'Humaniste" (*Essais de Théodicée,* §405). As a Spanish example of the late sixteenth or early seventeenth century, I noted the following title: "Discurso de las letras humanas llamado el humanista, compuesto por el maestro Francisco Cespedes, Cathedratico de prima de Rethorica en la Universidad de Salamanca" (Pedro Roca, *Catálogo de los manuscritos que pertenecierón a D. Pascual de Gayangos existentes hoy en la Biblioteca Nacional* [Madrid, 1904] p. 227, no. 643; this is now cod. 17736, as I was informed by Ramón Paz).

64. Apparently the term *Humanismus* was coined in 1808 by F. J. Niethammer to denote the educational theory that tried to defend the traditional place of classical studies in the school curriculum (Walter Rüegg, *Cicero und der Humanismus* [Zürich, 1946], p. 2ff.). Goethe (*Dichtung und Wahrheit,* bk. XIII, published 1814) uses the term in the sense of humanitarianism (my attention was called to this passage by Dino Bigongiari).

65. For the relation between theology, medicine, and philosophy in Italy, see Hastings Rashdall, *The Universities of Europe in the Middle Ages,* 2d ed., ed. F. M. Powicke and A. B. Emden, vol. 1 (Oxford, 1936), p. 261ff. There is some Aristotelianism in the writings of Urso and other Salerno masters (cf. Kristeller, *Studies in Renaissance Thought and Letters,* pp. 517–19), and there was a group of theologians and canonists at Bologna in the twelfth century who were influenced by Abelard. Yet the regular connection between medicine and Aristotelian philosophy, which was to become characteristic of Italian science, appears for the first time in the writings of Taddeo of Florence (late thirteenth century). See Bruno Nardi, "L'averroismo bolognese nel secolo XIII e Taddeo Alderotto," *Rivista di Storia della Filosofia* 4 (1949): 11–22.

66. The influence of the school of Paris upon the earliest Italian Aristotelians ought to be investigated further. The earliest tangible fact seems to be the notice that Gentile da Cingoli, who became a teacher of logic and philosophy at Bologna around 1300, attended a course on Aristotle by Johannes Vate who appears at Paris around 1290 (Martin Grabmann, *Mittelalterliches Geistesleben,* vol. 2 [Munich, 1936], p. 265ff.). It is well-known that Peter of Abano, the supposed founder of the school of Padua, studied at Paris and was in personal relations with Jean de Jandun. As late as 1340 the physician Gentile da Foligno is reported to have advised the ruler of Padua to send twelve youths to Paris to study the arts and medicine (Heinrich Denifle and Émile Chatelain, *Chartularium Universitatis Parisiensis,* II [Paria, 1891]), p. 558).

67. Martin Grabmann, "Studien über den Averroisten Taddeo da Parma," *Mittelalterliches Geistesleben,* vol. 2, pp. 239–60; *id.,* "Der Bologneser Averroist Angelo d'Arezzo," *ibid.,* pp. 261–71. Peter of Abano and Gentile da Cingoli belong to the same period. Urbano of Bologna would seem to belong to the second half of the fourteenth century. Anneliese Maier, "Eine italienische Averroistenschule aus der ersten Hälfte des 14. Jahrhunderts," *Die Vorläufer Galileis im 14. Jahrhundert* (Rome, 1949), pp. 251–78; Martin Grabmann, "Gentile da Cingoli, ein italienischer Aristoteleserklärer aus der Zeit Dantes," *Sitzungsberichte der bayerischen Akademie der Wissenschaften, Philosophisch-Historische Abteilung,* Jahrgang 1940, Heft 9 (published 1941). P. O. Kristeller, "A Philosophical Treatise from Bologna Dedicated to Guido Cavalcanti," in *Medioevo e Rinascimento: Studi in Onore di Bruno Nardi,* vol. 1 (Florence, 1955), pp. 425–63. See also, Zdzislaw Kuksewicz, *Averroïsme Bolonais au XIVe siècle* (Wroclaw, 1965); *id., De Siger de Brabant à Jacques de Plaisance* (Wroclaw, 1968).

68. Pierre Duhem, "La tradition de Buridan et la science italienne au XVIe

siècle," *Etudes sur Léonard de Vinci,* vol. 3 (Paris, 1913), pp. 113–259; *id.,* "La dialectique d'Oxford et la scolastique italienne," *Bulletin Italien* 12 (1912) and 13 (1913). Marshall Clagett, *Giovanni Marliani and Late Medieval Physics* (New York, 1941). Curtis Wilson, *William Heytesbury* (Madison, Wis., 1956). Theodore E. James, "De primo et ultimo instanti Petri Alboini Mantuani" (Ph.D. diss., Columbia University, 1968).

69. For this Italian Aristotelianism, see Friedrich Ueberweg, *Grundriss der Geschichte der Philosophie,* 12th ed., vol. 3 (Berlin, 1924), p. 22ff. Jakob Brucker, *Historia critica philosophiae,* vol. 4, pt. 1 (Leipzig, 1743), p. 148ff. Carl von Prantl, *Geschichte der Logik im Abendlande,* vol. 4 (Leipzig, 1870), pp. 118ff., 176ff., 232ff. Ernest Renan, *Averroès et l'averroïsme* (Paris, 1852; rev. ed., 1861). Clagett, *Giovanni Marliani.* Eugenio Garin, *La filosofia* (Milan, 1947), vol. 1, pp. 338–52 and vol. 2, pp. 1–65. Bruno Nardi, *Sigieri di Brabante nel pensiero del Rinascimento italiano* (Rome, 1945). P. O. Kristeller, "Renaissance Aristotelianism," *Greek, Roman and Byzantine Studies* 6 (1965): 157–74. Charles B. Schmitt, *A Critical Survey and Bibliography of Studies on Renaissance Aristotelianism* (Padua, 1971).

70. Usually the introduction of English dialectic in Italy is attributed to Paul of Venice at Padua after 1400. Yet Peter of Mantua, whom Prantl and Duhem treat as an author of the fifteenth century because of the publication date of his treatises, lived during the fourteenth century and probably died in A.D. 1400. He taught at Bologna and may have been the first Italian follower of the Oxford School. See the letter addressed to him by Salutati (note 13), and Novati's footnote which gives several biographical data and references to manuscripts, all unknown to historians of philosophy. A manuscript with logical works of Peter is in the Columbia University Libraries. The text of the "loyca Ferebrigh" appears in the library of the Franciscans in Assisi as early as 1381 (cf. Giuseppe Manacorda, *Stoiria della scuola in Italia* [Milan, n.d.], pt. 2, p. 361). However it is known that Peter of Mantua studied at Padua before beginning to teach at Bologna in 1392. See Roberto Cessi, *Athenaeum* 1 (1913): 130–31. A. Segarizzi, *Atti della I. R. Accademia di Scienze, Lettere ed Arti degli Agiati in Rovereto,* 3d ser., 13 (1970): 219–48. Cesare Vasoli, "Pietro degli Alboini da Mantova 'scholastico' della fine del Trecento e un'Epistola di Coluccio Salutati," *Rinascimento* 14 [n.s. 3] (1963): 3–21. James, "De primo et ultimo instanti Petri Alboini Mantuani."

71. After having joked about the Barbaric names of the English logicians, Bruni continues: "Et quid Colucci ut haec ioca omittam quid est inquam in dialectica quod non Britannicis sophismatibus conturbatum sit?" (*Leonardi Bruni Aretini Dialogus de tribus vatibus Florentinis,* ed. Karl Wotke [Vienna, 1889], p. 16).

72. For some of the humanist controversies see Remigio Sabbadini, *Storia del ciceronianismo* (Turin, 1885).

73. For Stoic elements in Pomponazzi, see Léontine Zanta, *La renaissance du Stoicisme au XVIe siècle* (Paris, 1914). For Platonic elements in Pomponazzi see essay 2.

74. Ernest Renan, *Averroès et l'averroïsme,* 2d ed. (Paris, 1861). Renan's work has been superseded for the thirteenth century by Pierre Mandonnet, *Siger de Bra-*

bant et l'averroïsme latin au XIIIe siècle, 2d ed., 2 vols. (Louvain, 1908–11). There is a widespread belief that Renan has been entirely superseded by Mandonnet, but this is obviously not true for the fourteenth and later centuries. The more recent article by M. M. Gorce, "Averroïsme," *Dictionnaire d'Histoire et de Géographie Ecclésiastique* 5 (1931): 1032–92, does not supersede Renan either, although it supplements him in a few details. Gorce largely follows Renan for the later period and does not correct any of his major mistakes. There is a fairly large literature on Pomponazzi, and a monograph on Cesare Cremonini by Léopold Mabilleau, *Étude historique sur la philosophie de la Renaissance en Italie* (Paris, 1881). See also Bruno Nardi, *Saggi sull'Aristotelismo padovano dal secolo XIV al XVI* (Florence, 1958). M. A. Del Torre, *Studi su Cesare Cremonini* (Padua, 1968).

75. An important contribution to the latter problem has been published by J. H. Randall, Jr., "The Development of Scientific Method in the School of Padua," *Journal of the History of Ideas* 1 (1940): 177–206, reprinted in his *The School of Padua and the Emergence of Modern Science* (Padua, 1961), pp. 13–68. Giovanni di Napoli, *L'immortalità dell'anima nel Rinascimento* (Turin, 1963); Martin Pine, "Pietro Pomponazzi and the Immortality Controversy" (Ph.D. diss., Columbia University, 1965).

76. For the contributions of the Aristotelians to sixteenth-century science, see Lynn Thorndike, *A History of Magic and Experimental Science,* vols. 5–6 (New York, 1941). For Galilei's connection with Italian Aristotelianism, see Randall, "The Development of Scientific Method in the School of Padua." I should like to add the following detail: Everybody knows Galilei's statement that the nobility of a science depends on the certainty of its method rather than on the dignity of its subject matter (*Opere,* Edizione Nazionale, vol. 6 [1896], p. 237 and vol. 7 [1897], p. 246). Remembering this statement, I was surprised to find among Pomponazzi's Questions on the first book of Aristotle's *de anima* the following one: "Nobilitas scientiae a quo sumatur. Quaestio est a quo sumatur magis nobilitas scientiae, an a nobilitate subiecti an a certitudine demonstrationis vel aequaliter ab ambobus" (Luigi Ferri, "Intorno alle dottrine psicologiche di Pietro Pomponazzi," *Atti della Reale Accademia dei Lincei,* 2d ser., 3 [1875–76], pt. 3, p. 423). Pomponazzi does not give a clear answer as does Galilei, but it is obvious that Galilei's statement is not an isolated aphorism, but a conscious answer given to a traditional question debated in the Aristotelian schools of philosophy. See Eugenio Garin, *La Disputa delle Arti nel Quattrocento* (Florence, 1947), p. xiiiff.

77. Most of these notions go back to Renan and have been repeated ever since, especially by French scholars. As I hope to have shown elsewhere, there is no evidence for the existence of an Alexandrist school in the sixteenth century; there is hardly a uniform Averroist tradition, especially not in the sense used by Renan, who fails to distinguish between the use made of Averroes as a commentator and the adherence to specific Averroist doctrines such as the unity of the intellect; there was no distinctive school of Padua, especially not in the fourteenth century, but merely a broad movement of Italian Aristotelianism in which the university of Padua came to play a leading role during the sixteenth century. Many philosophers listed by Renan as representatives of the Paduan school actually never lived in that city; the tradition

that the Paduan Aristotelians were atheists and freethinkers is mainly based on un-verified anecdotes and insinuations that developed in France during the seventeenth and eighteenth centuries when the freethinkers of that period were looking for fore-runners and their orthodox opponents had no reason to defend the memory of thinkers who had tried to compromise between reason and faith in a way that was no longer considered permissible or possible by either side. P. O. Kristeller, "Petrarch's 'Averroists,' " *Bibliothèque d'Humanisme et Renaissance* 14 [*Mélanges Augustin Renaudet*] (1952): 59–65; *id.*, "The Myth of Renaissance Atheism and the French Tradition of Free Thought," *Journal of the History of Philosophy* 6 (1968): 233–43; *id.*, "Paduan Averroism and Alexandrism in the Light of Recent Studies," in *Aristotelismo Padovano e Filosofia Aristotelica: Atti del XII Congresso Internazionale di Filosofia* 9 (Florence, 1960): 147–55.

78. On the question of Latin and *volgare* as discussed by the humanists, see Remigio Sabbadini, *Storia del ciceronianismo*, pp. 127–36. I do not agree with his presentation of the problem. The orations of Romolo Amaseo, and the similar one of Sigonius, were primarily defenses of Latin as a field of study, without any intention to abolish the *volgare*. We still need a history of the Italian literary language that would show its gradual expansion, at the expense of Latin and also of local dialects, according to the various regions of Italy as well as to the various branches of literary expression. The problem was formulated by Burckhardt, *Die Kultur der Renaissance*, p. 418. See Kristeller, *Studies in Renaissance Thought and Letters*, pp. 473–93.

79. P. O. Kristeller, "The Modern System of the Arts," *Journal of the History of Ideas* 12 (1951): 496–527 and 13 (1952): 17–46, reprinted in *Renaissance Thought II: Papers in Humanism and the Arts* (New York, 1965), pp. 163–227.

6. RENAISSANCE PHILOSOPHY AND THE MEDIEVAL TRADITION

1. See, among many other discussions, the symposium led by Dana Durand and Hans Baron and published in the *Journal of the History of Ideas* 4 (1943): 1–74. Wallace K. Ferguson et al., *The Renaissance* (New York, 1953 and 1962). *The Renaissance*, ed. Tinsley Helton (Madison, Wis., 1961). Herbert Weisinger, "Renaissance Accounts of the Revival of Learning," *Studies in Philology* 44 (1948): 105–18. For a comprehensive history of the Renaissance concept, see W. K. Ferguson, *The Renaissance in Historical Thought* (Boston, 1948). *Zu Begriff und Problem der Renaissance*, ed. August Buck (Darmstadt, 1969).

2. Two classical books on the fifteenth century, Jacob Burckhardt, *Die Cultur der Renaissance in Italien* (Basel, 1860, and many later editions), and Johan Huizinga, *The Waning of the Middle Ages*, trans. F. Hopman (London, 1924), focus on Italy and the Low Countries, respectively; and the considerable difference of their outlook derives to a large extent from this fact.

3. For example, classical humanism occupied a much more central position in the fifteenth century than did the *ars dictaminis* in the twelfth or thirteenth centuries, al-

though the latter may be considered to some extent as the predecessor of the former. Moreover, those historians who stress the medieval antecedents of Renaissance humanism are apt to find them in the twelfth rather than in the thirteenth century.

4. This was done on a large scale by E. R. Curtius, *Europäische Literatur und lateinisches Mittelalter* (Bern, 1948), trans. by Willard R. Trask as *European Literature and the Latin Middle Ages* (New York, 1953). Cf. P. O. Kristeller, "Renaissanceforschung und Altertumswissenschaft," *Forschungen und Fortschritte* 33 (1959): 363–69.

5. For example, St. Augustine occupies a very important place in the work of Petrarch, but Petrarch's approach to St. Augustine is quite different from that of most medieval followers of St. Augustine. Cf. Nicolae Iliescu, *Il canzoniere petrarchesco e Sant'Agostino* (Rome, 1962). P. O. Kristeller, *Studies in Renaissance Thought and Letters* (Rome, 1956), pp. 355–72; and essay 4, p. 76.

6. Étienne Gilson, *Les idées et les lettres,* 2d ed. (Paris, 1955), p. 192: "La Renaissance, telle qu'on nous la décrit, n'est pas le moyen âge plus l'homme, mais le moyen âge moins Dieu. . . ." I am aware of the qualification ("telle que l'on nous la décrit") and of the more perceptive remarks made by the same scholar elsewhere, especially in his paper, "Le moyen âge et le naturalisme antique," *Archives d'histoire doctrinale et littéraire du Moyen Age* 7 (1932): 5–37.

7. Charles S. Baldwin, *Ancient Rhetoric and Poetic* (New York, 1924). Donald L. Clark, *Rhetoric in Greco-Roman Education* (New York, 1957). H.-J. Marrou, *Histoire de l'éducation dans l'antiquité* (Paris, 1948). See essay 12.

8. H.-J. Marrou, *Saint Augustin et la fin de la culture antique* (Paris, 1938). Pierre Courcelle, *Les lettres grecques en Occident: De Macrobe à Cassiodore* (Paris, 1943). William H. Stahl, *Roman Science* (Madison, Wis., 1962).

9. E. K. Rand, *Founders of the Middle Ages* (Cambridge, Mass., 1928).

10. Joseph Mariétan, *Problème de la classification des sciences d'Aristote à St. Thomas* (Fribourg, 1901). Martin Grabmann, *Geschichte der scholastischen Methode,* vol. 2 (Freiburg i. Br., 1957), pp. 28–54. Marrou, *Saint Augustin,* p. 187ff. P. O. Kristeller, "The Modern System of the Arts," in *Renaissance Thought II: Papers on Humanism and the Arts* (New York, 1965), pp. 163–227. *Artes Liberales,* ed. Josef Koch (Leyden and Cologne, 1959). *Arts libéraux et philosophie au Moyen Age* [Actes du quatrième congrès international de philosophie médiévale, Montreal, 1967] (Montreal and Paris, 1969).

11. In the Italian vernacular of the thirteenth and fourteenth centuries, the word "grammatica" came to stand for the Latin language.

12. Fausto Ghisalberti, "Giovanni del Virgilio espositore delle 'Metamorfosi,' " *Giornale Dantesco* 34 (1933): 31ff. Eva M. Sanford, "The Manuscripts of Lucan," *Speculum* 9 (1934): 278–95; *eadem,* "Juvenal," in *Catalogus Translationum et Commentariorum,* vol. 1, ed. P. O. Kristeller (Washington, D.C., 1960), pp. 175–238. Cf. essay 5, note 47. The prevailing view that classical studies declined in the thirteenth century has been qualified to some extent by E. K. Rand, "The Classics in the Thirteenth Century," *Speculum* 4 (1929): 249–69. See also Helene Wieruszowski, "Rhetoric and the Classics in Italian Education of the Thirteenth Century," *Studia Gratiana* 11 [*Collectanea Stephan Kuttner* 1] (Bologna, 1967): 169–207.

13. Louise R. Loomis, *Medieval Hellenism* (Lancaster, Pa., 1906). Bernhard Bischoff, "Das griechische Element in der abendländischen Bildung des Mittelalters," *Byzantinische Zeitschrift* 44 (1951): 27–55. K. M. Setton, "The Byzantine Background to the Italian Renaissance," *Proceedings of the American Philosophical Society* 100 (1956): 1–76. Robert Devreesse, *Les manuscrits grecs de l'Italie méridionale* [Biblioteca Vaticana, *Studi e Testi* 183] (Vatican City, 1955). Roberto Weiss, "The Greek Culture of South Italy in the Later Middle Ages," *British Academy, Proceedings*, 37 (1951): 23–50; *id.*, "The Study of Greek in England during the Fourteenth Century," *Rinascimento* 2 (1951): 209–39.

14. J. T. Muckle, "Greek Works Translated Directly into Latin before 1350," *Mediaeval Studies* 4 (1942): 33–42 and 5 (1943): 102–14. For translations from the Arabic and other languages, see Moritz Steinschneider, *Die europäischen Übersetzungen aus dem Arabischen bis Mitte des 17. Jahrhunderts* (Graz, 1956). George Sarton, *Introduction to the History of Science*, 3 vols. (Baltimore, 1927–1948).

15. *Catalogus Translationum et Commentariorum*, 3 vols., ed. P. O. Kristeller and F. Edward Cranz (Washington, D.C., 1960–76), especially the article on Alexander of Aphrodisias by F. Edward Cranz (1: 77–135), the article on St. Gregory Nazianzen by Sister Agnes Clare Way (2: 43–192), and the article on Theophrastus by Charles B. Schmitt (2: 239–322). See also R. J. Durling, "A Chronological Census of Renaissance Editions and Translations of Galen," *Journal of the Warburg and Courtauld Institutes* 24 (1961): 230–305. Vito R. Giustiniani, "Sulle traduzioni latine delle 'Vite' di Plutarco nel Quattrocento," *Rinascimento* 12 [n.s. 1] (1961): 3–62.

16. For Leonardo Bruni's translation of the Pseudo-Aristotelian *Oeconomica*, see Hans Baron, *Humanistic and Political Literature in Florence and Venice at the Beginning of the Quattrocento* (Cambridge, Mass., 1955). Josef Soudek, "The Genesis and Tradition of Leonardo Bruni's Annotated Latin Version of the (Pseudo-) Aristotelian 'Economics,' " *Scriptorium* 12 (1958): 260–68; *id.*, "Leonardo Bruni and His Public: A Statistical and Interpretative Study of His Annotated Latin Version of the (Pseudo-)Aristotelian Economics," *Studies in Medieval and Renaissance History* 5 (1968): 49–136.

17. K. M. Setton, "The Byzantine Background to the Italian Renaissance." Deno J. Geanakoplos, *Greek Scholars in Venice* (Cambridge, Mass., 1962). See also essay 7. For a comparison between the medieval and humanist translations of Aristotle, see P. O. Kristeller, *Studies in Renaissance Thought and Letters* (Rome, 1956), p. 339ff.

18. On medieval rhetoric in general, see Charles S. Baldwin, *Medieval Rhetoric and Poetic* (New York, 1928). Richard McKeon, "Rhetoric in the Middle Ages," *Speculum* 17 (1942): 1–32. For the *ars dictaminis*, see Charles H. Haskins, *Studies in Medieval Culture* (Oxford, 1929). For further literature, see P. O. Kristeller, "Matteo de 'Libri, Bolognese Notary of the Thirteenth Century, and his *Artes Dictaminis*," *Miscellanea Giovanni Galbiati* II (Milan, 1951): 283–320; *id.*, "Un'*Ars Dictaminis* di Giovanni del Virgilio," *Italia medioevale e umanistica* 4 (1961): 181–200.

To my knowledge, it has not been noticed that Gunzo of Novara (tenth century) in his well-known letter to the monks of Reichenau followed the scheme of the parts of a letter which was to be common in the theoretical treatises on *dictamen* (Gunzo, *Epistola ad Augienses* . . . , ed. Karl Manitius [Weimar, 1958]). This scheme is based on the ancient doctrine of the parts of speech, to be sure. But it is a new thing to use the parts of speech as parts of the letter, adding the salutation which has no equivalent in the speech. Hence, it appears that the practice of letter writing preceded in this respect (and perhaps in other ways) the theory of the *dictamen*, and that the origin of such characteristic theories as the six parts of the letter must be traced back beyond the earliest extant writers on *dictamen*.

19. Kristeller, "Un'*Ars Dictaminis* di Giovanni del Virgilio."

20. For a characteristic discussion of this question, see P. O. Kristeller, "An Unknown Correspondence of Alessandro Braccesi with Niccolò Michelozzi, Naldo Naldi, Bartolommeo Scala, and other Humanists (1470–1472) in Ms. Bodl.Auct.F.2.17," in *Classical, Medieval, and Renaissance Studies in Honor of Berthold Louis Ullman*, vol. 2 (Rome, 1964), pp. 311–63.

21. Richard McKeon, "Rhetoric in the Middle Ages," *Speculum* 17 (1942): 1–32, hardly discusses the *dictamen*. Yet see now James J. Murphy, *Rhetoric in the Middle Ages* (Berkeley, Calif., 1974).

22. This is quite evident from the manuscripts containing the *Rhetoric* and described in the *Aristoles Latinus, Codices*, 3 vols., ed. George Lacombe and others (Rome, 1939; Cambridge, 1955; Bruges and Paris, 1961). Commentaries on Aristotle's *Rhetoric* were composed by such scholastic philosophers as Aegidius Romanus, Guido Vernanus of Rimini, and Johannes de Janduno but not by any of the professional rhetoricians or *dictatores* prior to the fifteenth century. In the Greek manuscript tradition, the *Rhetoric* does not appear among the ethical works of Aristotle. See André Wartelle, *Inventaire des manuscrits grecs d'Aristote et de ses commentateurs* (Paris, 1963).

23. Several *dictatores* claim philosophical importance for their subject in their prefaces. Cf. Helene Wieruszowski, "*Ars Dictaminis* in the Time of Dante," *Medievalia et Humanistica* (1943): 95–108, at 105.

24. See essay 5 and essays 13 and 14. See also Alfredo Galletti, *L'Eloquenza dalle origini al XVI secolo* [*Storia dei generi letterari italiani*] (Milan, 1904–38). For humanist rhetoric, see Charles S. Baldwin, *Renaissance Literary Theory and Practice* (New York, 1939). Donald L. Clark, *Rhetoric and Poetry in the Renaissance* (New York, 1922). O. B. Hardison, *The Enduring Monument* (Chapel Hill, N.C., 1962).

25. Augusto Campana, "The Origin of the Word 'Humanist,' " *Journal of the Warburg and Courtauld Institutes* 9 (1946): 60–73. Giuseppe Billanovich, "Da autorista ad umanista," in *Wort und Text, Festschrift für Fritz Schalk* (Frankfurt, 1963), pp. 161–66. See also pp. 99 and 283–84 above.

26. W. H. Woodward, *Studies in Education during the Age of the Renaissance* (Cambridge, 1906). Eugenio Garin, *Il pensiero pedagogico dello umanesimo* (Florence, 1958).

27. Ferguson, *The Renaissance in Historical Thought*. Herbert Weisinger, "Renaissance Accounts of the Revival of Learning," *Studies in Philology* 45 (1948): 105–18.

28. Saul Lieberman, *Greek in Jewish Palestine* (New York, 1942); *id.*, *Hellenism in Jewish Palestine* (New York, 1950). F. C. Grant, *Roman Hellenism and the New Testament* (New York, 1962). Edwin Hatch, *The Influence of Greek Ideas on Christianity*, ed. F. C. Grant (New York, 1957). Charles N. Cochrane, *Christianity and Classical Culture* (London, 1944), credits the Church fathers and even St. Augustine with philosophical originality on many points where they actually depend on Stoic or Neoplatonic sources (see my review in *The Journal of Philosophy* 41 [1944]: 576–81). The literature on the classical influences on the Church fathers is far too large to be cited here in detail.

29. Martin Grabmann, *Die Geschichte der katholischen Theologie* (Freiburg, 1933; reprint ed., Darmstadt, 1961). A. M. Landgraf, *Einführung in die Geschichte der theologischen Literatur der Frühscholastik* (Regensburg, 1948). Joseph de Ghellinck, *Le mouvement théologique du XIIe siècle*, 2d ed. (Brussels and Paris, 1948).

30. Franz Ehrle, *Der Sentenzenkommentar Peters von Candia* (Münster, 1925). Ricardo Garcia Villoslada, *La Universidad de Paris durante los estudios de Francisco de Vitoria* (Rome, 1938). P. O. Kristeller, *Le Thomisme et la pensée italienne de la Renaissance* (Montreal and Paris, 1967), appearing in English translation, without the two supporting Latin texts, in *Medieval Aspects of Renaissance Learning*, ed. and trans. Edward P. Mahoney (Durham, N.C., 1974), pp. 27–91.

31. Roland H. Bainton, *Here I Stand: A Life of Martin Luther* (New York, 1950). Heiko A. Oberman, *The Harvest of Medieval Theology* (Cambridge, Mass., 1963).

32. Grabmann, *Die Geschichte der katholischen Theologie*. Carlo Giacon, *La seconda scolastica*, 3 vols. (Milan, 1944–50). Frederick Copleston, *A History of Philosophy*, vol. 3 (Westminster, Md., 1953).

33. See essay 4. E. H. Harbison, *The Christian Scholar in the Age of the Reformation* (New York, 1956). Pontien Polman, *L'élément historique dans la controverse religieuse du XVIe siècle* (Gembloux, 1932). Albert Hyma, *The Christian Renaissance* (New York, 1924).

34. Especially by Étienne Gilson, *L'esprit de la philosophie médiévale*, 2d ed. (Paris, 1944); *id. History of Christian Philosophy in the Middle Ages* (New York, 1955). I do not deny, of course, that the medieval philosophers were Christians and that their philosophy, for this and other reasons, must be distinguished from that of their Islamic and Jewish contemporaries. Yet to my knowledge the term "Christian philosophy" is not used by any of the medieval thinkers whom Gilson has in mind, and this fact seems to me significant.

35. Erasmus uses the terms *philosophia Christi* and *philosophia Christiana* repeatedly, especially in the prefaces of his *Enchiridion* and his edition of the *New Testament* (*Ausgewählte Werke*, ed. Annemarie and Hajo Holborn [Munich, 1933], pp. 5–7, 9, 139ff.). For Justinus Martyr, the crucial passage is found in the *Dialogus cum Tryphone*, ch. 8, vol. 1, ed. Georges Archambault (Paris, 1909), p. 40: "διαλογιζόμενός τε πρὸς ἐμαυτὸν τοὺς λόγους αὐτοῦ ταύτην μόνην εὕρισκον φιλοσοφίαν ἀσφαλῆ τε καὶ σύμφορον. Οὕτως δὴ καὶ διὰ ταῦτα φιλόσοφος ἐγώ." For the idea in Justin and other early Apologists, see M. V. Engelhardt, *Das Christenthum Justins des Märtyrers* (Erlangen, 1878), pp. 223–31. Carl Christian Clemen, *Die religionsphilosophische Bedeutung des stoisch-christlichen Eudaemonismus in*

Justins Apologie (Leipzig, 1890). J. Quasten, *Patrology*, vol. I (Utrecht, 1950), pp. 196, 220.

36. Ernest Renan, *Averroès et l'averroïsme* (Paris, 1852). Pierre Mandonnet, *Siger de Brabant et l'averroïsme latin au XIII e siècle*, 2d ed. (Louvain, 1908–1911). Stuart MacClintock, *Perversity and Error: Studies on the "Averroist" John of Jandun* (Bloomington, Ind., 1956).

37. Bruno Nardi, *Sigieri di Brabante nel pensiero del Rinascimento italiano* (Rome, 1945); *id., Saggi sull'Aristotelismo Padovano dal secolo XIV al XVI* (Florence, 1958).

38. P. O. Kristeller, *Il pensiero filosofico di Marsilio Ficino* (Florence, 1953), pp. 18–20, 346–49.

39. J. F. von Schulte, *Die Geschichte der Quellen und Literatur des canonischen Rechts*, 3 vols. (Stuttgart, 1875–1880). Stephan Kuttner, *Repertorium der Kanonistik*, vol. I (Vatican City, 1937). Joseph de Ghellinck, *Le mouvement théologique au XIIe siècle*, 2d ed. (Brussels and Paris, 1948).

40. Friedrich Karl von Savigny, *Geschichte des römischen Rechts im Mittelalter*, 2d ed., 7 vols. (Heidelberg, 1834–1851). Hermann Kantorowicz, *Studies in the Glossators of the Roman Law* (Cambridge, 1938). Donald R. Kelley, *Foundations of Modern Historical Scholarship* (New York, 1970); *id.,* "Historical Thought and Legal Scholarship in Sixteenth-Century France" (Ph.D. diss., Columbia University, 1962).

41. Guido Kisch, *Humanismus und Jurisprudenz* (Basel, 1955); *id., Erasmus und die Jurisprudenz seiner Zeit* (Basel, 1960). Domenico Maffei, *Gli inizi dell'umanesimo giuridico* (Milan, 1956).

42. Pierre Mesnard, *L'essor de la philosophie politique au XVIe siècle* (Paris, 1936).

43. The beginning sentence of Chrysippus' treatise on law has been preserved because it was inserted verbatim in the *Corpus Iuris* (Dig., I, 3, 2, citing "Marcianus libro primo institutionum"). Cf. Hans von Arnim, *Stoicorum Veterum Fragmenta*, vol. III (Leipzig, 1903), pp. 77, no. 314 (who mentions Marcianus, but not the *Corpus Iuris*).

44. *De ordine*, II, 8, 25. *De vera religione*, 31, 58. *De libero arbitrio*, I, 6. Cf. Étienne Gilson, *Introduction à l'étude de Saint Augustin*, 3d ed. (Paris, 1949), p. 168. St. Thomas Aquinas, *Summa Theologiae*, Ia–IIae, q. 91–95. Cf. also Gratian, *Decretum*, Dist. I, C.7.

45. Pierre Duhem, *Études sur Léonard de Vinci*, 3 vols. (Paris, 1906–13). Ernest Moody, "Galileo and Avempace," *Journal of the History of Ideas* 12 (1951): 163–93, 375–422. Marshall Clagett, *Giovanni Marliani and Late Medieval Physics* (New York, 1941); *id., The Science of Mechanics in the Middle Ages* (Madison, Wis., 1959). Anneliese Maier, *Die Vorläufer Galileis im 14. Jahrhundert* (Rome, 1949); *eadem, An der Grenze von Scholastik und Naturwissenschaft*, 2d ed. (Rome, 1952); *eadem, Zwischen Philosophie und Mechanik* (Rome, 1958); *eadem, Ausgehendes Mittelalter*, 2 vols. (Rome, 1964–77). A. C. Crombie, *Augustine to Galileo* (London, 1952). Edward Rosen, "Renaissance Science As Seen by Burckhardt and His Successors," in *The Renaissance*, ed. Tinsley Helton (Madison, Wis., 1961), pp. 77–103.

46. L. C. MacKinney, *Early Medieval Medicine* (Baltimore, 1937). Henry E. Sigerist, "The Latin Medical Literature of the Early Middle Ages," *Journal of the History of Medicine* 13 (1958): 127–46. Augusto Beccaria, *I codici di medicina del periodo presalernitano* (Rome, 1956).

47. Cf. Kristeller, *Studies in Renaissance Thought and Letters*, p. 495ff. P. O. Kristeller, "Beitrag der Schule von Salerno zur Entwicklung der scholastischen Wissenschaft im 12. Jahrhundert," in *Artes Liberales*, ed. Josef Koch (Leyden and Cologne, 1959), pp. 84–90.

48. For Galen, see R. J. Durling, "A Chronological Census of Renaissance Editions and Translations of Galen," *Journal of the Warburg and Courtauld Institutes* 24 (1961): 230–305. For Hippocrates, see Pearl Kibre, "Hippocratic Writings in the Middle Ages," *Bulletin of the History of Medicine* 18 (1945): 371–412; *eadem*, "Hippocrates Latinus," *Traditio* 31–33 (1975–77), to be continued.

49. W. H. Stahl, *Roman Science* (Madison, Wis., 1962).

50. George Sarton, *Introduction to the History of Science*, 3 vols. (Baltimore, 1927–48). Marshall Clagett, *The Science of Mechanics in the Middle Ages* (Madison, Wis., 1959); *id., Archimedes in the Middle Ages*, vol. 1 (Madison, Wis., 1964) and vol. 2 (Philadelphia, 1976).

51. Paul Lawrence Rose, *The Italian Renaissance of Mathematics* (Geneva, 1975).

52. Alexandre Koyré, *Etudes Galiléennes*, 3 vols. (Paris, 1939). Edward Rosen, "Renaissance Science As Seen by Burckhardt and His Successors," in *The Renaissance*, ed. Tinsley Helton (Madison, Wis., 1961), pp. 77–103. Anneliese Maier also makes fewer claims than Duhem or others.

53. Marshall Clagett, *Giovanni Marliani and Late Medieval Physics* (New York, 1941). J. H. Randall, Jr., *The School of Padua and the Emergence of Modern Science* (Padua, 1961); *id., The Career of Philosophy: From the Middle Ages to the Enlightenment* (New York, 1962). Curtis Wilson, *William Heytesbury* (Madison, Wis., 1956).

54. Dana B. Durand, "Tradition and Innovation in Fifteenth-Century Italy," *Journal of the History of Ideas* 4 (1943): 1–20. "Strabo," by Aubrey Diller and P. O. Kristeller, in *Catalogus Translationum et Commentariorum*, vol. 2, ed. P. O. Kristeller and F. Edward Cranz (Washington, D.C., 1971), pp. 225–33.

55. See the monumental work by Lynn Thorndike, *A History of Magic and Experimental Science*, 8 vols. (New York, 1923–1958).

56. D. P. Walker, *Spiritual and Demonic Magic from Ficino to Campanella* (London, 1958). Frances Yates, *Giordano Bruno and the Hermetic Tradition* (London, 1964).

57. Friedrich von Bezold, *Das Fortleben der antiken Götter im mittelalterlichen Humanismus* (Bonn, 1922). Jean Seznec, *La survivance des dieux antiques* (London, 1940), trans. by Barbara F. Sessions as *The Survival of the Pagan Gods* (New York, 1953). Edgar Wind, *Pagan Mysteries in the Renaissance* (New Haven, 1958).

58. *Aristoteles Latinus, Codices*, 3 vols., ed. George Lacombe et al. (Rome, 1939; Cambridge; 1955, Bruges and Paris, 1961), Lorenzo Minio-Paluello, *Opuscula* (Amsterdam, 1972). Fundamental still are the chapters contributed by the late Msgr. Auguste Pelzer to the first two volumes of Maurice De Wulf's *Histoire de la philo-*

sophie médiévale, 6th ed., 3 vols. (Louvain, 1934–47), 1: 64–80 and 2: 25–58, of which the second is omitted in the English translation by E. C. Messenger (London, 1935–38). Of Messenger's "definitive" translation, only the first volume has appeared (New York, 1952).

59. Anneliese Maier, *Zwei Grundprobleme der scholastischen Naturphilosophie,* 2d ed. (Rome, 1951).

60. See notes 45 and 51.

61. See notes 52 and 53. For the influence of Buridan in Italy, see G. Federici Vescovini, "Su alcuni manoscritti di Buridano," *Rivista critica di storia della filosofia* 15 (1960): 413–27. The dependence of the early Galileo on the commentaries of sixteenth-century Jesuits on Aristotle's *Physics* has been studied by William A. Wallace, *Galileo's Early Notebooks* (Notre Dame, Ind., 1977).

62. Kristeller, *Studies in Renaissance Thought and Letters,* pp. 339–42. Soudek, "The Genesis and Tradition of Leonardo Bruni's Annotated Latin Version"; *id.,* "Leonardo Bruni and His Public." Much bibliographical and other material on the humanist translations of Aristotle has been collected by F. Edward Cranz but not yet published. Eugenio Garin, "Le traduzioni umanistiche di Aristotele nel secolo XV," *Atti e Memorie dell'Accademia Fiorentina di Scienze Morali 'La Colombaria'* 16 [n.s. 2] (1947–50): 50–104.

63. For Alexander of Aphrodisias, see F. Edward Cranz in *Catalogus Translationum et Commentariorum,* vol. 1, ed. Kristeller, pp. 77–135 and vol. 2, ed. Kristeller and Cranz, pp. 411–22.

64. Ernest Moody, "Galileo and Avempace," *Journal of the History of Ideas* 12 (1951): 163–93, 375–422.

65. Alexandre Koyré, *Etudes Galiléennes,* 3 vols. (Paris, 1939). Ernst Cassirer, *Das Erkenntnisproblem,* vol. 1, 3d ed. (Berlin, 1922); *id.,* "Galileo's Platonism," in *Studies and Essays in the History of Science, Offered in Homage to George Sarton* (New York, 1946), pp. 276–97. For so-called Pythagorean influences, see also Erich Frank, *Plato und die sogenannten Pythagoreer* (Halle, 1923).

66. J. P. Mullally, *The Summulae Logicales of Peter of Spain* (Notre Dame, Ind., 1945). I. M. Bochenski, *Formale Logik* (Freiburg and Munich, 1956), trans. by Ivo Thomas as *A History of Formal Logic* (Notre Dame, Ind., 1961). Ernest A. Moody, *Truth and Consequence in Mediaeval Logic* (Amsterdam, 1953). Philotheus H. Boehner, *Medieval Logic* (Chicago, 1952). Lorenzo Minio-Paluello, *Twelfth Century Logic,* 2 vols. (Rome, 1956–58). Lambertus M. De Rijk, *Logica Modernorum,* vol. 1 (Assen, 1962). Peter of Spain, *Tractatus,* ed. Lambertus M. De Rijk (Assen, 1972).

67. Curtis Wilson, *William Heytesbury* (Madison, Wis., 1956). For the later repercussions of the medieval logical tradition see also Neal W. Gilbert, *Renaissance Concepts of Method* (New York, 1960).

68. Mario Nizolio, *De veris principiis,* 2 vols., ed. Quirinus Breen (Rome, 1956).

69. Perry Miller, *The New England Mind,* 2 vols. (Cambridge, Mass., 1939–1953). Walter J. Ong, *Ramus: Method and the Decay of Dialogue* (Cambridge, Mass., 1958); *id., Ramus and Talon Inventory* (Cambridge, Mass., 1958). Gilbert, *Renaissance Concepts of Method.* Wilhelm Risse, *Die Logik der Neuzeit* (Stuttgart, 1964).

70. Giovanni di Napoli, *L'immortalità dell'anima nel Rinascimento* (Turin, 1963). Martin Pine, "Pietro Pomponazzi and the Immortality Controversy" (Ph.D. diss., Columbia University, 1965). P. O. Kristeller, "Pier Candido Decembrio and His Unpublished Treatise on the Immortality of the Soul," in *The Classical Tradition: Literary and Historical Studies in Honor of Harry Caplan* (Ithaca, N.Y., 1966), pp. 536–58. See essay 10. P. O. Kristeller, "A Thomist Critique of Marsilio Ficino's Theory of Will and Intellect," in *Harry Austryn Wolfson Jubilee Volume, English Section*, vol. 2 (Jerusalem, 1965), pp. 463–94; *id.*, *Le Thomisme et la pensée italienne de la Renaissance* (Montreal and Paris, 1967), pp. 104–23; *id.*, *Medieval Aspects of Renaissance Learning*, ed. and trans. Edward P. Mahoney (Durham, N.C., 1974), pp. 79–90.

71. Cf. Leonardo Bruni Aretino, *Humanistisch-Philosophische Schriften*, ed. Hans Baron (Leipzig and Berlin, 1928). Eugenio Garin, "Le traduzioni umanistiche di Aristotele nel secolo XV," *Atti e Memorie dell'Accademia Fiorentina di Scienze Morali 'La Colombaria'* 16 [n.s. 2] (1947–50): 55–104. Cf. also the studies by Josef Soudek cited in note 16.

72. Kristeller, *Studies in Renaissance Thought and Letters*, pp. 340–41.

73. P. O. Kristeller, "The Moral Thought of Renaissance Humanism," *Renaissance Thought II: Papers on Humanism and the Arts* (New York, 1965), pp. 20–68.

74. For the influence of Aristotle's *Poetics* in the sixteenth century, see Baxter Hathaway, *The Age of Criticism* (Ithaca, N.Y., 1962); and esp. Bernard Weinberg, *A History of Literary Criticism in the Italian Renaissance*, 2 vols. (Chicago, 1961). An analogous study for his *Rhetoric* has not yet been undertaken, as far as I know. See essay 14.

75. *Timaeus a Calcidio translatus commentarioque instructus*, ed. J. H. Waszink (*Plato Latinus*, ed. Raymond Klibansky, vol. 4 [London, 1962]).

76. Raymond Klibansky, *The Continuity of the Platonic Tradition during the Middle Ages* (London, 1939). See also essay 3.

77. *Dionysiaca*, 2 vols. (Paris and Bruges, 1937) where all known Latin translations are given in parallel columns, along with the Greek text.

78. *Corpus Platonicum Medii Aevi, Plato Latinus*, ed. Raymond Klibansky, 4 vols. (London, 1940–1962). Proclus, *The Elements of Theology*, ed. E. R. Dodds (Oxford, 1933, rev. ed., 1963). Proclus, *Tria Opuscula*, ed. Helmut Boese (Berlin, 1960); cf. my review in *The Journal of Philosophy* 54 (1962): 74–78. Proclus, *Elementatio Theologica, translata a Guilelmo de Moerbeke*, ed. C. Vansteenkiste, *Tijdschrift voor Philosophie* 13 (1951): 263–302, 491–531.

79. The Platonism of Aquinas is emphasized by Arthur Little, *The Platonic Heritage of Thomism* (Dublin, 1949), and played down by R. J. Henle, *Saint Thomas and Platonism* (The Hague, 1956). Yet, other studies have shown that Aquinas' doctrine of participation is influenced by Proclus and occupies a significant place in his thought. See L.-B. Geiger, *La participation dans la philosophie de S. Thomas d' Aquin* (Paris, 1942). Cornelio Fabro, *La nozione metafisica di partecipazione secondo S. Tommaso d'Aquino* (Milan, 1939; 2d ed., Turin, 1950; 3d ed., Turin, 1963); *id.*, *Participation et causalité selon S. Thomas d'Aquin* (Louvain, 1961).

80. Proclus, *Elements of Theology*, ed. Dodds, p. xxxii. Klibansky, *Continuity of*

the Platonic Tradition, p. 28. An edition of the text is being prepared by Loris Sturlese.

81. Edmond Vansteenberghe, *Le cardinal Nicolas de Cues* (Paris, 1920), esp. pp. 413–16 and 436–38. See also Nicolaus de Cusa, *De docta ignorantia,* ed. Ernst Hoffmann and Raymond Klibansky (Leipzig, 1932) for references given in the apparatus and in the index. P. O. Kristeller, "A Latin Translation of Gemistos Plethon's *De fato* by Johannes Sophianos dedicated to Nicholas of Cusa," in *Nicolò Cusano agli inizi del Mondo Moderno* (Florence, 1970), pp. 175–93.

82. Kristeller, *Studies in Renaissance Thought and Letters,* pp. 368–71.

83. Eugenio Garin, "Ricerche sulle traduzioni di Platone nella prima metà del sec. XV," in *Medioevo e Rinascimento: Studi in onore di Bruno Nardi,* vol. 1 (Florence, 1955): 339–74; *Supplementum Ficinianum,* ed. P. O. Kristeller, vol. 1 (Florence, 1937; reprint ed., 1973), pp. clvi–clvii.

84. Kristeller, *Studies in Renaissance Thought and Letters,* p. 38ff.; *id.,* "Florentine Platonism and Its Relations with Humanism and Scholasticism," *Church History* 8 (1939): 201–11.

85. A.-J. Festugière, *La révélation d'Hermès Trismégiste,* 4 vols. (Paris, 1950–1954). Wilhelm Kroll, *De oraculis Chaldaicis* (Breslau, 1894). Hans Lewy, *Chaldaean Oracles and Theurgy* (Cairo, 1956).

86. Kristeller, *Il pensiero filosofico di Marsilio Ficino,* pp. 16–20.

87. See the letter to Martinus Uranius reproduced by Klibansky, *Continuity of the Platonic Tradition,* pp. 45–47.

88. Kristeller, *Studies in Renaissance Thought and Letters,* p. 223.

89. Augustinus Steuchus, *De perenni philosophia,* in 10 books, with a preface to Paul III (Lyon, 1540; reprint ed., Basel, 1542). The edition of 1552, cited in the catalogue of the Bibliothèque Nationale, does not exist; I examined the respective copy which has the shelf mark R 1782, and it turned out to be a copy of the 1542 edition, in which the Roman numeral x on the title page had been erased, making the year MDXLII appear as MD LII with a blank space. It is also included in the author's *Opera omnia* (Paris, 1578; Venice, 1591, 1601). In the edition of 1591 the text appears in vol. III, f. 1–207v. Agostino Steuco was born in Gubbio ca. 1497 and died in Venice in 1548. In 1538 he was named Prefect of the Vatican Library and Bishop of Kisamos in Crete by Paul III. See *Enciclopedia Italiana* 32 (Rome, 1936): 726 (by Giuseppe Riciotti); *Enciclopedia Cattolica* 11 (Vatican City, 1953), cols. 1332–33 (by Gioacchino Paparelli); Th. Freudenberger, *Augustinus Steuchus [Reformationsgeschichtliche Studien und Texte,* 64–65] (Münster, 1935); A. S. Ebert, "Agostino Steuco und seine Philosophia perennis," *Philosophisches Jahrbuch* 42 (1929): 342–56, 510–26 and 43 (1930): 92–100. Julien Eymard d'Angers, "Epictète et Sénèque d'après le *De perenni philosophia* d'Augustin Steuco (1496–1549)," *Revue des Sciences Religieuses* 35 (1961): 1–31; Charles B. Schmitt, "Perennial Philosophy: From Agostino Steuco to Leibniz," *Journal of the History of Ideas* 27 (1966): 505–32; *id.,* "Prisca Theologia e Philosophia Perennis: due temi del Rinascimento italiano e la loro fortuna," in *Il pensiero italiano del Rinascimento e il tempo nostro,* ed. Giovannangiola Tarugi (Florence, 1970), pp. 211–36. Giovanni di Napoli, "Il concetto di 'Philosophia Perennis' di Agostino Steuco nel quadro della tematica

rinascimentale," in *Filosofia e cultura in Umbria tra Medioevo e Rinascimento* [*Atti del quarto Convegno di Studi Umbri*] (Gubbio, 1966), pp. 399–489.
90. Matthias Meier, *Descartes und die Renaissance* (Münster, 1914). Léon Blanchet, *Les antécédents historiques du "Je pense, donc je suis"* (Paris, 1920). Joseph Politella, *Platonism, Aristotelianism and Cabalism in the Philosophy of Leibniz* (Philadelphia, 1938). Ernst Cassirer, *Die platonische Renaissance in England und die Schule von Cambridge* (Leipzig, 1932), trans. by James Pettegrove as *The Platonic Renaissance in England* (New York, 1955).

Part Three: Renaissance Thought and Byzantine Learning

7. ITALIAN HUMANISM AND BYZANTIUM

1. For the general bibliography of our subject, I should like to cite the following works: N. H. Baynes, *Byzantine Studies and Other Essays* (London, 1955). *Byzantium*, ed. N. H. Baynes and H. St. L. B. Moss (Oxford, 1949). H. G. Beck, *Kirche und theologische Literatur im byzantinischen Reich* (Munich, 1959). R. R. Bolgar, *The Classical Heritage and Its Beneficiaries* (Cambridge, 1954). Robert Devreesse, *Introduction à l'étude des manuscrits grecs* (Paris, 1954); *id., Les manuscrits de l'Italie méridionale* (Vatican City, 1955). Albert Ehrhard, *Überlieferung und Bestand der hagiographischen und homiletischen Literatur der griechischen Kirche von den Anfängen bis zum Ende des 16. Jahrhunderts*, 2 vols. (Leipzig, 1937–1952). Karl Krumbacher, *Geschichte der byzantinischen Literatur*, 2d ed. (Munich, 1897). Émile Legrand, *Bibliographie hellénique*, 4 vols. (Paris, 1885–1906). Remigio Sabbadini, *Le scoperte dei codici latini e greci ne' secoli XIV e XV*, 2 vols. (Florence, 1905–1914). J. E. Sandys, *A History of Classical Scholarship*, 3d ed., vol. 1 (Cambridge, 1921). Ihor Ševčenko, "The Decline of Byzantium Seen through the Eyes of Its Intellectuals," *Dumbarton Oaks Papers* 15 (1961): 167–86. Basile Tatakis, *La philosophie byzantine* (Paris, 1949). Marie Vogel and Viktor Gardthausen, *Die griechischen Schreiber des Mittelalters und der Renaissance* (Leipzig, 1909). Georg Voigt, *Die Wiederbelebung des classischen Alterthums*, 3d ed., 2 vols. (Berlin, 1893).

2. William H. Stahl, *Roman Science* (Madison, Wis., 1962).

3. Pierre Courcelle, *Les lettres grecques en Occident, De Macrobe à Cassiodore* (Paris, 1943).

4. Charles H. Haskins, *Studies in the History of Mediaeval Science*, 2d ed. (Cambridge, Mass., 1927). J. T. Muckle, "Greek Works Translated Directly into Latin before 1350," *Mediaeval Studies* 4 (1942): 33–42 and 5 (1943): 102–14. George Sarton, *Introduction to the History of Science*, 3 vols. (Baltimore, Md., 1927–1948). A. Siegmund, *Die Überlieferung der griechischen christlichen Literatur in der lateinischen Kirche bis zum zwölften Jahrhundert* (Munich-Pasing, 1949). Moritz

Steinschneider, *Die europäischen Übersetzungen aus dem Arabischen bis Mitte des 17. Jahrhunderts* (Graz, 1957). *Catalogus Translationum et Commentariorum*, ed. P. O. Kristeller and F. Edward Cranz, 3 vols. (Washington, D.C., 1960–76).

5. Robert Devreesse, *Les manuscrits grecs de l'Italie méridionale* (Vatican City, 1955). Marcello Gigante, *Poeti italobizantini del secolo XIII* (Naples, 1953). Barlaam Calabro, *Epistole greche*, ed. Giuseppe Schirò (Palermo, 1954). Kenneth Setton, "The Byzantine Background to the Italian Renaissance," *Proceedings of the American Philosophical Society* 100 (1956): 1–76.

6. Bernhard Bischoff, "Das griechische Element in der abendländischen Bildung des Mittelalters," *Byzantinische Zeitschrift* 44 (1951): 27–55. Louis R. Loomis, *Medieval Hellenism* (Lancaster, Pa., 1906). Roberto Weiss, "The Translators from the Greek of the Angevin Court of Naples," *Rinascimento* 1 (1950): 195–226; *id.*, "The Study of Greek in England during the Fourteenth Century," *Rinascimento* 2 (1951): 209–39; *id.*, "The Greek Culture of South Italy in the Later Middle Ages," *Proceedings of the British Academy* 37 (1951): 23–50; *id.*, "England and the Decree of the Council of Vienne on the Teaching of Greek, Arabic, Hebrew and Syriac," *Bibliothèque d'Humanisme et Renaissance* 14 (1952): 1–9; *id.*, "Lo studio del greco all'abbazia di San Dionigi durante il medio evo," *Rivista di storia della chiesa in Italia* 6 (1952): 426–38; *id.*, "Lo studio del greco all'Università di Parigi," *Convivium*, n.s. 2 (1955): 146–49.

7. *Corpus Platonicum Medii Aevi, Plato Latinus*, ed. Raymond Klibansky, 4 vols. (London, 1940–1962). See my reviews in the *Journal of Philosophy* 37 (1940): 695–97, 53 (1956): 196–201, and 62 (1965): 14–17.

8. The main exceptions are Plato, Proclus, and Sextus Empiricus for the Greek philosophers not connected with the Aristotelian tradition, and Demetrius (*de elocutione*) and Isocrates (*ad Demonicum*) for the rhetorical authors. Cf. Muckle, "Greek Works Translated into Latin." Sabbadini, *Le scoperte*, 2:264 (for Isocrates). None of these authors was completely translated during the Middle Ages. See essay 13, notes 52 and 53.

9. Moritz Steinschneider, *Die arabischen Übersetzungen aus dem Griechischen* (Graz, 1960). Richard Walzer, *Greek into Arabic* (Oxford, 1962). 'Abd al-Raḥmān Badawī, *La transmission de la philosophie grecque au monde arabe* (Paris, 1968).

10. For translations of Planudes, see Krumbacher, *Geschichte der byzantinischen Literatur*, pp. 544–46. For the Greek translations of St. Augustine, see Michael Rackl, "Die griechischen Augustinusübersetzungen," in *Miscellanea Francesco Ehrle*, 1 [Biblioteca Vaticana, *Studi e Testi* 37] (Rome, 1924): 1–38.

11. E. H. Wilkins, *Life of Petrarch* (Chicago, 1961), pp. 33–34, 136. Giovanni Gentile, "Le traduzioni medievali di Platone e Francesco Petrarca," *Studi sul Rinascimento* (Florence, 1936), pp. 23–88. Petrarch's manuscript of the medieval Latin version of Plato's *Phaedo* has been identified as Paris. lat. 6567 A by Lorenzo Minio-Paluello (*Plato Latinus*, vol. 2 [London, 1950], p. xii). Petrarch's Greek manuscript of Homer has been identified as Ambr. J 98 inf. by Agostino Pertusi (*Leonzio Pilato fra Petrarca e Boccaccio* [Venice and Rome, 1964], pp. 62–72), Petrarch's Greek Plato more tentatively as Paris. gr. 1807 by Élisabeth Pellegrin (*La Bibliothèque des Visconti et des Sforza, Ducs de Milan, au XVe siècle* [Paris, 1955], p. 310. Cf. Pertusi, *Leonzio Pilato fra Petrarca e Boccaccio*, p. 18).

12. Pertusi, *Leonzio Pilato fra Petrarca e Boccaccio*. The fact that Pilato did not merely tutor Boccaccio but also was appointed by the city authorities of Florence "ad docendam grammaticam grecam et licteras grecas" and received a salary from 1360 to 1362 has been recently documented by Gene A. Brucker ("Florence and Its University, 1348–1434," in *Action and Conviction in Early Modern Europe, Essays in Memory of E. H. Harbison*, ed. Theodore K. Rabb and Jerrold E. Seigel [Princeton, N.J., 1969], pp. 220–36, at 231–33).

13. Giuseppe Cammelli, *I dotti bizantini e le origini dell'umanesimo*, 3 vols. (Florence, 1941–1954).

14. For the later period, see Deno J. Geanakoplos, *Greek Scholars in Venice* (Cambridge, Mass., 1960).

15. Sabbadini, *Le scoperte*, 1:43–71. E. W. Bodnar, *Cyriacus of Ancona and Athens* (Bruxelles, 1960).

16. This idea was first suggested to me by James Hutton.

17. Some Greek letters of Lianoro to Tortelli are found in the well-known ms. Vat. lat. 3908.

18. Deno J. Geanakoplos, "The Discourse of Demetrius Chalcondyles on the Inauguration of Greek Studies at the University of Padua in 1463," *Studies in the Renaissance* 21 (1974): 118–44.

19. Karl Müllner, *Reden und Briefe italienischer Humanisten* (Vienna, 1899), pp. 3–56.

20. Berlin, ms. lat. oct. 374. See Herbert Meyer, "Ein Kollegheft des Humanisten Cono," *Zentralblatt für Bibliothekswesen* 53 (1936): 281–84. Alexandre Oleroff, "L'Humaniste dominicain Jean Conon et le Crétois Jean Grégoropoulos," *Scriptorium* 4 (1950): 104–7. For another manuscript of Cono, see Sister Agnes Clare Way, "Gregorius Nazianzenus," in *Catalogus Translationum et Commentariorum*, vol. 2, ed. P. O. Kristeller and F. Edward Cranz (Washington, D.C., 1971), pp. 43–192, at 113, 142–43.

21. P. O. Kristeller, *Studies in Renaissance Thought and Letters* (Rome, 1956), pp. 337–53.

22. K. K. Mueller, "Neue Mittheilungen über Janos Laskaris und die Mediceische Bibliothek," *Centralblatt für Bibliothekswesen* 1 (1884): 332–412. Börje Knös, *Un ambassadeur de l'hellénisme, Janus Lascaris, et la tradition gréco-byzantine dans l'humanisme français* (Uppsala and Paris, 1945).

23. Emil Jacobs, "Francesco Patricio und seine Sammlung griechischer Handschriften in der Bibliothek des Escorial," *Zentralblatt für Bibliothekswesen* 25 (1908): 19–47; J.-Th. Papademetriou, "The Sources and the Character of *Del Governo de'Regni*," *Transactions and Proceedings of the American Philological Association* 92 (1961): 422–39, at 434–37.

24. For Poliziano, see *Mostra del Poliziano* [Florence, Istituto Nationale di studi sul Rinascimento], *Catalogo*, ed. Alessandro Perosa (Florence, 1955). For Ficino, see Martin Sicherl, "Neuentdeckte Handschriften von Marsilio Ficino und Johannes Reuchlin," *Scriptorium* 16 (1962): 50–61. P. O. Kristeller, "Some Original Letters and Autograph Manuscripts of Marsilio Ficino," in *Studi di Bibliografia e di Storia in Onore di Tammaro De Marinis*, vol. 3 (Verona and Vatican City, 1964), pp. 5–33. For Ermolao Barbaro, see note 21. For Leonardo Bruni, see Cosimo Stor-

naiolo, *Codices Urbinates Graeci Bibliothecae Vaticanae* (Rome, 1895), p. 38 (cod. 32), p. 39 (cod. 33), p. 48 (cod. 42), and pp. 149–50 (cod. 97). Sotheby & Co., *Catalogue of Nineteen Highly Distinguished Medieval and Renaissance Manuscripts . . . The Property of Sir Sydney Cockerell . . .* (London, April 3, 1957), p. 15, no. 10, where the opinion of Miss Barbour is cited. The manuscript was reportedly acquired by Martin Bodmer (Genève-Cologny), but an enquiry which I addressed to Mr. Bodmer obtained only an evasive reply.

25. *La stampa greca a Venezia nei secoli XV e XVI, Catalogo di Mostra* [Venice, Centro arti e mestieri, Fondazione Giorgio Cini], ed. Marcello Finazzi (Venice, 1968).

26. For the case of Alexander of Aphrodisias and a few other authors, see *Catalogus Translationum et Commentariorum*, 3 vols., ed. P. O. Kristeller and F. Edward Cranz (Washington, D.C., 1960–76), especially the articles by Cranz (1:77–135 and 2:411–422). For the translations of Aristotle, see *Aristoteles Latinus*, ed. George Lacombe et al., 3 vols. (Rome, 1939; Cambridge, 1955; Bruges and Paris, 1961). Eugenio Garin, "Le traduzioni umanistiche di Aristotele nel secolo XV," *Atti e Memorie dell'Accademia Fiorentina di Scienze Morali "La Colombaria,"* 16 [n.s. 2] (1947–1950, published 1951): 55–104. For the translations of Plato, see *Plato Latinus*, ed. Klibansky. Raymond Klibansky, *The Continuity of the Platonic Tradition during the Middle Ages* (London, 1939 and 1950). Eugenio Garin, "Richerche sulle traduzioni di Platone nella prima metà del secolo XV," in *Medioevo e Rinascimento, Studi in onore di Bruno Nardi,* vol. 1 (Florence, 1955), pp. 339–74.

27. For the *Plato Latinus*, see note 7. Proclus, *Tria Opuscula*, ed. Helmut Boese (Berlin, 1960). See my review in the *Journal of Philosophy* 59 (1962): 74–78.

28. For an important example, see Josef Soudek, "The Genesis and Tradition of Leonardo Bruni's Annotated Latin Version of the (Pseudo-) Aristotelian 'Economics,' " *Scriptorium* 12 (1958): 260–68; *id.,* "Leonardo Bruni and His Public: A Statistical and Interpretative Study of His Annotated Latin Version of the (Pseudo-) Aristotelian Economics," *Studies in Medieval and Renaissance History* 5 (1968): 49–136.

29. A vast bibliography of Greek and Latin editions of Aristotle published in the fifteenth and sixteenth centuries is being prepared by F. Edward Cranz. See now his *A Bibliography of Aristotle Editions 1501–1600* (Baden-Baden, 1971).

30. Kristeller, *Studies in Renaissance Thought and Letters,* pp. 340–42. Paul Lawrence Rose and Stillman Drake, "The Pseudo-Aristotelian *Questions in Mechanics* in Renaissance Culture," *Studies in the Renaissance* 18 (1971): 65–104.

31. For Galen, see R. J. Durling, "A Chronological Census of Renaissance Editions and Translations of Galen," *Journal of the Warburg and Courtauld Institutes* 24 (1961): 230–305. For the *Geography* of Ptolemy, see Dana B. Durand, "Tradition and Innovation in Fifteenth-Century Italy, 'Il primato dell'Italia' in the Field of Science," *Journal of the History of Ideas* 4 (1943): 1–20, at p. 4. For Hippocrates, see Pearl Kibre, "Hippocrates Latinus," *Traditio* 31–33 (1975–77), to be continued.

8. BYZANTINE AND WESTERN PLATONISM IN THE FIFTEENTH CENTURY

1. Milton V. Anastos, "Pletho's Calendar and Liturgy," *Dumbarton Oaks Papers* 4 (1948): 183–305. François Masai, *Pléthon et le Platonisme de Mistra* (Paris, 1956). Ludwig Mohler, *Kardinal Bessarion als Theologe, Humanist und Staatsmann*, 3 vols. (Paderborn, 1923–1942). P. O. Kristeller, *Il pensiero filosofico di Marsilio Ficino* (Florence, 1953). Eugenio Garin, *Giovanni Pico della Mirandola* (Florence, 1937); *L'opera e il pensiero di Giovanni Pico della Mirandola nella storia dell'Umanesimo*, 2 vols. [Mirandola, Convegno internazionale, September 15–18, 1963] (Florence, Istituto nazionale di studi sul Rinascimento, 1965). Bohdan Kieszkowski, *Studi sul Platonismo del Rinascimento in Italia* (Florence, 1936).

2. Basile Tatakis, *La philosophie byzantine* (Paris, 1949), pp. 281–314. Cf. M. Boivin le Cadet, "Querelle des philosophes du quinzième siècle," *Mémoires de Littérature tirés des registres de l'Académie Royale des Inscriptions et Belles-Lettres* 2 (1736): 715–29. Cf. *ibid.*, 3 (1772): 281–87, where a letter relating to the controversy by Bessarion is published. None of these accounts is adequate or complete.

3. Dante, *Inferno*, IV, 131.

4. Petrarch, *Trionfo della Fama*, III, 4–6. Cf. P. O. Kristeller, *Eight Philosophers of the Italian Renaissance* (Stanford, 1964), p. 169.

5. Raymond Klibansky, *The Continuity of the Platonic Tradition During the Middle Ages* (London, 1939).

6. Bruno Nardi, *Saggi sull'aristotelismo padovano dal secolo XIV al XVI* (Florence, 1958). J. H. Randall, Jr., *The School of Padua and the Emergence of Modern Science* (Padua, 1961). P. O. Kristeller, *La tradizione aristotelica nel Rinascimento* (Padua, 1962); *id.*, "Renaissance Aristotelianism," *Greek, Roman and Byzantine Studies* 6 (1965): 157–74; and essay 2. Charles B. Schmitt, *A Critical Survey and Bibliography of Studies on Renaissance Aristotelianism* (Padua, 1971).

7. Charles B. Schmitt, "Perennial Philosophy," *Journal of the History of Ideas* 27 (1966): 505–32. Cf. essay 6.

8. The most Platonist passages are found in the *Somnium Scipionis*, in the *Tusculan Disputations*, and in the *Orator*. The translation of the *Timaeus* covers 27d–37c, 38c–43b, 46b–47b of the text.

9. Apuleius, *De deo Socratis; De Platone et eius dogmate*. Cf. Willy Theiler, *Die Vorbereitung des Neuplatonismus* (Berlin, 1930).

10. *Hermès Trismégiste*, ed. A. D. Nock and A.-J. Festugière, vol. 2 (Paris, 1945), pp. 296–355.

11. (Platonis) *Timaeus a Calcidio translatus commentarioque instructus* [*Corpus Platonicum Medii Aevi, Plato Latinus*, ed. Raymond Klibansky, vol. 4], ed. J. H. Waszink (London and Leyden, 1962). The translation extends to p. 53c of the text.

12. For Victorinus, see his *Traités théologiques sur la Trinité*, 2 vols., ed. Paul Henry and Pierre Hadot (Paris, 1960).

13. Cf. P. O. Kristeller, *Studies in Renaissance Thought and Letters* (Rome, 1956), pp. 355–72.

14. *Corpus Philosophorum Medii Aevi, Aristoteles Latinus, Codices,* 3 vols., ed. George Lacombe et al. (Rome, 1939; Cambridge, 1955; Bruges and Paris, 1961).

15. Moritz Steinschneider, *Die europäischen Übersetzungen aus dem Arabischen* (Graz, 1956). J. T. Muckle, "Greek Works Translated Directly into Latin before 1350," *Mediaeval Studies* 4 (1942): 33–42 and 5 (1943): 102–14.

16. *Corpus Platonicum Medii Aevi, Plato Latinus,* ed. Raymond Klibansky, 4 vols. (London, 1940–62): vol. 1: *Meno interprete Henrico Aristippo,* ed. Victor Kordeuter and Carlotta Labowsky (1940); vol. 2: *Phaedo interprete Henrico Aristippo,* ed. Lorenzo Minio-Paluello (1950); vol. 3: *Parmenides usque ad finem primae hypothesis necnon Procli Commentarium in Parmenidem, Pars ultima adhuc inedita interprete Guillelmo de Moerbeka,* ed. Raymond Klibansky and Carlotta Labowsky (1953); vol. 4: *Timaeus, a Calcidio translatus commentarioque instructus,* ed. J. H. Waszink (1962). Proclus, *Tria Opuscula,* ed. Helmut Boese (Berlin, 1960). Proclus, *The Elements of Theology,* ed. E. R. Dodds, 2d ed. (Oxford, 1963). Proclus, *Elementatio Theologica, translata a Guilelmo de Moerbeke,* ed. C. Vansteenkiste, *Tijdschrift voor Philosophie* 13 (1951): 263–301, 492–531. Martin Grabmann, *Guglielmo di Moerbeke O. P.* (Rome, 1946).

17. Cornelio Fabro, *Participation et causalité selon S. Thomas d'Aquin* (Louvain, 1961); *id., La nozione metafisica di partecipazione secondo S. Tommaso d'Aquino,* 3d ed. (Turin, 1963). P. O. Kristeller, *Le thomisme et la pensée italienne de la Renaissance* (Montreal, 1967); *id., Medieval Aspects of Renaissance Learning* (Durham, N.C., 1974). A commentary on Proclus' *Elements of Theology* by the Dominican Berthold of Moosburg is now being published by Loris Sturlese.

18. See note 4.

19. *Renaissance Philosophy of Man,* ed. Ernst Cassirer, P. O. Kristeller, and J. H. Randall, Jr. (Chicago, 1948), pp. 47–133 (English translation by Hans Nachod). Cf. P. O. Kristeller, "Petrarch's 'Averroists,' " *Bibliothèque d'Humanisme et Renaissance* 14 (1952): 59–65; *id.,* "Il Petrarca, l'Umanesimo e la Scolastica a Venezia," in *La Civiltà Veneziana del Trecento* (Florence, 1956), pp. 147–78.

20. Eugenio Garin, "Ricerche sulle traduzioni di Platone nella prima metà del sec. XV," in *Medioevo e Rinascimento, Studi in onore di Bruno Nardi,* vol. 1 (Florence, 1955), pp. 339–74. P. O. Kristeller, "Marsilio Ficino as a Beginning Student of Plato," *Scriptorium* 20 (1966–1967): 41–54.

21. Agostino Pertusi, *Leonzio Pilato fra Petrarca e Boccaccio* (Venice and Rome, 1964), p. 18.

22. We now know that Leontius Pilatus was appointed as lecturer of Greek at the University of Florence 1360–1362; see Gene A. Brucker, "Florence and Its University, 1384–1434," in *Action and Conviction in Early Modern Europe, Essays in Memory of E. H. Harbison,* ed. Theodore K. Rabb and Jerrold E. Seigel (Princeton, N.J., 1969), pp. 220–36, at 231–32. For Leontius, see Pertusi, *Leonzio Pilato.*

23. See note 20.

24. Marsilius Ficinus, *Opera omnia,* vol. 2 (Basel, 1576; reprint ed., Turin, 1959), p. 1537.

25. The decree was not enforced, according to Alan Cameron, "The Last Days of the Academy at Athens," *Proceedings of the Cambridge Philological Society* 195

(1969): 7–29. I am indebted for this reference and for other information to Leonardo Tarán.

26. Henri Alline, *Histoire du texte de Platon* (Paris, 1915), esp. pp. 174–280. *Plato manuscripts: A Catalogue of Microfilms in the Plato Microfilm Project, Yale University Library*, ed. Robert S. Brumbaugh and Rulon Wells, 2 parts (New Haven, Conn., 1962). Tatakis, *La philosophie byzantine*, pp. 133–34. Pertusi, *Leonzio Pilato*, pp. 500–2. Karl Krumbacher, *Geschichte der byzantinischen Literature*, 2d ed. (Munich, 1897), p. 524. *Greek Manuscripts in the Bodleian Library* (Oxford, 1966), p. 14–15, no. 5. Martin Sicherl, "Platonismus und Textüberlieferung," *Jahrbuch der österreichischen byzantinischen Gesellschaft* 15 (1966), pp. 201–29.

27. Tatakis, *La philosophie byzantine*, pp. 161–210.

28. *Hermès Trismégiste*, ed. Nock and Festugière, vol. 1, pp. xlix–li (where Psellos' editorship is discussed but doubted).

29. *Oracula magica Zoroastris cum scholiis Plethonis et Pselli*, ed. Johannes Opsopoeus (Paris, 1599, first printed in 1589). For Ficino's translation, see his *Opera*, vol. 2, pp. 1939–45.

30. Chumnos' *Antitheticum adversus Plotinum* was published in Friedrich Creuzer's edition of Plotinus, vol. 2 (Oxford, 1835), pp. 1413–30, and in Migne, *Patrologia Graeca*, vol. 140, cols. 1404–37. Cf. Jean Verpeaux, *Nicéphore Choumnos* (Paris, 1959), pp. 17–23, 141–46. Ševčenko, *Etudes sur la polémique entre Théodore Métochite et Nicéphore Choumnos* (Brussels, 1962). In late manuscripts, the text usually appears under the name Kanikles or Charicles. Cf. Valentino Capocci, *Codices Barberiniani Graeci*, vol. 1 (Vatican City, 1958), p. 104, cod. 84.

31. Martin Sicherl, "Neuentdeckte Handschriften von Marsilio Ficino und Johannes Reuchlin," *Scriptorium* 16 (1962): 50–61, at 52 and 61. Cf. Nicolaus Methonensis, *Refutatio institutionis theologicae Procli Platonici*, ed. J. Th. Voemel [Procli Diadochi et Olympiodori in Platonis Alcibiadem Commentarii, vol. 4] (Frankfurt, 1825).

32. *Procli Diadochi Tria Opuscula*, ed. Helmut Boese (Berlin, 1960). Isaak Sebastokrator, *Zehn Aporien über die Vorsehung*, ed. Johannes Dornseiff [Beiträge zur klassischen Philologie 19] (Meisenheim, 1966). Isaak Sebastokrator, *De malorum subsistentia*, ed. James John Rizzo [Beiträge zur klassischen Philologie 42] (Meisenheim, 1971).

33. André Wartelle, *Inventaire des manuscrits grecs d'Aristote et de ses commentateurs* (Paris, 1963). A more detailed list is being prepared by Paul Moraux of the Free University, West Berlin. Dieter Harlfinger, *Die Textgeschichte der pseudo-aristotelischen Schrift, περὶ ἀτόμων γραμμῶν* (Amsterdam, 1971). Klaus Oehler, *Antike Philosophie und byzantinisches Mittelalter* (Munich, 1969), pp. 272–86. Paul Moraux et al., *Aristoteles Graecus*, vol. 1 (Berlin, 1976).

34. The *Commentaria in Aristotelem Graeca* include the commentaries by Michael of Ephesus on the *Nicomachean Ethics* (vol. 20) and on the *Parva Naturalia* (vol. 22), those of Eustratius on the *Nicomachean Ethics* (vol. 20) and on the *Analytica Posteriora* (vol. 21). Also Stephanus' commentary on the *Rhetoric* (vol. 21, pt. 2) and Sophonias' paraphrase of the *De anima* (vol. 23) are Byzantine. For further commentaries, see Wartelle, *Inventaire des Manuscrits*.

35. For the medieval translation of Eustratius' and Michael of Ephesus' commentaries on the *Nicomachean Ethics*, see *Aristoteles Latinus, Codices*, vol. 1 (Rome, 1939), p. 97.

36. Tatakis, *La philosophie byzantine*. Krumbacher, *Geschichte der byzantinischen Literatur*.

37. For the translations of Ovid, Cicero, Boethius, Augustine, and other Latin authors by Maximus Planudes, see Krumbacher, *Geschichte der byzantinischen Literatur*, p. 545. Cf. Michael Rackl, "Die griechischen Augustinübersetzungen," *Miscellanea Francesco Ehrle*, vol. 1 [Biblioteca Vaticana, *Studi e Testi* 37] (Rome, 1924), pp. 1–38. For Greek translations of Aquinas, see note 44.

38. See note 1.

39. Pléthon, *Traité des Lois*, ed. Charles Alexandre and Augustin Pellissier (Paris, 1858; reprint ed., Amsterdam, 1966).

40. On Plethon and the attribution of the oracles to Zoroaster, see Joseph Bidez and Franz Cumont, *Les mages hellénisés*, 2 vols. (Paris, 1938). For Plethon's commentary, see note 29.

41. For Plethon's copy of the Orphic hymns, see R. and F. Masai, "L'oeuvre de Georges Gémiste Pléthon," *Académie Royale des sciences, des lettres, et des beaux-arts de Belgique, Bulletin de la Classe des Lettres, et des Sciences morales et politiques*, 5th ser., 40 (1954): 536–55, at 546. For the complete text of Plethon's treatise on the differences between Plato and Aristotle, see Migne, *Patrologia Graeca*, vol. 160, cols. 881–932. At the beginning, there is a characteristic attack on Averroes.

42. The *De fato* is a chapter (bk. II, ch. 6) from Plethon's *Laws*. It is printed in *Traité des Lois*, ed. Alexandre and Pellissier, pp. 64–78.

43. Georges Scholarios, *Oeuvres complètes*, ed. Louis Petit, X. A. Siderides, and Martin Jugie, vol. 4 (Paris, 1935), pp. 1–116.

44. Scholarios composed epitomes of Thomas' *Summa contra Gentiles* and of his *Summa Theologiae*, parts I and Ia-IIae (*Oeuvres*, vols. 5–6, [1931–1933]). He also translated Thomas' commentary on Aristotle's *Physics*, books I-II, and his treatise *De fallaciis*, as well as Petrus Hispanus and Gilbertus Porretanus (*Oeuvres*, vol. 8 [1936]).

45. *Oeuvres*, vol. 4, p. 4.

46. Migne, *Patrologia Graeca*, vol. 160, cols. 979–1020, at 981.

47. Cf. Mohler, *Kardinal Bessarion*, and Masai, *Pléthon et le Platonisme de Mistra*. For Gaza, see Alfred Gercke, *Theodoros Gazes* (Greifswald, 1903). Theodore Gaza's *De fato*, ed. John Wilson Taylor, University of Toronto Studies, Philological Series, vol. 7 (Toronto, 1925). For Michael Apostolis, see Deno J. Geanakoplos, *Greek Scholars in Venice* (Cambridge, Mass., 1962), pp. 73–110. For Andronicus Callistus, see Giuseppe Cammelli, "Antronico Callisto," *La Rinascita* 5 (1942): 104–21, 174–214.

48. Venice, 1523; reprint ed., Frankfurt, 1965.

49. Remigio Sabbadini, "Briciole umanistiche V," *Giornale storico della letteratura italiana* 18 (1891): 230–41. "Briciole umanistiche XXII," *ibid.* 43 (1904): 253–54. Giorgio Castellani, "Giorgio da Trebisonda maestro di eloquenza a Vicenza e a Venezia," *Nuovo Archivio Veneto* 11 (1896): 123–42. See also, John Monfasani,

George of Trebizond: A Biography and A Study of His Rhetoric and Logic (Leiden, 1976).

50. For the translations of Plato, see Raymond Klibansky, "Plato's Parmenides in the Middle Ages and the Renaissance," *Medieval and Renaissance Studies* 1 (1941–1943): 281–330, at 289–304. Garin, "Ricerche sulle traduzioni di Platone," pp. 372–73. For the translations of Aristotle, see Eugenio Garin, "Le traduzioni umanistiche di Aristotele nel secolo XV," *Atti e Memorie dell' Accademia Fiorentina di Scienze Morali "La Colombaria"* 16 [n.s. 2] (1947–50, published 1951): 55–104.

51. *Gesamtkatalog der Wiegendrucke* 4183. For the Greek and Latin text, see Mohler, *Kardinal Bessarion*, vol. 2.

52. It was printed by Sweynheym and Pannartz, the two Germans who introduced printing into Italy.

53. Bessarion's correspondence with Ficino, Argyropulus, Fichet, Perotti, Omnibonus Leonicenus, Filelfo, Panormita, and others is published in Mohler, *Kardinal Bessarion*, vol. 3.

54. Beriah Botfield, *Prefaces to the First Editions of the Greek and Roman Classics* (London, 1861), pp. 68–78.

55. Mohler, *Kardinal Bessarion*, 3: 343–75.

56. The beginning and end of Andreas Trapezuntius' treatise was published by F. A. Zaccaria, *Iter Litterarium per Italiam* (Venice, 1762), pp. 127–34. I hope to study and publish these treatises in collaboration with John Monfasani and Frederick Purnell.

57. Paris, *Bibliothèque Nationale*, ms. lat. 6284.

58. *Discussiones Peripateticae* (Venice, 1571; enlarged ed. Basel, 1581).

59. Edmond Vansteenberghe, *Le cardinal Nicholas de Cues* (Paris, 1920; reprint ed., Frankfurt, 1963).

60. *Ibid.*, pp. 29–30. For his return from Constantinople, see Cusanus, *De docta ignorantia*, ed. Raymond Klibansky (Leipzig, 1932), p. 163. (I was reminded of this passage by Morimichi Watanabe.)

61. Klibansky, "Plato's Parmenides in The Middle Ages and the Renaissance." For the translation of Proclus' *Platonic Theology*, see Raymond Klibansky, *Proceedings of the British Academy* (1949), p. 11. H. D. Saffrey, "Sur la tradition manuscrite de la Théologie Platonicienne de Proclus," in *Autour d'Aristote, Recueil d'Etudes . . . offert à Monseigneur A. Mansion* (Louvain, 1955), pp. 387–430. P. O. Kristeller, *Iter Italicum*, 2 vols. (London and Leyden, 1963–67), 1:8.

62. P. O. Kristeller, "A Latin Translation of Gemistos Plethon's *De fato* by Johannes Sophianos dedicated to Nicholas of Cusa," in *Nicolò Cusano agli Inizi del Mondo Moderno* (Florence, 1970), pp. 175–93.

63. See Kristeller, *Il pensiero filosofico de Marsilio Ficino*, ch. 2.

64. Ficinus, *Opera Omnia*, vol. 2, p. 1537.

65. Kristeller, *Il pensiero filosofico di Marsilio Ficino*, p. 460. For the remark on Averroes, see *Opera*, p. 327.

66. *Supplementum Ficinianum*, ed. P. O. Kristeller, vol. 2 (Florence, 1937; reprint ed., 1973), p. 104.

67. Eugenio Garin, "Per la storia della cultura filosofica del Rinascimento,"

Rivista critica di storia della filosofia 12 (1957): 3–21; *id.*, "Platonici bizantini e platonici italiani," *Studi sul platonismo medievale* (Florence, 1958), pp. 153–219. A. Keller, "Two Byzantine Scholars and Their Reception in Italy," *Journal of the Warburg and Courtauld Institutes* 20 (1957): 363–70. Cf. Kristeller, *Iter Italicum*, 1:184.

68. Vat. Ottob. lat. 2966.

69. Kristeller, *Studies in Renaissance Thought and Letters*, pp. 164–65.

70. *Opera Omnia*, vol. 2, pp. 1939–45.

71. *Ibid.*, p. 899.

72. See notes 1 and 2. Francesco da Diacceto, Ficino's pupil and successor, wrote and probably lectured on both Plato and Aristotle. See Kristeller, *Studies in Renaissance Thought and Letters*, pp. 287–336. For Patrizi, see *Discussiones Peripateticae* (Venice, 1571; enlarged edition, Basel, 1581). In the sixteenth century a comparison between Plato and Aristotle was attempted, among others, by the following scholars: Bernardinus Donatus (*De Platonicae atque Aristotelicae philosophiae differentia*, printed with, and apparently based on, Plethon's treatise [Venice, 1540]. Sebastian Fox Morcillo (*De naturae philosophia seu de Platonis et Aristotelis consensione* [Louvain, 1554]. Jac. Carpentarius (*Platonis cum Aristotele in universa philosophia comparatio* [Paris 1573]. Gabriel Buratellus (*Praecipuarum controversiarum Aristotelis et Platonis conciliatio* [Venice, 1573]). Jacopo Mazzoni (*De triplici hominum vita . . . methodi tres . . . in quibus omnes Platonis et Aristotelis . . . discordiae componuntur* [Cesena, 1576]; *id.*, *In universam Platonis et Aristotelis philosophiam praeludia, sive de comparatione Platonis et Aristotelis* [Venice, 1597]). Frederick Purnell, "Jacopo Mazzoni and his comparison of Plato and Aristotle" (Ph.D. diss., Columbia University, 1971). A Latin translation of Plethon's treatise by Nicolaus Scutellius (s. XVI) is found in Vienna, Nationalbibliothek, ms. 10056, f. 155–221v.

Part Four: Renaissance Concepts of Man

INTRODUCTION

1. Étienne Gilson, *Les idées et les lettres*, 2d ed. (Paris, 1955), p. 192.

2. Eugenio Garin, "La 'dignitas hominis' e la letteratura patristica," *La Rinascita* 1 (1938): 102–46.

3. Eugenio Garin, *Ritratti di umanisti* (Florence, 1967), p. 187. On the subject as a whole, see Giovanni Gentile, "Il concetto dell'uomo nel Rinascimento," *Il pensiero italiano del Rinascimento*, 3d ed. (Florence, 1940), pp. 47–113. Eugenio Garin, *Der italienische Humanismus* (Bern, 1947). Charles E. Trinkaus, *Adversity's Noblemen: The Italian Humanists on Happiness* (New York, 1940); *id.*, *In Our Image and Likeness*, 2 vols. (Chicago, 1970). Giuseppe Saitta, *Il pensiero italiano nell'umanesimo e nel rinascimento*, vol. 1 (Bologna, 1949).

9. THE DIGNITY OF MAN

1. For many of the texts discussed in this paper, see the English translations and notes in *The Renaissance Philosophy of Man*, ed. Ernst Cassirer, P. O. Kristeller, and J. H. Randall, Jr. (Chicago, 1948). See also P. O. Kristeller, *Eight Philosophers of the Italian Renaissance* (Stanford, Calif., 1964).

2. *Apologie de Raimond Sebond* (Essais II, 12), in *Essais*, ed. Jean Plattard, vol. 2, pt. 1 (Paris, 1947), p. 168ff. and *passim*. Cf. Donald M. Frame, *Montaigne's Discovery of Man* (New York, 1955), pp. 62–73, 104–5.

3. "[M]agnum miraculum est homo . . .": *Asclepius* 6, in *Corpus Hermeticum*, ed. A. D. Nock and A.-J. Festugière, vol. 2 (Paris, 1945), pp. 301–2. Cf. G. Pico della Mirandola, *De hominis dignitate*, . . . ed. Eugenio Garin (Florence, 1942), p. 102.

4. Cf. *Academica posteriora* I, 4, 15: "a rebus occultis . . . ad vitam communem."

5. *Timaeus*, 34 b ff.

6. Lotharii Cardinalis (Innocentii III) *De miseria humane conditionis*, ed. Michele Maccarrone (Lugano, 1955). Cf. *Two Views of Man*, ed. and trans. Bernard Murchland (New York, 1966), pp. 1–60.

7. In his preface, Innocent III states that he may in a future work describe the dignity of human nature (*De miseria*, ed. Maccarrone, p. 3). Bartholomaeus Facius states at the beginning of his treatise that he is writing about the excellence of man since Pope Innocent had not carried out his promise to write about the subject: Bartholomaei Faccii *de excellentia ac prestantia hominis . . . liber*, in Felinus Sandeus, *De rebus Siciliae epitome*, ed. Marquardus Freherus (Hanau, 1611), pp. 149–68, at 149. Giannozzo Manetti, after having discussed man's excellence according to his body, his soul, and his whole nature, cites and refutes Innocent III among the authors opposed to his own thesis: Janocius de Manectis, *De dignitate et excellentia hominis libri IV* (Basel, 1532), pp. 169, 183–85, 209ff; *idem*, ed. Elisabeth R. Leonard (Padua, 1975), pp. 102, 111–12, 117ff., and *passim*. Cf. Giovanni Gentile, *Il pensiero italiano del Rinascimento*, 3d ed. (Florence, 1940), pp. 90–113.

8. Pétrarque, *Le traité de sui ipsius et multorum ignorantia*, ed. L. M. Capelli (Paris, 1906), pp. 24–25. Cf. the translation and notes by Hans Nachod, in *Renaissance Philosophy of Man*, ed. Cassirer, Kristeller, and Randall, pp. 58–59.

9. Francesco Petrarca, *Le familiari*, vol. 1, ed. Vittorio Rossi (Florence, 1933), p. 159; *Renaissance Philosophy of Man*, ed. Cassirer, Kristeller, and Randall, p. 44. Cf. Augustine, *Confessions* X, 8.15, and Seneca, *Epistles* 8.5.

10. See essay 5.

11. See note 7. Cf. Gentile, *Il pensiero italiano*, p. 92. P. O. Kristeller, "The Humanist Bartolomeo Facio and His Unknown Correspondence," in *From the Renaissance to the Counterreformation, Essays in Honor of Garrett Mattingly*, ed. Charles H. Carter (New York, 1965), pp. 56–74, at 68, 73–74.

12. P. O. Kristeller, "The Humanist Bartolomeo Facio," pp. 68, 74. Charles Trinkaus, *In Our Image and Likeness*, 2 vols. (Chicago, 1970), 1: 210–13, 408–9.

13. P. O. Kristeller, *Medieval Aspects of Renaissance Learning*, ed. and trans. Edward P. Mahoney (Durham, N.C., 1974), pp. 95–158.

14. See H. W. Wittschier, *Giannozzo Manetti* (Cologne and Graz, 1968). Cf. note 7.

15. P. O. Kristeller, "Florentine Platonism and Its Relations with Humanism and Scholasticism," *Church History* 8 (1939): 201–11; *id.*, "Giovanni Pico della Mirandola and His Sources," in *L'Opera e il pensiero di Giovanni Pico della Mirandola nella storia dell'umanesimo: Convegno internazionale*, vol. 1: *Relazioni* (Florence, 1965), pp. 35–133, at 56–57.

16. *Theologia Platonica* XIII, 3, *Opera* (Basel, 1576), vol. 1, pp. 295–98; *Théologie Platonicienne*, vol. 2, ed. R. Marcel (Paris, 1964), pp. 223–29. Cf. P. O. Kristeller, *The Philosophy of Marsilio Ficino* (New York, 1943), p. 119.

17. Kristeller, *Philosophy of Marsilio Ficino*, pp. 106–8.

18. *Theologia Platonica* XIV, 2–5, *Opera* (Basel, 1576), pp. 307–14. *Théologie Platonicienne*, ed. Marcel, vol. 2, pp. 250–66.

19. *Theologia Platonica* XIV, 3. *Théologie Platonicienne*, ed. Marcel, vol. 2, p. 256.

20. Kristeller, *Philosophy of Marsilio Ficino*, p. 120.

21. *Theologia Platonica* XIII, 3. For a comparison with Francis Bacon's notion of the dominion of man over nature, see P. O. Kristeller, "Ficino and Pomponazzi on the Place of Man in the Universe," *Studies in Renaissance Thought and Letters* (Rome, 1956), pp. 279–86, at 285.

22. Kristeller, *Studies in Renaissance Thought and Letters*, pp. 279–86. Gentile, *Il pensiero italiano*, pp. 80–81.

23. Pico, *De hominis dignitate*, ed. Eugenio Garin (Florence, 1942), p. 18.

24. Eugenio Garin, *La cultura filosofica del Rinascimento italiano* (Florence, 1961), pp. 231–40.

25. Kristeller, "Giovanni Pico," p. 53.

26. Johannes Picus, *Commentationes*, 2 vols. (Bologna, 1496; Hain 12992).

27. Pico, *De hominis dignitate*, ed. Garin, p. 102. Ficinus, *Theologia Platonica* XIV, 3, *Opera* (Basil, 1576). *Théologie Platonicienne*, ed. Marcel, vol. 2, p. 257.

28. *De hominis dignitate*, ed. Garin, p. 102.

29. *Ibid.*, p. 104. Cf. Plato, *Protagoras* 321 b–d.

30. *Ibid.*, p. 106.

31. For the history of this notion, see Arthur O. Lovejoy, *The Great Chain of Being* (Cambridge, Mass., 1953). For Pico, cf. Ernst Cassirer, *Individuum und Kosmos in der Philosophie der Renaissance* (Darmstadt, 1963), pp. 88–90, trans. by Mario Domandi as *The Individual and the Cosmos in Renaissance Philosophy* (New York, 1963), pp. 84–85.

32. Avery Dulles, *Princeps Concordiae: Pico della Mirandola and the Scholastic Tradition* (Cambridge, Mass. 1941), pp. 15–16.

33. Kristeller, "Giovanni Pico," p. 53.

34. *De hominis dignitate*, ed. Garin, pp. 266–68.

35. *Ibid.*, p. 300.

36. *Ibid.*, pp. 300–2.

37. *Ibid.*, p. 302.

38. *Ibid.*, p. 304.

39. *Ibid.*

40. John Herman Randall, Jr., *The School of Padua and the Emergence of Modern Science* (Padua, 1961). P. O. Kristeller, "Renaissance Aristotelianism," *Greek, Roman and Byzantine Studies* 6 (1965): 157–74.

41. Petrus Pomponatius, *Tractatus de immortalitate animae*, ed. Gianfranco Morra (Bologna, 1954), ch. 1, p. 38; *Renaissance Philosophy of Man*, ed. Cassirer, Kristeller, and Randall, p. 282.

42. Pomponatius, *Tractatus de immortalitate animae*, ch. 14, ed. Morra, pp. 184–204; *Renaissance Philosophy of Man*, ed. Cassirer, Kristeller, and Randall, pp. 353–63.

43. *Ibid.*

44. P. O. Kristeller, "Two Unpublished Questions on the Soul of Pietro Pomponazzi," *Medievalia et Humanistica* 8 (1955): 76–101, at 89–90.

45. Garin, *La cultura filosofica*, pp. 231–40. Kristeller, "Giovanni Pico," p. 53.

10. THE IMMORTALITY OF THE SOUL

1. Jacob Burckhardt, *Die Kultur der Renaissance in Italien*, 13th ed. (Stuttgart, 1922), sect. 2, ch. 3, pp. 106–15.

2. *Ibid.*, sect. 2, pp. 97–126.

3. Giovanni Di Napoli, *L'immortalità dell'anima nel Rinascimento* (Turin, 1963). Eurenio Garin, *La cultura filosofica del Rinascimento italiano* (Florence, 1961), pp. 93–126. P. O. Kristeller, "Pier Candido Decembrio and His Unpublished Treatise on the Immortality of the Soul," in *The Classical Tradition: Literary and Historical Studies in Honor of Harry Caplan*, ed. Luitpold Wallach (Ithaca, N.Y., 1966), pp. 536–58.

4. P. O. Kristeller, *The Philosophy of Marsilio Ficino* (New York, 1943), pp. 344–45.

5. P. O. Kristeller, "The Humanist Bartolomeo Facio and His Unknown Correspondence," in *From the Renaissance to the Counter-Reformation: Essays in Honor of Garrett Mattingly*, ed. Charles H. Carter (New York, 1965), p. 68.

6. Erwin Rohde, *Psyche: Seelenkult und Unsterblichkeitsglaube der Griechen*, 2d ed. (Freiburg i. Br., 1898).

7. Plato, *Phaedo*, esp. 76d–77a. Cf. R. L. Patterson, *Plato on Immortality* (University Park, Pa., 1965).

8. Plotinus, *Ennead* II, 2–3, and IV, 7.

9. *De anima*, III, 4–5.

10. "Animam autem non possunt occidere" (*Ev. Matth.* 10:28). "Qui odit animam suam in hoc mundo, in vitam aeternam custodit eam" (*Ev. Joh.* 12:25). These are the only scriptural passages cited in the Lateran decree of 1513 (see note 24).

11. Kristeller, "Pier Candido Decembrio," pp. 553–55. To the literature cited there, we may now add: Richard Heinzmann, *Die Unsterblichkeit der Seele und die Auferstehung des Leibes: eine problemgeschichtliche Untersuchung der frühscholas-*

*tischen Sentenzen- und Summenliteratur von Anselm von Laon bis Wilhelm von Aux-
erre [Beiträge zur Geschichte der Philosophie und Theologie des Mittelalters,* vol.
40, no. 3] (Münster, 1965).

12. Augustine, *De immortalitate animae* and *De quantitate animae* (*Oeuvres* 1, 5,
2, ed. Pierre de Labriolle [Paris: Desclée, 1939]). Cf. also Harry A. Wolfson, "Immortality and Resurrection in the Philosophy of the Church Fathers," *Religious Philosophy* (Cambridge, Mass., 1961), pp. 69–103, who fails, however, to acknowledge a sharp distinction between the concept of immortality, rooted in Greek
philosophy, and that of resurrection, based on scripture.

13. Cf. *Summa Theologiae* I, q. 75, a. 6.

14. *Opus Oxoniense* 4, d. 43, q. 2; *Reportata Parisina* 4, d. 43, q. 2. Sofia Vanni
Rovighi, *L'immortalita dell'anima nei maestri francescani del secolo XIII* (Milan,
1936), pp. 197–233. Cf. Kristeller, "Pier Candido Decembrio," p. 553.

15. Averroes, *Commentarium magnum in Aristotelis de anima libros,* ed. F. Stuart
Crawford (Cambridge, Mass., 1964).

16. Thomas Aquinas, *De unitate intellectus,* in his *Opuscula philosophica,* ed. J.
Perrier (Paris, 1949), pp. 71–120; trans. and annotated by Bruno Nardi (Florence,
1947).

17. See note 3.

18. Kristeller, *Philosophy of Marsilio Ficino* p. 346.

19. *Ibid,* pp. 332 and 348.

20. *Ibid.*

21. Edward P. Mahoney, "The Early Psychology of Agostino Nifo" (Ph.D.
diss., Columbia University, 1966).

22. He wrote commentaries on several Platonic dialogues and a defense of Plato
against Georgius Trapezuntius. Cf. Friedrich Lauchert, *Die italienischen literarischen Gegner Luthers* (Freiburg, 1912), pp. 239–40. P. O. Kristeller, *Medieval
Aspects of Renaissance Learning,* ed. and trans. Edward P. Mahoney (Durham,
N.C., 1974), pp. 138–39. Richard Lemay, "The Fly against the Elephant: Flandinus
against Pomponazzi on Fate," in *Philosophy and Humanism: Renaissance Essays in
Honor of Paul Oskar Kristeller,* ed. Edward P. Mahoney (New York, 1976), pp.
70–99.

23. P. O. Kristeller, "Giovanni Pico della Mirandola and His Sources," in
*L'Opera e il pensiero di Giovanni Pico della Mirandola nella storia dell'umanesimo:
Convegno internazionale,* vol. 1: *Relazioni* (Florence, 1965), pp. 35–133, at 63.

24. J. D. Mansi, *Sacrorum Conciliorum nova et amplissima collectio,* vol. 32
(Paris, 1902), col. 842–43. For the decree of Vienne (1311), see vol. 25 (Venice,
1782), col. 411. Felix Gilbert, "Cristianesimo, Umanesimo e la Bolla 'Apostolici
Regiminis' del 1513," *Rivista storica italiana* 79 (1967): 976–90. John M. Headley,
"Luther and the Fifth Lateran Council," *Archiv für Reformationsgeschichte* 64
(1973): 55–78.

25. Di Napoli, *L'immortalità dell'anima nel Rinascimento,* pp. 277–338. Étienne
Gilson, "Autour de Pomponazzi," *Archives d'histoire doctrinale et littéraire du
Moyen Age* 63 (1961 [published 1962]): 163–279; *id.,* "L'affaire de l'immortalité de
l'âme à Venise au debut du XVIe siècle," in *Umanesimo europeo e umanesimo*

veneziano, ed. Vittore Branca (Florence, 1963), pp. 31–61. Martin Pine, "Pietro Pomponazzi and the Immortality Controversy, 1516–1524" (Ph.D. diss., Columbia University, 1965).

26. Petrus Pomponatius, *Tractatus de immortalitate animae*, ed. Gianfranco Morra (Bologna, 1954), ch. 15, pp. 232–38, translated by William H. Hay in *The Renaissance Philosophy of Man*, ed. Ernst Cassirer, P. O. Kristeller, and J. H. Randall, Jr. (Chicago, 1948), pp. 377–81.

27. *Ibid.*, chs. 2–8. The short discussion of Plato (chs. 5–8) is ignored by Gilson.

28. *Ibid.*, ch. 4.

29. *Ibid.*, ch. 1.

30. *Ibid.*, ch. 7.

11. THE UNITY OF TRUTH

1. Morton White, *Toward Reunion in Philosophy* (Cambridge, Mass., 1956).

2. Richard H. Popkin, *The History of Scepticism from Erasmus to Descartes* (Assen, 1960). Charles B. Schmitt, *Gianfrancesco Pico della Mirandola (1469–1533) and His Critique of Aristotle* (The Hague, 1967); *id., Cicero Scepticus* (The Hague, 1972).

3. *Tractatus de immortalitate animae*, Prologue and ch. 15.

4. P. O. Kristeller, "The Myth of Renaissance Atheism and the French Tradition of Free Thought," *Journal of the History of Philosophy* 6 (1968): 233–43.

5. Lynn Thorndike, *Science and Thought in the Fifteenth Century* (New York, 1929), pp. 24–58. Coluccio Salutati, *De nobilitate legum et medicinae*, ed. Eugenio Garin (Florence, 1947). *La disputa della arti nel Quattrocento*, ed. Eugenio Garin (Florence, 1947). Giulio F. Pagallo, "Nuovi testi per la 'Disputa delle arti' nel Quattrocento . . . ," *Italia Medioevale e Umanistica* 2 (1959): 467–81. A "sermo habitus in initio studii sub questione de praestantia medicinae et scientiae legalis" by Julianus Bononiensis dates from the early fourteenth century (ms. Vat. lat. 2418; cf. P. O. Kristeller, *Iter Italicum*, 2 vols. [Leyden, 1963–67], 2: 313). See essay 5, note 27.

6. It flourished in the sixteenth century. Yet the fifteenth-century humanist Lapo da Castiglionchio wrote a *comparatio inter rem militarem et studia literarum* that occurs in several manuscripts (e.g., Florence, ms. Ricc. 149, f. 64–84; cf. *Iter Italicum*, 1: 187).

7. Leonardo da Vinci, *Paragone: A Comparison of the Arts*, ed. I. A. Richter (London, 1949).

8. For Mussato's poetic reply to the Dominican friar Johanninus de Mantua, see *Thesaurus Antiquitatum et Historiarum Italiae*, ed. Jo. Georg. Graevius, vol. 6, pt. 2 (Leyden, 1722), cols. 59–62. Petrarch, *De sui ipsius et multorum ignorantia*, ed. L. M. Capelli (Paris, 1906). *Invective contra medicum*, ed. P. G. Ricci (Rome, 1950). Giovanni Boccaccio, *Genealogie deorum gentilium libri*, ed. Vincenzo Romano, 2 vols. (Bari, 1951), bks. XIV and XV (2: 679–785). Colucii Salutati *De laboribus Herculis*, ed. Berthold Louis Ullman, 2 vols. (Zurich, 1951). Around the middle of

the fifteenth century, a Regular Canon, Timoteo Maffei, wrote a similar treatise addressed to Nicolaus V and entitled *In sanctam rusticitatem* that appears in a number of manuscripts (e.g. Florence, Laurenziana, ms. Ashb. 690, fasc. 2; cf. *Iter Italicum*, 1: 89–90).

9. Edgar Wind, *Pagan Mysteries in the Renaissance* (New Haven, 1958).

10. See note 2.

11. Eugene F. Rice, Jr., *The Renaissance Idea of Wisdom* (Cambridge, Mass., 1958), pp. 187–90.

12. Montaigne, *Essais*, ed. Jean Plattard, vol. 2, pt. 1 (Paris, 1947), p. 326.

13. For Gianfrancesco Pico, see Charles B. Schmitt, *Gianfrancesco Pico della Mirandola*. For Montaigne, see Donald M. Frame, *Montaigne's Discovery of Man* (New York, 1955), pp. 57–73.

14. Ernst Cassirer, *The Individual and the Cosmos in Renaissance Philosophy*, trans. Mario Domandi (New York, 1963), pp. 28–31.

15. P. O. Kristeller, *The Philosophy of Marsilio Ficino* (New York, 1943), pp. 27–29.

16. *Ibid.*, pp. 320–23.

17. *Ibid.*, pp. 316–20.

18. *Ibid.*, pp. 25–27.

19. P. O. Kristeller, "Giovanni Pico della Mirandola and His Sources," in *L'Opera e il pensiero di Giovanni Pico della Mirandola nella storia dell'umanesimo: Convegno internazionale*, vol. 1: *Relazioni* (Florence, 1965), pp. 35–133. Cf. P. Kibre, *The Library of Pico della Mirandola* (New York, 1936). For his Cabalism, see Joseph L. Blau, *The Christian Interpretation of the Cabala in the Renaissance* (New York, 1944). François Secret, *Les kabbalistes chrétiens de la Renaissance* (Paris, 1964).

20. Jo. Picus, *Opera* (Basel, 1572), pp. 63–113. Pico della Mirandola, *Conclusiones*, ed. Bohdan Kieszkowski (Geneva, 1973).

21. See Kristeller, "Giovanni Pico," p. 63.

22. *De hominis dignitate*, ed. Eugenio Garin (Florence, 1942), pp. 138–42.

23. Eugenio Garin, *La cultura filosofica del Rinascimento italiano* (Florence, 1961), p. 239.

24. Charles B. Schmitt, "Perennial Philosophy: From Agostino Steuco to Leibniz," *Journal of the History of Ideas* 27 (1966): 505–32. See essay 6, note 89.

Part Five: Philosophy and Rhetoric from Antiquity to the Renaissance

12. CLASSICAL ANTIQUITY

1. Richard Volkmann, *Die Rhetorik der Griechen und Römer*, 2d ed. (Leipzig, 1885; reprint ed., 1963). Hans von Arnim, *Leben und Werke des Dio von Prusa*

(Berlin, 1898). Wilhelm Kroll, "Rhetorik," in Pauly-Wissowa, *Real-Encyklopaedie der klassischen Altertumswissenschaft, Supplementband 7* (Stuttgart, 1940), cols. 1039–1138. Charles S. Baldwin, *Ancient Rhetoric and Poetic* (New York, 1924). Heinrich Lausberg, *Handbuch der literarischen Rhetorik*, 2 vols. (Munich, 1960). George Kennedy, *The Art of Persuasion in Greece* (Princeton, N.J., 1963); *id., The Art of Rhetoric in the Roman World* (Princeton, 1972). William R. Roberts, *Greek Rhetoric and Literary Criticism* (New York, 1963). Josef Martin, *Antike Rhetorik* (Munich, 1974). See also: H.-I. Marrou, *Histoire de l'éducation dans l'antiquité* (Paris, 1948), trans. by George Lamb as *A History of Education in Antiquity* (London, 1956). Donald L. Clark, *Rhetoric in Greco-Roman Education* (New York, 1957). Eduard Norden, *Die antike Kunstprosa*, 5th ed., 2 vols. (Stuttgart, 1958). Wesley Trimpi, "The Ancient Hypothesis of Fiction: An Essay on the Origins of Literary Theory," *Tradito* 27 (1971): 1–78; *id.*, "The Quality of Fiction: The Rhetorical Transmission of Literary Theory," *ibid.* 30 (1974): 1–118. Aldo D. Scaglione, *The Classical Theory of Composition* (Chapel Hill, N.C., 1972).

2. Werner Jaeger, *Paideia: die Formung des griechischen Menschen*, 4th ed., 4 vols. (Berlin, 1959), 1: 364–418 ("Die Sophisten). Heinrich Gomperz, *Sophistik und Rhetorik* (Leipzig, 1912; reprint ed., 1965).

3. Aristophanes, *Clouds*. Plato, *Apology*.

4. Plato, *Gorgias* 462c–465e.

5. Friedrich Wilhelm Blass, *Die attische Beredsamkeit*, 2d ed. 3 vols. (Leipzig, 1887–98).

6. Plato, *Phaedrus* 227a–234c.

7. Plato, *Menexenus* 236d–249c.

8. Thucydides II, 35–46.

9. Plato, *Phaedrus* 258d and *passim*.

10. Jaeger, *Paideia*, 3: 105–225. For Isocrates' claim to be a philosopher, see *De antidosi*, 175ff. and 270ff.; cf. Jaeger, *Paideia*, 3: 396, n. 13.

11. Friedrich Solmsen, *Die Entwicklung der aristotelischen Logik und Rhetorik* (Berlin, 1929); *id.*, "The Aristotelian Tradition in Ancient Rhetoric," *American Journal of Philology* 62 (1941): 35–50, 169–90.

12. Aristotle, *Rhetorica* I, 1, 1354a 1. See also the many passages where the rhetorical argument (*enthymema*) is compared with the syllogism. For the theory of the passions, see *Rhetorica* II, 1–11.

13. Johannes Stroux, *De Theophrasti virtutibus dicendi* (Leipzig, 1912). The treatise *De elocutione* attributed to Demetrius Phalereus (edited with Aristotle's *Poetics* by W. Rhys Roberts, Loeb Classical Library [Cambridge, Mass., 1965]) has Peripatetic elements and was probably written in the first century A.D. (cf. Stroux, *De Theophrasti virtutibus dicendi*, p. 257 and 271).

14. *Stoicorum Veterum Fragmenta*, ed. Hans von Arnim, 4 vols. (Leipzig, 1903–26; reprint ed., Stuttgart, 1964), 1: 21–23 (Zeno, fragments 74–84); 2: 95–96 (Chrysippus, fragments 288–98).

15. Modestus van Straaten, *Panétius* (Amsterdam, 1946), p. 160.

16. Sextus Empiricus, *Adversus Mathematicos* II, who cites repeatedly Critolaus the Peripatetic. A treatise on rhetoric by the Epicurean Philodemus has been partly

preserved: *Philodemi volumina rhetorica,* ed. Siegfried Sudhaus, 2 vols. (Leipzig, 1892–96; reprint ed., Amsterdam, 1964).

17. On Proclus' contributions to literary criticism, see James A. Coulter, *The Literary Microcosm* (Leyden, 1976). *Anonymi et Stephani in Artem Rhetoricam commentaria* [*Commentaria in Aristotelem Graeca,* vol. 21, pt. 2], ed. Hugo Rabe (Berlin, 1896). Syrianus, *Scholia in Hermogenem,* in *Rhetores Graeci,* ed. Christian Walz, 9 vols. (Stuttgart, 1832–36; reprint ed., 9 vols. in 10, Osnabrück, 1968), vol. 4 (1833), and vol. 7, pt. 1 (1833).

18. Hans von Arnim, *Leben und Werke des Dion von Prusa* (Berlin, 1898).

19. *Rhetores Graeci,* ed. Walz, vols. 4; 5; 7, pts. 1 and 2. Another influential work which was also the subject of commentaries was the *Progymnasmata* of Aphthonius (*ibid.,* vols. 1 and 2). The rhetorical work by Menander (*ibid.,* vol. 9 [1836], pp. 127–330) deals exclusively with epideictic oratory.

20. Demetrius, *De elocutione* IV, 223–40. See Sykutris, "Epistolographie," in Pauly-Wissowa, *Real-Encyclopädie der classischen Altertumswissenschaft, Supplementband 5* (Stuttgart, 1931): 185–220. *Epistolographi Graeci,* ed. Rudolf Hercher (Paris, 1873).

21. Paul Wendland, *Die hellenistisch-römische Kultur in ihren Beziehungen zu Judentum und Christentum* (Tübingen, 1907), pp. 39–53, tries to connect the early Christian homily with the diatribe of the popular philosophers of the period.

22. Karl Krumbacher, *Geschichte der byzantinischen Literatur,* 2d ed. (Munich, 1897; reprint ed., New York, n.d.), pp. 450–98. George L. Kustas, *Studies in Byzantine Rhetoric* (Thessaloniki, 1973). Cf. Herbert Hunger, "Aspekte der griechischen Rhetorik von Gorgias bis zum Untergang von Byzanz," *Österreichische Akademie der Wissenschaften, Philosophisch-Historische Klasse, Sitzungsberichte* 277 (1972), no. 3; *id., Die hochsprachliche profane Literatur der Byzantiner,* vol. 1 (Munich, 1978), pp. 62–196 (Rhetorik) and pp. 197–239 (Epistolographie).

23. *Rhetores Graeci,* ed. Walz, vols. 2; 4; 5; and 7.

24. The collections attributed to Demetrius and to Libanius or Proclus are included in *Epistolographi Graeci,* ed. Hercher, pp. 1–13. For the whole subject, see Sykutris, "Epistolographie," Pauly-Wissowa, *Supplementband 5.* Giles Constable, *Letters and Letter-Collections* (Turnhout, 1976), p. 8.

25. See note 1. See also J. F. D'Alton, *Roman Literary Theory and Criticism* (London, 1931). M. L. Clarke, *Rhetoric at Rome* (London, 1966). Edilbert P. Parks, *The Roman Rhetorical Schools as a Preparation for the Courts Under the Early Empire* (Baltimore, Md., 1945). *Rhetores Latini minores,* ed. Karl Felix von Halm (Leipzig, 1863).

26. Cicero, *Orator* 4–19. Cicero, *pro Archia poeta* 2–4: "studiis humanitatis . . . liberalissimisque studiis." Cf. Hans Kurt Schulte, *Orator: Untersuchungen über das ciceronische Bildungsideal* (Frankfort, 1935).

27. *Orator* 8–10.

28. Cf. Seneca, *Epist.* 116, 5; cf. van Straaten, *Panétius,* p. 365, fragment 114. Cicero, *De officiis* I, 15, 46; II, 3, 13–4, 15.

29. *Stoicorum Veterum Fragmenta,* ed. von Arnim, vol. 3, p. 49, l. 7 (Chrysippus, frag. 202); p. 49, ll. 24–25 (frag. 204); p. 51, l. 20 (frag. 214); p. 72, ll.

19–20 (frag. 293); p. 120, 11. 15–26 (frag. 471); p. 139, 1. 17 (frag. 516); p. 140, 11. 12–20 (frag. 521); p. 148, 1. 42-p. 149, 1. 1 (frag. 560). Cf. *Epicurea*, ed. Hermann Usener (Leipzig, 1887; reprint ed., Rome, 1963), frags. 219–21, 227b. Cicero, *de finibus* I, 13, 42 (frag. 397). Sextus, *Adv. math.* XI, 167ff.

30. Cicero coins the term *qualitas* and excuses its novelty because he wants to render the term *poiotes* which also in Greek is a technical term of philosophy and not a popular word (*Academica posteriora* I, 6, 24–7, 25). In nearly 2,000 years, the word has become a part of "ordinary language" in English as in most other modern languages.

31. Thucydides I, 140–44.

32. *Rhetores Latini minores*, ed. Halm, pp. 153–304, 596–606.

33. On the chancery practice of the Roman emperors and the early popes, see Harry Bresslau, *Handbuch der Urkundenlehre für Deutschland und Italien*, 3d ed., 2 vols. (Berlin, 1958), 1: 184ff. and 190ff. Cassiodore's *Variae* consist of letters and documents connected with his activity as chancellor of Theodoric; cf. Bresslau, 1: 103–4 and *passim*.

34. *Rhetores Latini minores*, ed. Halm, pp. 447–48 (ch. 27: "De epistolis").

35. Edward Kennard Rand, *Founders of the Middle Ages* (Cambridge, Mass., 1928).

36. Martianus Capella, *De nuptiis Philologiae et Mercurii*, ed. Adolf Dick (Leipzig, 1925). Books III-IX are each dedicated to one of the seven arts. Book V deals with rhetoric.

37. H.-I. Marrou, *Saint Augustin et la fin de la culture antique*, 4th ed. (Paris, 1958), pp. 211–35: "Les sept arts libéraux."

38. Sextus Empiricus, *Adversus mathematicos* (not considered by Marrou).

13. THE MIDDLE AGES

1. Charles S. Baldwin, *Medieval Rhetoric and Poetic* (New York, 1928). Richard McKeon, "Rhetoric in the Middle Ages," *Speculum* 17 (1942): 1–32. James J. Murphy, *Medieval Rhetoric: A Select Bibliography* (Toronto, 1971); *id.*, *Rhetoric in the Middle Ages* (Berkeley, Calif., 1974); *Medieval Eloquence*, ed. James J. Murphy (Berkeley, 1978). For important aspects of medieval rhetoric not discussed in this essay, see Ernst Robert Curtius, *Europäische Literatur und lateinisches Mittelalter* (Bern, 1948). Franz Quadlbauer, "Die antike Theorie der *genera dicendi* im lateinischen Mittelalter," *Österreichische Akademie der Wissenschaften, Sitzungsberichte* 241 (1962), no. 2. For Italy, see Alfredo Galletti, *L'eloquenza dalle origini al XVI secolo* [*Storia dei generi letterari italiani*] (Milan, 1904–38).

2. The Arabic tradition does not seem to have played a role in the history of rhetoric as it did in philosophy and the sciences. Cf. S. A. Bonebakker, *Materials for the History of Arabic Rhetoric* (Naples, 1975).

3. *The Rhetoric of Alcuin and Charlemagne*, ed. and trans. Wilbur S. Howell (Princeton, N.J., 1949; reprint ed., New York, 1965). Luitpold Wallach, *Alcuin and Charlemagne* (Ithaca, N.Y., 1959).

4. Cora E. Lutz, "Martianus Capella," in *Catalogus Translationum et Commentariorum*, vol. 2, ed. P. O. Kristeller and F. Edward Cranz (Washington, D.C., 1971), pp. 367–81.

5. P. O. Kristeller, "The Historical Position of Johannes Scottus Eriugena," in *Latin Script and Letters A.D. 400–900: Festschrift Presented to Ludwig Bieler* (Leyden, 1976), pp. 156–64. Marie Thérèse d'Alverny, "Les *Solutiones ad Chosroem de Priscianus Lydus* et Jean Scot," in *John Scot Érigène et l'Histoire de la Philosophie* (Paris, 1977), pp. 145–60.

6. *Gunzo, "Epistola ad Augienses," und Anselm von Besate, "Rhetorimachia"*, ed. Karl Manitius (Weimar, 1958).

7. William D. Patt, "The Early *Ars dictaminis* as Response to a Changing Society," *Viator* 9 (1978): 133–55.

8. See note 6. Ernst Dümmler, *Anselm der Peripatetiker* (Halle, 1872). Cinzio Violante, "Anselmo da Besate," *Dizionario biografico degli Italiani* 3 (1961): 407–9.

9. E. A. Quain, "The Medieval *Accessus ad auctores*," *Traditio* 3 (1945): 215–64. R. W. Hunt, "The Introductions to the *Artes* in the Twelfth Century," in *Studia Mediaevalia in honorem admodum Reverendi Raymundi Josephi Martin* (Bruges, ca. 1949), pp. 85–112. R. B. C. Huygens, *Accessus ad Auctores* (Leyden, 1970).

10. Isidorus Hispalensis, *Etymologiae sive Origines*, ed. W. M. Lindsay (Oxford, 1911), bk. II, ch. 24, sec. 3: "Philosophiae species tripartita est: una naturalis, quae Graece Physica appellatur . . . altera moralis, quae Graece Ethica dicitur . . . tertia rationalis, quae Graeco vocabulo Logica appellatur."

11. Martin Grabmann, *Die Geschichte der scholastischen Methode*, vol. 2 (Freiburg, 1911; reprint ed., Graz, 1957), pp. 28–48 and *passim*.

12. Eva M. Sanford, "Juvenalis," in *Catalogus Translationum et Commentariorum*, vol. 1, ed. P. O. Kristeller (Washington, D.C., 1960), pp. 193–94: "Bernardus (Carnotensis) dicebat hoc (i.e., cui parti philosophie supponatur) non esse in actoribus quaerendum, cum ipsi nec partes philosophiae nec de philosophia tractant." Cf. Helen Rodnite Lemay, "Guillaume de Conches' Division of Philosophy in the *Accessus ad Macrobium*," *Mediaevalia* 1 (1977): 115–29: "Cui parti philosophie supponatur minime querendum est dum non uni soli parti sed omni supponitur" (p. 122).

13. S. Thomas de Aquino, *Expositio super librum Boethii de Trinitate*, ed. Bruno Decker (Leyden, 1955), p. 167 (q. 5, a. 1): "Ad tertium dicendum quod septem liberales artes non sufficienter dividunt philosophiam theoricam." Cf. Joseph Mariétan, *Problème de la classification des sciences d' Aristote a St. Thomas* (Fribourg, 1901), p. 193.

14. *Commentum Bernardi Silvestris super sex libros Eneidos Virgilii*, ed. Wilhelm Riedel (Greifswald, 1924); *Commentum Bernardi Silvestris super sex libros Eneidos Virgilii*, ed. Julian Ward Jones and Elizabeth Frances Jones (Lincoln, Neb., 1977). J. R. O'Donnell, "The Sources and Meaning of Bernard Silvester's Commentary on the Aeneid," *Mediaeval Studies* 24 (1962): 233–49. Fausto Ghisalberti, "Arnolfo d'Orléans, un cultore di Ovidio nel secolo XII," *Memorie del R. Istituto*

Lombardo di scienze e lettere, Classe di lettere, scienze morali e storiche 24 [3d ser., 15] (1932): 157–234. Arnulfus Aurelianensis, *Glosule super Lucanum* [*Papers and Monographs of the American Academy in Rome,* 18], ed. Berthe M. Marti (Rome, 1958).

15. Mary Dickey, "Some Commentaries on the *De inventione* and *Ad Herennium* of the Eleventh and Early Twelfth Centuries," *Medieval and Renaissance Studies* 6 (1968): 1–41. Karin Margareta Fredborg, "The Commentary of Thierry of Chartres on Cicero's *De inventione*," *Cahiers de l'Institut du Moyen Age grec et latin* (University of Copenhagen), no. 7 (1971): 1–36; *eadem,* "Petrus Helias on Rhetoric," *ibid.,* no. 13 (1974): 31–41; *eadem,* "The Commentaries on Cicero's *De inventione* and *Rhetorica ad Herennium* by William of Champeaux," *ibid.,* no. 17 (1976): 1–39. John O. Ward, "Artificiosa Eloquentia in the Middle Ages" (Ph.D. diss., University of Toronto, 1972); *id.,* "The Date of the Commentary on Cicero's *De inventione* by Thierry of Chartres and the Cornifician Attack on the Liberal Arts," *Viator* 3 (1972): 219–73; *id.,* "From Antiquity to the Renaissance: Glosses and Commentaries on Cicero's *Rhetorica,* in *Medieval Eloquence,* ed. Murphy, pp. 25–67. Nicholas M. Haring, "Thierry of Chartres and Dominicus Gundissalinus," *Mediaeval Studies* 26 (1964): 271–86. On Alanus, see Harry Caplan, "A Mediaeval Commentary on the *Rhetorica ad Herennium,*" *Of Eloquence: Studies in Ancient and Mediaeval Rhetoric,* ed. Anne King and Helen North (Ithaca, N.Y., 1970), pp. 247–70. *Alain de Lille,* ed. Marie Thérèse d'Alverny (Paris, 1965), pp. 52–55. James J. Murphy, "Cicero's Rhetoric in the Middle Ages," *Quarterly Journal of Speech* 53 (1967): 334–49.

16. Eduard Norden, *Die antike Kunstprosa,* vol. 2, 5th ed. (Stuttgart, 1958), pp. 688–93, 724–31.

17. For the extensive bibliography, see McKeon, "Rhetoric in the Middle Ages"; Murphy, *Medieval Rhetoric;* and Patt, "The Early *Ars Dictaminis* as Response to a Changing Society." Charles H. Haskins, *Studies in Medieval Culture* (Oxford, 1929; reprint ed., New York, 1958), pp. 170–92, and *passim.* Ernst Hartwig Kantorowicz, *Selected Studies* (Locust Valley, N.Y., 1965), pp. 194–212, 247–63. Helene Wieruszowski, *Politics and Culture in Medieval Spain and Italy* (Rome, 1971), pp. 331–77, and *passim.* Giles Constable, *Letters and Letter-Collections* [*Typologie des sources du Moyen Age Occidental,* 17] (Turnhout, 1976); *id.,* "The Structure of Medieval Society According to the *Dictatores* of the Twelfth Century," in *Law, Church, and Society: Essays in Honor of Stephan Kuttner,* ed. Kenneth Pennington and Robert Somerville (Philadelphia, 1977), pp. 253–67. James R. Banker, "The *Ars dictaminis* and Rhetorical Textbooks at the Bolognese University in the Fourteenth Century," *Medievalia et Humanistica,* n.s. 5 (1974): 153–68. Emil J. Polak, *A Textual Study of Jacques de Dinant's "Summa dictaminis"* (Geneva, 1975). Carol D. Lanham, *Salutatio Formulas in Latin Letters to 1200* (Munich, 1975). H. M. Schaller, "Die Kanzlei Kaiser Friedrichs II," *Archiv für Diplomatik* 4 (1958): 264–327. Franz-Josef Schmale, "Die Bologneser Schule der *Ars dictandi,*" *Deutsches Archiv für Erforschung des Mittelalters* 13 (1957): 16–34. Giuseppe Vecchi, *Il magistero delle "artes" latine a Bologna nel medioevo* (Bologna, 1958). The largest collection of texts is still: Ludwig Rockinger, *Briefsteller und Formelbücher*

des eilften bis vierzehnten Jahrhunderts (Munich, 1863–64; reprint ed., New York, 1961).

18. Francesco Novati, *La giovinezza di Coluccio Salutati* (Turin, 1888), pp. 66–121; *id., Freschi e minii del Dugento* (Milan, 1908), pp. 299–328. Harry Bresslau, *Handbuch der Urkundenlehre für Deutschland und Italien*, 3d ed., vol. 1 (Berlin, 1958), pp. 583–635.

19. *Monumenta Germaniae Historica, Legum Sectio V: Formulae Merowingici et Karolini Aevi*, ed. Karl Zeumer (Hanover, 1886). The only formulary attached to a compiler's name is that of Marculfus and dates from the seventh century (*ibid.*, pp. 36–106).

20. Constable, *Letters and Letter-Collections*, pp. 30–31. Patt, "The Early *Ars dictaminis* as Response to a Changing Society."

21. Gunzo, "*Epistola ad Augienses*", ed. Manitius, pp. 19–57. The parts may be characterized as *salutatio* (p. 19), *exordium* (p. 19), *narratio* (p. 21), *argumentatio* (p. 42), and *conclusio* or *peroratio* (p. 55). For the parts of the speech in ancient Roman rhetorical treatises, see Heinrich Lausberg, *Handbuch der literarischen Rhetorik*, vol. 1 (Munich, 1960), pp. 148–49.

22. Charles H. Haskins, "Albericus Casinensis," in *Casinensia*, 2 vols. (Montecassino, 1929), 1: 115–24. Alberici Casinensis *Flores rhetorici*, ed. D. M. Inguanez and H. M. Willard (Monte Cassino, 1938). Anselmo Lentini, "Alberico," *Dizionario biografico degli Italiani* 1 (1960): 643–45. Hugh H. Davis, "The *De rithmis* of Alberic of Monte Cassino," *Mediaeval Studies* 28 (1966): 198–227. Herbert Bloch, "Montecassino's Teachers and Library in the High Middle Ages," in *La scuola nell'Occidente latino dell'alto medioevo* [*Settimane di studio del Centro Italiano di Studi sull'Alto Medioevo*, 19], 2 vols. (Spoleto, 1972), 2: 563–605, at 587–99. The manuscript in Leningrad, Public Library, cod. Lat. O v XVI 3, contains Alberic's *breviarium de dictamine, de rithmis, de orationibus, de epistolaribus modis* and *de encliticis*. It is being studied by Paul F. Gehl (Chicago) and Konrad Krautter (Konstanz).

23. For France, see Léopold Delisle, "Les écoles d'Orléans au douxième et au treizième siècle," *Annuaire Bulletin de la Société de l'histoire de France* 7 (1869): 139–54. Noël Valois, *De arte scribendi epistolas apud Gallicos Medii Aevi Scriptores Rhetoresve* (Paris, 1880; reprint ed., New York, 1964). For England, see Noël Denholm-Young, "The Cursus in England," *Collected Papers on Mediaeval Subjects* (Oxford, 1946), pp. 26–55. For Spain, see Charles Faulhaber, *Latin Rhetorical Theory in Thirteenth and Fourteenth Century Castile* (Berkeley, Calif., 1972); *id.,* "Retóricas Clásicas y Medievales en Bibliotecas Castellanas," *Ábaco* 4 (1973): 151–300. Juan Gil de Zamora, *Dictaminis Epithalamium*, ed. Charles Faulhaber (Pisa, 1978). For Germany, see Walter Kronbichler, *Die "Summa de arte prosandi" des Konrad von Mure* (Zurich, 1968).

24. Francesco Novati, "Di un' *ars punctandi* attribuita a Francesco Petrarca," *R. Istituto Lombardo di scienze e lettere, Rendiconti* 2d ser., 42 (1909): 82–118.

25. Francesco Di Capua, *Il ritmo prosaico nelle lettere dei papi*, 3 vols. (Rome, 1937–56); *id., Scritti minori*, 2 vols. (Rome, 1959). Gudrun Lindholm, *Studien zum mittellateinischen Prosarhythmus* (Stockholm, 1963). Tore Janson, *Prose Rhythm in Medieval Latin from the 9th to the 13th Century* (Stockholm, 1974).

26. Banker, "The *Ars dictaminis* and Rhetorical Textbooks"; *id.*, "Giovanni di Bonandrea and Civic Values in the Context of the Italian Rhetorical Tradition," *Manuscripta* 18 (1974): 3–20. The writings of Boncompagnus, Guido Faba, Giovanni di Bonandrea, Laurentius de Aquilegia, and Johannes Bondus de Aquilegia were frequently copied in the fourteenth and even in the fifteenth century. *Dictamen* treatises were composed in the fourteenth century by Giovanni del Virgilio (cf. P. O. Kristeller, "Un'*ars dictaminis* di Giovanni del Virgilio," *Italia Medioevale e Umanistica* 4 [1961]: 181–200); by Francesco da Buti (ms. Angelica 1375 and Freiburg 167) [cf. Kristeller, "Un'*ars dictaminis*," p. 190] and ms. Bodl. lat. misc. e. 52); by Dominicus Bandinus (Brussels ms. 1561–84 and Seville, ms. 7–5–2); and in the fifteenth century by Nicolaus Vulpis (Seville, Colombina, ms. 5–3–27, f. 175).

27. Boncompagnus, *Breviloquium,* ed. Joseph Vecchi (Bologna, 1954). *Testi riguardanti la vita degli studenti a Bologna nel secolo XIII,* ed. Virgilio Pini (Bologna, 1968). Cf. Virgilio Pini, "Boncompagno da Signa," in *Dizionario biografico degli Italiani* 11 (1969): 720–25; J. Purkart, "Boncompagno of Signa and the Rhetoric of Love," in *Medieval Eloquence,* ed. Murphy, pp. 319–31; Robert B. L. Benson, "Protohumanism and Narrative Technique in Early Thirteenth-Century Italian 'Ars Dictaminis,' " in *Boccaccio: Secoli di vita, Atti del Congresso Internazionale: Boccaccio 1975* (Los Angeles, 1975), ed. M. Cottino-Jones and Edward F. Tuttle (Ravenna, 1979), pp. 31–50. Giancarlo Alessio, "La tradizione manoscritta del *Candelabrum* di Bene da Firenze," *Italia Medioevale e Umanistica* 15 (1972): 99–148. Virgilio Pini, "La *Summa de vitiis et virtutibus* di Guido Faba," *Quadrivium* 1 (1956): 41–152. Charles B. Faulhaber, "The *Summa dictaminis* of Guido Faba," in *Medieval Eloquence,* ed. Murphy, pp. 85–111. Bonus Lucensis, *Cedrus Libani,* ed. Giuseppi Vecchi (Modena, 1963). P. O. Kristeller, "Matteo de'Libri, Bolognese Notary of the Thirteenth Century, and his *Artes dictaminis,*" *Miscellanea G. Galbiati,* vol. 2 [*Fontes Ambrosiani,* 26] (Milan, 1951), pp. 283–320. Guido Zaccagnini, "Giovanni di Bonandrea dettatore e rimatore . . . ," *Studi e Memorie per la storia dell'Università di Bologna* 8 (1924): 211–48. James R. Banker, "Giovanni di Bonandrea and Civic Values in the Context of the Italian Rhetorical Tradition," *Manuscripta* 18 (1974): 3–20. For Giovanni del Virgilio, see Kristeller, "Un'*ars dictaminis.*" A group of unknown grammatical treatises by this author is found in Seville, ms. 81-6-6.

28. A *dictamen* treatise by Johannes Odonecti vocatus Baptista de Sancto Johanne Maurianensi nativus sed studii Bononiensis alumnus appears in Magl. VIII 1412 (Kristeller, *Iter Italicum,* 2 vols. [London and Leyden, 1963–67], 1:133; cf. Banker, "The *Ars dictaminis* and Rhetorical Textbooks," p. 166, n. 33, who dates it to the fourteenth century), in Ricc. 669 (cf. *Iter Italicum,* 1: 195), and in Seville 7-5-2 (cf. Faulhaber, "Retóricas Clásicas y Medievales en Bibliotecas Castellanas," pp. 226–27, no. 197.).

29. Kristeller, "Matteo de'Libri," p. 288.

30. M. A. von Bethmann-Hollweg, *Der Civilprozess des gemeinen Rechts in geschichtlicher Entwicklung,* vol. 6 (Bonn, 1874), pp. 148–59.

31. Arturo Palmieri, *Rolandino Passaggeri* (Bologna, 1933).

32. Edmond Faral, *Les arts poétiques du XIIe et du XIIIe siècle* (Paris, 1924; reprint ed., 1962). *Three Medieval Rhetorical Arts,* ed. James J. Murphy (Berkeley,

Calif., 1971); cf. Traugott Lawler, *Speculum* 48 (1973): 388–94. E. Gallo, "The *Poetria nova* of Geoffrey of Vinsauf," in *Medieval Eloquence,* ed. Murphy, pp. 68–84. His connection with Bologna depends on the authorship of another treatise on *dictamen;* cf. Vincenzo Licitra, "La *Summa de arte dictandi* di Maestro Goffredo," *Studi Medievali,* 3d ser., 7 (1966): 864–913. Giovanni Mari, "I trattati medievali di ritmica latina," *Memorie dell'Istituto Lombardo di scienze e lettere* 20 [3d ser., 11] (1899): 373–496. Traugott Lawler, *The "Parisiana poetria" of John of Garland* (New Haven, Conn., 1974).

33. "Numquam enim memini me Tullium legisse. . . . Verumtamen nunquam Tullii depravavi rethoricam nec eam imitari volentibus dissuasi" (preface of his *Palma,* in Carl Sutter, *Aus Leben und Schriften des Magister Boncompagno* [Freiburg i. Br., 1894], pp. 105–6). "Rhetorica compilata per Tullium Ciceronem iudicio studentium est cassata, quia nunquam ordinarie legitur, immo tanquam fabula vel ars mechanica latentius transcurritur et docetur." This statement is followed by a critical comment on the prologue of the *De inventione* (*Boncompagni Rhetorica novissima,* ed. Augusto Gaudenzi, in *Bibliotheca Juridica Medii Aevi: Scripta anecdota glossatorum,* vol. 2, ed. Augusto Gaudenzi [Bologna, 1892], p. 251).

34. J. P. Schneyer, *Repertorium der lateinischen Sermones des Mittelalters für die Zeit von 1150–1350* [*Beiträge zur Geschichte der Philosophie des Mittelalters* 43], 7 vols. (Muenster, 1969–76).

35. Harry Caplan, *Mediaeval Artes Praedicandi,* 2 vols. (Ithaca, N.Y., 1934–36). Thomas M. Charland, *Artes Praedicandi* (Ottawa, 1936). See also the article by Richard Rouse in *The Renaissance of the Twelfth Century,* ed. R. L. Benson and Giles Constable (forthcoming).

36. Albertano da Brescia, a layman, composed several sermons and also a treatise on preaching, entitled *Ars loquendi et tacendi.* Cf. Galletti, *L'Eloquenza,* pp. 467–68. Aldo Checchini, "Un giudice del secolo decimoterzo, Albertano da Brescia," *Atti del R. Istituto Veneto di scienze, lettere ed arti* 71, pt. 2 [8th ser., 14, pt. 2] (1911–12): 1423–95. Marta Ferrari, "Intorno ad alcuni sermoni inediti di Albertano da Brescia, *Atti dell'Istituto Veneto* 109 (1950–51): 69–93.

37. See McKeon, Murphy, and others (see note 17).

38. Otto of Freising (*Gesta Friderici* I, bk. 2, ch. 30, ed. Georg Waitz [Hanover, 1912], p. 136) reports how the emperor Barbarossa in 1155 interrupted a speech addressed to him by the envoys of the city of Rome: "cursus verborum illorum . . . more Italico longa continuatione periodorumque circuitibus sermonem producturis interrupit." The speech is given in ch. 29 (pp. 135–36), but probably not *verbatim.*

39. The work has been edited by Augusto Gaudenzi in *Bibliotheca Juridica Medii Aevi: Scripta Anecdota glossatorum,* vol. 2 (Bologna, 1892), pp. 249–97.

40. Guido Faba, *Parlamenti ed epistole,* in Augusto Gaudenzi, *I suoni, le forme e le parole dell'odierno dialetto della città di Bologna* (Turin, 1889). *Le dicerie volgari di Ser Matteo de' Libri da Bologna secondo una redazione pistoiese,* ed. Luigi Chiappelli (Pistoia, 1900). Matteo dei Libri, *Arringhe,* ed. Eleonora Vincenti (Milan and Naples, 1974). Eleonora Vincenti, "Matteo dei Libri e l'oratoria pubblica e privata nel '200," *Archivio Glottologico Italiano* 54 (1969): 227–37. *Le dicerie di Ser Filippo Ceffi,* ed. Luigi Biondi (Turin, 1825). Giuliana Giannardi, "Le

'Dicerie' di Filippo Ceffi," *Studi di filologia italiana* 6 (1942): 5–63. Carlo Frati, " 'Flore de parlare' o 'Somma d'arengare' attributa a Ser Giovanni fiorentino da Vignano in un codice marciano," *Giornale storico della letteratura italiana* 61 (1913): 1–31, 228–65. A collection of Latin *arengae* is found in Berlin ms. lat. fol. 68; cf. *Archiv der Gesellschaft für ältere deutsche Geschichtskunde* 8 (1843): 826–27. The word *arenga* usually stands for public speech. The term is also used by Harry Bresslau (*Handbuch der Urkundenlehre*, vol. 1, p. 48) and following him by other scholars for the first part of a document. Bresslau citres a passage from Guido Faba, but this use of the term is rare and secondary. It merely means that some introductions of letters and documents were worded in the style of public speeches.

41. The anonymous *Oculus Pastoralis* is published in Lodovico Antonio Muratori, *Antiquitates Italicae Medii Aevi* IX (Arezzo, 1776), col. 787–856. Cf. Dora Franceschi, "L'Oculus pastoralis e la sua fortuna," *Atti dell'Accademia delle scienze di Torino* 99 (1964–65): 205–61. Joh. Viterbiensis, *De regimine civitatum*, ed. Gaetano Salvemini, in *Bibliotheca Juridica Medii Aevi: Scripta Anecdota glossatorum*, vol. 3, ed. Augusto Gaudenzi (Bologna, 1901), pp. 217–80. Fritz Hertter, *Die Podestàliteratur Italiens im 12. und 13. Jahrhundert* (Leipzig and Berlin, 1910).

42. G. L. Haskins and Ernst Kantorowicz, "A Diplomatic Mission of Francis Accursius and his Oration before Pope Nicholas III," *English Historical Review* 58 (1943): 424–47.

43. I expressed similar views in my paper "Humanism and Scholasticism in the Italian Renaissance" which appeared first in *Byzantion* 17 (1944–45): 346–74 and is reprinted in this volume as essay 5. It seems that in our age an idea remains unnoticed unless it is properly labeled and emphasized through titles, abstracts, and indices. An idea, even when expressed in an entire paragraph, cannot be "retrieved." There is still a difference between an attentive human reader and a computer or its programmer. See also Galletti, *L'Eloquenza*, pp. 413–537.

44. Rolandinus Patavinus, *Cronica* [*Rerum Italicarum Scriptores* VIII, 1], ed. Antonio Bonardi (Città di Castello, 1905–8), p. 64, bk. IV, chap. 10: "[S]urrexit iudex imperialis Petrus de Vinea. . . . Proposuit autem illam auctoritatem Ovidii: 'Leniter, ex merito . . .' [*Heroides*, V, 7–8] et aptata sapienter auctoritate intencioni, disputavit et edocuit populum. . . .''

45. The speech begins: "Sed me Parnasi deserta per ardua dulcis raptet amor. Georgicorum III° [291–92]. Hodierno die . . ." Cf. Attilio Hortis, *Scritti inediti di Francesco Petrarca* (Trieste, 1874), p. 311.

46. Kristeller, *Iter Italicum*, 1: 160.

47. Sandra Karaus, "Selections from the Commentary of Bartolinus de Benincasa de Canulo on the *Rhetorica ad Herennium*, with an Introduction" (Ph.D. diss., Columbia University, 1970). An article by Karaus Wertis on the subject will appear in *Viator*. For the document, see Emilio Orioli, *La cancelleria pepolesca* (Bologna, 1910), pp. 65–67.

48. Banker, "The *Ars dictaminis* and Rhetorical Textbooks," p. 154 and p. 165, n. 10. Emil Polak, *A Textual Study of Jacques de Dinant's "Summa Dictaminis"* (Geneva, 1975). André Wilmart, "L'*Ars arengandi* de Jacques de Dinant," *Analecta Reginensia* [Biblioteca Vaticana, *Studi e Testi* 59] (Vatican City, 1933), pp.

113–51. A fragmentary commentary on the *Ad Herennium* by Jacobus de Dinanto is found in Modena, ms. Est. lat. 714 (Alpha F 5, 3), f. 69–84 (communication of John O. Ward and James R. Banker).

49. Karaus, "Selections from the Commentary of Bartolinus."

50. George Lacombe, *Aristoteles Latinus, Codices,* vol. 1 (1939), pp. 77–78.

51. Martin Grabmann, "Eine lateinische Übersetzung der pseudo-aristotelischen *Rhetorica ad Alexandrum* aus dem 13. Jahrhundert," *Sitzungsberichte der bayerischen Akademie der Wissenschaften, Philosophisch-historische Abteilung* (1931–32), Heft 2. The edition is based on Vat. lat. 2995, and the translation attributed to William of Moerbeke. Another version of the same text is found in Urbana, University of Illinois Library, ms. Xf 881.A 8.XL, f. 38–48. Cf. Lacombe, *Aristoteles Latinus, Codices,* pp. 78–79.

52. Bernice Virginia Wall, *A Medieval Latin Version of Demetrius' "De elocutione"* (Washington, D.C., 1937). The text is based on the same Urbana manuscript, f. 48–51v, and the translation is dated to the thirteenth century (*ibid.,* p. 51). Cf. Bernard Weinberg ' in *Catalogus Translationum et Commentariorum,* vol. 2, ed. P. O. Kristeller and F. Edward Cranz (Washington, D.C., 1971), p. 28, who assigns the translation to the fourteenth century.

53. Kurt Emminger, "Studien zu den griechischen Fürstenspiegeln" (Ph.D. diss., Munich, 1913). The text is given from three manuscripts (pp. 14–22) and assigned to the late twelfth century (p. 11). The translation was cited in the fourteenth century by Walter Burley, Geremia da Montagnone, and Guglielmo da Pastrengo. Cf. Remigio Sabbadini, "Una traduzione medievale del πρὸς Δημόνικον di Isocrate e una umanistica," *R. Istituto Lombardo di scienze e lettere, Rendiconti,* 2d ser., 38 (1905): 674–87. It should be noted that the three authors who cite the translation treat it as a work of moral philosophy.

54. See p. 62. James J. Murphy, "The Scholastic Condemnation of Rhetoric in the Commentary of Giles of Rome on the *Rhetoric* of Aristotle," in *Arts libéraux et philosophie au Moyen Age* [Actes du quatrième congrès international de philosophie médiéval, Montreal, 1967] (Montreal and Paris, 1969), pp. 833–41; *id.,* "Aristotle's *Rhetoric* in the Middle Ages,"*Quarterly Journal of Speech* 52 (1966): 109–15. The medieval translation of Aristotle's *Poetics* survives in only two manuscripts, whereas a Latin version of Averroes' *Paraphase* was more widely diffused.

55. Andre Wartelle, *Inventaire des manuscrits grecs d'Aristote et de ses commentateurs* (Paris, 1963).

56. Aristotle, *Rhetorica* II, 1–11.

57. Charles H. Lohr, "Medieval Latin Aristotle Commentaries," *Traditio* 23 (1967): 313–413; 24 (1968): 149–245; 26 (1970): 135–216; 27 (1971): 251–351; 28 (1972): 281–396; and 29 (1973): 93–197. *Id.,* "Renaissance Latin Aristotle Commentaries," *Studies in the Renaissance* 21 (1974): 228–89; continued in *Renaissance Quarterly* 28 (1975): 689–741; 29 (1976): 714–45; and 30 (1977): 681–745, with further installments to follow.

58. Aegidius Romanus: Lohr, *Traditio* 23 (1967): 334–35, no. 12. Guido Vernanus: Lohr, *Traditio* 24 (1968): 192, no. 6. Johannes Buridanus: Lohr, *Traditio* 26 (1970): 181, no. 45. Johannes de Janduno: Lohr, *Traditio* 26 (1970): 214–15, no.

17. Stuart MacClintock, *Perversity and Error: Studies on the "Averroist" John of Jandun* (Bloomington, Ind., 1956), p. 126, no. 15.

14. THE RENAISSANCE

1. Donald L. Clark, *Rhetoric and Poetry in the Renaissance* (New York, 1922; reprint ed., 1963). Charles S. Baldwin, *Renaissance Literary Theory and Practice* (New York, 1939; reprint ed., 1959). Osborne B. Hardison, Jr., *The Enduring Monument* (Chapel Hill, N.C., 1962). For Italy, see Alfredo Galletti, *L'Eloquenza dalle origini al XVI secolo* [*Storia dei generi letterari italiani*] (Milan, 1904–38). For England, see Wilbur S. Howell, *Logic and Rhetoric in England, 1500–1700* (Princeton, N.J., 1956). For Germany, see Samuel O. Jaffe, *Nic. Dybinus, Declaracio oracionis de beata Dorothea: Studies and Documents in the History of Late Medieval Rhetoric* (Wiesbaden, 1974). Klaus Dockhorn, "Rhetorica movet: Protestantischer Humanismus und karolingische Renaissance," in *Rhetorik: Beiträge zu ihrer Geschichte in Deutschland vom 16.–20. Jahrhundert,* ed. Helmut Schanze (Frankfort, 1974), pp. 17–42.

2. See essay 6. Hanna Gray, "Renaissance Humanism: The Pursuit of Eloquence," *Journal of the History of Ideas* 24 (1963): 497–514. Jerrold E. Seigel, *Rhetoric and Philosophy in Renaissance Humanism* (Princeton, 1968). Lorenzo Valla went further and considered rhetoric as a substitute for philosophy, and this is significant, but not typical. Cf. Hanna-Barbara Gerl, *Rhetorik als Philosophie: Lorenzo Valla* (Munich, 1974). See also Ernesto Grassi, "Can Rhetoric Provide a New Basis for Philosophizing? The Humanist Tradition," *Philosophy and Rhetoric* 11 (1978): 1–18, 75–97.

3. William H. Woodward, *Vittorino da Feltre and Other Humanist Educators* (Cambridge, 1897); *id., Studies in Education During the Age of the Renaissance, 1400–1600* (Cambridge, 1906). Eugenio Garin, *L'educazione in Europa, 1400–1600* (Bari, 1957); *id., Il pensiero pedagogico dello Umanesimo* (Florence, 1958).

4. Hans Baron, *The Crisis of the Early Italian Renaissance,* 2 vols. (Princeton, N.J., 1955; rev. ed., 1 vol., Princeton, N.J., 1966); *id., Humanistic and Political Literature in Florence and Venice at the Beginning of the Quattrocento* (Cambridge, Mass., 1955). Lauro Martines, *The Social World of the Florentine Humanists* (Princeton, 1963).

5. Charles Trinkaus, *Adversity's Noblemen* (New York, 1940); *id., In Our Image and Likeness,* 2 vols. (Chicago, 1970). Giuseppe Saitta, *Il pensiero italiano nell'Umanesimo e nel rinascimento,* vol. 1 (Bologna, 1949). Eugenio Garin, *Der italienische Humanismus* (Bern, 1947); *id., La cultura filosofica del Rinascimento italiano* (Florence, 1961); *id., L'età nuova* (Naples, 1969). Francesco Tateo, *Tradizione e realtà nell'Umanesimo italiano* (Bari, 1967).

6. P. O. Kristeller, "The Impact of Early Italian Humanism on Thought and Learning," in *Developments in the Early Renaissance,* ed. Bernard S. Levy (Albany, N.Y., 1972), pp. 120–57.

7. See essay 6.

8. P. O. Kristeller, "The Modern System of the Arts," *Renaissance Thought II* (New York, 1965), pp. 162–227.

9. Remigio Sabbadini, *Le scoperte dei codici latini e greci ne' secoli XIV e XV,* 2 vols. (Florence, 1905–14).

10. For general bibliographical information about the writings of the humanists, see Georg Voigt, *Die Wiederbelebung des classischen Alterthums,* 3d ed., 2 vols., ed. Max Lehnerdt (Berlin, 1893). Vittorio Rossi, *Il Quattrocento* (Milan, 1949), P. O. Kristeller, *Iter Italicum,* 2 vols. (London and Leyden, 1963–67).

11. See essay 2.

12. E. N. Tigerstedt, "Observations on the Reception of the Aristotelian Poetics in the Latin West," *Studies in the Renaissance* 15 (1968): 7–24. The sixteenth-century commentators on the *Rhetoric* include Daniel Barbarus, Petrus Victorius, M. A. Maioragius, Franciscus Portus, and Ant. Riccobonus. See F. Edward Cranz, *A Bibliography of Aristotle Editions 1501–1600* (Baden-Baden, 1971), pp. 162–63. The *Rhetoric* and *Poetics* were not included in the Aldine edition of the Greek Aristotle (5 vols., 1495–98), but in his collection *Rhetores Graeci* (1508). Cf. Lorenzo Minio-Paluello, "Attività filosofico-editoriale dell'umanesimo," *Opuscula* (Amsterdam, 1972), pp. 483–500.

13. For Demosthenes, see Ludwig Bertalot, *Studien zum italienischen und deutschen Humanismus,* ed. P. O. Kristeller, vol. 2 (Rome, 1975), pp. 398–99. For Demetrius, see Bernard Weinberg, in *Catalogus Translationum et Commentariorum,* vol. 2, ed., P. O. Kristeller and F. Edward Cranz (Washington, D.C., 1971), pp. 27–41.

14. George L. Kustas, *Studies in Byzantine Rhetoric* (Thessaloniki, 1973). Annabel M. Patterson, *Hermogenes in the Renaissance* (Princeton, N.J., 1970). John Monfasani, *George of Trebizond* (Leyden, 1976); *id.,* "Byzantine Rhetoric and the Renaissance" (forthcoming). Herbert Hunger, *Die hochsprachliche profane Literatur der Byzantiner,* vol. 1 (Munich, 1978), ch. 2 (rhetoric) and ch. 3 (epistolography), pp. 65–239.

15. Monfasani, "Byzantine Rhetoric and the Renaissance."

16. Philippus Callimachus, *Rhetorica,* ed. K. F. Kumaniecki (Warsaw, 1950). For Fichet, see P. O. Kristeller, "An Unknown Humanist Sermon on St. Stephen by Guillaume Fichet," *Mélanges Eugène Tisserant* 6 [Biblioteca Vaticana, *Studi e Testi* 236] (Vatican City, 1964), pp. 459–97.

17. *Ibid.*

18. *Le Epistole "De imitatione" di Giovanfrancesco Pico della Mirandola e di Pietro Bembo,* ed. Giorgio Santangelo (Florence, 1954). Erasmus, *Il Ciceroniano,* ed. Angiolo Gambaro (Brescia, 1965). Remigio Sabbadini, *Storia del Ciceronianismo* (Turin, 1885). Izora Scott, *Controversies Over the Imitation of Cicero as a Model for Style* (New York, 1910).

19. See note 12.

20. See Kristeller, *Iter Italicum.*

21. Galletti, *L'Eloquenza,* pp. 538–94. Karl Muellner, *Reden und Briefe italienischer Humanisten* (Vienna, 1899). For an early example of university speeches, see Gerard Fransen and Domenico Maffei, "Harangues universitaires du XIVe siècle," *Studi senesi* 83 (1971): 7–22.

22. The most famous example is Giovanni Pico's oration which was never delivered. For other examples, see P. O. Kristeller, "Giovanni Pico della Mirandola and His Sources," in *L'Opera e il pensiero di Giovanni Pico della Mirandola*, vol. 1 (Florence, 1965), pp. 52–53.

23. P. O. Kristeller, *Medieval Aspects of Renaissance Learning*, ed. and trans. Edward P. Mahoney (Durham, N.C., 1974), pp. 60–62. John W. O'Malley, "Some Renaissance Panegyrics of Aquinas," *Renaissance Quarterly* 27 (1974): 174–93. Luciano Gargan, *Lo studio teologica e la biblioteca dei domenicani a Padova nel tre e quattrocento* (Padua, 1971), p. 79. For orations in praise of St. Jerome by Vergerio and others, see Eugene F. Rice, *St. Jerome in the Renaissance*, forthcoming from the Johns Hopkins University Press.

24. John W. O'Malley, "Preaching for the Popes," in *The Pursuit of Holiness in Late Medieval and Renaissance Religion*, ed. Charles Trinkaus and Heiko Oberman (Leyden, 1974), pp. 408–40; id., *Praise and Blame in Renaissance Rome* (Durham, N.C., 1979). See also, John M. McManamon, S.J., "The Ideal Renaissance Pope: Funeral Oratory from the Papal Court," *Archivum Historiae Pontificiae* 14 (1976): 9–70.

25. Emilio Santini, *Firenze e i suoi "Oratori" nel Quattrocento* (Milan, 1922); id., "La *Protestatio de iustitia* nella Firenze medicea del sec. XV," *Rinascimento* 10 (1959): 33–106.

26. P. O. Kristeller, *Studies in Renaissance Thought and Letters* (Rome, 1956), p. 105.

27. Giles Constable, *Letters and Letter-Collections* (Turnhout, 1976), pp. 39–41. A. Gerlo, "The Opus *de Conscribendis Epistolis* of Erasmus and the Tradition of the *Ars Epistolica*," in *Classical Influences on European Culture A.D. 500–1500*, ed. R. R. Bolgar (Cambridge, 1971), pp. 103–14. Cecil H. Clough, "The Cult of Antiquity: Letters and Letter Collections," in *Cultural Aspects of the Italian Renaissance*, ed. Cecil H. Clough (Manchester and New York, 1976), pp. 33–67.

28. Aldo Scaglione, *Ars grammatica* (The Hague, 1970). W. Keith Percival, "The Grammatical Tradition and the Rise of the Vernaculars," in *Historiography of Linguistics*, 2 vols. [*Current Trends in Linguistics*, ed. Thomas A. Sebeok, vol. 13, pt. 1 (The Hague, 1975)], vol. 1, pp. 231–75; id., "Renaissance Grammar: Rebellion or Evolution?" in *Interrogativi dell'Umanesimo*, vol. 2, ed. Giovannangiola Secchi Tarugi (Florence, 1976), pp. 73–90. G. A. Padley, *Grammatical Theory in Western Europe 1500–1700: The Latin Tradition* (Cambridge, 1976).

29. Eduard Norden, *Die antike Kunstprosa*, vol. 2 (Stuttgart, 1958), p. 767.

30. "[A]t philosophia ac dialectica non solent ac ne debent quidem recedere ab usitatissima loquendi consuetudine et quasi a via vulgo trita et silicibus strata," Lorenzo Valla, *Disputationes dialecticae*, bk. I, chap. 3, in his *Opera omnia* I (Turin, 1962), p. 651.

31. Hanna H. Gray, "History and Rhetoric in Quattrocento Humanism" (Ph.D. diss., Harvard University, 1956). Eduard Fueter, *Geschichte der neueren Historiographie*, 3d ed. (Munich, 1936; reprint ed., New York, 1968). Donald J. Wilcox, *The Development of Florentine Humanist Historiography in the Fifteenth Century* (Cambridge, Mass., 1969). Nancy S. Struever, *The Language of History in the Renaissance* (Princeton, N.J., 1970). Donald R. Kelley, *Foundations of Modern*

Historical Scholarship (New York, 1970). Eckhard Kessler, *Petrarca und die Geschichte* (Munich, 1978).

32. Enrico Maffei, *I trattati dell'arte storica dal Rinascimento al sec. XVII* (Naples, 1897). Beatrice Reynolds, "Shifting Currents of Historical Criticism," in *Renaissance Essays from the Journal of the History of Ideas*, ed. P. O. Kristeller and P. P. Wiener (New York, 1968), pp. 115–30. Girolamo Cotroneo, *I trattatisti dell' "Ars historica"* (Naples, 1971).

33. See note 12.

34. Bernard Weinberg, *A History of Literary Criticism in the Italian Renaissance*, 2 vols. (Chicago, 1961).

35. Marvin T. Herrick, *The Fusion of Horatian and Aristotelian Literary Criticism, 1531–1555* (Urbana, Ill., 1946). Baxter Hathaway, *The Age of Criticism* (Ithaca, N.Y., 1962). Francesco Tateo, *"Retorica" e "Poetica" fra Medioevo e Rinascimento* (Bari, 1960).

36. Charles Trinkaus, "The Unknown Quattrocento Poetics of Bartolommeo della Fonte," *Studies in the Renaissance* 13 (1966): 40–122.

37. Francesco Patrizi da Cherso, *Della Poetica*, ed. Danilo Aguzzi Barbagli, 3 vols. (Florence, 1969–71).

38. P. O. Kristeller, "The Origin and Development of the Language of Italian Prose," *Renaissance Thought II*, pp. 119–41. For the humanists and the visual arts, see Michael Baxandall, *Giotto and the Orators* (Oxford, 1971).

39. See note 5. Francesco Tateo, *Tradizione e realtà nell' umanesimo italiano*. P. O. Kristeller, "The Moral Thought of Renaissance Humanism," *Renaissance Thought II*, pp. 20–68.

40. Léontine Zanta, *La renaissance du stoïcisme au XVIe siècle* (Paris, 1914). Jason L. Saunders, *Justus Lipsius* (New York, 1955). Richard H. Popkin, *The History of Scepticism from Erasmus to Descartes* (Assen, 1960). Charles B. Schmitt, *Cicero Scepticus* (The Hague, 1972).

41. Neal W. Gilbert, *Renaissance Concepts of Method* (New York, 1960), pp. 74–81, 129–44. Wilhelm Risse, *Die Logik der Neuzeit*, vol. 1 (Stuttgart, 1964), chs. 1–3. Cesare Vasoli, *La dialettica e la retorica dell'Umanesimo* (Milan, 1968).

42. Mario Nizolio, *De veris principiis*, ed. Quirinus Breen, 2 vols. (Rome, 1956). Walter J. Ong, *Ramus, Method, and the Decay of Dialogue* (Cambridge, Mass., 1958). *Testi umanistici su la Retorica*, ed. Eugenio Garin et al. (Rome, 1953).

43. P. O. Kristeller, "Renaissance Aristotelianism," *Greek, Roman and Byzantine Studies* 6 (1965): 157–74.

44. Eugenio Garin, "Le traduzioni umanistiche di Aristotele nel secolo XV," *Atti e Memorie dell'Accademia Fiorentina di Scienze Morali "La Colombaria"* 16 [n.s. 2] (1947–50): 55–104. F. Edward Cranz, *A Bibliography of Aristotle Editions, 1501–1600; id.*, "Alexander Aphrodisiensis," in *Catalogus Translationum et Commentariorum*, vol. 1, ed. P. O. Kristeller (Washington, D.C., 1960), pp. 77–135. Bruno Nardi, "Il commento di Simplicio al *De anima* nelle controversie della fine del secolo XV e del secolo XVI, *"Saggi sull'Aristotelismo Padovano dal secolo XIV al XVI* (Florence, 1958), pp. 365–442.

45. Leonardo Bruni Aretino, *Humanistisch-Philosophische Schriften*, ed. Hans

Baron (Leipzig-Berlin, 1928). P. O. Kristeller, "Un codice padovano di Aristotele postillato da Francesco ed Ermolao Barbaro," *Studies in Renaissance Thought and Letters,* pp. 337–53. Eugene F. Rice, *The Prefatory Epistles of Jacques Lefèvre d'Etaples and Related Texts* (New York, 1972).

46. Josef Soudek, "Leonardo Bruni and His Public: A Statistical and Interpretative Study of His Annotated Latin Version of the (Pseudo-)Aristotelian *Economics,*" *Studies in Medieval and Renaissance History* 5 (1968): 51–136.

47. Charles H. Lohr, "Renaissance Aristotle Commentaries," *Studies in the Renaissance* 21 (1974): 228–90; *Renaissance Quarterly* 28 (1975): 689–741; 29 (1976): 714–45; and 30 (1977): 681–745; with further installments to follow.

48. P. O. Kristeller, "Florentine Platonism and Its Relations with Humanism and Scholasticism," *Church History* 8 (1939): 201–11.

49. Eugenio Garin, "Ricerche sulle traduzioni di Platone nella prima metà del sec. XV," in *Medioevo e Rinascimento: Studi in onore di Bruno Nardi,* vol. 1 (Florence, 1955), pp. 339–74. P. O. Kristeller, "Marsilio Ficino as a Beginning Student of Plato," *Scriptorium* 20 (1966): 41–54.

50. Quirinus Breen, "Three Renaissance Humanists on the Relation of Philosophy and Rhetoric," *Christianity and Humanism* (Grand Rapids, Mich., 1968), pp. 1–68.

51. Hier. Fracastorius, *Naugerius sive de poetica dialogus,* ed. Ruth Kelso and Murray W. Bundy (Urbana, Ill., 1924).

52. Luigi Firpo, *Bibliografia degli scritti di Tommaso Campanella* (Turin, 1940), pp. 116–19, no. 22; cf. pp. 166–68, no. 50; and pp. 176–77, no. 62.

53. Francesco Patrizi, *Della historia dieci dialoghi* (Venice, 1560), *Della poetica: La deca istoriale* (Ferrara, 1586), *Della Poetica: La deca disputata* (Ferrara, 1586). Cf. *Testi umanistici su la Retorica,* ed. Garin et al.

54. See note 37. This edition includes the two decads of 1586 and several additional sections previously unpublished and preserved in autograph manuscripts.

55. Kristeller, "Modern System of the Arts," pp. 189–216.

56. Meyer Howard Abrams, *The Mirror and the Lamp: Romantic Theory and the Critical Tradition* (New York, 1953).

57. Thomas Cook, *The New Universal Letter Writer* (Montpelier, Vt., no date, but early nineteenth century; copy owned by Julius S. Held). Lawrence M. Brings, *Clever Introductions for Chairmen* (London, 1958).

58. There has been an interesting recent attempt to revive rhetoric as a rival to philosophy: Chaïm Perelmann and Lucie Olbrechts-Tyteca, *La nouvelle rhétorique: Traité de l'argumentation,* 2 vols. (Paris, 1958), trans. by J. Wilkinson and P. Weaver as *The New Rhetoric: A Treatise on Argumentation* (Notre Dame, Ind., 1969).

Index